NATION OF DEVILS

NATION OF DEVILS

DEMOCRATIC LEADERSHIP
AND THE
PROBLEM OF OBEDIENCE

STEIN RINGEN

Yale
UNIVERSITY PRESS
New Haven & London

Published with assistance from the foundation established in memory of
Calvin Chapin of the Class of 1788, Yale College.

Yale University Press books may be purchased in quantity for educational,
business, or promotional use. For information, please e-mail sales.press@yale.edu
(U.S. office) or sales@yaleup.co.uk (U.K. office).

Set in Simoncini Garamond type by Newgen North America.
Printed in the United States of America.

Library of Congress Cataloging-in-Publication Data
Ringen, Stein
Nation of devils : democratic leadership and the problem of obedience /
Stein Ringen.
p.   cm.
Includes bibliographical references and index.
ISBN 978-0-300-19319-0 (alk. paper)
1. Democracy—Great Britain.   2. Democracy—United States.   3. Obedience—
Political aspects—Great Britain.   4. Obedience—Political aspects—United States.
I. Title.
JN900.R56 2013
320.941—dc23   2013003467

A catalogue record for this book is available from the British Library.

This paper meets the requirements of ANSI/NISO Z39.48–1992
(Permanence of Paper).

10 9 8 7 6 5 4 3 2 1

For Aaron, Lola, Cosmo and Trilby

CONTENTS

PREFACE:
THE FUTILITY OF POWER

"I thought I could do something different from any Conservative prime minister before me. But I couldn't. Shops were closing, people were losing their homes—all the things I went into politics to avoid—and I was almost powerless to do anything about it."
—John Major in *The Guardian,* 22 September 2012

My first aim in this book is to explain how governments get things done and make things happen. I lean on the eminent thinkers on power such as Max Weber and Joseph Nye, whom I follow, although not without disagreement. I learn from the great users of power back to the Persian and Roman emperors and to the modern ruthless ones such as Bismarck and de Gaulle and democratic ones such as Roosevelt and Eisenhower, all of whom I admire. I take inspiration from Niccolò Machiavelli, who, when he observed the decline of Italy in the sixteenth century, thought it a good idea to use his experience to advise the young Florentine prince with some straight talk about the art of rule.

I think it no less a good idea to speak truth to those who are supposed to govern us today. They are not doing well. I hope I have something to say to them. I've been doing policy analysis for nearly forty years. I've worked as a government official, both as a head of ministerial research and later an assistant director general in the Ministry of Justice in my native Norway, and in the unwieldy bureaucracy of the United Nations in New York. I have experience as a management consultant and a political journalist. I trained in Norway and have lived and worked in many countries—Britain, France, Germany, the United States, Sweden and elsewhere—and benefit, I hope, from the comparative outlook that comes from a formative grounding in a small country and then a cosmopolitan life.

Good government is in part a moral issue, but it is effectiveness that preoccupies me here. A full analysis should confront two questions: how can a government dispense necessary rule, and how can the population protect itself against excessive rule? My concern is with the first of these questions. I have tried to answer the second one as well as I have been able to elsewhere, in particular in a previous book called *What Democracy Is For,* and I do not have much to add to that account.

The first aim of the book, to explain how governments get things done, is pulled together in the first half of the final chapter. The basic lesson is elementary: Put no trust in power. Seek authority and apply leadership.

My second aim is to speak to our contemporary decline and to the leaders in America and Britain. Strangely enough, since it is democratic government that preoccupies me, I draw from the start on an authoritarian experience, that of South Korea. I know it well, and it has much to tell us about power and leadership. But my main cases are the United States and Britain. They should be beacons for the democratic world, but have been reduced to substandard governance. The democratic family needs their inspiration and is not getting it.

For Britain, I rely on my own studies, having had my home there for more than twenty years and having come to despair over the utter misrule in public affairs in that country (to quote the heading the editors of the *Financial Times* put on a comment of mine at the beginning of the 2010 election campaign: "Misrule has made things worse for Britain"). For the United States, I follow in the footsteps of Alexis de Tocqueville, who observed democracy in America in the 1830s, and benefit from the eye of the outsider sharpened by stints as an immersed visitor. But I also step out of his shadow. He then affirmed democracy in America. I now question its existence.

This second part of my analysis I pull together in the final chapter's second half. Leadership is built on respect. Democratic leadership is built on the respect that comes from democratic quality. I want my message to be clear: Your systems are dysfunctional. You must reform. You owe it to your people and to the world. I beseech you, you *must* improve your democracies.

1

THE POWERLESSNESS OF POWERFUL GOVERNMENT

. . . he finds himself surrounded by many who believe
they are his equals, and because of that he cannot
command or manage them the way he wants.
　　　　　　　　　　—Niccolò Machiavelli, *The Prince,* chapter 9

"If the state is to exist, the dominated must obey the authority claimed by the powers that be." So said Max Weber, the greatest of German political thinkers, in a famous lecture at Munich University in 1919 under the title "Politik als Beruf."[1] That might seem cynical, like a eulogy for dictatorship, but it is nothing of the kind. Serious governments want to rule. But also their populations want them to rule, to rule appropriately, of course, but therefore clearly to rule. Hence, in the American Declaration of Independence, "to secure these rights, Governments are instituted among Men." We citizens want rule because we need rule for order, fairness and protection. We need to hold the tyranny of government at bay but we also want, in our own interest, our governments to defeat our tyranny over them. The problem, then, is *obedience.*

THE PUBLIC GOOD

Macho men want the government off their backs but are dead wrong, as the bankers of the world learned after 2007 when the cost in money and esteem of radical deregulation caught up with them. When people live in society, it is government that prevents them from falling into the war of all against all that the philosopher Thomas Hobbes believed was the natural state of affairs, and it is government that makes it possible for us to live lives that are useful for ourselves and others. The painter Ambrogio Lorenzetti gave this knowledge life in fourteenth-century Italy with his frescoes in the Palazzo Pubblico in Siena, where he created allegories of good government with happy people building their future in a city of order and of bad government with idle people in a crumbling world. The Norwegian Johan Bojer, in *The Last Viking,* his early twentieth-century epic of the winter fisheries in northern Norway in the age of sail, saw the magic at work where life is raw. A fjord is teeming with fish, the fishermen scramble for a take in the bounty, a minor civil war breaks out until the regulator arrives and restores order: linesmen in that part of the fjord, netsmen in the other. "A thousand men were transformed from animals to human beings again." On today's testing ground for progress, in Africa, the economist Paul Collier, in *The Bottom Billion,* sees a near perfect correlation: where government works, the economy works, and where the economy works there is government at work.

No wonder Aristotle praised "he who first founded the state [as] the greatest of benefactors. For man, when perfected, is the best of animals, but when separated from law and justice, he is the worst of all."[2]

In his first inaugural address, at the birth of the American republic, President George Washington defined the job of government as "the discernment and pursuit of the public good." Citizens left to their own devices are interested in their various little private goods, and at each other's throats. Governments are instituted to cut through that chaos and create a new reality that is public. They must discern: the public good must be defined, explained and made accepted. They must pursue: the dominated must be made to obey, preferably by being made to want to obey.

LEADERS

Governments must get two things done. They must make policy and they must put their policies to work in society. S. E. Finer, in *The History of Government,* calls it decision making and decision implementing. In political reporting in the press, "politics" is almost always about the making of policy, as it is in a great deal of writing in political science. The government is victorious when it is able to get its programme enacted and it loses when the opposition is able to defeat it. Well and good, those are tricky problems—but not the endgame problems. In making policy work, the challenge is just as much or more in implementation. Decisions are everything for the members of the political class, but for society they are nothing unless they are implemented.

For example, on the 13th of February 2009, the United States Congress approved President Barack Obama's near $800 billion economic stimulus package. That was only two weeks after his inauguration and was, rightly, seen as a great victory. However, the money thereby allocated was supposed to flow through to hundreds of projects around the country in infrastructural investments, schools, employment, social security, health care and much more. The decision by Congress on that day was only to make the money available. What would flow through was yet to be seen.

An indication of some of what might happen was by coincidence on display in the Helsinki newspaper *Hufvudstadsbladet* in Finland the very next day. The Finnish government had launched its own stimulus package a few months earlier. A review by the paper revealed that in at least some areas very little of what was intended had reached its objective. For reasons of legal wrangling and logistical problems, intended credits to businesses through a government loans agency were being held up, as was intended support to local municipalities through another government agency to stimulate housing construction.

President Obama's package was inspired in part by the initiatives of President Franklin D. Roosevelt in 1933, but Roosevelt did much more than to get money allocated. In his first one hundred days he not only summoned Congress and kept it working in emergency session to push through fifty major recovery laws, but also followed up by creating a raft of new government agencies to carry allocated money into projects in the real economy.[3] In 2009, it took less than a week after Congress had approved the spending for reporting to emerge in the press about difficulties of implementation. Political posts remained unfilled in the new administration, and political leadership was not in place in several cabinet departments and lower-level agencies, including the Treasury, the result being a danger of at least delays in the implementation of policies that were seen to be urgent.[4] Congress earmarked at least $20 billion for energy efficiency projects in towns and cities across the country, which would have to be carried out by local agencies that had few plans in place and were without experience of or capacity for projects on the necessary scale.[5] President Obama had won a victory in Congress, but the significance for American society of that victory would depend on the administration's ability to practically get the money put to use. A year later, the president's popularity had collapsed, in part because of a widespread perception in the country that a great deal of his stimulus money had been siphoned off for pork-barrel projects with little or no relevance for economic recovery. And on the effects of the stimulus package for the economy, and how its multiple projects unfolded, the jury is still out.[6]

Likewise in Britain. In late 2011, the chancellor of the exchequer, George Osborne, tempered his austerity with some public works plans to stimulate economic activity and growth. But half a year on, referring to "squabbling" and "plans left to gather dust on desks," the director general of the Confederation of Business Industries, John Cridland, "strongly criticised the government for the 'really disappointing' implementation of its growth plans, asking: 'Where are the diggers on the ground.'"[7]

FOLLOWERS

Whenever anyone wants to rule or lead, it is *others* they must manage— that amorphous mass of people who must obey but are inclined not to. That is a fact of life in the running of businesses as well as the governing of countries. For governance, it is a fact in democracies as in autocracies. Always, the craft of governing is about winning over reluctant and sometimes hostile others to not frustrating, and sometimes even to supporting, your intentions. President Harry Truman knew this when he handed power to his successor, Dwight D. Eisenhower, and predicted, not without schadenfreude: "Poor Ike. He'll sit right here, and he'll say do this, do that!! And nothing will happen—it won't be a bit like the army."[8] Jonathan Powell, who was Tony Blair's chief of staff, remembers how Blair's term in office started: "A new prime minister pulls all the levers of power and nothing happens."[9] Rule has everything to do with those, from a government's point of view, confounded *others*.

Why is that? Charles Lindblom, the eminent political scientist, has put it succinctly: "Many people constantly try to change the social world. An explanation of their failure more plausible than that of inertia is to be found in the great number of other people who are vigorously trying to frustrate social change."[10]

Governors bring burdens down upon the governed, principally taxes and regulations. Therefore, the governed dislike what their governors impose on them. Therefore, they are looking for excuses to persuade themselves that they are entitled to disregard the will of those they for their own psychological gratification call "the politicians." Therefore, aspiring leaders must deny them reasons for refusing to make themselves followers.

It takes a lot. It is no good, said the philosopher Immanuel Kant in his attempt at a treaty for perpetual peace, to assume that people are angels. We need institutions that can maintain order in a nation of devils. Institutions are of various kinds, such as rules and culture. Good rules control devils. Good cultures make it difficult for people to be devils. There must be control and there is no reason to be romantic about it: there are devils aplenty, small and large, and leaders need to manage them.

But not everything and everyone can always be controlled. "Rule, to last," observes Henry Kissinger, speaking of China, "needs to translate force into obligation."[11] At the height of the debate over bank reform in Britain following the recession of 2008, the head of C. Hoare, the country's most eccentric (and highly profitable) old-school bank, said: "We have had this massive scare, but what was the cause? A lack of moral compass and a lack of understanding of the nature of debt and civic responsibility. Changing capital ratios will not change that."[12] There needs to be an acceptance in people's minds, and in the way they see each other, of the validity of order. There needs to be *understanding*. Let's be straight about it: there needs to be some morality and some shared sense of the moral in the cultural fabric we live within. For Kant, those institutions that can control devils are possible even among non-angels, but only if they have the intelligence to understand that "public conduct" requires that they check each other. Carl Schmitt, a legal scholar in Weimar Germany (whose reputation as a political thinker survived his later allegiance to Nazism), writing nearly a century ago, saw democracy somewhat mysteriously as a matter of shared identity between the rulers and the ruled which was possible only "for a people who really think democratically."[13] Forty years ago, when there was fear that democracy might crumble under the competition from authoritarianism, the Trilateral Commission asked Michel Crozier, Samuel Huntington and Joji Watanuki to analyse the possible "crisis of democracy." Their report was conditionally optimistic. "Democracies can work *provided* their publics truly understand the nature of the democratic system, and particularly if they are sensitive to the subtle interrelationship between liberty and responsibility."[14]

SETTLEMENT

Some countries have found their way to a habit of leaders governing well and followers cooperating willingly. There is, in the language of Samuel Huntington and Francis Fukuyama, political order. But that apparent simplicity is deceptive. Under the surface is a rough confrontation between instinctive antagonists, between the governed and the governors. Only some countries, at some times, have the good fortune that the confrontation has been resolved. We could call it a covenant, or a contract, but that's a bit grand. It's more of a deal, or better still a settlement, a *settlement of order.*

The modern study of democracy was inaugurated by the French aristocrat Alexis de Tocqueville in his observations in *Democracy in America,* published in two volumes in 1835 and 1840. He found much to admire, in particular in his first volume. He found a settled confrontation. The American Constitution gives representatives the power they need to govern but also restrains that power in a system of checks and balances. Citizens were enmeshed in networks of associations that reduced their dependency on the state. The represented could trust their state to be benevolent.

But in his second and more pessimistic volume, he also found that an established settlement could disintegrate into what he called "soft despotism": a creeping erosion of freedom within a shell of democratic formality, which citizens allow to fester out of greed and indifference, gradually and hardly perceptively.

The American settlement was soon not only to disintegrate but to collapse into civil war when the destructive force of slavery in the republic of equality could no longer be contained. Whether a new settlement was found is debatable, but President Franklin Roosevelt's reforms could be seen as a quest. If that succeeded for a while, as it appeared during the Eisenhower presidency, it again collapsed under the strains of the war in Vietnam and the civil rights movement at home. These influences have not yet been resettled, and to that we must now add to the American scene, as we will see, a fair dose of Tocquevillian soft despotism.

WORKABLE OR NOT

Democracies are normal or dysfunctional. In normal systems, the machinery churns on to the making and implementation of policy. It's like a normal car. It may have some scratches but you assume that the steering works so that you can set off and drive without lurching into the ditch. When a leader takes up office in a normal democracy, he or she can take it that the country is reasonably governable. We should take care not to ask for perfection, which is not available and the aspiration to which is self-defeating and destructive, but we should ask for and expect workability. Most democracies are in this meaning normal—which is why democracy has prospered, advanced and outdone the competition.[15]

In dysfunctional systems, the machinery is defunct and good government not available, either because necessary decisions do not get made or, if made, are not implementable.[16] In the next chapter, we will see how New Labour in Britain was given all the power a democratic government could dream of but that "a strong government was defeated by a weak system of governance." In America, Barack Obama fought a brilliant election campaign in 2008 and came to power as the most attractive leader since Ronald Reagan. But when he settled into office thinking that Washington could be made to work according to the textbook, he was overwhelmed by vicious subversion. Good government depends on a combination of functional institutions and competent leadership. If institutions are dysfunctional, no competence can save the day. But also, functional institutions are only a necessary condition and never a sufficient one. There is still the problem of obedience.

This defines the two ways that governments can fail: in a normal democracy if they are unable to work the system and in a dysfunctional one because the system is unworkable. This also corresponds to my two aims in this book, to speak to leaders about how to lead when the system is workable and how to reform when it is not. Leadership I'm able to discuss in general terms, but reform needs more specific context, which I find in the cases of America and Britain.

So this is a book of two parts: an essay about rule into which is inserted a treatise on misrule in America and Britain.

I start with normal democracies in mind and stay in that mindset for a good deal of time until I get properly back to the problem of obedience in Chapters 8 and 9, and zoom in on the cases of the United States and Britain, where the comfort of normality gradually breaks down.

THE AMERICAN PREDICAMENT

I introduce one of those cases, Britain, in the next chapter, but not the other one, the United States. That case emerges gradually until it takes centre stage in the last chapters. In fact, however, it is present all the way, if at first quietly. America has declined to the model dysfunctional democracy. I want to understand why. That evolves around the relationship between the rulers and the ruled, around trust, leadership, authority, settlement— finally around political culture. This—culture—is another theme which emerges gradually until, like the American case, it becomes *the* theme. In many democracies now, but in America in particular, a profound distrust in politics has taken hold so that the foundations of good government are eroding or have eroded. Inequalities at shocking levels are allowed to fester, even celebrated. That great American engine of progress, social mobility, is grinding to a halt. Most people are excluded from the benefits of economic advancement. The have-mores are allowed to buy political influence at the expense of democracy, leaving the have-lesses with no reason to believe that public policy might be for their good. The population is divided into "them" and "us" who live in different worlds. There is no sense of shared destiny and no shared deliberation about what is and should be common and public. The very idea of government as an instrument of good is challenged, perhaps abandoned. Being a politician is disreputable and contempt of politics a free-for-all. The press, with its 24/7 schedule, hounds leaders away from their business of ruling and has in large measure made itself partisan and aggressive, to the neglect of its duty of information and of providing an arena for the big conversation.[17] It is common sense that decision making in the American system is heavy going, but the predicament now is that dysfunction goes all the way to the foundations, to the political culture. This is *new*. The challenge now, therefore, is not so much about this or that reform as about the capacity for reform altogether and about escaping entrenched governmental grid-lock. That is the difficult problem I land myself with toward the end of this essay. I deal with it as a matter of cultural revolution. I reach back to the progressive tradition in American history, only recently interrupted. I turn to the president (the presidency being the remaining functional in-stitution) and recommend that he reconnects with that tradition and pulls the American people into a soul-searching exercise in deliberation over their union, social and political, and their democracy and government. It is a matter of repairing a fractured culture so that there might be hope that settlement, political order and good government could be restored.

SOME ASSUMPTIONS

Obviously, I set out on this journey with a baggage of ideas and assump-tions, and it might be helpful to lay out what some of them are.

On human nature. I go by an understanding of humanity that is in-spired by Aristotle. Human beings have the potential for nobility but are not noble by instinct. They need what I have elsewhere called "social an-chorage." They need to be trained, supported and guided. They need to be governed. It is not in isolation but in togetherness that we can realise our potential. Human beings are stable, they are as they are and good enough. Institutions differ, those influences that train, support and guide. The public good is realised in the building and nurturing of institutions that guide each of us toward the realisation of our noble potential.[18]

On democracy. Democracy is a method more than a purpose. The ar-guments for democratic government are two: that it, being under popular control, should protect citizens against oppression, and, that it being by consent, should be effective. It is not enough for a democracy to be demo-cratic and no democracy should be lauded for just being a democracy. If it can't be effective it will decline democratically as well.

On participation. Participation is like motherhood: one cannot be against it. But it is a slippery idea. If it means giving citizens a share in day-to-day decision making, for example through intensive use of refer-endums and the like, then, sad is it may be, participation from below is

9

not conducive to good government. It gives leaders too little power to dominate followers and others too much power to subvert governors. Hard libertarians and soft advocates of participatory democracy have in common that they believe people to be instinctively of sound and rational character and judgement. But they are not, which is why leadership from above is the essence. Citizens are best served by delegating decision making to representatives. On the other hand, if governors are to get their doings accepted, they need to involve citizens so that they feel they are not being treated arbitrarily or in a dictatorial manner. This is a different form of participation—I prefer to think about it as deliberation—in which governors pull citizens into their orbit, or co-opt them. Needless to say, participation in this meaning is separated from manipulation by a very thin line.

On governing. I identify with "the governor" and want him or her to succeed. I want those of us who reflect on democracy to think more about effectiveness than we have been inclined to. When democratic government is challenged, it is the inability to deliver that makes the challenge credible and dangerous. This way of looking at it reduces somewhat the presence of "the people." My excuse for thus looking down upon the people from up high is that it is in their (our) interest that they (we) are governed. Governance is a getting-done contest, not a beauty contest.

On governance. Some political scientists (in the "new governance" literature) believe that governance has become more complex than it was in simpler olden times and that contemporary democratic governments are increasingly constrained in the options available to them. Understanding governance, then, is a matter more of observing the environment governments work within than how they operate. This is a case of the more things change, the more they are the same. If you think governance in the age of bureaucracy is complex, spare a thought for medieval kings and their courts. Governments have *always*—read Finer's *History of Government*—struggled with making things happen. On this, nothing has changed and there is no new complexity. In the next chapter, I introduce two case studies, one government that had everything against it and succeeded and one that had everything for it and failed—in both cases by the way they operated. I defend the old-fashioned view that governance is a craft that some master and others don't (wherefore I also defend the old-fashioned method of working through examples of leaders exercising that craft). However, there *are* also new realities of constraint. One such influence, which I will return to, is from economic globalisation. Political power is up against economic power. Globalisation benefits economic power to the detriment of political power and has increased the capacity of those who control capital to constrain government action. That's a more difficult environment for governments, and in some ways a recent one. But it is different by down-to-earth changing power relations more than new-fangled "complexity." What makes for dysfunction is too much power where it should not be, in the hands of those whose interest is in disobedience, and too little where it should be, in the hands of governors. Reform in dysfunctional democracies is about shutting out unwanted power more than about straightening out complexities.

On writing political science. I start from straight and simple questions: What is a government? What do governments do? How can they get it right? I want my answers to be in the same spirit. To that end, I will observe governance as a matter of persons acting and reacting. Governments consist of many things and we need to pick them apart. Basically, they consist of people. A government is a group of *persons*—we usually call them ministers, and sometimes I call them governors, meaning those who (supposedly) govern. A bureaucracy is made up of *persons*—we usually call them officials. A nation is made up of *persons*—we usually call them citizens. The problem with the analysis of "systems" is that people tend to disappear except as collectives and masses. As so often, I follow Max Weber: "Concepts such as 'state,' 'associations,' 'feudalism,' and the like designate certain categories of human interaction. Hence it is the task of sociology to reduce these concepts to 'understandable' action, that is, without exception, to the actions of participating individual men."[19] I will sometimes engage with writings that approach it differently, as need dictates, and sometimes not when I feel I don't have to. My sorrow is that, however I have tried, I have not been able to make this book shorter than it is.

2

HOW TO DO IT WELL
AND BADLY

... friendship which is bought with money and not
with greatness and nobility, does not last and yields nothing.

... must none the less make himself feared in such a way
that, if he is not loved, at least he escapes being hated.

—The Prince, chapter 17

The ingredients of analysis are thereby in place. The question is how governments rule. The business of government is the public good. The problem is obedience. (I will eventually redefine it to loyalty, but for now obedience will do.) Obedience must be extracted from the dominated. That is done by pull, that of good governance, and by push, that of robust institutions.[1] When these influences come together, there is settlement and order. In a democracy, government is for the people. They then owe their governors obedience. But that obedience must still be earned, and is earned when governors with effect pursue the public good.

With this backdrop in mind, let's turn to two case studies, one of failure and one of success.

In Britain in 1997, an ideologically committed regime of eighteen years was thrown out and a new regime of opposite colours was voted in with a monumental majority. The new leaders aimed, they said, to change the direction of social development in the country and were given an undisputed mandate and unrivalled means to do so. A laboratory thus opened up in which an experiment was unfolding of a government with abundant democratic power. What came of it?

In 1948, a country appeared on the global map under the name of the Republic of Korea. It was a non-nation, an arbitrary half of what had been Korea, itself destroyed physically and morally by Japanese colonial rule and the fallout from the Second World War, and to suffer further destruction by the devastations of the Korean War from 1950 to 1953. Yet in two short generations, in the greatest development story ever told, it had become one of the world's biggest economies and a stable democracy. How could that happen?[2]

THE GREAT BRITISH FLOP

New Labour won a magnificent victory in 1997, taking 418 of 659 seats in the House of Commons. Labour was back in power after eighteen years in opposition and a painful process of soul-searching to remake itself into a credible party of government. It pushed out a demoralised competitor who then for a long time was not even able to mount an opposition to be noticed. It won two more elections with huge majorities and held on to undisputed power into its third term. It was ambitious, idealistic, self-righteous and activist, and no doubt sincere in its wish for change. It was also competent, under the joint, if uneasy, leadership of a gifted publicist, Mr. Blair, and a shrewd economic manager, Mr. Brown.

My fascination with this experiment comes not from it being a Labour experiment but from it being a power experiment. But it also comes from the person of Mr. Blair. Governance grows out of leadership, and here was a man determined to lead from the front. He seemed to have the ability: young, energetic, engaging and original. "I was and remain first and foremost not so much a politician of traditional left or right, but a moderniser."[3] His memoir, *A Journey*, is cool, full of anecdotes and insights, and well presented. But as you get into his story, as into his period in office, there is just a bit too much display and not enough substance. His governance was activism in all things which, however, resulted in failure in most things.

Is that too harsh a judgement? Now that New Labour is history, there is predictably an industry of writing about it. The best insider accounts are Mr. Blair's own memoirs, those of his chief of staff, Jonathan Powell, which we encountered in the previous chapter, and Michael Barber's *Instruction to Deliver*, which we will meet later on. These are great books: intelligent, informative, funny, and self-deprecating on the endless cock-ups that are endemic in government. But they are also strategic books that use self-critical charm to secure the reputation of their own enterprise as imperfect but basically sound.

But I'm having none of this exoneration by flirtation. I read Mr. Blair and on page 574, when he is contemplating the end of his reign, meet this: "Nonetheless, what was done was significant and will last." But if you ask me, the patient reader of those 574 pages, what "what was done" is, I am at a loss. There were some achievements, the greatest one the peace in Northern Ireland. Devolution, in particular to Scotland, was a constitutional innovation, but a bad one: it opened for the breakup of the union. But on its progressive agenda, the experiment was a no-nonsense failure. Politically, the aim was to create a centre-left force that would establish itself as the natural government; that led to the Conservative-Liberal coalition in 2010. Economically, the aim was stable growth; that led to the crash of 2008. And socially, my own particular analysis, the aim was to break with the Thatcherite legacy of rising inequality; that led to an even more unequal Britain.

Non-insider accounts are predictably more critical. The best of these is *Off Message* by Bob Marshall-Andrews, a respected barrister and a Labour MP of thirteen years whom *The Daily Telegraph* called "the leader of Labour's own opposition." His assessment of Mr. Blair's premiership is that he perfected "a presidential system [without] the checks and balances necessary in such a form of democratic government" and that he used that power so that "the recurring theme was legislation aimed systematically at the curtailment and withdrawal of liberty."[4]

In economic policy Mr. Brown was king: authoritative, ambitious, determined, confident. He boasted to have broken the cycle of boom and bust. We now know it was not to be. However, in my study of New Labour governance I found that its economic policy had failed *before* the economy fell into crisis. That was not easy to see. There was steady economic growth. Mr. Brown was an impressive chancellor of the exchequer and there was much to suggest force and determination in his economic management. The true record had to be excavated with archaeological attention and detail. That excavation revealed that for all the effort Mr. Brown invested into the British economy, there was little to show for it in outcomes. It looked so good. There were new policies here, there and everywhere. The economy was expanding. But it did not stack up. Of effort there was much; of achievement little. I am referring, to repeat, to the period up to 2007 and those, from the government's point of view, good years.

There was no shortage of ambition and assertiveness.[5] In a keynote speech to the Fabian Society in January 2006, Mr. Brown spoke of how the government was "moving Britain forward." He underlined his values, those of fairness, liberty and justice. The purpose New Labour gave itself was to break with the legacy of Margaret Thatcher. However, after ten years of New Labour rule, Britain was untouched as a society of entrenched inequality. The line from Mrs. Thatcher to Mr. Blair and Mr. Brown was one of conspicuous continuity.[6] The surprising verdict on the experiment was that power had not delivered.

Strategy

Mr. Brown's slogan "prudence for a purpose" (in his 1998 budget speech in Parliament) brilliantly captured his philosophy of economic policy. *Prudence* was his approach to the budget. *Purpose* was to nudge social trends in the direction of justice. This would happen through careful step-by-step economic management from budget control to social outcomes, along the lines in the model below.

To assess the success or failure of a government, the analysis needs, first, to separate ends and means. Stages 1, 2 and 3 in the model capture the means of economic policy. No government can succeed unless it is able to spend money, but spending money is obviously no government's purpose. When government ministers claim success by pointing out that they have increased spending in some area or passed a law on some matter,

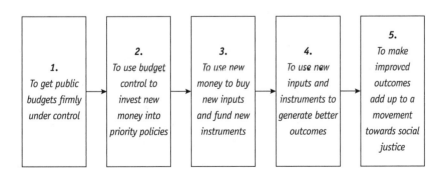

| 1.
To get public budgets firmly under control | 2.
To use budget control to invest new money into priority policies | 3.
To use new money to buy new inputs and fund new instruments | 4.
To use new inputs and instruments to generate better outcomes | 5.
To make improved outcomes add up to a movement towards social justice |

they are cheating. Success comes when, and only when, new money or laws generate better outcomes.

Once we are clear about means and ends, the analysis needs to follow through to stages 4 and 5 and observe whether there are improvements in outcomes and whether such improvements are a result of the government's efforts and policies. No final assessment can be made in any other way than through outcomes.

Following through to outcomes is astonishingly difficult for the political mind, which is naturally geared to the battle over decision making. In *The New Machiavelli,* Jonathan Powell says, rightly: "The purpose of government is to make things happen."[7] His own story, however—and he is probably not even aware of it as he inevitably observes events as they looked from inside Downing Street—is told completely in the language of what the government did, of inputs, and with no analysis of what those inputs did for outcomes out there in society.

The decade from 1997 to 2007 was one of great change. There was high employment and rising standards of living. There was less hardship, even among those on the lower reaches of the income distribution. But for all this, government policies had contributed little or nothing.

This was paradoxical. Mr. Brown managed his budgets shrewdly. He started by slashing public spending in his first three years to get control and only then went on to put new money into priority policies. Total public spending went up from 36 per cent of national income in 1999 to 43 per cent in 2005. Spending on education increased by 4.3 per cent per year in real terms from 1999 to 2007; in schools specifically by 6 per cent, and per pupil by 6.4 per cent. New schools were built and more teachers hired. Spending on the National Health Service increased by 50 per cent in real terms in five years from 2002, resulting in new hospitals built and more doctors and nurses hired. Spending on criminal justice policies were lifted from a level of 2 per cent of national income to 2.5 per cent (from 1999 to 2005), resulting among other things in an increase in police staffing. The chancellor also devised new instruments for his purposes, notably the Working Families Tax Credit for combating child poverty, introduced in 1999, from 2003 reshaped into the Child and Working Tax Credits, designed to bring more income to needy families and to encourage people into work and up the job ladder. However, as we follow events through the steps in the model above, we find that the potential contained in budget control and new inputs gradually petered out, so that by the time we get to outcomes which were supposed to add up to a shift toward social justice, there was no force left.

After ten good years for New Labour, income inequality and health inequality had increased, the prevalence of ill health remained stubbornly high by European comparison, child poverty was rising, social mobility was stagnant, and the school system was as ever an arena of class division and its perpetuation.

Here, in some more detail, is the intricate dialectic of a government's competence and failure:

1. Were the budgets economically responsible? Yes. The record up to 2007 on taxes, spending and borrowing is a display of fiscal control and efficiency. The level of public investment was lifted upward. Borrowing was held to a cautious level by both historical standards in Britain and comparative standards in Europe. Spending increased, but not beyond what was covered painlessly by new taxes.

2. Were the budgets politically effective? Yes. There were considerable changes in the structure of spending, reflecting the government's priorities and manifesto commitments. The government was able to increase spending in its priority areas more than it increased aggregate spending and more than it increased taxes.

3. Did budgetary prudence lay the ground for high and steady economic growth? No. Stable economic growth was already there when New Labour took over and was handed to the new government as a gift, continued at a steady pace until 2007, and then collapsed in spite of the chancellor's careful husbandry.

4. In Mr. Brown's flagship policy, did additional investments and new instruments aimed to redistribute income to low-income families carry through to lower rates of child poverty? No. New Labour inherited a trend of reduced child poverty but was unable to maintain that trend. Paradoxically, in the years after the introduction of tax credits, the child poverty rates moved back onto an upward trend.

5. Did additional investments in criminal justice policies carry through to reducing crime? No. Crime was on a falling trend when Labour came to office, but after 2002, when Labour was putting serious new

money into the system, measured crime fell less than it had been up to that time.

6. Did additional investments in health services carry through to improvements in health? Probably not. In large measure, if not totally, the new money was wasted. Average health status probably improved, but that was in continuation of long-term trends. Health inequalities increased. Increased investments in the NHS were balanced out by a loss of productivity.

7. Did additional investments in schools carry through to improvements in education? Probably marginally, but at poor value for money. The pupil experience probably improved, at least in primary schools. School performance indicators had long shown steady improvements, and there was no new upward thrust in these trends following New Labour's additional investments in schools and education.

8. Did New Labour policies in the period from 1997 to 2007 add up to a turning of the tide in Britain toward more social justice? No. Britain became more unequal under New Labour and was by 2007 a more unequal society than even where the Conservative governments had left off.

Economic Growth

Economic growth was integral to the New Labour story, but the truth about New Labour and economic growth is not that New Labour made economic growth but that economic growth made New Labour. Budget control was easy. There were improvements to observe in many social trends and various hardships as measured by social indicators were pushed back.[8]

But that in itself is not evidence of effective policies. Economic growth creates progress in standards of living directly, without going through public policies. Any government will cash in on the benefits that flow from economic growth, but when that government is not the architect of economic growth, as New Labour was not, then neither are the benefits that flow directly from economic growth to that government's particular credit.

In recent British history, there was a moderately progressive period from about 1994 to about 2004. That was the product of two influences:

stable economic growth, which started in 1994, and stability in the distribution of income, which ended in 2004. While these influences coincided, there was some change for the good in social distributions. The rate of child poverty, for example, had been rising steadily from about 15 per cent in the mid-1970s to a high of 34 per cent in 1993–94, when it started to fall. The Labour government inherited a rate of child poverty on a downward move (at 33 per cent in 1997–98) which continued to fall to 28 per cent in 2004–5. From then on, however, when underlying inequality increased, the rate of child poverty increased again, up to between 30 and 31 per cent by 2006–7.[9] We saw the same influence in unemployment. From a peak of 3 million in 1993, the number of the unemployed fell steadily to about 1.5 million in 2001, when it first flattened and then started to rise again from 2007. And we saw it in crime. Here, a long trend of increasing rates ended around 1994 and then started to fall, but around 2004–5 that downward trend petered out.

This progressive period covered the last years of the Conservative regime and the first years of New Labour's regime. During John Major's years in office, income inequality was roughly stable, but during Mr. Blair's years it increased again. It increased in particular after 2004 when the effects of the government's policies should have been coming through and should have started to push inequality back. Only the first years of New Labour's regime could in this meaning be said to be progressive, the years *before* Mr. Brown's new investments in priority policies should have produced progressive results.

What Went Wrong?
Some elementary explanations can be dismissed. Many governments are unable to rule as they wish for want of means. But that was not Mr. Brown's problem. We can also dismiss explanations that go to a lack of will. New Labour hardly promised a Scandinavian-type welfare state, but it had made social justice the purpose of its economic policy.

Nor is incompetence a persuasive explanation. It is true that Mr. Brown failed to understand that artificial growth generated by hot air in the financial services industry was a bubble, but so did almost everyone else. Otherwise, he was on top of the budget. The New Labour team was suspicious of and cautious with power. Governments often fail because they become overconfident, but the reshaping of the Labour Party by

Messrs. Blair and Brown consisted of it coming to terms with the limits of power.

If any of these explanations had been pertinent, the New Labour saga would have been trivial. But none of this applies. The New Labour story is a mystery. It should have been a tale of success but collapsed into failure.

Mistaken Policies

The policy mistakes were numerous. On the distribution of income, the government failed those at the bottom of the distribution and gave too much to those at the top. To avoid the increase in inequality, which was the undoing of its social ambition, it would have needed better social policies for the poor and more determined taxation of the rich. It was not necessary to be radical, just a touch more generosity at one end and a touch more determination at the other end.

On child poverty, it underestimated the amount of spending needed and overestimated the effectiveness of targeted policies. Most of its new money came from reallocations within the social security budget. Targeted transfers are usually too complicated to be effective, and were certainly so in this case. It was too convoluted and time consuming for those in need to get access to tax credits; too many who should have support lost out and too many who should not got included, resulting in massive mispayments.[10]

On criminal justice, the government overestimated the effectiveness of reactive control and underestimated the need for preventive measures. It would for its crime policies have been better served by, for example, more support for families at the cost of less additional money in policing and prisons.

On health care, there were two serious mistakes. As with criminal justice, it overestimated the effectiveness of reactive care, where it made most of its investments, and underestimated the need for public health and preventive measures, where it invested next to nothing. Also, health care spending was increased too much too quickly. The NHS had since its inception worked under strict budget discipline. Additional investments were undoubtedly needed, but the additional money was put in so quickly and with so much political fanfare that the system as a whole let its guard down on budget discipline. As a result, a great deal of the additional investment was lost, including in a wage bonanza for existing staff, and productivity declined.

On education, more money went in but centralised management and detailed controls intensified and productivity was allowed to slip.

The System of Governance

However, "mistaken policies" is not much of an explanation in this case. This was a competent government. The real question is this: why did not competence do better?

The combination, in the public services, of more money and less productivity is a clue. Why would doctors and teachers respond to more money with working less productively? The answer is found in the way the government treated the professions. Its public management relied heavily on targets, performance indicators, league tables and the like. If you asked any professional in the NHS or in schools at the time, he or she would bore you to death with complaints about their burden of targets, monitoring, form filling and box ticking. This kind of management comes with two side-effects to drain efficiency. One is the investment of time and energy in beating the system for the purpose of satisfying targets. A second is to discourage initiative, flexibility and drive. Rigidly schematic targets, controls and performance indicators present themselves to workers as oppressive disincentives.

By its style of management, the government put public professionals under command. It failed to mobilise them for its reforms and instead alienated them by its heavy-handedness. The response of the professions was a silent revolt against an aggressive style of management by an authoritarian government.

The inability to mobilise people for its cause was also a factor in the government's failure in its flagship policy on child poverty. Breaking free from the heritage of child poverty would have required an investment in the political culture ahead of the economic one. But Mr. Brown was entirely technocratic. The government did not mount an attack on Britain's culture of accepting poverty and did not rally the nation behind a shared commitment to repay its debt to its children.[11]

Anyone who explores the making of public policy in Britain in some detail will not fail to see how centralised the system has become (on which more in Chapter 8). All policies emanate and are managed from Whitehall, and preferably from Downing Street. The rest of the country is on the receiving end, more under command than in partnership. The House of Commons is not a partner in governance. Local government is bereft of autonomy. Cabinet government was abolished. A once proud and independent civil service has been demoted to servitude. With such centralisation, a government has nothing to fall back on but commands and dictate. The absence of mobilising policies under New Labour is legion. The professions were not rallied and encouraged. The population was not mobilised to rid the nation of the shame of child poverty. Neighbourhoods were not mobilised against the scourge of anti-social behaviour. People were not mobilised to take care of their own health. The government *did;* everyone else was *done to.* One can object to this kind of governance on grounds of civil liberty; my complaint is with effectiveness.

A country of 60 million people cannot be run by a handful of politicians in the capital. It needs to be governed through leadership in which the government persuades *others,* from civil servants to citizens, that its project is worthy. It must encourage them to engage with and work for that project. No government can succeed by force of its own effort. It can only succeed if it is able to mobilise the effort of the millions. That it cannot do by command, which is counterproductive, but only by leadership and by showing citizens confidence and professionals trust. New Labour, for all its showmanship and spin, mishandled the art of leadership. Thereby, in defiance of its carefully cultivated scepticism of power, it nevertheless came to overestimate its power and squander it in its own way.

Political power is dangerous for its holder. A strongly centralised structure of governance—presidential without checks and balances according to Mr. Marshall-Andrews—puts too much power of decision making in the hands of too few people and denies those lone decision makers necessary protections against the intrinsic tendency for things to go wrong. Too much power is a recipe for mistaken policies. It makes it too easy for too few people to decide too much. It deprives those decision makers of the caution that comes with the awareness that their decisions will be checked and double-checked and scrutinised by others with independent authority.

It was finally this misunderstanding about power and command that was at the heart of the failure of the New Labour leaders. That misunderstanding came on further display when Mr. Brown succeeded Mr. Blair as prime minister in 2007—confirming the old wisdom that no one who is desperate to be leader is competent to be leader—and instead of reintroducing cabinet government, as he had promised, brought a reign of terror to Downing Street.[12] His control freakery became legend until he himself spilled the beans at the opening of the final television debate in the 2010 election campaign: "There is a lot to this job. I don't get all of it right. But I do know how to run the economy, in good times and in bad." A leader who thinks he runs the economy and, what is worse, believes himself when he says he does, is of course doomed.[13]

The difficulty for New Labour was not in the making of policy; indeed they legislated like madmen and launched new policies left and right. But they failed in implementation. It was not that Blair & Company did not recognise the difficulty. In 2001 they set up a "delivery unit" in the prime minister's office with Mr. Blair's full personal authority behind it to bully everyone else in Whitehall to follow through and follow up. The head of the unit, Michael Barber, has accomplished the feat of writing a witty and readable memoir of his time as chief implementer. "We made mistakes. Certainly I did. We took on too much, not all of it central to changing the system." That was early on; later, he says, they learned to prioritise. But when you read on through his long and ever shifting lists of priorities, you see that they were all over the place and that while much was prioritised very little was ever de-prioritised.

New Labour never managed to articulate anything like a clear project of purpose for itself (in part because the personal animosity and at times warfare between Mr. Blair and Mr. Brown was much stronger and more brutal than the outside world knew, as subsequently laid bare in Jonathan Powell's memoirs). Without a project to discipline itself and to serve as a cover for a bit of ruthlessness, the government was, in spite of itself and its own awareness of the danger of taking on too much, never able to get down to the necessary prioritising. They slipped up on the first rule of strategy, according to the management guru Michael Porter: that a sound strategy starts with having the right goal. Therefore they also failed in the ultimate rule: that the essence of strategy is choosing what not to do.

Mr. Blair and Mr. Brown inherited a system that Mrs. Thatcher had been relentlessly centralising. It was easy to make policy, but there was not enough order to prevent bad ones and not enough obedience to implement good ones. Had they broken with that legacy, they might have succeeded. Instead, they continued to centralise and condemned themselves to ever harder effort for ever less gain. Given the designs they worked within, they didn't have a chance.

THE GREAT KOREAN SUCCESS

South Korea's remarkable transition was, as is generally recognised, state led.[14] However, to make sense of that established wisdom we need to understand in some detail how that state worked and just what kind of leadership it provided. Very early, social policy became an indispensible instrument in embryonic initiatives that started the ball rolling on to a fully fledged welfare state. In *The Korean State and Social Policy,* my colleagues and I take the Korean governments' use of social policy as a prism through which we observe their governance. Ever since Bismarck invented the modern welfare state in Germany in the 1880s, social policies have been recognised to be, among other things, instruments of order, state building, rule, social control, efficiency and legitimacy. Our analysis is in that tradition.

Backdrop

Late-twentieth-century South Korea was a nation that could not have been predicted fifty years earlier. Three great achievements had been realised. Poverty was turned to prosperity, dictatorship was turned to democracy, and a social safety net was spread in the population, so that eventually no significant section is excluded from the benefits of economic advancement.

To put these achievements in perspective, consider the great contemporary development story, that of China. If we set the take-off for modernisation in South Korea to the end of the Korean War, in 1953, and the take-off in China to the end of the perversely named Great Leap Forward, around 1961, then China should by now have achieved what South Korea had managed about ten years ago. In fact, China has copied only one of Korea's three achievements, that of economic growth, but has so far failed to achieve both social security and democracy.

Here are some of the milestones in South Korea's remarkable voyage:

1945–48   American military government

1946–55   Land reform

1948   Formal division of Korea into North and South

1948–60   The First Republic under President Syngman Rhee, until he was forced to resign and leave the country for exile in Hawaii. Democratic constitution but increasingly authoritarian in practice. Uneasy industrialisation and the emergence of deeply corrupt crony capitalism. Influx of American voluntary agencies.

1950–53   The Korean War

1960–61   The Second Republic, established as a parliamentary democracy but unable to provide effective rule

1961   First military coup, bloodless

1961–63   Military dictatorship under Park Chung Hee as chairman of the Supreme Council for National Reconstruction. The creation of the Korean Central Intelligence Agency. Emergence of "the developmental state."

1961–80   South Korea's emergence as an Asian "tiger" economy

1963–72   The Third Republic under Park Chung Hee as president. Soft authoritarianism. The articulation of industrial modernisation as the project of national resurrection. The advent of the welfare state. The "koreanisation" of the voluntary sector. Emergence of state-directed *chaebŏl* monopoly capitalism.

1970–79   Cultural revolution of mass mobilisation in the *Saemaul* movements, first the rural New Community Movement and then the urban-industrial New Factory Community Movement

1972   Second military coup, as a coup within the coup, violent

1972–81   The Fourth Republic under the Yushin Constitution. Military dictatorship under Park Chung Hee as president until he was shot dead by his own security chief in 1979, probably in a drunken brawl.

1979   Third military coup, violent

1980–87   The Fifth Republic under Chun Doo Hwan as president. Continuation of military dictatorship. Continued strong economic growth.

1987   Attempt to continue authoritarian rule fails in the face of nationwide uprisings

1987–98   The Sixth Republic. Democratic constitution, gradual re-democratisation, winding down of "the developmental state." The presidency remains in the hands of the old guard, first under Roh Tae Woo, a former general, and then Kim Young Sam, the first civilian president since 1961. Authoritarian habits linger.

1997   Democratic consolidation with the election of Kim Dae Jung as president. The East Asian financial crisis hits Korea severely with mass unemployment as one result.

1997–98   The Tripartite Commission and the Grand Social Pact

1998–   Welfare reform and *chaebŏl* reform. The end of "the developmental state" and the normalisation of the state and of state-society relations.

The Project

In the first half of the twentieth century, Korea, an old and proud nation, was humiliated by Japanese colonialism and destroyed by war and division. It had to start afresh. It did that by adopting a project that grew out of its history: the resurrection of a nation that could stand proud in the world. That was the guiding vision in both Koreas, in the North, at least initially, as well as the South, but with the difference that in the South the project was established and survived as one of modernisation.

Authoritarian rule, although painful, turned out to be progressive for South Korea. It brought will and ability to a project that was so clearly articulated and firmly established that it overpowered even the dictators who defined it.

Economic Advancement

South Korea took off to economic advancement under authoritarian rule. These authoritarian governments were, on one hand, pretty far out toward one extreme in the use of force to maintain power, but also, on the other hand, pretty far out toward the other extreme in delivering effective governance. This combination of being strong in the use of force and effective in the delivery of governance is the specific feature of South Korean authoritarianism. These were not tin-pot dictators. They were in all their reprehensibility also sophisticated in the sense of seeing themselves as, and being, agents of a project to which they bound themselves.

Park Chung Hee was a straitlaced military technocrat. Yet, when in power, he saw that "mess" was inevitable and that non-state actors could not just be put in their place in a chain of command. Only those who were weak and whom he did not need because they had no useful service to offer him did he push down and away. That was the destiny of the trade unions. Those who might have been able to stand up to him, and whom he could make use of, he co-opted. In the business community he encountered a pack of profiteers who had enriched themselves during the years of Syngman Rhee, and whom he despised and was minded to put away in jail and leave there. But instead, he entered into a, for him, unholy alliance with big business and gave in to a particular kind of state-directed monopoly capitalism steeped in corruption that must have been distasteful to him. Instead of nationalising the voluntary sector, and thereby ridding himself of a threatening network of civil agencies involved in (potential) grass-roots activism—the dread of any dictator—he again struck a deal with the devil that allowed voluntary agencies to continue working and growing in return for delivering services he needed to have delivered to the population but that his governments did not have the economic or administrative capacity to deliver themselves.

The state-business alliance in Korea is well known. Less well known has been the alliance of state and voluntary sector, an alliance that sits oddly with the idea that in authoritarian South Korea public policy flowed directly from the strong state. The Korean welfare state was made by the presidency. But in implementation, the management of the welfare state was in the hands of a broad coalition of state, business and voluntarism. When we observe these coalitions at work, we see a very strange kind of strong state. It does call the shots and instructs its partners about what is expected of them. But also it does work *with* partners. What we see is not a state doing the job but a state co-opting others to get it done for it in some kind of togetherness, with give and take on both sides.

The Korean rulers, certainly President Park, dealt with their own apparatus of government in much the same way. They set themselves up to be in charge. They hired people they trusted, purged those they disliked, promoted those who were faithful, and spied on those who were suspect. But then, on this understanding of who was in charge, they turned to flattery. They pulled officials into the orbit of power, listened to them, consulted with them and allowed them dignity and importance. They created institutions for their participation in all manner of consultative bodies. They engaged advisers and experts whom they did not patronise but gave platforms of influence in advisory agencies. The skill that stands out here is the skill of co-optation.

Even a state with dictatorial strength is not likely to be able to shape events in its country if it makes itself a power state only. It is impossible for any state to *command* its society to be efficient. If it wants not just control but also things to happen, there is no other way than to mobilise others and encourage them to efficiency. Even the South Korean state, which during the main build-up of modernisation was centralised, hierarchical, powerful and ruthless was in governance at the mercy of others whom it had to rely on in order to impose its will. It certainly had the means of coercion, and the will and ability to use them, but those means and that strategy were of use to it mainly for protecting itself. The forcing of others to efficiency with the help of raw coercion is not available to any state. Only rulers who are able to understand this and to rule accordingly, however strong they be, have the potential to be effective. President Park, unusually among autocrats, seems to have stumbled upon a keen awareness of this complexity of governance and was able to govern with much care and a good deal of restraint in spite of a total absence of fear in the use of force.

The conventional interpretation of the Korean state is "strong." But that does not capture the delicate balance between force and restraint that was the essential characteristic of Korean authoritarianism. There was force but also direction, there was repression but also vision, there was brutality but also mobilisation. These governments used their strength to be able to rule, but then governed with the help of restrained strength. The identity of this state is to be found not in power but in the *use* of power, in its ability to use strength rationally and prudently so as to make things—astonishing things—happen in and to Korean society. Korean modernisation grew out of state practices that differed sharply in their two manifestations. While in dispensing force the governments were self-sufficient and reliant only on the apparatus of state under their command, in dispensing governance they were dependent on non-state actors. In the preservation of power they *commanded* servility; in governance they *asked for* compliance.

Democracy

It was in its ability to mobilise society that this state displayed its competence. It mobilised its own servants. It mobilised experts. It mobilised the population to self-betterment in the *Saemaul* movements. It used occupational welfare to mobilise businesses and workers. It turned foreign voluntarism into a national capacity and mobilised it for the management of social services.

Mobilisation is a strategy with consequences. Those who are mobilised survive, live, prosper and are given clout. Many authoritarian regimes have preferred to crush society; in South Korea, in contrast, society was built up. The price of mobilisation is to allow others influence. The officials and experts who were mobilised used their influence to fortify the modernisation project. They were apolitical, but they were men of the world and brought an ethos of worldly sophistication to the partnership with their masters. They looked to the advanced countries of the world and saw, for example, that there would be no modern Korea without a welfare state. The rural people and factory workers and their families were mobilised in a cultural revolution of countless *Saemaul* projects. They were thereby given a voice so that the government that had given them that voice could not turn around at will and ignore what they said. Businesses and voluntary agencies were made partners in governance.

By the strategy of mobilisation, the authoritarian rulers not only led Korea to economic development but also built it up as a society rich in institutions. In the civil service a centuries-old meritocratic tradition of bureaucratic rationality survived to some degree. Institutional meeting grounds were created in which masters and servants collaborated and civil servants were given importance. The role of expert adviser was made prominent and, again, institutions were created for serious and durable deliberations over public policy. The *Saemaul* movements created quasi-government institutions across the country and pulled millions of ordinary Koreans into organisational activity. Tripartism was a tested technique in industrial relations long before Kim Dae Jung made a success of it in the driving through of labour market flexibility in the aftermath of economic crisis.

The strong state dominated society, but also, paradoxically, filled it with life. The society it bequeathed to democracy was not monolithic but a pluralistic one of vibrant institutions. How fundamentally different this was from the legacy of authoritarianism in Russia and Eastern Europe! There, autonomous institutions had been crushed and when the old regimes were swept away there was nothing for the new ones to work with. They had to start from scratch and build up institutions again, from business via civil society to public administration. That process has been difficult and has after more than twenty years still long to run for a new normality to be found. In Korea, there was much less difficulty. Authoritarianism was overtaken by its own bequest, the constitution was quickly redrafted, and democratic rule took over without counterrevolution. The institutions of a reasonably pluralistic order were there, alive and well, and democracy could find its footing in a gradual process of transition until consolidated ten years after the breakthrough.

If civil society is made up of those institutions which live and operate in the space between individuals and the state, then authoritarianism in Korea was of a kind that worked with and stimulated such institutions and let civil society thrive. Here, finally, lies the answer to the double mystery of affluence and democracy. The secret is institutional pluralism in spite of autocracy. Korea could grow economically because the state provided leadership and let that leadership work through a varied network of institutions. It could shift with relative ease from autocratic to democratic rule because the institutions a democracy needs to be able to operate were already in place.

VISION AND RESTRAINT

No easy comparison should be made between a turn-of-the-century democratic government in Britain and twenty-six years of authoritarian rule in Korea at an earlier stage. Circumstances are, to put it carefully, different. But the two examples have something in common in the origins of success and failure. In both cases, the explanation lies not in power but in the *use* of power.

In the Korean case it was conspicuous how the governments were pursuing a project—or a vision or purpose or narrative, it has many names. Joseph Nye calls it "a state's grand strategy, its leaders' theory and story about how to provide for its security, welfare and identity" and argues that the first step in effective governance is "clarity about objectives."[15] Korea's objective was to reclaim (in the words of historian Bruce Cumings) its place in the sun, that was to happen through modernisation, and modernisation meant industrial development. This was an articulated vision from the beginning of authoritarian rule. In 1963, two years after his coup and ahead of presidential elections, General Park defined this idea of purpose, project and priority with absolute clarity: "I want to emphasize and reemphasize that the key factor of the May 16 Military Revolution was in effect an industrial revolution in Korea. Since the primary objective of the revolution was to achieve a national renaissance, the revolution envisaged political, social and cultural reforms as well. My chief concern, however, was economic revolution."[16]

It was also the right project. The Koreans lived in poverty. Their leaders offered them an escape from misery. They made their project even more the right one by wrapping into it a promise of social security. The governments were authoritarian but their project was credibly for the public good. That was made yet more credible by their ability to deliver.

This project gave direction to governance. What has been called "the developmental state" was single-mindedly dedicated to orchestrating industrial development and economic growth. Neither rulers nor country had any doubt what the show was about. But it was also a project that constrained the rulers. The reason the dictators were prudent in governance and worked *with* non-state actors and stimulated the development of non-state institutions is that they could not be more dictatorial in governance without sacrificing the project which they themselves had made their raison d'être. The Koreans were unfortunate to have to suffer brutal authoritarianism but fortunate that when they were to have authoritarianism, they got intelligent autocrats. (In Europe, the Greeks—and others—should be so lucky as to have had authoritarianism of this kind instead of what they have had: bad authoritarianism and bad democracy.)

In the New Labour story, the project was ambiguous, if there was any at all. New Labour should have had a project—to break away from the legacy of Mrs. Thatcher and introduce a melody of social justice into public policy—but no such vision was articulated so as to be binding on public policy. After an initial honeymoon, no one knew what New Labour was about beneath the fog of obfuscation the government spread around itself, and in hindsight it is easy to see that in economic policy Messrs. Blair and Brown were just surfing on their lucky wave of economic growth, until the absence of project caused them to lose balance when the economy came tumbling down. When Mr. Brown, in the autumn of 2007 and shortly after having become prime minister, in a *spectacle son et lumière* of combined political cowardice, bad judgement and inept footwork that destroyed the authority of his premiership, pulled back from calling an election that he would have won, and compounded his mistake by trying to cover it over with another one when he wanted us to believe that the bad poll that had scared him had nothing to do with it, he gave as his reason that he wanted more time to develop the government's vision. After ten years in office!

In the introduction to his memoirs, Mr. Blair describes the British people as "brave, determined and adventurous" but also as people "who need a vision, a concept, a sense of our place in the world."[17] I don't think it is a particularly unfriendly reading of the book to say that thereafter there is not much vision in sight, except that Labour must be New Labour for the purpose of being in government.

The experience is reminiscent of another failed leadership, that of President Jimmy Carter in the United States. In the words of historian Nigel Hamilton, "Carter failed to apply the two most fundamental elements of command: the need to impose a clear vision that others can ascribe to, and the ability to delegate to others if that vision is to be carried out successfully."[18]

Both my British and Korean stories are about governments that were solidly in power—meaning able to make policy—in different ways, but in power. The stories differ, however, in the implementation of policy. The Korean rulers were without scruples in their use of hard power to stay in control, but for their time and place unexpectedly sophisticated in the use of soft power in governance. Once in control, they preferred to co-opt rather than to command. As authoritarian rulers go, they were uncharacteristically prudent in the way they dealt with their *others*.

In British democracy, there is no need for ruthless power for a government to stay in office, but once there its problem of governance is much the same as for any government. Success rests on smartness and sophistication and elegance in the use of power. In governance, the New Labour bosses were much harder than they should have been. They understood the limits of power for staying in control and were soft with their potential enemies, in particular in the financial services industry. But they did not similarly grasp the limits of power in their dealings with those who worked for them in the civil and public services. In their respective contexts, the Korean leaders were command-adverse and the British leaders command-prone.

Dictators usually deal with the confrontation between governors and governed by suppressing it—until they are unable to keep the lid on, as in Eastern Europe in 1989 and in North Africa in 2011. The Korean dictators were different. They went beyond suppressing the confrontation to managing it by having it absorbed in a network of institutions. That also did not last, but when it broke what followed was not chaos but orderly transition.

In Britain, the New Labour experiment revealed an unsettled confrontation. Citizens were surprisingly compliant, reelecting Mr. Blair twice, but government workers were unforgiving. Working in a centralised system of command and control had alienated public servants so that by the time Mr. Blair took up office, the habit of cooperation had been broken and the government did not have an apparatus at its disposal that just got on with it.

It should have been the other way. In democratic systems, followers have a duty of compliance, and we should have expected that duty at work in the British case. In an autocratic system, there is coercion but not duty, and we should have expected ineffective rule in the Korean case. But these examples show that democratic governments can put no trust in duty and that non-democratic ones can be effective. Obedience must be created. Others have it in their power to refuse it. It falls on leaders to lead so that underlings see them as someone who deserves their obedience.

The secret of effective government lies in how power is used. Every wielder of power from time immemorial has known that, or if not discovered it to his detriment—as did President George W. Bush when he both at home and abroad overestimated what he could do with power and neglected the art of elegance in its use, and became one of the least, perhaps *the* least, successful presidents in American history. It is even common sense what it is in the use of power that contains the potential for making it effective. It's *restraint* that can generate obedience to power. That was known to be the recipe of success for the first ever successful emperor.

When Darius I consolidated the Persian Empire around 500 BCE, he conquered, defeated and put down revolts. But it was by restrained power that
he held the empire together. He did not as a rule crush those he defeated,
but preferred to co-opt by making cooperation attractive and allowing the
defeated to maintain their customs in religion, language and ways of life.[19]
Suetonius, the great and gossipy biographer of Roman emperors, ascribes
successful governance by Julius (Caesar), Augustus and Tiberius to restrained rule. Augustus, for example, like Darius, "nearly always restored
the kingdoms which he conquered to their defeated dynasties."[20] When
these emperors later failed, it was because they became used to power and
threw restraint aside. A later effective ruler with great power who also
had the gift of restraint was Otto von Bismarck, who was not quite the
"iron chancellor" he has been made out to be. "The key to his success lay
in a marvellous combination of strength and restraint," writes historian
Norman Davies. "He built up positions of great power, only to disarm his
opponents with carefully graded concessions that made them feel relieved
and secure."[21] The Korean dictators stumbled on the same wisdom. They
had iron fists and were ready to show it, but they preferred to give others
something, even when they disliked the gift they had to make, and incite
them to collaborate.

Those who are given power are rendered lonesome. They are not
liked, they are envied, they are suspected, they are despised and plotted
against. He who is lonesome can get nothing done without the help of others. When those others are prone to disliking him, he must flatter them to
lure them away from their suspicion and to dispose them to work for him.
If he lets the wrath of his power fall down upon them, he can crush their
opposition but not make them his allies. To obtain that, he must give them
something. Tiberius, for example, although all-powerful, "left a great deal
of public business to the magistrates and the ordinary process of law [and
let the consuls] grow important again."[22] As did Park in Korea vis-à-vis
his officials and advisers. The only way for a ruler to defeat the tyranny of
others is to pay those others something of what they appreciate so as to
dissuade them from using against him some of their counterpower. A government that wants something done in and for its country cannot rely on
force. Its leaders should be determined in what they want to do, in vision,
and restrained in the way they do it, in the use of power.

3

HOW TO USE POWER

These ways can win a prince
power but not glory.

—The Prince, chapter 8

The New Labour story is confusing. This was a government with power that for all its activism was of little consequence. It may also be difficult to come to grips with the Korean story, or at least my interpretation that it was not power but a particular and in some ways restrained use of power that accounts for success. This does not make sense. Powerless governments are inconsequential but powerful ones rule. Is that not so by definition?

Not necessarily. The British experience is not even all that unusual. On taking up the American presidency in 1977, Jimmy Carter enjoyed Democratic majorities in both houses of Congress. Yet, "Tax reform: defeated. A new consumer protection agency: defeated. Election Day voter registration: scuttled before reaching the floor of the House. Health-care reform: defeated. A proposal to tie the minimum wage to the average manufacturing wage: defeated. An overhaul of outdated labour relations laws: successfully filibustered in the Senate."[1] It's not a mechanical question of power. Powerful governments can be impotent. Seemingly weak ones can punch above their weight. Power does not necessarily get things done.

The idea that effective governance flows from powerful governments should be relegated to the book of myths, the sooner the better. In

British political thinking, for example, it has been established dogma that the political process should produce governments with decisive power. That has been the excuse for a perverse election system that, along with low voter turnout, has produced solid majority governments backed by as little as 25 per cent of the electorate. This dogmatic thinking was so firmly established that, although the theory had been disproved by the New Labour experience, the idea of effective coalition government after the 2010 election was almost impossible to grasp for most people in the commentariat.

And not only in British thinking: "All you have to do is look at how many minority or weak coalition governments there are around the world who can't deliver something big in their own country, but basically just teeter on the edge, because they can't put together the votes to do anything consequential, because of the divided electorate." This was Robert Gates, at the time the U.S. secretary of defence, speaking in 2010.[2] But let me offer that gentleman a lesson about things consequential, and one not from lofty presupposition but from real life. In the British election campaign in 2010 there were signs in the beginning that the parties might come together for much needed reform in long term and old age care, but the issue quietly dropped off the radar again. As I see it, this would count as "something big" (although for a defence secretary bigness perhaps depends on guns). Over the years, strong majority governments had allowed a functioning arrangement of care associated with the National Health Service to slowly fall apart, at the cost of economic loss and suffering for millions of elderly and needy people. At the time, although too late, when even a feeble attempt to start thinking about a repair failed, it was already fifteen years since Germany, long accustomed to coalition governments and the best governed country in Europe (among the big ones), had had the foresight to preempt this difficult consequence of population aging by introducing a long-term care insurance effective enough to cope with the problem and flexible enough to adjust to changing economic and demographic conditions.

For his fear of weak coalition governments, Gates should further consider the case of Denmark. In a world of fractured confidence, since 1973 (the start of the data series) Danish citizens' satisfaction with their governments and political system has consistently *increased*. During that same period, no government, coalition or not, received a majority of the national vote and not a single party had a legislative majority in the Danish parliament. Whether any of these governments delivered something big in their country is perhaps debatable, but they did at least deliver a well-governed country, which unfortunately cannot be said of all democracies, and certainly not of the one from which Mr. Gates gazes out upon the world. Quinton Mayne, who has analysed this remarkable case, ascribes Danish political satisfaction to what he calls "municipalization," which, Mr. Gates will be surprised to hear, consists of weak coalition governments giving away even some of the little power they have. "By the end of the 1980s, municipalities had assumed wide-ranging spending and decision-making powers [and as a result] political power was no longer monopolized by national politicians in Copenhagen but rather came to be shared between national and local politicians. Whereas prior to municipalization national electoral losers justifiably felt their needs and preferences were excluded when salient public policies were decided, thanks to municipalization national electoral losers were able to exercise influence over the direction of important policy decisions through local politics."[3]

Mr. Gates in fact gets it totally wrong. Effective governance is a subtle business. It is not strength that makes for greatness but authority and leadership. The strong governments Mr. Gates may like perhaps have some capacity to deliver something big but also to make mistakes on a big scale. He should know, having been involved in American and British strong government bigness in the wars in Iraq and Afghanistan. What governments need is protection against mistakes; blank cheques to deliver things big make them lose their way. I will return to this central theme in good government in some detail in Chapter 6, starting from the premise that in political decision making, things go wrong when nothing is done to prevent it.

GOVERNMENT

What is a government? Not as easy to say as one might think. Or, for a related concept, what is a state? Sometimes it is the central government as opposed to regional or local authorities. When he unified Germany, Bismarck wanted a strong *state* that could dominate the *Länder*. At other times it is something completely different, for example the same as a country or nation. We may say that states go to war against each other, or do we mean governments or countries? In the field of welfare state studies, welfare states are sometimes certain countries, such as the Scandinavian ones, and sometimes a set of policies, such as pensions and health care, as in for example "the British welfare state."

And it's no less confusing with the concept of power. What is it that makes someone powerful? Let me quote from an e-mail from a colleague: "Power is a contested concept, but my behavioural definition comes pretty close to the common usage of the dictionary—the ability to get things done (i.e., to affect others to get the outcomes you want). If one distinguishes the resources (hard and soft) that produce power from the desired behavioural outcomes, then a government has the power resources that it has but whether it can translate those resources into desired outcomes depends upon the context and its skills in power conversion."[4] Well, if so, what is it that makes a government powerful? Is it resources or resource conversion, or is it ability or skill—or is it not anything that a government has but rather a relationship between the rulers and the ruled? Possibly it is some of all of that, but, at least for me, it is confusing to put so many different things into one concept. I am interested in the association between power and the ability to get things done, but if power *is* the ability to get things done that's a non-analysis. If I insist that power and ability are not one and the same thing and that it is interesting to investigate how they are linked, I need definitions that separate the two components I want to analyse and that do not make them the same thing.

A *government* is a body of persons governing a nation. This is the definition of the *Oxford English Dictionary,* in my opinion an excellent definition.[5] It says what a government is—a body of ministers—and what it does: govern a nation.

Some would find this a narrow and formalistic concept. They may argue that the civil service is not only engaged in executing orders from its political bosses but that it wields real power of its own that influences the character and direction of governance and that a realistic definition of "government" should recognise this and acknowledge that a government is really the entire system that generates governance.

I disagree with that kind of logic. Such "realist" definitions tend to become unwieldy, so that we can never pin this thing government down.

I think we need to unwrap the system that generates governance and explore what goes on inside it. For me, the relationship between the political bosses and their civil servants, for example, is very much a part of the mystery of governance (which I return to in Chapter 7), and I don't want to hide that mystery away in a definition that says that both bosses and servants are parts of the same thing. I want a definition that encourages me to ask how it comes about that servants do as their bosses want, if that's what they do.

The "governing a nation" part is still a bit iffy. Do governments in fact govern? That's the question I am exploring, and it may then seem to be jumping ahead to include it as an assumption in the definition. But any government worthy of the name is at least in the business of governing, although it is always open to question whether it really does, or how well and effectively.

This definition of government helps me to go on and define some other concepts. If governments are in the business of governing, the activities and outcomes they produce (or not) is what constitutes *governance.*

If a government governs a nation, what is a nation? A *country* is a territory defined by established borders. Often a nation is the same as a country: the country of Iceland is a nation. But not always. Kurds insist that there is a Kurdish nation although there is no Kurdish country. In North America, native American tribes are often said to be nations, as in the Iroquois Nations. When people consider themselves to constitute a nation, that identity tends to be linked to a territory which they think of as in some meaning theirs (although many members of the nation may live elsewhere, even all or most of them, as when the Jews were dispersed). A *nation,* then, is the synthesis of a people and its territory. Where the territory in question is a country, the nation is the synthesis of people and country.

If that defines government and nation, what is a state? In common parlance, it is often the same, again, as a country or nation. Hence, a *nation-state* is a country defined as a political entity. Or it can mean more or less the same as government: when a government acts it is the state that acts. But it is probably better to say that the government acts on behalf of the state, in which case the state is more (durable) than the government but less than the country or nation. Let's say that the *state* is the site of political power in a nation and its institutions that work "from above."

Governments may govern nations, to which people belong, but people are usually said to live in societies. A *society* is a group of people— sometimes the people of a nation, as when we say "Norwegian society"— and their institutions that work "from below."

WHAT DO GOVERNMENTS DO?

The business of government is obviously done on a grand scale. It is therefore not difficult to lay out the complexities of it all, as can be seen in the learned literature. For John Dunn, the ambition to rule tends to be defeated by the cunning of unreason, no less today that in earlier times. For Margaret Levi, in her presidential address to the American Political Science Association in 2005, the combined efforts of the great thinkers and the massive body of recent research in political science, history and economics have taken us no further than that we may foresee somewhere in the future "the emergence of a dynamic theory of effective government."[6] A school of thought that works from what seems to be an obvious idea that governments govern with the help of instruments has not even been able to find an agreed definition of what an instrument of governance is or to offer any coherent typology.[7] My good colleague Christopher Hood has suggested that governments rule with the help of "tools," but I am unable to follow him in that. At least the governors I have seen have had no tools in their hands that they could put to use to get things done. Hood's government tools are the control over information, control over economic and other resources, authority in the form of legal powers, and organisational controls over people, land, equipment and so on. But these are not tools stored in a box in the government's offices that ministers can reach into when they want to do a bit of governing. They are scattered around in the vast apparatus of administrations and agencies, and beyond. To put them to use, government ministers have to get armies of officials and ordinary people to work together. That's not something they can just decide to do and get on with. They have to mobilise countless *others* to get done what they want done. Said Charles I—we are now in the 1640s—shortly before others cut his head off: "There is more to the doing than bidding it be done."[8]

Almost all approaches to the understanding of governance in political science that I am aware of seem to be in fright of what they are up against. They treat "government" as a monstrosity of tentacles, organs, connectors, reachers and levers of all kinds all over the place in patterns that are beyond easy observation and finally ungraspable. A system of governance, as opposed to a government, is obviously a behemoth that it is difficult to make sense of if treated as a singular thing.[9] That's what John Dunn finds, but without getting much further than observing that in complex systems intentions often get confounded, which is just a confirmation of Murphy's law that when things can go wrong they do go wrong. Margaret Levi wants to make sense of the behemoth with a "dynamic theory," but that's as vain a hope as anyone could harbour. Those who want to explain government with the help of "theory" leave us in the dark about what the theory they are searching for might look like or how we would recognise it if we saw it—or what the question is to which "theory" could be the answer. They are really doing little more than using fancy language to tell us over and over again that complicated systems are complicated. Nor does the language of instruments and tools take us far, as we will see as we go along.

I think we should go about it differently. We have to find somewhere to start and we should start with something that is simple enough to describe with ordinary language. We need to debunk the mystery of the behemoth and get down to observing the nitty-gritty of practical government business. No useful purpose is served by lamenting endlessly the complexities of the world. Everyone knows of its complexity; what is wanted from social scientists is simplicity and a grasp of the essential. My hunch is that we learn more by asking simple questions than by being sophisticatedly theoretical. I have let myself be guided by Richard Rose, who long ago put to us the question "in plain man's language" of what governments *do?*[10]

WHAT DO THEY DO IT WITH?

On his re-election in 2004, President George W. Bush said, "I earned capital in the campaign, political capital, and now I intend to spend it." He was right; the election had put him and the Republican Party firmly in power. But two years later, in the 2006 midterm elections, his government was in tatters and never recovered.

When the Labour Party won its great election victory in Britain in 1997, and should have been able to govern in any way it wanted, it seemed to back away from using the power it had won and went on to govern with a surprising absence of what many observers would have thought of as Labour policies.

The British government had power but was reluctant to use it. The American president was eager to use his but squandered it. Were these governments powerful? Perhaps not, as Jonathan Powell learned: "The main thing that a prime minister himself notices on entering Downing Street for the first time is how illusory power really is. When you are in opposition you are convinced that, if only you can get through the door, you can start making things happen. But power, like the crock of gold at the end of the rainbow, is never there when you arrive."[11]

Power

Political scientists tend to define power as the ability to get things done. I think they have made a mistake. Here, for once, but also rather basically, I disagree with Max Weber, who is (the modern) father of the established definition: "Power is the probability that one actor within a social relationship will be in a position to carry out his own will despite resistance."[12] But that cannot be right. Whatever power is, it is not a probability. At the very least, it is what makes for a probability. Nor do I agree with James Coleman that "the power of an actor resides in his control over valuable events."[13] This is to get ahead of things. Power is prior to control, and actors can have much power and little control or little power and much control. Nor with Raymond Aron's version that "power is the capacity to do, make or destroy."[14] Too fast again. Capacity does not flow directly from power. All American presidents are equal in being "the most powerful man in the world," but they are everything but equal in capacity. Even if you insist that they are also different in power, you would find them vastly more different in capacity. Mr. Reagan was not a success and Mr. Nixon a failure because one had power and the other not. The latter failed not for want of power but because he was overcome by paranoia and destroyed it for himself. These classical definitions conflate the thing power and the outcome of its use. In methodological language, they do not separate independent from dependent variables, which is a recipe for confused analysis.

Following Weber, it has become commonplace to think of power as something that is "relational," or, as we have seen above, "behavioural." But that is the view I want to overturn. No, I say, power is not relational and not behavioural! Getting someone to do what they otherwise would not, is *not* power. Power is something that may enable someone to influence someone else in that way. It is true that power mainly comes to play in relationships, but that is not to say that it *sits* in relationships. If you have a gun, you have the power that comes from having a gun, and you can get me to give you my money. If you try to rob someone who turns out to also have a gun, that changes the relationship, but not because you no longer have the power of a gun. It's because suddenly there are two people who both have the same power.

Power is something someone *has,* full stop. If you are the prime minister with a majority in the legislature in a government culture in which ministers obey the prime minister and parliamentary majorities the government, you have power (until your colleagues turn against you). Power is there or not, you have it or not, it does not present itself once you start behaving but is prior. It does not sit in any relationship between people; it sits squarely with persons. It is messy to start analysis from a definition that wraps into a single concept things so different as resources, behaviours, capacities, probabilities, relations, instruments, tools, skills and so on. We help ourselves by keeping it simple.

In an important contribution, Joseph Nye has distinguished between hard, soft and smart power.[15] Hard power is the ability to command, soft power the ability to persuade, and smart power the productive combination of hard and soft. That simple distinction is ingenious, and its author has himself used it to good effect, from reflections on foreign policy to reflections on leadership. But I am not comfortable with the language. I think commanding and persuading are very different things, so much so that we should not say that both are types of power. Commanding sits close to power, persuading is more distant from it.

Power is at play when *governors* are up against *others.* The governor is the one who wants something done; the others are those he depends on affecting to make it happen. There are situations where governors are autonomous and depend on no one, and in that sense are in absolute power. If I want a fried egg and have an egg and a pan, I just do it. But that's trivial; it is when governors rely on others that it is meaningful to reflect on power. For governments there are certainly always others out there.

Power is of two types: the power of governors over others and the power of others over governors. Power sits on both sides of the exchange.

It is not what governors bring to bear on others, but something that both governors and others bring to bear on each other. If the governor is all powerful, others must do as they are told. If others are all powerful, the governor is reduced to begging them to give him what he needs from them. The difference between commanding and persuading is this: Commanding is what governors can do with effect to the degree that *they* hold power. Persuading is what they must do to the degree that *others* hold power.

At one extreme, the governor is able to command others to obey. Here, power is on his side. If your country has a conscription army and you are conscripted, you have to serve. And if the government decides to take the country to war, you must go and fight.

At the other extreme, the governor has no power to command and can rely on nothing but persuasion. Now it is others who hold power. The governor wants something of them, but it is entirely for them to decide whether or not to comply. On the morning of the 9th of April 1999, British health officials issued a warning to prospective parents against trying for the millennium baby, since the story was out that the 9th and 10th of April were the best days, out of concern that the health services might not cope if unusually many women were to come to childbirth at the same time on the night that health workers wanted to be out celebrating. In this case, the government could inform and encourage, but the power of action was fully in the hands of others, in this case prospective parents.

In real life, there are never extreme cases where power sits either with the governors or with others. The governor may hold the upper hand so that others are obliged to follow, but others are never completely without counter-power. Even in the conscription example, although it is correct to say that the government has the power of command, it is still too strong to say that others have to obey. The soldier who must go to the battlefield has at least the power to fight badly. And before that, you *can* refuse conscription, if to great cost. You must be prepared to break the law and to suffer the punishment that follows, or possibly to go into hiding or exile. At the other extreme, it may be entirely for others to decide whether or not to let themselves be persuaded, but when your government asks something of you, you are under pretty strong pressure to comply. In the 9th of April case, the government's persuasion may well have worked since there was no rush of mothers-to-be nine months later.

It has been suggested to me that there is no symmetry between governors and others and that we should not say that both sides have power as if they were equals. Perhaps power is what governments have while others have something a bit less, such as capacity to resist. I disagree. My argument goes the other way. Political thinkers tend to award the government side too much power and to admit the side of others too little and underestimate how desperately governments are at the mercy of *others* that ministers run up against the moment they step out of their comfortable offices. "This [says Stalin to Bulgakov in John Hodge's play *Collaborators*] is what it's like when you govern. You sit here, in an office in Moscow. And out there, there's a hundred million peasants who cannot read. They hate you. They don't trust you. But you have a country to run. Targets to fulfil. An industrial base to secure, to expand. You have cities waiting to be fed. No one says it's easy."[16] It is useful that we remind ourselves of how dependent governors are on other people, and how little control they have over them, by putting that dependency in the hard language of power. Others are *not* limited to resisting. They have the power to undo those who are charged with ruling them. Remember Professor Lindblom: what stands in the way of the governor is "the great number of other people who are vigorously trying to frustrate." And not just trying. Those in whose interest it is to evade governance—special interests we say, but we all have special interests—often have not only the will but also the power to frustrate.

The power of governors, how strong it may appear, is always limited since it always has to be exercised over someone, which is to say over persons with will of their own. Not even enslaving someone else gives you the control you may think, because although the slave becomes dependent on you, you also make yourself dependent on him. Plantation slaves in the Americas, who lived under the most brutal human disempowerment ever invented, were never without counter-powers. They knew that their masters depended on their labour for their business and could use that knowledge to sabotage and subvert. The owners knew that the slaves knew of their dependence on them and both knew that the slaves could implicitly—or explicitly, for example by escaping—threaten with inefficiency. The slaves would extract concessions from their owners who, at least when reasonably rational, knew that they had to accommodate to some degree their interests and demands.[17]

It is true that it sometimes appears that governments can just command and get on with it and override resistance. For example, the British, Spanish and Italian governments in 2003 decided to join the war in Iraq against massive opposition in their populations. But at least in the British case, not without trouble from others. As late as a week before the invasion, the commander of the British forces, Admiral (later Lord) Michael Boyce, demanded a written assurance from the prime minister that the war would be legal in international law so that British troops would not be at risk of indictment for war crimes. That assurance the prime minister was forced to give in a letter. Behind the demand was a threat of not obeying the war order.[18]

It is also true that it is often difficult for others to mobilise the power they hold, particularly if it requires spontaneous action by a very large number of people. But significant others are not always many. For example, the ministerial top civil servants, on whom ministers are dependent, make up only the same number as the number of ministers. If they should get together over lunch and decide to all go back to their respective ministers and advise in a coordinated manner against the government's plan to reorganise the social security administration, that plan would be dead in the water. If you think this sort of thing does not happen in government offices, you have not worked there. On the eve of D-Day in 1944, Churchill "dictated an instruction that de Gaulle was to be flown to Algiers, in chains if necessary, and a letter to the General ordering him out of Britain. The aid who received the instruction ignored it. Eden had the letter burned."[19] And when the others are many, their power is awesome once mobilised. When circumstances conspired so that people in East Berlin in 1989 gelled into togetherness, the police state crumbled and was unable to prevent them from tearing down the wall behind which they had for years been locked in.

What is gained by locating power to both sides of the exchange is clarity about this: ruling is not a one-way street where some rule by the force of power and others are done to and can only react. It is a game in which princes and knaves do battle and both sides bring heavy armaments to the confrontation. The thing to understand about power and rule is that power is *always* necessary but *never* sufficient. It is the licence to rule, but no more than a driving licence says how good a driver the holder is does power say how good a getter-done the governor is. Governors need power and must show it. That is the way to get respect and be the ones others listen to. But after that, it's manoeuvring against the power of others.

The difference between George W. Bush in 2004 and Tony Blair in 1997 is that the former thought he could rely on power to enforce action while the latter was distrustful of it. Blair, in spite of holding power, went on to make great use of persuasion—but overdid it and became ridiculous for his abuse of spin. He should have listened to Lafayette who, working for the American revolution, took care to "not talk too much—to avoid saying foolish things."[20] Bush went on to disregard Congress at home and allies abroad, found himself without friends among the many others he was dependent on, and was to learn painfully how little a governor can rely on power. *He* should have listened to his wiser colleague, President Václav Havel of the Czech Republic, who, while still a dissident, made his great contribution to the theory of power in what he called "the power of the powerless."[21] And how right he was. The soviet economies in Russia and Eastern Europe were not only slow but eventually collapsed because all-powerful governments were unable to get powerless people to be efficient workers in their rational systems of command. These governments were thought to be strong because they were able to hold on to office by force, but all the while their people were engaged in revolt. "We tried to do better," said Prime Minister Viktor Chernomyrdin, "but everything turned out as normal."[22] The authoritarian governments in South Korea were ruthless in suppressing opposition to their hold on power, but in governance it was restraint, not force, that enabled them to be effective agents of economic development.

Authority

Governors and others are up against each other. The governor is the initiator. He is the one who wants something and he needs to affect others to obtain it. If others agree with him, the game is simple and he gets his way. If they do not agree, the governor has a problem. Usually, at least some more or less significant others are more or less strongly, sometimes very strongly, disinclined to oblige. Affecting reluctant others, then, is the crux of the matter.

The governor can command or persuade. The more power he can lean on, the more he can command. The more the power of others, the more he must rely on persuasion. The governor's dilemma is that the more he needs to use persuasion, the more that is because others hold power. But why should reluctant others with power let themselves be persuaded? This does not add up. You cannot persuade someone to do as you want when they do not want to do it and have the power to do as they will. There is something missing in the equation.

Now, persuasion *is* possible and leaders are often very persuasive. But governors who want to persuade others to dance to their tune need something to back up their persuasiveness, something that will make others listen even when they are inclined not to, something that will change their minds and behaviours in a way that they do not spontaneously see to be in their interest. Again, that cannot be power, because the reason the governor has to turn to persuasion is that he does not have enough power to command.

Power on the side of the governor is what makes others obey commands. What makes them accept persuasion is *authority.* A governor with authority can persuade reluctant others to go along with his wishes, or even make them believe that what he wants of them is really what they want too.

We need to *separate:* as capacity does not flow directly from power, neither does power translate directly into authority. At the end of the Crusader period in Jerusalem, when Saladin was threatening the city, its defence was in the hands of Baldwin, the "leper-king." He had power but was concerned that his illness deprived him of capacity. "It's not fitting that a hand so weak should hold power when the Arab aggression presses upon the Holy City." When the king died, power passed to Guy of Lusignan, but in a messy court intrigue behind the backs of most of the barons, wherefore he "certainly lacked authority"—and the defence of the city faltered.[23]

Power comes to the governor from various resources that he controls. A business leader who has the power to hire and fire those who work for him can hire on the condition of obedience, and maintain obedience by the threat of firing. He has the power he has, and others, however reluctant, have no option but to accept or get out.

Authority is a more elusive commodity. It comes not so much from resources but is something that appears to sit in the person. Some people, it is often said, have natural authority. George Washington, whose "presence bedazzled people" and who was a "natural leader," had authority in abundance, and was so aware of it that he hardly spoke in the Constitutional Convention because he knew that if he did he would stifle further debate and was content to influence the proceedings by his "tacit blessing."[24] Bismarck ruled Prussia and Germany from 1862 to 1890 as chancellor, and engineered the unification of Germany, without any conventional political base and through his forceful and complex personality—and the king's backing.[25] Eisenhower was a monumental leader in both war and peace, in part, says the historian Nigel Hamilton, thanks to having the gift: "From the time he was a child the people around [him] wanted to win his affection and his approval."[26] Others become persons of authority when they are put into positions of leadership; they seem to grow with their position and become authoritative, sometimes slowly and gradually. The case of Harry S. Truman comes to mind. But position does not guarantee authority. By the end of his tenure, President Bush had so little authority that when a reluctant Congress was forced to bail out American banks in 2008, it did so more in spite of than because of his efforts at persuasion. Tony Blair started his premiership with authority in abundance; however, it was gradually worn down by bad policies, excessive spin, and plain wear and tear.

Leaders make themselves authoritative by the way they manage. For President Eisenhower, a balanced budget was a given. That brought him the authority, for example, to get others on board and share in the funding of the greatest infrastructural investment programme in the nation's history, the interstate highway system. The equivalent today would be a high-speed rail system, as President Obama recognised but had to give up at the first hurdle. His government is bigger than ever, richer than ever, mightier than ever and borrowing up to its neck, and still unable to maintain the nation's infrastructure, never mind to improve it.

The authority of a governor is in the eyes of others—just as beauty is in the eye of the beholder. And when underlings see that spark of authority, it works wonders. If servants acknowledge their superiors as "their lords," said the observant Machiavelli, they bear "natural affection" for them.[27] Authority is contained in the willingness of others to listen and be persuaded. No governor has any other authority than that which others see in him. He has the authority he is able to extract from those he wants to lead and that they are willing to award him. Authority enables governors to get others to do for them, but at the same time the governor is at the mercy of those same others for the authority he needs in order to lead them. The authority of a leader depends on his ability to trap reluctant others into seeing him as someone who deserves obedience. Authority, then, although appearing to belong to the governor, is really in the gift of those he wants to exercise authority over. The ultimate power of others is their ability to deny the governor the authority he needs to be able to affect them. That kind of power, explained Havel, is held even by those who appear utterly powerless. They may not be able to oppose actively or visibly, but as long as the governor is in any way dependent on them they can always subvert. Governing is a power business, but never only a power business. It is also, and always, a people business.

Legitimacy

Because of the flimsy futility of power, it is when governors have authority that they can be successful. They need to shine, to impose themselves, to dominate, and to define the agenda and the terms of competition. Caesar was not only a man of power and a great warrior but also a commanding presence. He "equalled, if he did not surpass, the greatest orators and generals the world had ever known. His prosecution of Dolabella unquestionably placed him in the first rank of advocates. Cicero confesses that he knew no more eloquent speaker than Caesar, and calls his style chaste and pellucid, not to say grand and noble."[28] President Obama is a leader of similar authority of brilliance, as he demonstrated in his commanding speech in Tucson, Arizona, on the 12th of January 2011 at the memorial service for those killed and wounded in the assault on Congresswoman Gabrielle Giffords and others the week before—and in the process redefined, for a while, political relations in Washington by making himself the commanding presence and reducing the standing of his opponents without even having to shame them.

Leaders extract authority from followers and then turn that same authority around to disciplining those same followers. The next question, then, is how to attract authority? What are the magnetic forces that pull authority out of others and give it to leaders? There are two such forces: first, as always, power, and then a wondrous magic called *legitimacy*.

Power and authority, we have seen, are different things but nevertheless related. When powerful people speak, others listen because the speaker is powerful. Sometimes, it is true, power may become an impediment to authority, for example if reluctant others are able use the governor's power against him as an excuse to persuade themselves that he does not merit their respect. The weapon de Gaulle's opponents were able to wield against him at the height of his powers, during what François Mitterrand called "the permanent *coup d'état,*" was the claim that he had made himself dictator. But usually governors speak with authority when they speak from a platform of power. They are in office, hold power, and can use that base to make themselves authoritative.

However, the authority that springs from power is crude and fickle. It rests, ultimately, on force, threat and sanction. It is extracted, it is taken, and it is therefore resented. It is authority that leaders cannot trust, that is not firm, and that others will revoke if they can. It *pushes* followers into settling with their leaders, but people who are only pushed are not happy. Power is necessary, but still only a platform from which to start the real business of governing. Power makes governors, but governors cannot govern by the force of power.

The authority that sits on legitimacy is something else; it is elegant and is given freely. This is the jewel in the crown in the game of governance that makes for stable, strong and reliable authority. It is magic because it makes people obey not because they must but because they want to. It *pulls* followers into a settlement which they see as rightful. The critical follower eyes those who claim authority over him and says (or not), OK, these are people who should be followed.

According to Weber, the sources of legitimacy are law, tradition and charisma. Above, I have wanted to improve on Weber in the understanding of power. I think there is also room for improvement in his treatment of legitimacy. He should have added a fourth source and included power. Power contributes directly to authority as we have seen. It also contributes to the magic of legitimacy, but not in the same direct way. The link between power and legitimacy is not power as such but, again, the way power is used. Underlings incline toward obeying a governor when they believe he is in office rightfully and exercises his power in a rightful way. Weber's sources of legitimacy account for the "being in office rightfully" part. We also need to account for the second part of "exercising power rightfully."

Legality breeds legitimacy. A legal government has the authority, for example, to get people to pay taxes because any government needs revenue to operate and a legal government has the right to collect it. When the colonists in New England said "No taxation without representation," they were claiming a right to withhold from an illegal government the authority to tax them.

Tradition breeds legitimacy. The reason President Bush was never completely without authority was that he spoke not only in his own capacity but on behalf of the Office of the President of the United States of America. Hence, even during the finance crisis of 2008, when his secretary of the treasury, Hank Paulson, was doing all the running, it was still essential that the president put the authority of the presidency behind the Treasury's policies.

And charisma breeds legitimacy. Jimmy Carter ran out of authority as president but was able to rebuild impressive personal authority for himself once he was free from the burdens of office.

Any governor will try to present himself as a charismatic leader and will call on legality and tradition with as much effect as he can. But these influences are by and large beyond his control. A governor is either exercising power lawfully or not, traditional authority either is attached to his office or not, and people, including leaders, are as they are—unattractive ones are unattractive and attractive ones attractive. Tony Blair was relieved when one of his ministers resigned: "Some are made for office. Some aren't. He wasn't. Simple as that."[29] A bland and uninspiring leader can try to beef up his act, but if he does not have charisma in his person, he has nowhere to find it. Gordon Brown was unable to be liked as prime minister and unable to do anything about it no matter how hard he tried.

The great uncertainty in the quest for legitimacy is the remaining influence of the way power is used. Governors perforce use power; those who are seen to do so for good purposes and with wisdom gain legitimacy in the eyes of their followers. A governor who is seen to use his power arbitrarily or recklessly forfeits legitimacy. He is seen as someone who should not be in office. When followers allow leaders power, they know that they are in danger. They are in danger of being abused and they are in danger being ignored while others, friends of the leaders, are privileged. To get followers to award them legitimacy, leaders need to reassure them about the way they will use their power.

The reassurances that followers want are of two kinds: the restrained use of power, as we have already seen, and, in addition, the fair use of power. Rulers who exercise restraint show the ruled that they do not use power abusively. Rulers who govern fairly show that they use power for the public good and not to the benefit of some at the detriment of others. Rulers who do not are unlikely to be seen as rulers who use power in a rightful way. One of the mistakes President Park in Korea made was to pamper his own district with government money and investments. This caused lasting resentment in other parts of the country. When the authoritarian regime weakened, that simmering resentment contributed to igniting the revolts that eventually brought it down.

Games of governments and others, we now see, are shaped in the main by three influences. First, *power.* It is power that defines the game and determines who is governor and who are others. A politician who is running for office becomes a governor by winning the office and assuming the power that comes with it. Until he does, he is only one of the others.

Second, *the use of power.* While power is more or less a given for the governor, the great variable is his use of it. This is the influence that is determined by his own doings. A leader with much power who is unable to use it well will pay the price in loss of respect. One with less power but more shrewdness in its use can be a leader of disproportionate consequence.

And third, the game is shaped decisively by *authority,* and in particular the authority that comes from legitimacy.

Power, then, is not at all the ability to affect others and get things done. It is only what puts someone in the office from which he is supposed to get things done. His ability then to move things, once he is in power and is the governor, depends *not* on the power that sits in his office, but on the intricate interplay of power, the uses of power, and authority.

THE PUBLIC GOOD

I am unable to define "the public good" once and for all as consisting of A, B, C and D, and probably no such definition is available. I can only suggest. The public good is that which is *ours,* and recognised and accepted to transcend the private and to be common and shared. It goes to order, protection and security. Governance for the public good is that which delivers the leaders' part of the settlement with the followers, that which is capable of extracting obedience. Crucially, it is fair governance.

Consent, finds Margaret Levi in *Consent, Dissent, and Patriotism,* depends on fairness, on *perceived* fairness. When you believe the governor is fair, that belief is for you a reason to obey him. What is done, and seen to be done, fairly is right. Leaders who are seen to govern fairly are seen to deserve obedience. I'm concerned, to repeat, with effectiveness and with governors' ability to deliver. A decisive part of what they should be effective for is fairness.

The force of the feeling of fairness, and even more unfairness, is strong. What turned the reluctant and conservative George Washington into a revolutionary, and many with him, was that he came to believe that the king and Parliament in London were treating the colonies unfairly (in taxation), that they were indifferent to their lot, and that they would persist in unfairness to their own benefit.[30] No doubt, this was the experience that led him to launch the independent American government as government for "the discernment and pursuit of the public good."

Governance is fair when no significant group in the population can successfully claim to be treated with blatant unfairness. Citizens look for unfairness in governance because unfairness is an excuse to withhold uncomfortable compliance. Governors who are to be effective must endeavour to deny citizens those excuses. To thus disarm them, they need to show themselves to be evenhanded.

There are two sides to perceived fairness, fairness in process and fairness in outcome. The process is fair when policy decisions are made correctly as the outcome of a fair tug of war in elections and parliamentary decision making. There is political equality and everyone has a fair say. No one can complain over decisions on the ground that they have not had a fair chance of influence in the process.

The outcome is fair, in addition, if the losers in the process are nevertheless treated fairly. In a normal democracy, the majority prevails. If it then takes all and disregards the minorities that are on the losing side, it is abusing its power. Minorities in this meaning are those who carry little weight in elections and parliamentary decision making and whose interests could be disregarded even in a fair tug of war between the competing interests that have clout. The disregard of minority interests is not only wrong but also unfair in the meaning of providing an excuse to deny a government respect, be it on the part of the minorities in question or of others who want to get at the government. The rich may, for example, use a government's inability to help the poor as an excuse for resisting taxation, on the argument that what they are asked to pay for is ineffective.

The fairness that depends on correct process can be engineered with the help of rules: free and fair elections, freedom of speech and association, a free press, transparent decision making, and so on. The fairness that depends on respect for minorities, however, can only to a lesser degree be ensured by rules. Minority rights can be legislated to bind the majority, for example the rights of handicapped persons, but if majorities are intent on disregarding minorities who cannot muster power of their own, it will be difficult to get protective legislation passed and to prevent discrimination in spite of legislation. Fairness, therefore, depends not only on rules but also on the various and elusive influences of culture.

There is a view that fairness depends on process only, for example that people are treated fairly if there is fair opportunity. But that is simplistic. For one thing, there is no fairness of opportunity if outcomes are unfair. The children of those who are poor and ignorant have a hard start in life by force of their parents' deprivation. Furthermore, it is not borne out by experience. Even the World Bank, that repository of neoclassical economic orthodoxy, has come to recognise that there are *two* conditions of justice: "equal opportunity" and "the avoidance of deprivation in outcomes."[31]

To return to Finer's distinction between decision making and decision implementing, this is the iron rule of policy effectiveness: there must be enough fairness in decision making to extract enough obedience from followers to enable enough decision implementing.

LEADERSHIP

Governments do things, I've said, but of course they don't. It is persons who do things, in our case ministers. Ministers get things done in society by getting others to do for them. When they do that by restrained power, they exercise leadership.

The restraint that leaders like Darius, Caesar, Augustus, Tiberius, Bismarck, and Park displayed gave them authority. It was not that they were paragons of constraint—they certainly were not—but because they acted in ways that were perceived to be restrained up against expectations at their time and in their place. Caesar was seen to be compassionate because "if he crucified the pirates who had held him to ransom, this was only because he had sworn in their presence to do so, and he first mercifully cut their throats."[32] Restraint, however relative it be, leads others to see virtue in their leaders and to see them as leaders who deserve to be obeyed.

In *American Caesars,* his panoramic exposé of the life and rule of twelve American presidents from Franklin D. Roosevelt to George W. Bush, Nigel Hamilton finds leadership to be the defining quality of the presidencies. Roosevelt, Eisenhower and Kennedy were not just powerful but monumental presidents, thanks to their ability to lead, from Roosevelt's "quality of soul" to Kennedy as "the last of the Great Caesars." These were men people (albeit not all) would jubilantly have followed through the gates of Hell. With Lyndon B. Johnson, his shortcomings were finally in leadership. Johnson's biographer Eric Goldman judged him to be a man of exceptional intelligence. He was enormously respected and admired in the first part of his term for his policies and his energy and effectiveness in pushing them through, in particular "the war on poverty," but when his policies failed (in the quagmire of the Vietnam War), he was deserted and found himself without followers, because finally "he could not command that respect, affection and rapport which alone permit an American president genuinely to lead."[33]

Leadership is the translation of power into authority, the ability, says Joseph Nye, "to orient and mobilise others for a purpose."[34] That is done by extracting authority from them so that they make themselves ready to be led.

While power is a given, it is leadership that is relational. It is built on the combination of initiative from above and acquiescence from below. The leader needs to bring to this relationship something that the followers like and believe in. There will not be leadership unless *others* accept and go along with it and make themselves followers. Those others always have it in their power to not follow. They do not have to revolt or resist outright; it is enough to do a bit of foot dragging, as did public sector workers in Britain in response to New Labour authoritarianism, in a display of how foot dragging can accumulate into implosion in the capacity of the public sector to deliver. Political leaders bring all nature of influences to bear on those they want to lead: power, position, legality, titles, laws, repute and so on, but all this those subject to being led can resist or subvert. Something more is needed, something that persuades the followers to let the leader lead the way.

Leadership in the polity works in the same way that the political economist Joseph Schumpeter argued that entrepreneurship works in the economy. Many people go into business. Of them, some turn out to be entrepreneurs. They are the ones who shape things beyond their own enterprise and influence the direction of economic activity and development. Entrepreneurship comes from grasping an idea for production, organisation or marketing, often an innovative idea, and turning it into a successful venture.

Likewise, many people go into politics. Of them, some turn out to have the stuff of political entrepreneurship. Successful leaders are those who are able to turn their more or less innovative ideas and programmes into policies that carry through to shaping ideas and developments in society. They have vision, show performance, deliver, and reap respect.

The successful entrepreneur is the businessman who believes in his own ideas, who puts himself on the line for their realisation, and who is able to make others believe in it and to lend him their support. He needs partners to put his idea into production, for example engineers, logisticians and marketing people. He needs workers who are prepared to engage in production, preferably by hard work and dedication. He needs bankers who are ready to trust him with their money. And he needs customers who will pay for what he needs them to buy. The entrepreneur is someone who has a good idea and is able to get *others* to go along with implementing it.

The successful political entrepreneur is someone who has faith in himself and the stomach for risk, and who has the good fortune to be in the right place at the right time. He needs to be determined and secure of himself and his mission. He must obviously be able to get himself into power, but once there he needs to make others believe in his determination. He needs partners and people to do the footwork, now officials and administrators in the place of engineers and workers. He needs backers, now legislators in the place of bankers. And he needs takers, now voters in the place of customers. He needs to get those *others* to accept him, in Machiavelli's words, as "their master."

THE MAGIC OF LEGITIMACY

So far, I have argued (1) that the problem is obedience, (2) that governments are up against others who are always reluctant, (3) that the final challenge in good government is implementation, (4) that the turning of power into performance depends on fairness and restraint, (5) that a settlement of order depends on institutions that bind governments and push followers into compliance, and (6) that such institutions reside in culture as much as in rules.

The deeper reasons behind those conclusions, I now add, is that power is not all it has been cracked up to be and that governance is also, and always, a people business. Sitting on power does not do governments much good. It gives them a certificate to direct things in the country but does not solve their problem of obedience. Power can at best and only sometimes control reluctant others, but not on its own get them into a settlement of willing cooperation. Governments can in only limited ways get their will by commanding. For the most part they depend on persuading. What governments need to muster if they are to be effective is authority and leadership. To shore that up, they will want the magic of legitimacy attached to themselves and their doings.

HOW TO BE A GOVERNMENT

. . . you cannot keep the friendship of those who
have put you there; you cannot satisfy them in the way
they had taken for granted, yet you cannot use strong
medicine on them, as you are in their debt.

                                        —*The Prince,* chapter 1

G overnments do one thing and one thing only: they give orders.
No other output or product comes from a government at work.
And even that is to put it too strongly. Sometimes their orders
are so meek as to be mere requests, for example when a government asks
the legislature to give it a budget, or just suggestions, for example when
it advises people to maintain their health by not smoking. We might have
said that all they do is to *speak.* They tell the legislature what laws to pass.
They tell their civil servants what laws and budgets to prepare. They tell
them to start implementing what the legislature has decided. And they tell
people out there in society to do what is expected of them according to the
law of the land and good sense. Sometimes they do not even do that. If the
legislature has passed a law on its own initiative, the government is on
the receiving end of orders from the lawmakers to implement what they have
decided. At other times they do a bit more; when a government holds delegated power it can give orders in society without having to take the trouble
of asking or pretending to ask the lawmakers for permission in each case.

But let's say that governments give orders. That is the full, complete
and unambiguous answer "in plain man's language" to the question of
what governments *do.*

It is worth stressing the point. Governments do very little. That is difficult to get across and is contrary to how we often think about governments wielding great powers. Often when we think about problems in society we also think about the many ways our governments could rectify them. If it is poverty they could, we say, transfer income. If it is inequality, they could tax the rich. If it is market distortion, they could regulate. But making up lists of things governments *could* do is, in response to the simple question of what they *do,* wrong language. Governments do not actually *do* the kinds of things we are accustomed to saying that they do. They tell others to do it. Governments do not for example regulate. They may order officials to impose new regulations on, say, banks, but after that it is anyone's guess what actually materialises by way of new rules and how the banks respond. It is interesting to reflect on what governments could and should do, but first we need to be clear about what they actually *do.*

TROUBLE

Part of my difficulty with Christopher Hood's parable of tools is that it is too clinical. His governments detect problems and act on them. So they do, of course, but not always. Often, very often, it is problems that call on the government rather than it on them. Governance is mysterious, messy and chaotic. Governments are pushed around and knocked off course by what Harold Macmillan, when British prime minister, called "events, dear boy, events."

Serious governments have programmes that they want to implement, but from their first day they discover that the world is not ready to sit by and let them conduct their business in peace. An oil depot goes up in flames. A train crashes. A stock trader is found to have gambled unsuccessfully on a monumental scale and to have put his bank in danger. Disgruntled civil servants leak official secrets. A union calls a strike. Lorry drivers block the motorways. The issue of food safety crowds itself on to the agenda after a media storm surrounding the death of a seven-year-old boy from *E. coli* infection transmitted to him from a playmate who had eaten an undercooked burger. A sex scandal forces a minister to resign, or a tax scandal prevents an anointed one from taking up office. The price of oil skyrockets. A national mining company is caught up in a mess of bribery in Africa. The prime minister, in a careless moment, is overheard calling his finance minister a coward and the press whips up a storm. Russia cuts off the flow of gas to Europe. A teenager goes on a rampage in his previous school and shoots dead eight pupils and three teachers. A war in Sierra Leone makes itself something that must be responded to. A hurricane hits New Orleans, a tsunami Japan. A newspaper has a scoop and finds immigration controls that are a sham, or a government computer system that is full of mistakes and running wildly over budget, or patients being left waiting for hours in emergency rooms. Terrorists explode a bomb in the City of London. One hundred economists sign a letter to the *Financial Times* calling for a change of direction in economic policy—or a corporate chief makes the same call to the same effect. A child under the supervision of the social services is abused to death by a parent. A pastor threatens a public burning of the Qur'an.

And so it goes on day in and day out in small and big ways. Events push themselves into governments' attention. Locusts, an aide to Mr. Obama is supposed to have called them, for the way they swarm down upon you without warning. A minister's day starts with the morning news and with setting in motion responses before noon to the troubles in front of him. Some get addicted to knocking down "stories." I know, I worked under such a minister and it was a mess. There was no plan or continuity in departmental work and we civil servants though our boss a fool and could not be bothered to exert ourselves. The degree to which the life of governments is chaotic cannot be overstated. "One of the strangest parts of politics," observed Tony Blair, "is how you get into situations of unbelievable controversy without ever meaning or wanting to."[1] The game of governors and others is rarely under the government's control. Others are always making trouble, sometimes big and sometimes small, sometimes in anger and sometimes for the hell of it, sometimes deliberately and viciously and sometimes by accident—but always there is trouble.

Take, as an example, Monday the 10th of May 2010, as seen from London. The Thursday before there had been the general election resulting in a hung Parliament and no single party with a majority to form a government. This had caused panic, and on the Monday leaders were still scrambling to cobble together a deal to provide the country with a government.

Europe that morning woke up to extreme anxiety about what would happen when the markets opened for trading. European Union finance ministers had in an emergency weekend meeting in Brussels agreed on a package to shore up debt-ridden European governments, in particular in Spain, Portugal and Ireland, which were in danger of seeing the cost of their debt rise to unsustainable levels and future credit to evaporate. In all, 750 billion euros of potential credit was made available to euro-zone governments, enough to liberate the most indebted ones from dependency on private finance and, or so one hoped, see off the wolves at the door. These reactions were in addition to a separate package agreed for Greece in the preceding week to save the Greek government from defaulting on its debt. It had been hoped that the Greek package would have been enough to reestablish trust in the euro, but toward the weekend that proved to have failed, so that the contagion was in danger of spreading to other southern European countries and beyond, forcing the finance ministers to put together a new rescue package of hitherto unimaginable proportions in the course of a day or two.

What the next days would bring in the markets was still unknown. They were in jitters for other reasons as well. On the Thursday, the Dow Jones Industrial Average had suddenly plunged 1000 points at 2:47 in the afternoon. That was probably a fluke, and most of the loss was recovered quickly, but on our Monday the incident had yet no explanation and there were fears that "something" was on the loose in the markets and that "someone" knew about it.

In the Gulf of Mexico, BP's attempt to block a deepwater oil blowout failed and masses of oil continued to gush into the sea and on to southern U.S. shores, resulting in not only huge environmental damage but also fears about the future of deep-sea oil exploitation and hence the supply and price of oil—and of a great British company.

If anyone was able to look further afar, in Thailand, Bangkok was becoming a battlefield between protesters who had barricaded parts of the centre and ever more heavily armed police and military in ways that looked as if they might spiral into civil war. In the Philippines, presidential elections that same day were in danger of collapsing in chaos, cheating and escalating violence.

That was the way the day started in London. Not your average political day, to be sure, but one to show that "politics" is a messy business in which in large measure what leaders must do is to react as best they can to events that are heaped on them from far outside of their control.

Chaos threatens any government to be knocked off course. In parts of John Major's period as prime minister in Britain, incessant events from within and outside of the government took hold in such a way that governance pretty much disintegrated. Some governments manage to keep some consistency of direction in public policy through the inevitable chaos that rages around them, and when they do we should recognise that as a considerable achievement. Policy problems, observed Aaron Wildavsky (the master of implementation analysis) in *Speaking Truth to Power,* are seldom solved, only worked on.

The significance of incessant events is that governments always face trouble in even getting themselves into the position of being able to give orders. Not only is giving orders all they can do, it is a constant battle for them just to be able to stand up, speak, be heard and listened to. Never mind the problem of getting people to obey; before that they must elbow their way through to a position of putting to them the orders they want them to heed.

And events are of course not necessarily random. There are people out there "vigorously trying to frustrate." If you want to make trouble for a government, the smart way is to derail it before it is able to start giving orders.

GOVERNMENT AGAIN

The body of persons that constitutes a government is in my way of thinking small. In British parlance the government is sometimes said to be the majority side in Parliament and to include both holders of ministerial office and their supporters on the back benches in both the lower and the upper houses. In my definition, the government is made up of only those who hold ministerial office.

Governments are sometimes also spoken of as if they are made up of both political bosses and their officials, at least higher officials. For example, when we say that governments run things, such as the public health service, those doing the running seem to be both those who give the orders and those who execute them. In my definition, the government includes only the bosses, the political appointees who are at the head of the ministries. Governments own or manage other institutions, but those institutions are not a part of the government: they work for it. All of them—ministerial departments, armies and navies, agencies of public ad-ministration, social services, railways, public hospitals, oil companies, uni-versities—are no part of the government. Masters never fully possess their servants (not even if they are their slaves). Servants are separate, always *others,* and may or may not cooperate and may or may not coordinate.

In some systems there are many political bosses. In the United States, each department has several higher- and lower-level secretaries and the holders of senior civil service posts are also often political appointees. In Britain now, about one hundred members of the majority side in Parlia-ment hold senior or junior ministerial office. It does not make much dif-ference for my purpose how wide a circle of political appointees I include, but it simplifies things to narrow it down to the holders of top political office.

A government, then, as I think of it, consists of those persons who make up the top political command, such as the Cabinet in the British case. It is the executive committee of a corporation made up of itself, of a legislature to which it reports, of a set of ministries and agencies which report to it, and of the courts that adjudicate over right and wrong in the conduct of the others.

A government then is not just a body of persons but a *small* body of persons, practically speaking a handful of men and women, say twenty or so in all. That crystallises our puzzle. How does it come about that so small a group of people can govern a nation? A government consists of people who are much like you and I: they have twenty-four hours in the day, they need to sleep, eat and take care of family matters, and possibly have some fun. How do they do it?

Governments rule with the help of ministries, directorates, the armed forces, accountants, social workers, local officials and so on. A gov-ernment has this vast machinery of governance at its disposal once it is in power. But that does not take it very far. It has to get the machinery to work for it. "From inside No. 10 looking outwards," found Michael Bar-ber, "the strong sense is of a small number of people trying to influence a vast, unwieldy and unmanageable bureaucracy."[2] And that's not even looking beyond the bureaucracy and into the country.

The puzzle is this: if, say, twenty people are to rule sixty million, those twenty are when all is said and done helpless. They are in power, but governing involves thousands and thousands of civil servants, officials and workers in a myriad of ministries, departments, directorates and other agencies. Indeed, it involves everyone who lives in the country, both those who are engaged in the apparatus of governance and everyone else who allow themselves to be governed.

A minister cannot so much as set up a meeting without getting a secretary to arrange it. What if the secretary refuses, ignores orders, forgets, misunderstands, goes out for a coffee? Or calls another secretary who refuses, forgets or messes up? Any minister who has been in office for more than two weeks can tell you stories about how the simplest things go wrong. Getting secretaries to follow up is of course the least of a minister's problems (although: in the early morning hours of the 2nd of May 1997, the day after his first great election victory, when Mr. Blair, the prime minister elect, was returning to London from his constituency and was on his way to the jubilant party festivities, "in one of these ridiculous mishaps that happen, we lost our way to the Festival Hall").[3] But he or she depends not only on their secretaries but on everyone else. Whatever they are to do they depend on someone else for it to materialise, and the government collectively on everyone. Some, their officials, they can command, but commanding is not of much use if those who are on the receiving end are disinclined to bother. Most, ordinary citizens in the ordinary business of life, cannot easily be commanded but must still be made to comply. The game of governors and others is extremely imbalanced: the few against the many—on the side of the governors a handful, on the side of the others the millions. Those who criticise my opinion that power sits on both sides of the exchange are right that there is no symmetry in it, but wrong in thinking I allocate too little power to the governors. The imbalance is to the detriment of the governors.

Take the spectacle in the United States in the days before the 11th of September 2010, the anniversary of the attack in 2001 on the World Trade Center in New York City and the Pentagon in Washington, D.C., of the pastor no one had heard of in a behind nowhere little church in a small town in Florida with a congregation of a handful, who threatened a burning of the Qur'an on the anniversary day. The rumours of his plan were enough to incite riotous demonstrations in Muslim countries, including Afghanistan, and to bring out the American commander, General Petraeus, to warn that the event might put American troops in danger. A major international confrontation threatened. The president of the United

States, the most powerful man in the world, used a press conference to urge the pastor to call off his stunt. Behind the scenes, the defence secretary, Robert Gates, the commander of the most powerful war machine of army, navy and air force ever seen in human history (the same man I quoted in the last chapter in praise of strong governments able to deliver something big in their country) spoke to the pastor by telephone and asked him—*asked* him, not told him—to desist from setting the world ablaze. So much for power! In this case it was the pastor who had the capacity to do, make and destroy, but if that leads you to defining power so that the pastor had it and the president and defence secretary not, you have slipped up in your definition. (And the pastor *did* desist, at least long enough for his stunt to become ineffective.)

ORDERS

Governments give orders to get decisions made and to get decisions once made acted upon.

In a normal democracy, decision making is the easy part. Of course, all kinds of things may go wrong already here. A government with a narrow majority may be held to ransom by renegades in its own ranks—it is enough to remember the case of Prime Minister John Major in Britain up to his defeat in 1997. But also governments with too big a majority may be unable to discipline their troops. President Jacques Chirac in France found himself in this position in 1997 when he was unable to rally his big majority in the National Assembly behind necessary reforms. He called a snap election to get himself a smaller majority that he could control, but miscalculated, lost not only some but all of his majority, and in one bold blow made himself a lame-duck president. Or governments may be in internal disarray and unable to agree with themselves, for example in multi-party systems where governments are often coalitions, in particular if antagonistic parties have to team up. Chancellor Angela Merkel's big coalition between the conservative and social democratic parties in Germany from 2006 to 2009 may be a case in point, although when Mrs. Merkel in 2009 got herself the centre-right coalition she wanted, she to her surprise found the better coalition even more difficult to manage. So decision making is never entirely easy and sometimes pretty tricky, but compared to implementation still easy.

The reason things are comparatively simple at this stage is that those involved are few and close to each other—ministers and their *near others*. Any government in a normal democracy that is in any way a functioning one will *ex officio* have the authority it needs to be able to order its near officials to do the planning it has to get done and is likely to find its officials willing and eager. Not necessarily and always, and not always efficiently, but usually: "Many Labour politicians had expected the civil servants they faced to be dyed-in-the-wool Thatcherites," says Jonathan Powell, "but after eighteen years of Tory government the civil servants were bored and desperate for change."[4] Also, the government and legislature should usually know each other well enough that the government will only by rare accident make a proposal to the legislature that it does not pretty much know will be accepted.

But a government that can get decisions made is still not ruling. A decision is only words on paper. It is entirely possible for a legislature to pass laws and have no one act on them. Remember the Russian Duma in the early years after the fall of communism. The reason I am unsatisfied with the language of tools or instruments is that it takes too much for granted, as if a decision that something should be done puts tools into the hands of the government to do it. That's to move too fast. Just as the government needs to get decisions made and may struggle with that, it also needs to get tools put to use and may struggle at least as much with that again.

A political decision contains second-round orders to implement its intention. The reason things now get more complicated is that there are many more *others* involved, and many who are *distant others*. Now the government is dependent not only on those who are inside its own circle, but on innumerable others many of whom live and work in the far corners of the country and have no involvement in decision making. That's why, concluded the political scientists Jeffrey Pressman and Aaron Wildavsky, "it's amazing that federal programs work at all."[5]

Second-round orders go first to the same officials in the same ministries who previously prepared the decision, but now as an order to put the decision into effect. That changes things dramatically. The government is dealing with the same people but in a different way. While it previously told its officials to prepare things on paper, it is now telling them to make things happen in life. As I know from my own experience as a government servant, planning is easy (and fun), implementation difficult (and frustrating). When it comes to implementation, governments must follow through and follow up and follow up again—and that is very, very, very trying and hard going.

Second, orders now flow not only from ministers to servants but also from ministries to underlying agencies with mainly implementing duties. These agencies usually do not play much of a role in the planning of decisions. They may have been asked to provide background into the planning, for example statistics or studies of logistics, but are mainly there to carry the burden of implementation. Say the government wants to increase the level of the income tax. The minister of finance gets her officials to draw up a proposal to the legislature with the necessary background material and does the political fine-tuning in a couple of rounds with her government colleagues and the relevant lawmakers. The minister puts the proposal to the parliament that puts the label of "law" on it—possibly with some modifications since legislators like to feel useful—and turns around and tells the same officials in her ministry to get the law put into effect. Those officials then turn to the relevant underlying agency, call it the Directorate of Tax Collection, which redesigns its system for extracting income taxes according to the new law and mobilises as best it can its innumerable local sub-offices to do the job. The world of implementing agencies is much larger than that of the ministries. These agencies are more removed from the centre of power and often spread out over the country and, from a minister's outlook, more anonymous, as is for them the minister.

No minister can ever take it for granted that she can easily get her ministry to do as she wants. Indeed, the enduring experience of holding government office is how difficult it is to get anything at all to move and be *done.* A new government may have won an election victory and be in control of the legislature, only to find that it has inherited a civil service that will not throw itself into active service for the new regime. When Aneurin Bevan became secretary for health in the Labour government in Britain in 1945 and set about creating the National Health Service against the grain of health policy planning during the war and under the pre-election coalition, he had to outmanoeuvre the top mandarins in his own ministry, who had been in charge of the planning he now rejected, and ally himself with younger officials whom he could count on to work loyally for his policy.[6]

A minister is obviously in a position to direct her officials to prepare the legislation she wants to push through, but no one can order officials to enthusiasm. Or for that matter to not make mistakes: In 2004, John Prescott, the British deputy prime minister, arranged a referendum in the northeast of England on devolved power to regions. He put much work into the campaign and "personally recorded a phone message saying, 'This is John Prescott, I am ringing to urge you to vote in next week's referendum.' They were to go out to households across the region in three bursts around teatime. Unfortunately, the technician programming the machinery had got the timing wrong so that thousands of sleepy households answered the phone at four thirty, five and five thirty in the morning."[7]

Even if a minister meets a competent and cooperative civil service, she must still animate the people who make up the service to put their backs into the job of changing the direction of policy. She must deal with inertia, with the instinct to continue to do things the way they have always been done and with inevitable institutional conservatism. In France, in 1976, "A plan was drawn up to transfer the Education Ministry out of its sprawling premises on the Left Bank and into the former NATO headquarters at the Porte Dauphine, a move which [Prime Minister Georges] Pompidou hoped would facilitate the reduction of the 'trade union squatters' who dominated the staff and impeded change."[8]

However, although all kinds of things may go wrong in the inner circle for all kinds of reasons—conflicts, quarrels, power struggle, paralysis, tugs-of-war over turf, mistakes and miscalculations, disobedience, back-stabbing, mischievous leaks to the press and what not—in the larger scheme of things this is still manageable. A ministry can be reasonably handled by any minister who is not completely without charm and administrative skill. But when she turns her hand to implementation proper, she will find herself on more wobbly ground and dependent not only on officials in her own secretariat but also on those Michael Lipsky called "street-level bureaucrats." To get a ministry to cooperate may be a bit of a frustration; to get the whole apparatus of agencies on different levels of responsibility and their thousands of managers and clerks to cooperate, coordinate and pull together is a nightmare.

For example, in the mid-1980s the Norwegian government decided it had to do something to get escalating social assistance expenditures under control. In previous years, the treatment of social assistance claims had been "objectivised" in the interest of administrative simplicity. More than previously, cases were decided by standardised formulae and less by scrutiny of each case separately. One result was that more social assistance was awarded and that recipients tended to stay on the rolls longer. The government decided to reverse procedures and impose more careful case-by-case scrutiny. However, it also knew that social workers in the mean-time had become attuned to the new administrative system and suspected that they approved of it both because it was less "degrading" for potential recipients and because it had proved to be more generous. It therefore not only told the social workers what they would have to do but set in motion a careful campaign of educating and informing them about the rationale of the new policy. The government got it done, but not simply by deciding that it should be done.[9]

Implementation is often local: services have to be delivered where people live and work. The trouble with implementation, therefore, is not only distance and that orders must travel down through multiple layers of administration as in a game of Chinese whispers, but also local interests and local government. Always, local people see things differently from how they are seen centrally. They think central authorities want to command them too much, do not understand local circumstances, and do not give them the resources they need to implement centrally decided policies. Local interests are always suspicious, and often contemptuous, of those people up there in the capital. Local governments always feel under siege and always want to protect, and if possible to extend, their domain of authority. Even local sub-agencies that are part of the central government's apparatus are often local in their identity and torn between their duty to execute orders from above and their inclination to see things from below.

But even that is not the end of it. The orders contained in political decisions also go out into the country to those who are really distant: to businesses, organisations, voluntary agencies, schools, families and to all the people who make them up as directors, workers, members, husbands, wives, pupils and so on. This is where things start to get not only difficult for the government, but desperate. It may be hell to get officials to cooperate and do what they are supposed to, but that is at least to deal with people whose job it is to obey orders from above. Once ministers are into telling ordinary people how to go about their business, they find themselves on very shaky ground indeed, considering that "people" include all sorts: capitalist tycoons, dysfunctional families, speeding motorists, teenage delinquents, underpaid teachers, tax cheaters, overzealous social workers, turf-protecting bureaucrats and sticklers for red tape, arrogant surgeons, businessmen on the take, reactionary unions, publicists and influence hawkers, demoralised transport workers, know-all professors, irresponsible journalists, drug dealers and mafiosi, manipulating advertisers, dumbing-down broadcasters, and libertarians who just want to be left alone. The line of command is now very long, for example from the minister of agriculture in his office to the prairie farmer who is tilling his soil. Will the order be heard, understood and respected? Those expected to obey and comply are numerous. How does a lonely commander get thousands and thousands of people to walk in tandem? What rights do ministers have to order? What duties do people have to let themselves be ordered and how inclined are they to obey what they are told is a duty? It may be a duty for citizens to obey the laws, but that is not much for a minister to lean on if anonymous citizens strongly dislike the laws imposed on them. Within ministries and agencies, ministers may hope to have support from a culture of administration: out there in the citizenry the culture may be very different, for example entrenched scepticism of "big government."

Finally, and of course importantly, the government now meets *interests,* in everything from local governments via union leaders to business captains. No matter what a government decides and in whatever area of policy, there will be persons and groups and institutions who see the orders they are asked to comply with to be contrary to their interests. If the government decides, for example, to lower the speed limits on motorways, it will find motorists, or some or many of them, to be against it and to have an interest in avoiding its consequences. These interests may be backed up by power, say mighty motoring organisations or a car industry in control of jobs. The government may want to impose its will on society, but society is a messy matter to deal with, made up of endless criss-crossing constellations that can and will counter, resist or frustrate the orders that flow from the centre.

A government meets counter-interests and counter-powers already within its inner circle and in the civil service. But that is nothing compared with the resistance it meets when it tries to push its orders beyond the inner circle and into the population. All governments want to think that their policies are popular, and sometimes they are—for some. But they will not have been long in office before they discover that ingratitude is the law of politics and the normal thanks they get for all the good they do.

PEOPLE BUSINESS

The *only* reason ministers issue orders is that their underlings do not want to do as they should. Good behaviour does not always depend on government orders. The economy rolls on and produces goods and services thanks to workers getting up in the morning, going to work and doing their jobs. The government does not have to sound a national 6:30 alarm and chase us off to the bus. When a government has to resort to giving orders, that is *always* because it needs to get others to do what they do not want. Not only are the governors few and the others many and distant, but also the governor is needy and the others unwilling, often strongly so.

To get others to take you seriously, you start by showing them your power. But once it is established that you are a governor with the power to command, your ambition to be effective bids you to pull back from the use of the power you have in your hands. You may hold it up as a threat, but if you unleash it except in the last resort you will get the power of others against you and fail in what you want to achieve. The prudent governor should leave power latent as much as possible and turn to persuasion. He needs to deflect others from unleashing their counter-power to frustrate him and should therefore endeavour to influence them toward *wanting* to oblige.

Followers are asked to obey against their self-interest. The public good is not something that sits in front of us for all to see and embrace instinctively. It must be created and obedience to it enforced. We need, said Aristotle, to be "perfected," which again, he said, depends on "law and justice." Washington, in his first inaugural address, made an almost identical call. National policy, he said, should be rooted in morality and public morality relies on the "eternal rules of order and right."

These appeals were, as you would expect from a thinker as great as the leader and a leader as great as the thinker, prescient. Perfection, or morality, depends on *two* influences, one that pulls and one that pushes. If governance is fair—according to justice and right—the governed are pulled into a settlement with their governors. But we humans, the devils we are, also need to be pushed by what Aristotle and Washington called "law" and "order." The job is not impossible, but it is not much good to sit back and send out orders that no one listens to, even if you are the most powerful kind of government. "The multifarious and very frank expressions that can be found on the Chinese Internet today is done almost entirely under pseudonyms. The authorities have banned the use of pseudonyms, but when 400 million people use them anyway, what can they do?"[10]

There are—and I here follow Tom Tyler in *Why People Obey the Law* —two broad ways. One way is to work instrumentally: to dominate those whose compliance the governor wants so that they do as they are told whether they like it or not. This is what ministers *must* do when they know that others will not comply freely and what they *can* do to the degree that they have power. It is a harsh and cumbersome way, and a way that may cause ministers and their government a loss of future political capital, and also a way that is only available to ministers in narrow circumstances when the balance of power is decidedly on their side. This is the fragility of authority when grounded in power only.

The other way is to work normatively: to influence people's mindsets, beliefs and preferences so as to neutralise antagonism and lure people into wanting to do as they should so that they do it by their own volition and do not have to be forced. Ministers must inform and educate their people, and touch their souls and stimulate their will. This is much the nicer way, and often the only possible way when the narrow circumstances are not available to allow bossy instrumentalism. It is also usually the more effective way. Leaders who are able to work normatively get their way not by force but through the magic of legitimate authority. It is difficult for leaders to get much done if they are unable to mobilise some of that magic. For the leader's intention to follow through to consequence, each servant must do as he is told and the servants collectively must coordinate and pull together. It won't work if those who work it don't *want* it to. The leader needs to influence their interests and to orient them to complying and working jointly. They must get them to be, at least to some degree, actively for their plans and not just passively not against.

The more a government is successful normatively and able to shape the culture of governance to its advantage, the less it depends on working instrumentally. Churchill as war leader in Britain was not much good at instrumental work. He was a messy, erratic and unpredictable manager, and had a way of riding hobby-horses and pursuing hairy-fairy projects that he got into his head were smart and urgent. But he was a master of the vision thing. He inspired those who worked for him, who, in spite of despair over his style of management, loved it for the excitement of his person. He gave his people confidence and determination and made them work together through the trials of the war.

Putting one's trust in instrumentality is heavy handed. Margaret Thatcher was a forceful leader who worked mainly instrumentally and who had no time for the normative stuff. She had vision but her method was to force it on people more than to rally them to her purpose. As a result, she failed, was deserted by her political friends and saw her reputation plummet. Ronald Reagan was also a man of vision, much the same as that of his friend Margaret Thatcher, but one who worked very differently from her. His strength was as a master of the normative art. That proved a successful strategy at the time and has enabled his reputation to grow after he stepped off the stage.

In their people business, then, governments should put some fear into their underlings with a display of power, then pull them from one side with the help of fairness and push them from the other side with the appeal to rules, conventions and the like. Getting this to work vis-à-vis officials is difficult and vis-à-vis citizens very difficult.

THE PUNY NATURE OF GOVERNMENT ACTION

So far, I have argued (1) that the problem is obedience, (2) that governments are up against others who are always reluctant, (3) that the final challenge in good government is implementation, (4) that the turning of power into performance depends on fairness and restraint, (5) that a settlement of order depends on institutions that bind governments and push followers into compliance, (6) that such institutions reside in culture as much as in rules, (7) that power is not all it has been cracked up to be, (8) that governance is a people business, (9) that managing the problem of obedience depends on authority and leadership, and (10) that the most solid authority is that which rests on the magic of legitimacy.

In this chapter I have found, in addition, that governments do one thing and one thing only: they give orders. But giving orders to effect turns out to be a difficult art. It is difficult to work one's way through the omnipresent troubles that keep governments bogged down and hinder them from even getting to the starting line and being the orderer, it is difficult because always when they give orders it is to people whose interest is in not doing as they are told, it is difficult because many underlings are distant and removed from the government's reach, and it is difficult because there is an intrinsic contradiction between the necessity of imposing orders on underlings and the desirability of inclining them to willing cooperation. Governments need power but depend for the most part on working with persuasion.

5

HOW TO GIVE ORDERS

So a prince has of necessity to be so prudent that
he knows how to escape the evil reputation attached to
those vices which could lose him his state.

—The Prince, chapter 15

Ministers do not have much of a repertoire to play on. They cannot spend money, they cannot deliver services, they cannot build roads. All they can do is to tell people—others, as always—to do things in the hope that they get off their backsides and cooperate enough for action to be set in motion resulting in money being spent, services delivered and roads built.

TYPOLOGY

Government orders are commands or signals. That dichotomy makes for a complete classification of orders by the kind of order. When a government gives an order, it is either commanding or signalling, or combining the two.

What a government can order done is also limited. It can order taxes to be paid, transfers to be given, or behaviours to change. That's all. It cannot order a new direction of social trends. It cannot order the economy to grow or traffic to flow. It cannot order a war to be won. It can hope that what it orders people to do follows through to such outcomes but it cannot order things to happen in society.

A complete typology of government action, then, is simple. It's all about orders. Orders are commands or signals and the objects are to get taxes collected, transfers distributed or behaviours changed.

ORDERS

An order is a command when compliance is compulsory. When governments lean on power and work instrumentally they command. Signals are suggestions and encouragements. When they muster authority and work normatively, they signal. In contrast to commands, compliance is not compulsory and there is no enforcement.

The relationship between commands and signals is that commands are useless unless backed up by signals, whereas signals are often used on their own. Surprisingly, it is the politics of signals, and not at all of commands, that is the constant in government action. Signals, messages, projects—it was President Bush the elder who called it "the vision thing." This is what a government that is to be successful must manage. We could *almost* say (although it would be false) that if you want to be a governor, forget commanding, which will only get you into trouble. The name of the game is signalling. Signals are orders, make no mistake about it: they are the smart way of getting people to do as they should but do not want.

Commands

Orders to officials are usually commands. It is not at the discretion of servants whether or not to do as they are told.

Orders to the citizenry sometimes come in the harsh form of a command, typically when we are told to pay taxes, but often a government is not in a position to lay down rules about what citizens should do, even in matters it thinks are important. For example, it is always considered a good thing and generally a duty of citizenship in a democracy that people participate in elections, but only a few democracies (such as Australia, Belgium and Brazil) have taken the step of making voting compulsory. A command of that kind would mostly be seen to be impractical or contrary to principles of liberty. When it cannot command, a government can do no more than to suggest and persuade.

Compliance may be compulsory, but that is not to say that commands will necessarily be complied with. Many other reactions are available to the reluctant recipient. He can refuse to obey. That may get him into trouble, but if he refuses he refuses and the order does not get followed. Or he can question the rightfulness of the order and claim a right to not follow it. The government cannot then (easily) just deal with him as a refusenik, and may be obliged to start a legal process to clarify the contested authority or may be forced to back down. Or he can manoeuvre around the order to avoid its consequences. If it is for an extra tax, it becomes more tempting to hide away some of one's income. Or a command may just be ignored in the hope that no one cares or notices. In some cities with heavy winters it is a duty on homeowners to keep the pavement outside their property free from snow, but also a popular sport to disregard that duty in the hope that someone else clears the snow away. Or it is possible to obey in appearance only: slowly, by working to rule, sloppily or with deliberate forgetfulness.

Commands do not work just by being issued. They need to be followed up. One lesson to me as a young government official in one of the innumerable courses in leadership I had to attend that stuck in my mind, and has later been ever reconfirmed, was from the experienced permanent undersecretary of my department: making decisions is simple, the difficulty is the follow-up. The governor needs first to explain and justify and encourage and to add the unavoidable doses of signals. And then he must persevere. If he thinks an order just gets implemented he is wrong. He needs to remind his officials, and to monitor and check and assess, and to check that they check those further down the line, and he needs to do that again and again and again. What is not followed up relentlessly does not get done. He also needs to encourage. He needs to stimulate his officials to want to do as they are told, and he needs to inform and animate citizens to accept the duty he is imposing on them and to reasonably do that in the spirit of his command. And finally, he needs to control. Compliance does not come by itself; there must be controls and threats of sanctions to curtail avoidance and evasion. People do not do as they are told without threats and coercion, sometimes for good reasons but often also out of malice, ignorance or mischief. Even when it makes sense to obey, we like not to. It makes perfect sense for drivers to stick to speed limits on highways, but something so simple and sensible as ensuring reasonable road safety takes draconian systems of surveillance, policing and threats of fines and confiscated licenses. It's horrible the amount of coercion that is needed for something so trivial, but it is a sad fact of life that reasonable order depends on the government spying on its people and repressing them to toe the line.

Regulations

When commands are standardised, we call them regulations. Regulations help or make people live "sensibly," for example by assuring that they make economic provisions for old age, and guide them in cooperation, for example in the workplace or market. The rationale is a belief that good behaviour will not be forthcoming on its own—sometimes because people are inclined to cheat on one another, sometimes because they are unable to coordinate on their own, sometimes because of defunct markets, and sometimes because of the tendency for things to go wrong. People need rules and often it falls on the government to provide them. Regulations are a government's instrument for distributing protection, be it fair protection (against discrimination, for example) or unfair (against unwanted competition, say).

Modern societies appear to be thoroughly and infuriatingly regulated, so much so that almost all those who aspire to govern make themselves popular by promising deregulation, something none of them are able to do when they get into office, at least beyond the symbolic. Why? Because overregulation is a myth.

Regulations are for efficiency, safety, quality, and justice. Regulations for efficiency (to help make things work, such as markets) include, for example, the regulation of property rights, rules of accountancy, commerce and advertisement, antitrust legislation, watchdog oversight over monopolies or near monopolies, rules for and oversight of weights and measures, rules of currency and legal tender, compulsory social insurance, compulsory education, standards of school curricula, and the duty of employers and retailers to collect taxes.

Regulations for safety are, for example, speed limits in road traffic, the use of protective equipment in factory work and other work safety rules, the prohibition of dangerous substances in food products, or of asbestos in housing, or of lead in household ceramics, the use of safety belts in cars, safety standards in electrical equipment, the use of nonflammable materials in furniture, the testing of toys, the use of building techniques to reduce the danger of fire—and so on endlessly.

Regulations for quality include, for example, date marking of food, architectural regulations for neighbourhood consistency and for protection of the heritage, testing and authorisation of drugs, censorship of pornography, rules of ethics in scientific research, the keeping of charlatans out of the natural medicine and health food businesses, rules of environmental protection and of activities in national parks, standards of emission from motor cars, the accreditation of professional authority (doctors, plumbers, accountants, bishops, car mechanics, social workers—in some countries higher-level university posts are open only to those who hold a doctorate), procedures for the application of new scientific skills in, for example, genetic manipulation, in vitro fertilisation and the like, quality certification of silver and gold, procedures of adoption and foster care, the accreditation of university courses, and the imposition of standards of journalism.

And regulations for justice include, for example, provisions for handicapped persons (wheelchair ramps, lifts, lavatories), anti-discrimination legislation, affirmative action in education and employment, duties on schools to provide special assistance to children with learning difficulties, the protection of workers' rights and of the right to unionisation, provisions on working hours, holiday entitlements, minimum wages and the like, requirements on employers to make allowances for working mothers and child-care needs, and procedures of organisational democracy, for example in trade unions.

The extremely complicated networks of regulations in banking and financial services, which are currently under intense scrutiny and debate in the wake of financial crisis, are difficult to comprehend and get right, in part because they are intended to serve many purposes at the same time: market efficiency obviously, but also consumer protection, product quality and justice.

Regulation is sometimes self-regulation. The government may impose a duty of regulation on, say, a professional body to regulate a field of activity but does not itself set the rules. In Britain, the General Medical Council registers doctors to practice medicine, and sometimes strikes practicing doctors off the register, and exercises oversight in medical practice. Or a business may set up its own regulator. The Press Complaints Commission, in Britain again, was supposed to uphold the press's own standards of ethics, such as they were, but with the tabloid phone hacking scandals in 2011 (which finally threw a spanner in the wheels of press baron Rupert Murdoch's monopolistic schemes) became a study in the sometimes impotence of self-regulation.

Signals

Once we start to look, we see the politics of signals wherever governments operate. And what we then see is everything from ruthless manipulation to honourable efforts to educate the public. It is essential for a government to talk about itself and its policies and to talk to its people about what it wants to do and expects of them. This is at the core of any government's necessary endeavour to define its purpose, to provide leadership, to get its policies accepted, to influence the political culture, to control the agenda, to communicate, to make itself understood, and to get people within and outside of government to cooperate. If a governor wants others to engage with him, he must tell them what he is up to, convince them that it is worthy, and give them the information they need to coordinate with one another.

But no less than with commanding is signalling a difficult art. During the ten years of Tony Blair's premiership in Britain the politics of signals fell into disrepute under the label of "spin." Blair and the people around him just kept talking too much. They exhausted their public. They were scheming and careless with the truth and, what is worse, were caught out at it. On the 11th of September 2001, as the Twin Towers in New York burned, a spin doctor in the British Department of Transport sent out an e-mail to her colleagues saying that it "is now a very good day to get out anything we want to bury." They talked up initiatives and intentions endlessly and talked down any uncomfortable fact and slack achievement. Their self-presentation on department Web sites was thick on boasting and thin on facts. They did what any government of any calibre must do, but they messed up on getting the melody right.[1] It's a fine balance, and poor old Blair was so eager to talk about himself that he kept chipping away at the authority he was trying to fortify. Better to remain silent and be thought a fool, said Abraham Lincoln, than to speak out and remove all doubt.

People are endlessly being told by their governments how to behave and what to do and not do. We are recommended to eat healthy food, to not smoke, to not drink and drive, to save more and spend less, or the other way around if the economy is lax, to take holidays at different times of the year, to use public transport, to practice safe sex, to keep children at home and off the streets at night, to not call out the doctor needlessly, to read worthy literature, to not litter the landscape, to like the opera, to buy home-made products, to pick up and dispose of dog droppings, to econo-mise with water and electricity, to wash our hands before eating, to pay careful attention to consumer information on food products, to make our-selves computer literate, to take exercise. Parents are encouraged to read to their children. Prime Minister Pierre Mendès France encouraged the French to drink more milk and less wine (in vain), and current govern-ments are encouraging them to not overindulge in vitamin pills and medi-cation (in vain again).

Businesses are encouraged to pay workers a decent salary, or to not give excessive pay rises, to take measures for workplace safety, to offer employees help with child care, to minimise noise and pollution, to invest in modern technology, to help workers improve their skills, to support neighbourhood civic activities, to make donations to symphony orchestras or universities, to support local libraries. Churches are encouraged to do charitable work among the poor, pharmacies to dispense free syringes to drug addicts, trade unions to explain to members the need to be respon-sible workers, lawyers to devote some of their time for legal assistance to those who cannot pay, doctors to be cautious with prescriptions. And so it goes on. Hardly anyone or any activity is free from advice about what to do or how to think. Campaigns for or against this or that are a constant feature of modern governance.

Silliness galore, of course—but far from only silliness. Governments need to inform, to explain, to sell their policies, to make themselves trusted or at least believed, to encourage, to persuade, and to manipulate when that is called for. A government must be seen and heard and make itself the centre of attention, and it must out-manoeuvre those trying to out-manoeuvre it. It needs to control the issues that become salient in the press and public awareness and not let others take hold of the agenda. It needs to lead and to display leadership.

All this is a battle. As much as the government wants to hold the cen-tre ground, others want to push it out: the opposition, the press, organised interests, pressure groups, think tanks. An ambitious government knows that it needs to fight for dear life day in and day out and not be pushed around. It needs to be in control and hold on to the position from which it is able to issue orders.

President Franklin Roosevelt invented the "fireside chat" with citizens by way of radio, to great effect and for which we today admire him. If ever there was a master of spin, it was that greatest of modern political leaders, Winston Churchill. His genius as war leader was in communication, in his speeches and his display of confidence, determination and energy. This was pure signal politics and contributed decisively to effort, morale and cooperation. Governments today live in a harsher environment in which leadership is less accepted and trust thin. Political gamesmanship has shifted into arenas dominated by media, 24/7 news, organised interests, single-issue pressure groups, and corporations with huge public relations departments and think tanks at their beck and call. Politics itself revolves strongly around agenda issues: battles over which issues political battle is to be fought over. This is a war of words more than of action. The moment the government is driven on to the defensive it is on the run. It simply must *speak,* more and more and ever more loudly, so as to subdue those others who threaten to bring it out of balance and off course. It has to force others into the position of responding to it, or be their victim. It has to conceal what it is unable to get done, make murky compromise look like decisive action and magnify its achievements. It will overdo it—but the risk of looking foolish is for nothing compared to the risk of allowing others the high ground. Spin is not something a government has the luxury of choosing to indulge in or not. It is the face of a government that rules.

A government needs the use of signals in its internal struggle to get its own administration to do what it wants of it. It is not enough to tell officials what to do, and often orders are counterproductive. Good political leaders inspire those who work for them. If they try to get things done by putting fear into their officials, they may get servitude but not efficiency.

Politicians of authority can establish the direction of policy and administration without resorting to crude orders. An example from high politics: Shortly after the Tiananmen Square massacre in Beijing in 1989, Deng Xiaoping called together his top generals and officials and thanked them for the decisive way in which they had crushed the rebellion—and then let them understand by the subtlest of signals what could not be commanded or said outright, that the direction of economic reform was to remain unchanged. A decisive moment in the history of China, since Deng won the day, eventually: the political crackdown was not to be followed by economic crackdown. Signal politics of consequence!

Soft signals have continued to play a very considerable part in the hard dictatorship of Chinese politics, for example through slogans such as to "build a new socialist countryside," or the "five guarantees" policy for rural households, or "to construct a harmonious society," all flagging up central government or party initiatives to encourage more resources to be channelled into rural development.[2] This no doubt reflects the complexity of getting intentions implemented in so huge and complicated a country as China and is no more strange than, for example, Franklin Roosevelt's brilliant New Deal.

The best leadership may be in wise action but *speaking* is still indispensable. A good government offers citizens goals which it suggest they take as theirs and be guided by in their own lives and in their cooperation with others. It informs and educates. It explains to them what it is they should want and persuades them that that is what they do want. "Cecil King records how a colleague once called on [Prime Minister Edward] Heath and tried to persuade him to set up a propaganda department responsible for explaining his policies to the world. His job, replied Heath, was to govern, not to explain. That remark explains a lot of Ted's mistakes, commented King."[3] Something similar may have contributed to Barack Obama's difficulties in his first term as president, according to the journalist Peter Baker: "The President who muscled through Congress perhaps the most ambitious domestic agenda in a generation finds himself vilified by the right, castigated by the left and abandoned by the middle. The figure of inspiration from 2008, neglected the inspiration after his election."[4]

The simplest form of signal is pure information, for example about the dangers of smoking or the wisdom of taking exercise, in the hope that people will behave sensibly if only they know the facts. Information campaigns may be followed by guidelines of behaviour, for example campaigns about healthy diets with rules of guidance (such as five to seven slices of bread a day, as recommended in a memorable campaign in Sweden in the mid-1980s, or five units a day of fruit or vegetables as recommended by a British government committee on nutrition in the late 1990s, so successfully that "your five" has established itself in daily parlance). Recommendations may be followed by positive incentives—those who invest in pension plans are rewarded with tax reliefs—or by negative disincentives—those who are so sinful as to continue to smoke in spite of good advice will have to pay the extra tax. Signals may be combined with commands, in which case the signals attach to the policy in question to encourage compliance.

For the rest, signals flow from governments in constant streams of information and indications, in everything from direct propaganda to body language. Perceived signals which are read from the way politicians and officials conduct their daily business are suggestive of the stature of a government, which again influences the feel-good factor in the population and trust and confidence. We look to the ladies and gentlemen of government and interpret what they say and how they behave. From this we make guesses about the government's intentions, and from that decisions about the kinds of action we see to be prudent. When politicians—or even more, heads of central banks—are asked about future prospects for interest rates, currency devaluations, or other questions to which it is commonly understood that they cannot answer truthfully if there is anything of interest to say, everyone listens less to what is said than to how it is said. When Secretary of State Colin Powell spoke to the Security Council of the United Nations on the 4th of February 2003 on the case for war against Iraq, in what was seen as a decisive moment in the American attempt to persuade reluctant governments and peoples around the world, press comments and analyses in the following days were heavy on style, on his command of the occasion and the degree to which his body language displayed confidence.

Of course, there are limits to persuasion, no less than to commanding. People have interests of their own and do not want to be persuaded. They have power and do not need to listen. They can organise and support each other in disobedience. Criminals are not easily persuadable. Those who have much to lose are not easily persuadable. Organised interests are not easily persuadable. The media, the indispensible messengers of persuasion, have interests in not being used and will trip up the persuader when they can. A governor cannot get much done just by being nice. He must also be able to be hard. But neither can he get much done by being hard without also being nice. Rule, returning to Joseph Nye, does not spring from softness alone, any more than from hardness alone, but from the combination, from smartness.

Since spin is now thought repugnant, it is worth driving home that there are very good reasons for governments to make use of signals, beyond the promotion of their own excellence.

- There will not be effective governance unless governors follow through to motivating the dominated to obey their authority. There will not even be authority since the governor needs to present himself and his project to the governed in order to extract authority from them. Underlings must be persuaded that they ought to obey and then nudged to actually complying: without persuasion no compliance. They must be educated and reminded in their "understanding of the nature of the democratic system, and particularly the subtle interrelationship between liberty and responsibility." The ruler must deliberate with his followers and get them to deliberate with one another. Citizens do not just *have* preferences: preferences are formed, and it is contained in good leadership to contribute to infusing citizens with a will to reason and cooperation. If there is to be a settlement of order, the governors must engage and explain what they are doing and how, and they must do that persuasively. They should pull citizens into their orbit and get close enough to govern them. This is the combination, in which signalling in its manifold forms is essential, that enables the government side to feed into a political culture of confidence and trust.
- A government is seen to work for the public good when it is able to explain what it is doing and why and to get its policies accepted as right and fair. Edward Heath was wrong to think he was under no obligation to explain; what is done must be propagated.
- Signals are the government's inputs into the necessary process in a functioning democracy of deliberation between itself and citizens, and within the citizenry, and to establishing and maintaining a shared identity between leaders and the led. Culture must be cultivated; deliberation is the fertiliser on which political culture can flourish.
- Governance depends on "vision" and there is no way of communicating a sense of purpose and direction other than to engage with the citizenry.
- Signals work. In South Korea, around 1990, it was becoming apparent that lower birth rates were followed by an increasingly distorted

gender ratio at birth, with the proportion of boys to girls rising to about 1.15. The government responded by prohibiting practices to predetermine the gender of unborn children and with a social campaign about the issue among medical workers and in the public. Within about ten years the gender ratio at birth had reverted back to the normal.[5] While mayor of Bogotá in two terms between 1995 and 2003, Antanas Mockus became famous for his imaginative use of stunts and campaigns of encouragement without coercion that were spectacularly effective, against the odds, in, for example, reducing the usage of water, bringing down the rate of homicide and traffic fatalities, and even getting citizens to pay extra taxes on a voluntary basis.

- If a government has an intention and can realise it through encouragement, it would be wrong to go about it in more complicated ways.
- Signals are helpful for morale. In 1942, the Ordnance Department of the U.S. Army commissioned a painting from Norman Rockwell of a machine gunman in need of ammunition and had posters of the painting, entitled *Let's Give Him Enough and On Time,* distributed to ordnance plants throughout the country to encourage production.[6]
- They are not coercive.
- If wrong or inadequate information is the cause of wrong or damaging action, the government should obviously inform.
- Signals can be used when commands are impossible or unethical or when the control of compliance is not practicable. Preventive health care is a case in point. If we could improve diets, reduce the consumption of junk food, cut down on smoking, avoid the abuse of alcohol, and increase physical activity there would be immeasurable gains to happiness and health, as well as to health care budgets. Policies to stem the AIDS epidemic have rested strongly on signals since other means, such as vaccination, have not been available and the direct regulation of sexual behaviour is not ethical or possible.
- Signals are cheap and may be an available policy when more costly measures are not affordable.
- Even when more decisive action is necessary, for example to command people to pay a bit more tax, commands need to be followed

up by persuasion. A government may be in its full and undisputed right to command people to pay taxes, but it must nevertheless *beg* them to do so. It must respond to their tacit question about why they should give up more of their hard-earned cash and free the taxpayer from the temptation to persuade himself that he has just cause to resist. When Gordon Brown (while chancellor) announced in his 2002 budget a modest increase in the social security tax to cover additional investments in the National Health Service, he and the prime minister were in a hospital the very same day in front of the television cameras getting themselves on the evening news talking to doctors and nurses about the urgent need for those investments. Likewise, on the 12th of July 2010 when the new British coalition government announced a controversial decentralisation within the National Health Service, Prime Minister David Cameron was in front of the cameras at the Royal Marsden Hospital in London discussing the merits of the reform with health workers there.

There are also bad reasons which may lead governments to the politics of signals. Primary among these is a reluctance or unwillingness to use stronger means when that would be right and then to use signals to conceal non-action. Is propaganda an easy way out for a government in the battle against smoking, compared to, for example, the banning of advertisement for cigarettes? A further bad reason is the often irresistible inclination to know-all-ism. Many of us no doubt have an urge to teach others about life; ministers for their sins are listened to and may find it difficult to keep quiet.

OBJECTS

At the heart of rule is the difficult business of taxing.

Taxes are sheer punishment for those on whom they are imposed. We good citizens sometimes boast that we pay our taxes with pleasure, but that is hyperbole. Taxes are always resented and always avoided if possible. When asked ahead of the 2010 midterm election what had surprised him most since taking office, President Obama answered, "The number of people who don't pay their taxes."[7] He had had several high-level appointments scuppered when it was revealed that the appointees, pillars of society, had cheated on paying taxes. One of the things shown up by the sovereign debt crisis in Europe is that democratic governments typically do not collect anywhere near the taxes they impose. The very problem of governance comes into sharp focus in the clash between the government's commands to citizens to give it money and the citizens' desire to hold on to the money they have. An object of the American Constitution was to create a state with the power to tax, the experience from the Revolutionary War being the impotence of a state without its own taxing power. One reason why the secessionist confederacy (as of 1861) faltered was that states and citizens refused the timid central government the authority to collect taxes. Hence Geoffrey Brennan and James Buchanan were entirely justified in taking *The Power to Tax* as the title of their treatise on government.

Transfers, in turn, are a government's main means for doing good and being seen to do good. While taxes are resisted, transfers are in incessant demand, both because citizens want as much as they can get and because ministers want to give away as much as they can. The clearing of outgoings in transfers and ingoings in taxes is the big problem for democratic governments, an unmanageable problem, it has been said, for example by James O'Connor in *The Fiscal Crisis of the State* and Claus Offe in *Contradictions of the Welfare State*—in analyses that have taken on a new credence with the post-2007 economic crisis. When Greek public finances imploded in 2009–10, this was the accumulated misery resulting from consecutive governments' failure to collect taxes from a notoriously tax-averse population.

Taxation is to get people to give up some of their money, but sometimes also to get them to live sensibly, as when indirect taxes are used to put a price on bad behaviour such as smoking or drinking. Transfers put resources in people's hands that enable them to do business or make ends meet, but sometimes also to influence their lifestyles, as when child allowance is paid to the mother because it is then more likely that it will be used for the good of the children than if fathers control it.

All through the history of government, citizens have hated their governments because they confiscate their money and property. This is at the heart of the always antagonistic relationship between a government and its people. But also giving is difficult. With transfers, governments are in danger of being too generous and of undermining their authority by being seen to be profligate or irresponsible. S. E. Finer lists mass bribery to buy popularity among the pressures that brought down democracy in ancient Athens. He quotes Aristotle advising the avoidance of "expensive yet useless public services."[8]

Behavioural policies can be equally troublesome. Here the danger is, as in that great British put-down, "nanny-statism," the government that interferes so much in people's lives that it gives them the excuse they are looking for to deny it respect.

Taxes

Taxes shift economic resources from households and organisations to government coffers. The purpose is to enable the government to buy and give. However, since their ability to tax is limited, governments will want to find ways of getting things done without outlays from their budgets. That they can do by directing or encouraging private interests to public purposes. When that is successful, we have non-tax taxation: citizens think they are not being taxed when they cash out for necessities. American workers think they do not pay any health care tax because their health care is paid through insurance, but that is a mirage. In fact, they are coerced to paying much more for their health care than do, for example, the British for their excellent freedom-of-choice care through the National Health Service.

Taxes can be hidden in other ways as well, mainly in the form of taxation through property, in kind and lottery. A government may take ownership of natural resources or production institutions and move output or profits into its own coffers. The Norwegian government holds ownership of the country's vast oil and gas resources and directs revenues to public budgets and government-owned savings. This is taxation by the logic that a government, at least a democratic one, is itself owned by the people who then also own its property and the income that flows from it. The state government of Alaska owns petroleum resources but returns some of the revenue to the people directly through an annual distribution to households.

Taxation in kind is mainly through extracted labour (but in exchange economies also in extracted goods, for example grain and other foodstuffs). The pyramids of Egypt and the mediaeval cathedrals of Europe are testimony to their rulers' ability to extract labour for their own ends. Taxation in kind survives in the form of military conscription (a form of extracted labour), but also in tax collection itself where employers usually (but not in for example France) collect their workers' wage tax and retailers the sales tax, and sometimes (as in for example Britain) banks collect the tax on interest.

In a state lottery the government persuades the many to give it money in return for a promise of high prizes to a few. This is the only known form of taxation for which taxpayers rush to the tax man and line up to be taxed. Although grossly inequitable it is perceived as fair and fun. It would not be much of a government that did not exploit this wonder for all it is worth.

Visible taxes are direct or indirect and are levied on persons and businesses. Direct taxes are on income and property. They are allocated by rules governing the tax base and the tax rates. The tax base specifies the income and property that is subject to taxation, the tax rates the level and distribution of the tax levied on that base. There is a trade-off between base and rates. A broad base pushes rates downward and toward a moderately progressive or flat distribution. Strongly progressive rates tend to contract the tax base by increasing exemptions and deductions. That again may make the real tax arbitrary in its distribution, depending on how exemptions and deductions are shaped and exploited, and may work back to undermining the legitimacy of the tax regime. In the United States, for example, the marginal rate in the federal tax on corporate profit is nominally 35 per cent, but profitable corporations typically pay 5 to 10 per cent, or nothing at all. These problems are compounded in the taxation of property by the endemic difficulty of realistic and fair assessment of property values. These trade-offs limit the scope for the use of direct taxation as an instrument of redistribution.

The most important indirect taxes are on consumer purchases, today usually collected as a value added tax (although the United States, backward as it is in practical governance, has still not got there). A general consumption tax is levied on all consumers. Its distribution is mostly flat relative to consumption and hence regressive to income (although for social reasons some "necessities," such as foods or children's clothing, are sometimes partly or fully exempt from the consumption tax).

Other indirect taxes are in the form of levies or fees on specific forms of consumption (such as tobacco and alcohol), on specific activities (hunting and fishing in national parks, for example, or driving on toll roads), or on services from government (from renovation to health care). European governments, from Hungary to Denmark, are taking to attaching a tax on unhealthy foods, partly for reasons of public health and partly to use the good cause of health to facilitate the nasty business of taxing.

Taxpayers seem to be less sensitive to indirect than to direct taxes. In the case of the consumption tax this is possibly because it has a peculiar virtue of fairness. Every citizen, rich and poor, is equal in basic material needs and all are taxed equally on this basic consumption. The acceptability of indirect taxes may also be helped by their being less visible than direct ones.

To preserve as much as possible their power to tax, which is imperative, governments should take great care with the way they "take it off them" (to use the words of Paul Keating, the former prime minister of Australia, which we will encounter again later on). Taxes should be fair, simple and non-provocative. A mild sleight of hand is advisable to dress them up in their best light and help citizens to feel the burden to be not intolerable. Fairness is, as always, perceived fairness and governments can help with that perception. But they cannot fool taxpayers, at least not much. If taxes are blatantly unfair, taxpayers will know it and you have a revolt on your hands. The more burdensome it is to do your taxes, for example to fill out the tax return and calculate your tax, the more the taxpayer will be an unhappy taxpayer. If taxes are in your face in your ordinary daily business, the more they provoke resentment.

Most tax systems fall short on these virtues, but the American system more than most, being "an absurdly complicated tax system that raises very little," as described by the *Economist*.[9] It is infuriatingly complicated. It massively hides away real taxes in non-tax taxation. And the mess of sales taxes, which differ between states and towns and are added on to every listed price as a constant rubbing-it-in-your-face that you cannot move about without some government dipping its hand into your pocket, is as if designed by conspiracy. American taxpayers might be surprised at what they would find if they moved to, for example, Norway. The income tax is mildly progressive. The VAT indirect tax is baked into listed prices and as good as invisible. And your tax return is a one-page form you receive from the tax man already filled in so that you only have to sign it. If it is wrong you can correct it, but usually it is right. The Norwegians are thought to be heavily taxed, but if you consider both up-front taxes and non-tax taxes, as well as what citizens get in return for their taxes, and the non-provocative way of taxation which eases the pain, the average Norwegian without doubt has a much better tax deal than the tax-downtrodden Americans. Wherefore they are also less dissatisfied with their taxes than are, for good reasons, the Americans.

Transfers

Transfers are goods governments give away. They shift resources from the government to households and organisations.

Subsidies are hidden transfers which operate inside the economy, the flip side of non-tax taxes. The government absorbs some of the costs of production so as to lower the price of goods, typically foods or public transport. Transfers to industries, for example agriculture or fisheries, are social subsidies as much as industrial policies, although it is not easy to determine who the beneficiaries are, for example how benefits and costs are shared between producers and consumers. Price subsidies are to the benefit of those who consume the subsidised goods, but some of the benefit is usually absorbed by producers. Free public services, which are of course never free, are fully subsidised by the government.

Open transfers are direct or indirect. Direct transfers are in the form of cash: to the poor and needy or to persons in contingencies, to prevent them from falling into poverty. In his state of the federation address in November 2010, President Dmitry Medvedev announced that the Russian government would be giving plots of land to parents who had at least three children; they are worried about low birth rates. Some tax exemptions or deductions are transfers in disguise, then sometimes called allowances, for example a married person's allowance or a cost-of-living allowance.

Indirect transfers are in kind: free or subsidised goods and services, such as education, health care, personal social care and the like.

Transfers can be means-tested (to those with less than a specified threshold of income or property), conditional (such as unemployment payments contingent on willingness to seek work), or universal (a child allowance to all parents with children and irrespective of income).

Transfers honour needs and interests in the population which are seen to be just and which it is assumed are not responded to adequately in markets. They may be for economic efficiency (health care is an invest-ment in human capital), behavioural efficiency (free education to encour-age young people to take more education), or justice (to prevent poverty and reduce inequality).

Charities are private transfers, be it to beggars in the street or in large-scale organised form. If a government is able to encourage private charity that would not materialise spontaneously, we could see that as a form of non-tax taxation. In the absence of that charity, the government might feel obliged or pressured to institute a transfer and hence have to raise the revenue to fund it through taxation.

As much as people hate taxes, they love transfers, those not in need no less than those in need. In London, all persons sixty or older receive free public transport. Although it is as foolish a social policy as can be imagined, and exceedingly expensive, the benefit is so robustly held on to by the middle class (such as myself) that even the budget-cutting govern-ment of 2010 could do nothing to change it.

What governments do when they want to distribute transfers is to allocate money. But money is a dangerous narcotic; ministers feel good when they give it away. Under New Labour in Britain, putting more money into the National Health Service became its own purpose, and even the next government, which defined itself by the need to rectify its predecessor's profligacy, committed, unwisely, to protecting spending on the NHS. In Norway, the centre-left coalition government that came into power in 2005 decided to increase the central government's subventions to municipalities in order to lift municipal finance to a sustainable level. There was jubilation and agreement all around that municipal finances had been made sound. But, as had happened in the NHS in Britain, the result of a rapid inflow of new money was that budget discipline broke down, the money was wasted in new bureaucracy and inefficiencies, and within two or three years the municipalities were back to their customary moaning about not getting enough money from the capital.

Behaviours

All government policies are behavioural, sometimes intentionally, and I have given a range of examples above of how eager governments are to get people to think right and live well. And sometimes unintentionally, as when good or bad "behavioural responses" follow as side effects of policies with other ends. Economists are obsessed with side effects, which they generally think are drains on efficiency, and for which they have invented fancy names such as "moral hazard," "rent seeking," "free riding," "justified envy" and other freemasonry terms of trade.

In addition to influencing how we behave, governments seek to influence how we think. We are back into the domain of informing, explaining, persuading and educating—and of political culture. Democracy needs citizens to "really think democratically." A democratic culture will not exist if it is not continuously maintained. Governors contribute to that by governing well and speaking well.

However, it is notoriously difficult to influence people to think or behave in a desired way with the help of government action (fortunately, we should probably say). The experience of getting people to wear safety belts in cars or to not smoke is that it takes hard, multiple and long-term efforts. The Cameron government in Britain fell in love with the idea of "nudging" and set up a "behavioural insight team" to devise nudge policies. It's a politically tempting idea. If you can nudge people to live well and do good, you don't have to legislate, tax, regulate and coerce. The ever sceptical House of Lords decided to see if there is anything to it through a subgroup of its respected science and technology committee. This group trawled the evidence and concluded that nudging without regulating is a gospel too good to be true.[10] To which should be added, however, that regulating without nudging is also a dead end.

So the politics of regulations is the great territory of behavioural politics. The government lays down rules to guide personal or corporate behaviour, and persons and corporations respond like angels when it is to their benefit and little devils when it is not.

As everything else in government, regulation can be done well or badly. There is a world of difference between sensible regimes of rules and what Derek Bok in *The Trouble with Government* calls "command-and-control regulations." The propensity of the latter, he found, is undermining good government in the United States (which, contrary to what some outsiders think, is steeped in rigid regulations), and is precisely what I in my New Labour study found had been at the heart of the implosion of efficiency in public services.

While we hate taxes and love transfers, people are strangely ambivalent about behavioural orders from their governments. Although we want guidance, we also resent being told how to live almost as much as we resent being taxed.

Are we overregulated? You may be but "we" are not. After the worst economic crisis since 1929, we must know that we are, at least in economic life, woefully underregulated. Remember what Johan Bojer saw in that Norwegian fjord: it was regulation that transformed men from animals to human beings again. You would think he was observing bankers and capitalists, not fishermen.

The Time Problem

Governments are constantly busy making new policies, laws and regulations—but often without clearing out old dead wood. The result is impenetrable complexity. When citizens cannot know what governance they are exposed to, it becomes increasingly difficult to persuade them that they should comply.

In *The Rule of Law,* Tom Bingham criticised British legislation for needlessly piling new laws on top of old ones. In taxation, governments latch on to one problem after another and introduce new provisions to deal with them, and before you know it the taxpayer cannot know what his duties are without the (expensive) assistance of a tax lawyer. In the constitutional arena, new conventions take hold and the constitution becomes ever more inconsistent. The American tax code has become hopelessly confused by new provisions incessantly being piled on top of old ones.

From time to time, there ought to be a clearing out of the clutter that builds up. Among Caesar's achievements was "the reduction of the civil law to manageable proportions, by selecting from the unwieldy mess of statutes only the most essential, and publishing them in a few volumes."[11] But it is usually easier to give in to political virility and add new provisions of one's own, needed or not, on top of the existing chaos.

THE TINY TOOLBOX

To recapitulate yet again, I have argued (1) that the problem is obedience, (2) that governments are up against others who are always reluctant, (3) that the final challenge in good government is implementation, (4) that the turning of power into performance depends on fairness and restraint, (5) that a settlement of order depends on institutions that bind governments and push followers into compliance, (6) that such institutions reside in culture as much as in rules, (7) that power is not all it has been cracked up to be, (8) that governance is a people business, (9) that managing the problem of obedience depends on authority and leadership, (10) that the most solid authority is that which rests on the magic of legitimacy, (11) that governments do one thing and one thing only: they give orders, and (12) that even holding on to the ground from which a government is able to issue orders is a battle.

I have now found, further, that orders are of two kinds, commands and signals. These are a government's only tools, however powerful it may look. While commands are heavy handed and commanding something ministers can do with success only occasionally, it is the politics of signals that is the great constant in government action, and normative governance—informing, educating, inspiring, leading—that is the secret of the art of ruling. But once you are into the delicate use of signals, into spin, which you cannot avoid, you are susceptible to overdoing it. You cannot make yourself authoritative without spin, but unless you are very surefooted, that same spin will make you ridiculous.

What governments can order done is also limited: taxes to be paid, transfers to be given and behaviours to change. Governments and ministers, then, for all their powers, do not have much to work with when they plunge into society to rule it.

6

HOW TO GET IT RIGHT

The prince who does not detect evils the moment
they appear is lacking in true wisdom; but few rulers
have the ability to do so.

—*The Prince,* chapter 13

New Labour in Britain was not only a government with power, mandate and money, it was a competent government with all those advantages. Yet its rule was a litany of failure. Its problem was not in getting policies made; rather it had it too easy on that front. Where it stumbled was in making workable policies. Good intentions are not enough. Competence is not enough. When a government has power and can make policy, its next problem is to avoid mistakes. You might think it a truism to advise governments to make good decisions. Sadly, it is all but.

THE PUBLIC GOOD

George Washington was right that government for the public good is a double challenge: discernment and pursuit. The policy must be worthy and right, but there is more to getting it right than not being wrong. What is decided must be implemented and made to work. The tiresome Mr. Blair was always "doing the right thing," but it does not help much to be right if the way you do it is ineffective or counterproductive. Good intentions do not make for governance, not even inspired intentions. It's about making things happen (as observed Mr. Powell). Where things do not happen there is no rule, however much the governor is sincere and intends there to be. What extracts obedience and makes for settlement on the part of the governor is that intentions follow through to action and action to consequences. Benign consequence, obviously, but consequence there must be.

We saw in Chapter 3 that legitimacy is the jewel in the crown of the game of governance; it's what makes others not only obey but want to obey. Legitimacy comes from rightful governors making rightful decisions in rightful ways. Governance is then fair and seen to be fair. Citizens have reason to obey and are denied reasons to disobey. Governments that make wrong decisions have no business being in power and will not be seen to be deserving of obedience. The trouble with government, found Derek Bok, reflecting on the erosion of government in the United States, in addition to the plight of command-and-control regulations, is the experience of perpetually poorly designed and inconsistent legislation. It's obvious, is it not: if our governments make a mess of it we will despise them, and if we despise them they cannot govern us. If they want our respect, they better get it right.

WHY THINGS GO WRONG

Political decision making is human decision making and in human decision making we are prone to mistakes. Our brains play tricks on us. Also, political decision making is a group activity, and in groups people play tricks on each other. In government no less than in business, even competent managers manage badly if their systems don't work.

Human Decision Making

We humans abhor error and gravitate toward certainty. But error is unavoidable and confusion the natural state of affairs for us poor human beings. Indeed, explains the writer Kathryn Schulz in a learned book, *Being Wrong*—she calls it "wrongology"—in a deep psychological meaning error is what enables us to learn, and is a fact of life that should be managed and not denied.

Neither you nor I, nor presidents nor ministers, are in control of his or her brain. We lie, and make ourselves believe that our lie is true. We think we know the facts when the facts we think we know are the ones we want to pertain. We pretend to know what we don't, and believe we do. We fall victim to distractions, ideology, prejudice, chauvinism, loony instincts and braggadocio. The psychologist Daniel Kahneman has given it a name: cognitive illusion—that false beliefs are accepted to be true—and has demonstrated that it is in the human condition to hold on to beliefs once embraced even when they are proved to be false. In a modern aphorism according to Nassim Taleb: "The person you are the most afraid of contradicting is yourself."[1] The philosopher Leszek Kołakowski called it "the law of infinite cornucopia": there is always an abundance of arguments in favour of any doctrine one for whatever reason wants to believe in. We fail when we try the notorious difficulty of managing two or more thoughts at the same time. "Eastern Airlines Flight 401 was preparing to land in Miami when a light on the control panel failed to illuminate. The three crewmembers in the cockpit became so focused on the problem that they didn't notice that the plane was continuing its descent on autopilot. The flight crashed in the Everglades, killing a hundred people."[2]

Therefore, intentions are not to be trusted. A political leader without intentions is useless, but leaders must ensure that intentions do not become master. And even more, ideology is not to be trusted. Ideologies are systems of intentions that fortify beliefs and instincts and tempt us toward unshakable certainty. They are a danger to liberty, argued the philosopher Isaiah Berlin. A danger to sound decisions too.

At its most basic, a decision is a combination of intention and implementation. Having to juggle no more than these two elements is enough for there to be a very considerable risk of getting decisions wrong. If you are devoted to a certain recipe for public policy, you will be tempted to resort to it as a panacea for all problems. The answer is lower taxes, said the conservative politician; what was the question?

Or more likely, the other way around, if you first set yourself on an intention such as to solve a problem or bring something good about, that wish works on your brain so as to tempt you to not reflect critically enough about what kind of action should be taken. If you wish to achieve something, it is easy to let yourself be persuaded that it can be done and difficult to caution yourself that the desirable may not be achievable or that the easier means may not be the best way, all the more so the more strongly you wish for it to happen. That's what happens when the pilot gets into his seat and says to himself, "Now let's get this thing flying," and overlooks some of the precautions he knows he should take. It is what happened, for example, when in the 2010 football World Cup Argentina was beaten 4 to 0 by Germany and the verdict the next day, in a headline in the *International Herald Tribune,* was that "Maradona's plan lacked a vital element: Defence."[3] How could a genius footballer neglect a plan of defence? It is not at all surprising. Diego Maradona (the Argentinean coach) had persuaded himself that his team would be on the offensive and in control of the match and that persuasion, since he had only yes-men around him, played the trick on his brain of preventing him from planning for an unwanted course of events.

This is a mistake political decision makers are notoriously prone to. If the intention is good and worthy, the brain goes mushy and tempts you to act as quickly as possible. It may even be risky to give too much consideration to practicalities out of fear that a feasibility study might reveal that no easy, quick or affordable action is available. When the British Parliament in 2005 said yes and amen to bringing the 2012 Olympics to London, they facilitated their decision by deceiving themselves about the cost—and soon found themselves saddled with a bill four times as high as the £2.35 billion price tag they had first nominally accepted.

This dictatorship of good intentions is what led the New Labour government in Britain astray in some of its most critical decisions. Mr. Brown's ambition was to reduce child poverty. He let himself be persuaded by the strength of that intention that it could be done on the cheap and that hopelessly complicated tax credit instruments would be practicable.

It is also what happened in the most fateful decision of the New Labour government, to go along with the Bush administration in the United States in the invasion of Iraq. Mr. Blair persuaded himself—as he said repeatedly, including when he in January 2010 testified before the British Iraq Inquiry and in his memoirs that were published in September the same year—that it was "the right thing to do." He came to lodge the intention so firmly in his mind that he forgot to consider the organisation of the occupation once the dictator was deposed and the implementation on the ground of what he thought was the right action. He was warned but was unable to listen, as revealed by the journalist Andrew Rawnsley: "President Jacques Chirac warned that the Americans and British were deluding themselves if they thought they would be welcomed in Iraq and asked Mr. Blair to realise that an invasion might precipitate civil war. As they left that meeting, Blair turned to his aid Stephen Wall and said, Poor old Jacques, he just doesn't get it, does he?"[4]

Top American politicians fell into the same trap. Vice President Dick Cheney, Defence Secretary Donald Rumsfeld and others allowed themselves to believe that the people of Iraq would embrace the occupiers in joy once Saddam Hussein was out of the way. There is in hindsight no disagreement that the war was launched without adequate and elementary planning.[5] For example, in a hearing before the Public Administration Committee of the House of Commons in Britain on the 16th of September 2010, the chief of the Defence Staff, Air Chief Marshal Sir Jock Stirrup (yes, that *is* his name) said that the military view was that the government at the time did not appreciate what it was taking on when it planned the invasion. In his memoirs, Mr. Blair himself describes the planning for the aftermath as "inadequate," "poor" and "not up to the mark."[6] It has often been commented on as incredible that American and British planning underestimated or overlooked the practical difficulties of occupation, but we should not be surprised. These were politicians who were firmly committed to overthrowing the regime in Iraq and who by the strength of that commitment fell into the trap of not thinking carefully enough about the consequences of invasion. In this case, the fallacy was stimulated by moralistic mindsets and strong ideological convictions, those of the neo-cons in the American administration, and in the case of Mr. Blair possibly by his religious convictions, which may have led him to ask more firmly about what was right than about how practically it should be done.[7] A chapter heading in a book by Gordon Goldstein analysing the disaster of America's war in Vietnam captures the essence brilliantly: "Conviction without rigor is a strategy for disaster."

Therefore, also, competence is not to be trusted. Skills training is a matter of acquiring the right competence for a specific task, but knowing how to perform a task is not enough to do it well. You have to apply what you know. In the following up from knowledge to application you are likely to forget, to overlook or to mess up. If there are five steps involved in performing a task, it is pretty likely that you will overlook something in at least one, and if so that's it for your task. Even if we act with great caution most of the time, details are likely to go wrong often enough for tasks to go wrong very often.

This is well known in high-skill professions, which have therefore learned to insure themselves against mistakes. Airline pilots, to return to them again, are trained to know everything about how to fly a plane, yet before starting they go through detailed checklists to ensure that they actually do what they know they must. It used to be thought that pilot competence was the key to safety, but it has been learned slowly and painfully how little competence can be trusted. So also in surgery, where checklists of elementary precautions that every surgeon knows he should take have proved to be dramatic life savers.[8]

The difficulty of getting it right is also well known to most of us in daily life. Making decisions on one's own is a recipe for mess. Say you are buying a new sofa. It needs to be comfortable, the right size for your room, the right colour and style, one your mother-in-law would approve of and so on. If you get one of these things wrong, you land yourself with a sofa you will not be content with. If therefore you are smart, you do what pilots and surgeons have learned to do: you subject your decision making to checks. For example, you get a companion to go with you to help you to consider all the details of deciding and to deliberate with you over each one. Without that help from a companion, who is really an informal checklist, you are likely to overlook some of the things you should consider and not give some of them enough thought.[9]

Checklists and companions are components in a system of decision making. The wise decision maker takes care to not rely on his own judgement only but to subject decisions to system. A checklist is an elementary way of disciplining your judgement in your own interest with the help of an imposed routine that forces you to take it step by step. A companion does much the same: she will say, "Should you not also take A, B and C into consideration? You like that colour but don't you think it will stand out too much from your other furniture?" When Eisenhower, who knew one or two things about management, took up office in the White House in 1953, he introduced modern headquarters-style administration (a novelty in a previously disorganised place). "Organization cannot make a genius out of a dunce," he would say. "But it can provide its head with the facts he needs, and help him to avoid misinformed mistakes."[10]

Group Decision Making

Group decision making should be safer than individual decision making, since there is the possibility that the members of the group control and correct each other. Indeed, that is the way we should wish political decision making to work. But it does not come by itself. Correcting arrangements need to be designed. Otherwise the danger is that group members fortify one another in gravitating to certainty. That is what is known as "groupthink." When you belong to a community of believers, the danger is that you persuade one another in your intentions and dissuade each other from critical deliberation. In government the dangers are in particular the hubris of power and the something-must-be-done syndrome, both of which influences weigh on the holders of office and lure them to doing what they ought not or what they ought in wrong ways.

As usual, power is as much trouble as it is good. Politicians who have won it are tempted to overestimate what it allows them to do and gives them the right to expect. When Mr. Bush trumpeted that he was about to start spending his political capital, it was unavoidable that things would go wrong. But also Barack Obama made the same mistake, although in his case out of not arrogance but carelessness. When he won his impressive election victory in 2008 and found himself not only president with a strong backing in the population but also the leader of a Democratic Party with majorities in both houses in Congress, everyone knew and spoke endlessly of the danger of inflated expectations. Everyone, from the president down and all political commentators, warned that expectations were massively unrealistic and would have to be reigned in.

But notwithstanding this awareness, which without doubt was entirely genuine, the president himself and the Democratic movement fell victims to the trappings of power. The president launched policies high and low and preached principle and idealism. It first looked good, but after no more than a year many Americans were in utter confusion about who their president was and in embarrassment about a man who talked so much but got, they thought, although wrongly, so little done.

The Democratic Party in Congress and its followers outside went punch drunk with power. They acted as if they thought, in spite of themselves, that with the power they had won they could have anything they wanted. This became manifest in the issue of health care reform. The president spoke of bipartisanship but could not help himself from acting as if he did not need it. His followers disregarded the need for unity and ego-trippers left and right allowed themselves to ride hobbyhorses relentlessly—public health insurance or nothing! health insurance for all but not for abortion!—and to mismanage the moment so that the president's battle came to stand with his own side and was there won only with the slimmest of majorities.

Gordon Brown, while chancellor of the exchequer during New Labour's good years, was overwhelmed by hubris. He was one of the leaders who had made the Labour Party electable by persuading it to be suspicious of power, but as a decision maker he still could not get himself to think that he did not have the right to get whatever he put his power behind. In his case, this showed up in his confidence that if he provided the inputs the outcomes would have to follow. He put massive new money into the National Health Service and took it for granted that it would carry through to more and better outcomes. He failed, however, to follow through into the translation of inputs into outcomes and neglected the necessity of mobilising the people who make up the health service to throwing themselves into the job of producing more outcomes from the inputs he gave them.

Do-something pressures come down on governments with relentless force. It comes from their own ambitions. Governments want to do good and are desperate to be of consequence. It comes from their constituents. The moment they are in office, those who feel they have put them there line up to get them to take up their particular causes. It comes from pressure groups. Every cause has a group working for it, and piling on the pressure for government action is what pressure groups do. It comes from the press, day in and day out exposing problems that the government is not up do dealing with. And it comes from the country. Through the government's window, the society it is responsible for governing looks like a catalogue of problems that cry out to it to be solved.

No single government can do all that much. There are infinitely more problems out there than any government can take on, never mind solve. Often there just are no solutions to even problems that are obvious, known and grave. President Eisenhower, when retiring, reflected that "he had longed to give the world peace but was only able to contribute a stalemate."[11]

Governments must choose what problems to take on and they must do that by asking what is practicable and solvable. This is difficult—it

105

really means deciding what problems to neglect—and the pressure and temptation to do more than is manageable is enormous.

AVOIDANCE OF MISTAKE

The challenge, then, is to avoid the mistakes that lie in lure, the mistake of trying too hard, of not de-prioritising and of not setting aside what cannot be done effectively, of overestimating one's powers and abilities, of letting intentions rule and not paying attention to the practicalities of follow-ups and implementation. A government that is to be effective needs to restrain itself. It needs to tie itself into a system of decision making that prevents it from going ahead when it is on the wrong track. Not even the keenest awareness of these risks is enough to avoid them. All politicians of any calibre have that awareness and still slip up. It is *system* that is needed: arrangements that pick up potential mistakes in time and prevent them from being let loose.

The Smartness of Slowness
When I moved to Britain from Scandinavia and from working in Norway and Sweden, I found that I had moved between very different cultures of policy planning. The Scandinavian countries are comparatively well governed, while Britain is on the lower end of government effectiveness among the established democracies.[12] One among many reasons for this difference is time. In Britain, once the government has opened a dossier, it is difficult for it to be allowed time to do the job properly. The pressures in Parliament and in the press are relentlessly for haste. This is one of the reasons why planning is inadequate and the quality of governance mediocre.

There is truth in the old wisdom that haste should be made slowly. "Many people observed that president Washington spoke slowly and took time to make decisions, letting plans ripen before enacting them. Politics gave him more time to deliberate than did warfare, and he made fewer mistakes as president than as a general on the battlefield. Hamilton concurred that the president consulted much, pondered much, resolved slowly, resolved securely. By delaying decisions he made sure that his better judgement prevailed over his temper. Jefferson did not rank Washington as a first-rate intellect, but he admitted that no judgement was ever sounder."[13] A couple of centuries later, in October 1957, the opposite approach was displayed when the Soviet Union announced that it had successfully fired a satellite, *Sputnik 1,* into orbit, and the Americans panicked to catch up. President Eisenhower ordered accelerated competition between the navy and army to develop America's own satellite. That led to a first launch attempt in December of the same year, an attempt that ended when the rocket exploded a few seconds after blastoff. A second attempt in February 1958 also failed when the rocket exploded within the first minute. "Making haste, unfortunately, only produced less speed."[14]

In Scandinavia, the routine is slow decision making. Indeed, in these countries, which have a high capacity for producing necessary decisions and for doing so in time, decision making is laboriously cumbersome. It may be worth explaining how in some detail and with a practical example.

When the Norwegian parliament in 2009 adopted a comprehensive pension reform, it was the culmination of a process that had started in 2001 and had moved forward in the usual lumbering way that major policy decisions are made. The slowness was not a result of deadlock; the reform was being taken forward relentlessly but without rush or panic.

The process toward decisions of this kind follows a fixed procedure that is prescribed in written regulations and established conventions and which it would normally be unthinkable, except in an emergency, to deviate from. The protection given by that procedure can be seen in what may happen when it is circumvented. A recent case was a major hospital reform in 2001, when the ownership of public hospitals was transferred from counties to the state, a reform that was rushed through with uncharacteristic political machismo. The result was the kind of mistake more associated with dysfunctional systems of decision making, such as in Britain. The very first thing that happened was that directors and chairman in new "health regions" awarded themselves salaries and compensations on a level until then unknown in Norwegian public service, falling effortlessly from day one into the language that if they were to carry serious responsibility they would have to recruit the best managers and therefore pay on a "competitive" level. The reform itself proved extremely expensive, brought on never-ending and still ongoing reorganisation, and has caused a deterioration of quality and confidence in the care system.

Here is how things work when taken forward as prescribed. A problem is identified that calls for some kind of public policy action or reform, and the government gets a nod from the *Storting,* the Norwegian parliament, to start planning toward a solution. It appoints a committee of study, usually made up of experts and some constituency representatives (typically of employers and unions), with a relatively precise mandate, to undertake a study of the issue and propose solutions. The committee will typically work three to four years and produce a comprehensive report, heavy on factual study, along with a joint proposal or majority and minority proposals. The next step is for the relevant ministry to distribute the report to interested parties throughout the country in what is known as "a hearing round," with a note of guidance on matters it in particular wants views on. The government will then produce a white paper to the parliament based on the committee's report and inputs from the hearing round, with a more or less precise outline of the action it thinks should follow. This will typically have taken another year or two. In the parliament, the white paper goes first to the relevant select committee, which works it over in detail and prepares a report, which will form the basis of a first plenary debate, again with more or less precise proposals or outlines for action. The parliament then holds a debate, more on principle than on detail. It may at this time bury the matter, but that would be highly unusual. We are now another year or so on. The report of the select committee and inputs in the debate, with or without a vote or votes, will be taken as instructions to the government for the preparation of legislation. That will take another year or two and culminate in what is known as a "proposition" to the parliament. There will typically be informal deliberations between the relevant ministry and the relevant select committee in the process. The proposition again goes to the relevant select committee, which again works it over and prepares a report, which again is the basis for the parliament to hold a debate in plenary, now culminating in a vote or series of votes to pass legislation.

At any time, a multitude of processes of this kind are in motion at different stages of advancement. The processes are slow but grind on relentlessly and produce grounded and deliberated decisions. Most processes will not be interrupted by a change of government, although a new government may for example marginally alter the composition or mandate of the occasional committee of study. In the case of the pension reform, the process started under a minority labour government, was carried forward under a minority centre-right coalition, and was finalised toward legislation under a majority centre-left government.

Basically, this kind of planning is a protracted process of deliberation. The virtue is that decision making is well prepared, solid and participatory, so that in most cases a reasonable consensus has been worked out, which will lend legitimacy to the eventual legislation.

No doubt there are many ways that rational decision making can be shaped, depending on political traditions in each country, and in Norway as elsewhere committees of study are sometimes used as a way of pushing troublesome issues into the long grass. The points made in this fairly detailed example, however, are first that expedited decision making does not come from hasty decision making, and, second, that there is virtue in having prescribed procedures for the preparation of major policies which individual ministers, who will always be tempted to haste, cannot easily circumvent.

The Blessing of the Back Room

A sensible government wants to avoid the issuing of orders that are foolish, unnecessary, impractical or unworkable. Once an order is issued, it is too late. The government is then committed to seeing it through. This is what happened to Mrs. Thatcher in the poll tax fiasco. She was not stopped in time and was trapped into pushing through a policy that could not be implemented. Of course, governments can do U-turns when they discover that they have got themselves into a fix, but U-turns are politically embarrassing—the most repugnant option in government, said the historian Barbara Tuchman, whereby mistakes are more often compounded than corrected.[15] "*You* turn if you want to," said Mrs. Thatcher, "the lady's not for turning."

If a minister or group of ministers are free to make decisions on their own without anyone standing in their way, they *will* get it wrong. All leaders know the danger of surrounding themselves with yes-men, but most are still tempted to do so. A wise minister would involve others to get her ideas checked before she launches a policy. She would know that anyone who embarks on a complicated venture must make sure to get a second opinion. Preferably, there should be procedures of decision making that oblige ministers to get others involved and prevent them from launching what has not been checked. If it is up to their own discretion, they will go ahead too quickly and without adequate planning and make a mess of it.

The two main mechanisms are autonomous advice and cabinet government. Autonomous advice comes from civil service autonomy or expert advisory bodies, or both. It is understood to be a duty on top officials or advisers to use their expertise to warn ministers when they are on track to a mistaken policy or have not planned carefully enough or paid sufficient attention to pertinent facts, and it may be a formal duty on ministers to have gone through a prescribed routine of civil service or expert vetting. This is uncomfortable for any minister, but necessary for good decisions. In a study of British legislation, the Hansard Society points to the lack of routine in the use of and consultation with independent expertise as one of the causes of persistently "bad law."[16]

In a dashing book on Second World War strategic planning in the United States and Britain, *Masters and Commanders,* the historian Andrew Roberts shows how the collaboration between Churchill and Alan Brooke (who later metamorphosed into Lord Alanbrooke) in Britain and Roosevelt and George Marshall in the United States (Brooke and Marshall being the respective top military commanders), and between the four of them, was a constant, hard, rough, aggressive battle about what should be done, when and how it should be done, and what should be avoided and what postponed. This collaboration was such that the two political bosses would mostly be unable to start anything without the acquiescence of their servants, and that they would repeatedly be thwarted in their intentions by vigorous resistance from below—luckily for the war effort, we must say, considering some of the schemes the political leaders inclined to. Of course, the masters checked the commanders too, but what is striking in the story is how the military commanders were able and determined to shoot down their masters' plans when they thought them ill advised. The necessity of having the commanders on board was built into the system. If a master was caught out having started to launch some planning of significance behind the back of his commander, the commander would be down on him like a ton of bricks, and it would be the master rather than the commander who would be embarrassed.

The strategies that emerged out of this vigorous decision making were the ones that survived both political and military vetting and the often aggressive confrontations between the two sides. Indeed, Roberts ascribes the Allied victory in the war to this system of decision making for its ability in large measure to prevent unworkable strategies or launching prematurely out of political impatience. Hence, the Allied invasion in France in 1944 was delayed two years beyond what the American political leadership had wanted, until Stalin had worn down Hitler so that Roosevelt and Churchill could knock him over.

The situation on the German side was completely different. Hitler as dictator had the ability to launch whatever he wanted, even when his generals recognised it to be self-defeating, and did not have servants around him with the ability to set him right when he was wrong. This, suggests Roberts, was finally why the Allies won, even though Germany had the superior fighting machine.

When a civil service is humiliated and put under command, as now in Britain, it ceases to be able or willing to do the job of holding ministers to the straight and narrow. In a report from the Committee on Public Accounts of the House of Commons in 2010, the Ministry of Defence is criticised in the strongest of terms for "having failed to exercise the robust financial management necessary to control its resources effectively in the long run. It has also failed to match its future plans to a realistic assessment of the resources available, [resulting in a likely shortfall] of up to £36 billion over the next ten years."[17] The committee heaps on further criticism of financial mismanagement and waste and then pins down the blame in unusually clear language: "the Accounting Officer has not discharged his responsibility to ensure that planned and committed expenditure across the defence budget represents value for money." The "accounting officer" of the department is its permanent undersecretary, the top civil servant, and the committee is explicit about "his responsibility."

With cabinet government, policy planning and decision making is collective. No minister is able to launch a policy without having gone through fixed routines for securing the pre-launch backing of his cabinet colleagues and all ministers know that they have co-responsibility. The alternative is what in Britain under Mr. Blair became known as "sofa government." When Mrs. Thatcher came to power in 1979, she inherited a system based on cabinet government and an independent civil service that she first had to work with. In about five years, however, she had reduced cabinet government to a formality, put the civil service (which she distrusted) under command, and shifted real decision making to informal settings. These were the conventions that New Labour inherited upon coming to power in 1997, and then perfected. It was a system in which very few checks had been maintained: no checks to make decision making prudent and deliberate, no checks from independent officials or experts, no checks from cabinet government, and no checks from proper scrutiny in Parliament. Decision making would be case-by-case in the hands of the prime minister and one or a few ministers who would sit down and sort matters out informally without participation by other ministers who did not need to know.

In his memoirs, Jonathan Powell is upset by the criticism of sofa government and resorts to the kind of language that shows the sting to have been felt: "This is nonsense." To demonstrate that the cabinet was thoroughly involved in decision making he writes: "We prepared intensively for each Cabinet meeting. Sally Morgan, and later Ruth Turner, would ring round all the members of the cabinet beforehand to see what was on their minds. Before the meeting itself, we would shuffle people in and out of Tony's den to resolve last-minute problems and agree on when Gordon Brown and John Prescott should be invited to intervene in the subsequent discussion."[18] Now there is a comedy of errors for you! And poor old Powell seems to believe that's what cabinet government would look like.

The problem with sofa government is, first, the informality. Decisions are made by stealth so that there is no explicit decision point. The space for misunderstandings is vast on what has been decided or whether a decision has been made. Second, decisions do not get checked. A minister wants to do something, gets the nod of the prime minister, or thinks he does, and is off. Or the prime minister hints at a policy, or a minister thinks he does, and off he is again.

More basically, with cabinet government the structure of decision making is made up of tight horizontal lines of communication between ministers who are involved in and informed about each other's planning as a matter of routing and who check and advise each other. With sofa government, the horizontal links between ministers are weak and decision making is made vertically in a messy network of ad hoc exchanges between the prime minister and departmental ministers. Much too much comes to depend on the single person who is the only permanent presence in decision making, the prime minister, and too few people contribute too little to thinking, planning, caution and deliberation.

The Security of Scrutiny

Public policy decision making in a democracy is supposed to be a partnership between the legislature and the government. In theory, the legislature decides and the government executes, but in parliamentary systems, such as in most European countries, the government, unless it is a minority government, is usually more or less in control of the legislature through its majority. In that situation, the reality of scrutiny in the legislature may wear thin. Britain is here an extreme case where constitutional conventions have settled so that the approval in Parliament of government initiatives is in most cases a mere formality, at least in the House of Commons. Parliament debates initiatives but for the most part engages in very little scrutiny proper of laws or budgets before putting its stamp of authority on them. Parliamentary debate is obviously important—but debate is not scrutiny. Scrutiny means to double-check in detail, but the House of Commons, which sometimes does debate well, does scrutiny badly.

The benefits of pre-decision scrutiny in the legislature are twofold. When a government knows that the lawmakers will turn over every stone in its proposals and push away what they find wanting, it cannot go to the legislature with proposals that are not properly prepared or worked through. In the absence of institutionalised scrutiny in the legislature, the government will be tempted to make haste and go to the lawmakers with poorly prepared proposals because it has no reason to fear that its proposals will be checked. Where pre-decision scrutiny is routine, the legislature is not likely to change much in what the government has proposed, but that is because the government will have had to anticipate what the lawmakers will accept and will usually have cleared its proposals with the legislature informally ahead of what it finally proposes. Lawmakers rejecting what the government proposes is not a sign of a strong legislature but of a system that does not work. When President Hamid Karzai in Afghanistan in March 2010 put before the Afghan national assembly a proposal to change the election law and had it rejected by a near to unanimous assembly, what we saw was not parliamentary power but governance in disarray.

The second advantage is that if more or less badly prepared proposals nevertheless slip through to the legislature, they are likely to be stopped or corrected before becoming law. Proper scrutiny goes to the devil in the detail, which debate in a large chamber never can.

Poor decision making is of course still possible, but with rigorous pre-decision scrutiny less likely. On the other side, the risk of bad decision making in the absence of proper scrutiny is very high. An illustrative case in Britain is that of indeterminate sentences for serious crimes. This was introduced in the Criminal Justice Act of 2003—a monster act of incomprehensibility in which MPs had no idea what they were letting through, according to Mr. Marshall-Andrews "one of the largest and worst pieces of criminal justice legislation in any century and one which has caused endless grief and injustice."[19] Under this provision, a minimum sentence is given by a court, but the convict will not be released after having served that tariff unless and until he or she can satisfy the Parole Board that he or she is fit for release. To that end, most convicts have to undertake various courses in what the Prison Service describes as "offending behavioural" or "cognitive skills" programmes. However, in some measure, probably in large measure, the required courses have not been available to convicts under indeterminate sentence. At any time, there may be around ten thousand prisoners serving indeterminate sentences in England alone. Many of these, an unknown number, have not been able to have their case for release heard, in what the Ministry of Justice euphemistically calls a "backlog." They just languish in prison with no knowledge about their future fate. This unbelievable state of affairs, which is unbefitting a society that wants to be civilised—a Kafka-like nightmare of a kind one expects to find in a Stalinist dictatorship—no doubt came about by accident. It is very unlikely that Parliament deliberately passed a law so perverse as to deprive prisoners of basic rights that were written into the law itself. That it nevertheless did pass a lock-them-up-and-throw-away-the-key law must be a result of some inadequacy of decision making. Had the House of Commons had effective procedures to double-check the government's proposals, it would not have been possible to just overlook that elementary provisions, necessary for the law to work as intended, were not in place. It would not even have been possible for the government to come to Parliament with a piece of legislation so shoddily prepared.

If you were to think ministers might have learned from that misery and improved their ways, think again. On the 31st of October 2011, the justice minister, Kenneth Clarke, was pushing another mess of a monster bill through Parliament with customary haste, the Legal Aid, Sentencing and Punishment of Offenders Bill. A former Labour minister, Chris Bryant, objected in the debate to the way it was done: "When government ministers come forward and say that we have to change the ordinary processes for the government's convenience, and we know we can do it because we have a majority, that ends up nearly always with bad legislation, because it doesn't get sufficient scrutiny. It certainly did when we were on that side of the House."

THE PROPENSITY TO MISTAKE

This is where we have arrived: I have argued (1) that the problem is obedience, (2) that governments are up against others who are always reluctant, (3) that the final challenge in good government is implementation, (4) that the turning of power into performance depends on fairness and restraint, (5) that a settlement of order depends on institutions that bind governments and that push followers into compliance, (6) that such institutions reside in culture as much as in rules, (7) that power is not all it has been cracked up to be, (8) that governance is a people business, (9) that managing the problem of obedience depends on authority and leadership, (10) that the most solid authority is that which rests on the magic of legitimacy, (11) that governments do one thing and one thing only: they give orders, (12) that even holding on to the ground from which a government is able to issue orders is a battle, and (13) that orders are commands or signals and that it is the politics of signals that is the great constant in government action.

In this chapter I have added that governments are notoriously prone to getting it wrong. Therefore, once in power, the job is to avoid mistakes. Neither good will nor dedication nor competence can be trusted. Good decision making depends on a good system of decision making in which decisions are checked and double-checked.

And that concludes the preparatory manoeuvres which, if I were a more pretentious man than I am, I might have called theory. We can thereby return to *the problem,* that of obedience, and confront that head on. I will deal with it in two steps, in order of difficulty, first with officials in the next chapter and then with citizens in the chapter thereafter.

7

HOW TO MAKE OFFICIALS OBEY

When, therefore, relations between princes and their
ministers are of this kind, they can have confidence in
each other; when they are otherwise, the result is
always disastrous for both of them.

—The Prince, chapter 22

A minister issues an order. The order hits an official. When that
happens, the default response is no response at all—nothing.
Civil servants are people and, like most people, proud and selfish.
The order tells the official to go out of his way and do something he has
not been inclined to. His selfishness tells him to avoid that. It deprives him
of freedom by subjecting him to the will of someone else as the servant of
a master. His pride tells him to oppose that.

This is not to say that no response is the expected response. It is
entirely possible. Officials disregard orders from above all the time, sometimes because they don't like them, sometimes because they forget or
could not care, and sometimes if orders are unclear, in which case doing nothing may be the safe thing. Or they take the lack of clarity as an
excuse for non-action. Even loyal officials often disregard orders. When
President Reagan started to show his age and lose his grip on policy, increasingly his "cabinet colleagues and staff acted according to what they
thought the president had in mind, or wanted, rather than what he actually instructed."[1] A secretary to the British cabinet during the Second
World War described the drafting of cabinet minutes as reporting "what
he thinks that they think they ought to have thought."[2]

But usually, in a normal democracy, it would be expected that officials respond to orders by more or less trying to do what they more or less think is wanted. However, there is nothing natural, god-given or obvious about that. It is not that orders are obeyed because they are issued; rather it is a bit of a mystery when officials do anything except nothing. And it is certainly a mystery if they respond well and efficiently. All this depends on causes and are things that must be explained.

THE DIFFICULTY

It can hardly be overstated how difficult it is for governments to get things done and to get it right. It is not enough to know of a problem, or to decide that should be dealt with, or to understand its nature and how it might be solved, or to decide what should be done, or to formulate policies or issue orders to that effect. All this must still follow through to the kind of implementation that produces outcomes than work. That's just plain *difficult*.

On the 13th of August 2012, in Norway, undoubtedly one of the best governed countries anywhere, the independent commission on the events of the 22nd of July 2011 issued its report of findings.[3] This was the notorious assault when a national terrorist drove a massive car bomb into the heart of the government compound in Oslo and exploded it, and then made his way to an island in a nearby lake where the youth organization of the Labour Party had its summer camp and went on a rampage to shoot down anyone among the participants he could get at. In all seventy-seven people were killed on that day and untold material damage caused.

The commission was charged with uncovering how this had happened. It concluded that the assault should not have been possible. The government compound should have had better security. Police routines should have been in place to prevent the terrorist from reaching the island, and once he was there the police should have been on the scene faster than they were. There was faulty security in the government compound and faulty operations and communications routines in the police. The commission furthermore found that these faults had been well known. The government and its relevant agencies were aware of the faults and had detailed analyses of deficient security and routines. The government had made plans for their rectification and issued decisions and instructions to get that done. All this was in place long before the events in 2011. But for all this awareness, analysis and decision making, implementation had failed. The commission found this to be the result of inadequate follow-ups by the government to its decisions, muddled lines of responsibility, poor quality of leadership in administrative agencies, and bad culture in those same agencies.

BUREAUCRACY AND MOBILISATION

The cardinal feature of the polity, said Finer, is "baron-management." The king "could give effect to his orders only through them [the barons]. Therefore they must be induced to give enthusiastic support (the best outcome) or acceptance (the next best) and discouraged from foot-dragging or, at the very worst, open resistance."[4] I'm not dealing with kings and barons, but the problem is the same. All governments *must* have acceptance from their officials and *want* enthusiastic service.

Good work in public services has two sources: it comes from energy on the part of individuals and from the many coordinating with each other. Ministers can order a job done, but neither energy nor coordination will follow unless underlings engage to make it happen.

The first thing bosses do to their servants to make them compliant is to slot them into a *bureaucracy*. Bureaucratic order is necessary if rulers are to hope for acceptance. But it does not do much toward enthusiastic support. On the contrary, bureaucratic rigidity is often off-putting and discouraging. Political bosses should therefore do more for and to their officials than to push them with bureaucracy. They should also use the pull of encouragement.

I say *should* because the encouragement of underlings from above is the great imponderable in leadership. Some leaders understand it and have a knack for it, some do not. Mr. Blair lost a valued minister in a scandal and was saddened by it, because "he was loved by his department (and believe me this is pretty rare)."[5]

Enthusiasm is not what one usually associates with public bureaucracies. Talleyrand, the eminent Napoleonic minister and diplomat, famously warned against too much zeal: "Surtout, pas trop de zèle." But that was from the point of view of the officials. Since bosses are unpredictable, it may be unsafe for underlings to work eagerly. Bosses, however, since they can give effect to their orders only through others, depend on those others *wanting* orders to be effected. Public services consist of people and cannot be effective unless those people work well.

All governments are constantly at work on their bureaucracies and endlessly engaged in reforms and reorganisations. Indeed, a treacherous trap for any ambitious government is to put too much trust in what can be done bureaucratically and with the help of commands and controls, and to neglect the need to encourage. If so, it may find itself in a downward spiral: it reorganises from above in ways that are discouraging from below, does not get the efficiency it is expecting, reorganises again and discourages yet more, and so on. That was the trap New Labour fell into in Britain and which contributes to explaining why its many initiatives did not follow through to much in outcomes.

Bureaucracy is magical, ideally akin to what the biologists Bert Hölldobler and Edward Wilson call "superorganisms." A minister exercises leadership by issuing orders that other members of the organisation, by force of the leader's authority, make their purpose. Purposeful action has been in motion since time immemorial and has caused structures to be established which work as signposts for workers today. From up high in the organisation, direction is imposed on individual members whereby each one by habituation gets on to doing whatever in their little turf is most conducive to the efficiency of the organism. In an ideal bureaucracy it would be right to say that the government runs everything.

All governments work with the help of big bureaucracies but— unfortunately for them and fortunately for everyone else—never ideal bureaucracies. In governance there is mess, trouble, events, mistakes, misunderstandings, conflict, competition, intrigue, resistance, inertia, disobedience and so on. Modern public administration is a never-ending merry-go-round of more or less desperate reorganisation and reform in a quest for something that "works." Most governments have separate ministries of public administration, which tend to carry dynamic names such as the Ministry of Administration and Reform (which was the Norwegian one, until it recently was reorganised yet again and became, mysteriously, the Ministry of Government Administration, Reform and Church Affairs).

The quest for bureaucratic perfection becomes a problem if in the interest of preventing resistance it is applied so heavily that it discourages support. The good bureaucracy is optimally fine-tuned, but the secret of bureaucratic fine-tuning has not yet been discovered. A top Ford Motors manager is supposed to have said, "Our crisis management model is this: Where we have centralised, we decentralise; where we have decentralised, we centralise." The fashion has now for some time been toward de-bureaucratisation, in the learned literature under the name of "new public management." Administrative structures are flattened, job specifications relaxed and project and group management across services and ministries encouraged, directions from above are issued as targets and goals rather than procedures, there is management by incentives, there are internal markets, and so on. It is a desperately moving field with little of robust knowledge or real expertise to fall back on.

To lift the spirit of officials from mere acceptance, what is further needed is *mobilisation,* the use of leadership to generate support from below with at least some enthusiasm. Here, ministers have the ordinary resources to play on of legality, tradition and charisma. But also, they control access to the enchanted territory of power. They have the means to flatter those who work for them by pulling them into their domain and giving them a share in the glory of power. If they do, they will be revered; if they refuse to share their gift, they will be hated.

The encouragement of public servants is much more difficult than the designing of public services. Bureaucracy is organisation; mobilisation is personal. It is psychological, it depends on human knowledge, it rests predominantly on the subtle use of signals and normative leadership, and it depends on getting the melody right in the specific context of culture, time and place. In a way, going back to the case studies we saw earlier, the Korean autocrats had it easy. Their national project of modernisation was inspiring in itself, and they worked in a Confucian culture of respect. The New Labour leaders in Britain inherited a demoralised civil service from the Thatcher years and were unable to break with that legacy.

WHO ARE THEY?

The people who work in the bureaucracies of government are of two kinds, those who are armed and those who are civil. I start with the armed ones because it is sometimes overlooked these days that governance without the threat of physical violence is impossible. Force, says Joseph Nye, "is to order as oxygen is to breathing, unappreciated until it becomes scarce."[6] When violent riots erupted throughout England in August 2011, the police were criticised, no doubt rightly, for not putting enough force quickly enough on to the streets to prevent the unrest from spreading.

The Armed Services

An important part of the answer to the question of how governments get people to do as they want is this: the government controls the guns. That is true today as it was in what we now think of as more raw and brutal olden times, when for example Machiavelli wrote that "the main foundations of every state are good laws and good arms."[7] Even the maintenance of ordinary, daily order in the most civilised society requires the presence of police as the visible threat of coercion. A government has the power to threaten people, including its servants, with arrest, interrogation, harassment, humiliation, imprisonment, and sometimes death.

Administrative force is surprisingly common once you look for it. The police are used routinely to strike down against tax evaders, illegal asylum seekers, welfare cheaters, those who park illegally, drive too fast or, for example, squat in unused property. Children are removed from unsafe homes and taken into care or brought to school against the will of their parents. Search for "dawn raids" on the Web and you will find innumerable such cases, often involving very harsh means.

Force is present in high politics as well. On the 27th of November 2008 Mr. Damien Green, Conservative member of Parliament and shadow minister for immigration, was arrested at his home in Kent by members of the counterterrorism command. Officers from the Metropolitan Police in London entered Parliament and conducted a search of his office there. His constituency offices and his two homes were also searched. Mr. Green was held and questioned for nine hours, then released on bail and was subsequently not charged with any offence. The raid was part of a police investigation into a series of leaks from the Home Office, on the instigation of its permanent undersecretary and on the argument that the leaks risked undermining the effective operation of the department. Mr. Green had had information from such leaks and had used it to put politically awkward questions to the government. There was a suspicion of conspiracy. A junior Home Office official with connections to the Conservative Party was arrested and suspended from service. The police had entered Parliament and searched Mr. Green's office without a warrant but with the permission of the relevant Parliament official. There were strong protests from members of Parliament over the police action, in particular the entry of officers into Parliament and their search of an office there and the demonstratively heavy-handed nature of the action. The government claimed it had nothing to do with the raid, washed its hands of the affair, and the furour died down. By the nature of things, it is not possible for outsiders to know just what was afoot behind the scenes, but in any event a very clear reminder was issued to both officials and politicians that the government has the power to unleash the police on them.

The apparatus of force divides in two main categories, the military and the police. In theory, the military is responsible for the use of force abroad or against external threats and the police for the use of force at home, but practically the military is a part of a government's apparatus of threat also against its own population. From time to time the military will be mobilised in the interest of domestic order, both because the police are sometimes not able to manage on their own and because it may be in the interest of a government to let the people see the colour of its steel. That happens regularly against labour and other unrest. It also happened, for example, in the United States on the 23rd of September 1957, when, in order to enable nine black children to attend Little Rock's Central High School, President Eisenhower "called the head of the US Army, General Maxwell Taylor and by nightfall some 500 paratroopers of the 101st Airborne Division had assumed positions in the centre of the city, with bayonets fixed. Governor Faubus went on national television to decry the 'warm red blood of patriotic citizens staining the cold, naked, unsheathed knives' of the airborne division's soldiers holding back the white mob, while Senator Richard Russell charged the president with using Hitler-like storm-trooper tactics on Ordinary Americans."[8] And again, for example, at the University of Mississippi in Oxford in September 1962 when about two thousand white students and troublemakers tried to stop the first ever black student from registering and local law enforcement and military forces were unwilling or unable to control the mob. "Finally, reluctantly the president [Kennedy] ordered regular army units to be flown from Tennessee to Oxford, just as Eisenhower had been compelled to do at Little Rock five years before."[9] Force was mobilised in these cases both to right wrongs—upholding the rights of individual citizens—and also, very much, to fortify the authority of the state.

So governments use and need their armed forces to exercise control over society—if, that is, as usual, they can control those services. For it is not quite correct as I said above that governments control the guns. The guns are still in the hands of others. It is therefore possible that those others control the government rather than it them. This is the case in many dictatorships, typically for example in North Korea. Finer's *History of Government* is full of armed mutinies. When people rose up against the regime of President Hosni Mubarak in Egypt in January 2011, they succeeded because the army refused to turn on the rebels (although in the interest of self-preservation). It is also possible that a government that is nominally in charge in what looks like a normal democratic situation may lose its control over those who wield the arms, and if so it is in serious trouble. On the 30th of September 2010, groups of angry police and security personnel in Ecuador, disgruntled with pay (and possibly with other grievances and motives), turned their guns on the democratically legal regime, stormed the national assembly, closed down the main airport in the capital, Quito, and forced the president, Rafael Correa, who was trying to reason with the mob, to take refuge in a hospital where he was held captive for more than ten hours. It was also guns that saved the regime when military forces loyal to the president stormed the hospital, in an operation involving about five hundred soldiers and exchange of gunfire, and rescued him back to the security of the presidential palace, from whence, obviously, a clearing out of "infiltrated elements" from the police was immediately unleashed, including the sacking of the national chief of police. A major factor in the collapse of the Fourth Republic in France, one that enabled de Gaulle to manoeuvre back into power and subsequently push through a new constitution to create the Fifth Republic and the strong presidency, was, says de Gaulle's biographer Jonathan Fenby, that the governments became "unable to rely on two bastions of the Republic, the police and the military. At the beginning of May 1958, a demonstration outside the National Assembly by right-wing police symbolised the ebbing control of the government."[10] I mentioned in Chapter 3 the threat of the British commander to not obey his government's orders ahead of the invasion of Iraq. Another example is the case of Israel, where the government is strongly dependent on the credible threat of force. One of the (many) difficulties with taking "the peace process" with the Palestinians forward to a two-state solution is that it might involve the forceful removal of Jewish settlers from the West Bank (as was done in the Sinai in 1982 and the Gaza Strip in 2005). Since substantial sections of the military are made up of Orthodox Jews or other personnel who are supportive of the settlement movement, there is a potential for disobedience or revolt in the military against an order to deploy against the settlers, a risk any Israeli government would be aware of and none could take, and that therefore limits their freedom of movement in the matter.

The poet Bertolt Brecht asked, when Caesar beat the Gauls, if there was not even a cook in his army. Well, there was and Caesar was, says Suetonius, well aware of it and of the power of his men and the need to win their loyalty: "Caesar loved his men dearly. He always addressed them not as 'soldiers' but as 'comrades,' which put them in a better humour, and he equipped them splendidly. By these means he won the devotion of his men as well as making them extraordinarily brave. There was not mutiny once during the Gallic war, which lasted ten years."[11]

The Military

The military is usually subdivided into various forces, typically the army, the navy and the air force. That is for reasons of administrative expediency, in the same way that the civil service is divided into ministries, but also to insert divide-and-rule into the organisation of services that are both necessary and dangerous. Because of the danger, their masters will split them up into specialised branches, which invariably get into conflict and competition with each other and are often manipulated to do so, in order to make it less likely that those who carry heavy arms could coalesce in threat or opposition.

The military brass often see themselves as an administrative aristocracy in force of carrying the heavy duty of defending the nation. They feel that they have a right to speak politically on matters of defence, for example to warn against inadequate military investments and budgets, and to be more at freedom to do so outside of internal budgetary processes than the representatives of other services. And when representatives of the military services speak critically in public about defence policy (or other matters), there is a touch of threat in the air. The nation is not only being advised; this is advice offered from a platform of strength that no one else in the political machine can match.

Military personnel are either professional or conscripted. A modern military service is unthinkable without a stratum of professional officers and specialists. For the rest, some democracies rely on the use of con-scripted foot soldiers, such as for example the Scandinavian countries and Israel, while others have fully professional services, such as Britain and the United States (except in emergency situations when additional personnel need to be conscripted). Conscription is in retreat, partly because it is seen as incompatible with modern high-tech warfare. France and Spain abolished conscription in 2001 and 2002, and Germany in 2011, but in a referendum in January 2013, the Austrians voted to retain conscription.

There is something very attractive in the principle of conscription: the people visibly sacrificing for and participating in the defence of their country and democracy. And there are democratic disadvantages to a fully professional force. It sets the military apart from the people, and a fully professional force represents more of a political threat than one based on conscription. Furthermore, it is probably easier for a government to go to war with a fully professional service than a conscription service—possibly too easy. A government that has the service of professional soldiers ab-dicates some of its responsibility to men and women who have agreed to be soldiers for pay and does not have to send ordinary boys and girls into battle and answer to them and their parents. That is all the more so since professional soldiers tend to be recruited heavily from lower social strata—and in the United States now heavily from the African American population—and may be seen as more expendable than conscripted av-erage youngsters. This may have been a contributing explanation of the relative readiness of the American and British governments to go to war in Iraq and the readiness of the same governments to send their soldiers to the danger zones in Afghanistan.

Historically, professional soldiers have often been mercenaries, and notoriously unreliable. In the Thirty Years' War in Europe (1618–48), semi-private armies roamed the continent, sometimes exchanging soldiers and sometimes in the service of one king and sometimes of his enemy. The use of mercenaries is far from extinct. Even a modern professional army is a mercenary force, only strictly national. The French Foreign Legion is not even that. It today boasts nearly eight thousand men and presents itself thus on the English-language version of its home page (one of four-teen non-French versions): "Whatever your origins, nationality or religion might be, whatever qualifications you may or may not have, whatever your social or professional status might be, whether you are married or single, the French Foreign Legion offers you a chance to start a new life." In Iraq, the American paramilitary company Blackwater became well known for providing very considerable armed services in collaboration with and outsourced from the American military force.

How large should the military machinery of a democracy be? The obvious answer is as small as possible. Military organisations are costly and dangerous. Defence budgets are notoriously difficult to control, and a big defence budget increases the difficulty of overall budget control. The defence department is a big purchaser, which at the other end means a big defence industry, with the government as its only or main client. This is the genesis of a garrison state. A military machine is a narcotic that tempts masters into using it. American governments have in recent times given in to that temptation, in Vietnam, where they were beaten, in Somalia, where they were humiliated, and in Iraq and Afghanistan, where they incurred monumental costs in life and treasure to little or no benefit to themselves or anyone else. The possession of heavy military might distorts national security policy toward excessive reliance on hard power and to overlook the benefits of soft power.

However, governments are nationalistically ambitious, and the larger ones want to be important players on the world stage. They see the weight of their military force not simply as a matter of defence but also to secure for themselves a place at the top table in international affairs. This is why Britain and France hold on to their very expensive nuclear weaponry al-though it is of no use militarily.

The United States is the paramount military power in the world, with nearly 1.5 million heavily armed and highly trained personnel in ac-tive service at home and on hundreds of installations and bases across the world. President Eisenhower, the general who understood that Amer-ica's strength abroad depends first on its economic strength at home, on leaving office in 1961 warned of the potentially uncontrollable "military-industrial complex." Now, fifty years on, his farewell address stands as one of the great presidential speeches in history and as magnificently heroic and prophetic. He, who knew more about military might than most, warned against the military's size and a permanent armaments industry of vast proportions and against the influence of this complex on American economic and social life, an influence, he said, that was "economic, political, even spiritual" and was "felt in every city, every statehouse, every office of the federal government"—and that was half a century ago.

The Police

The police are similar to the military in that they are part of a government's apparatus of force, but different in that they are (usually) less heavily armed and more autonomous. There is no ambiguity in principle about the political command to which the military owes obedience. The American president, for example, is the commander in chief, and it is the military's duty to obey the president's orders. Presidents, prime ministers and ministers of justice do not usually have the same unambiguous command over the police, at least the regular forces. The police have a duty to law and order and a duty to exercise that duty objectively and when necessary against the opportunistic will of the government of the day.

A police service can be unified, as in for example Britain, or divided into distinct sub-services, as for example in France. This may have something to do with how heavily armed the police are. In Britain, police officers do not routinely carry guns; in France they do. A more heavily armed police force starts to look like a military force, and governments may want to strengthen their control by divide-and-rule. There are also differences in the degree of centralisation and decentralisation and in the balance between uniformed and non-uniformed personnel. The more centralised, the stronger the political control; the more decentralised, the more the police force politically autonomous.

The function of the uniform is to attach authority to the police officer and to enable the officer to be identified so that everyone can know whom they are dealing with. The non-uniformed officer can operate more or less under cover. That is the first step toward a secret service, a service of police officers who are not known to the public to be police and who are in various ways, and for good or bad reasons, in the business of spying on the people (and their representatives) in the name of intelligence. In January 2011, it became known in Britain that the police had infiltrated

environmental activist movements with undercover officers who had operated as activists within the movements over many years. A secret police
force is necessary for the upholding of order, but also unavoidably represents a murky world that can be controlled only with great difficulty. Even
in Britain, rumours of political conspiracies in the secret services are not
held to be incredible.

Policing gives rise to a range of interesting questions which are nevertheless unanswerable. How large should the police force be? In Britain
the prevailing view has long been in favour of more police for the better
protection against crime, although there is little evidence that this is a robust correlation. How harsh should reactions against crime be and when
and for what reasons should offenders be locked up in jail? The United
States and Britain are democracies that have relied heavily on imprisonment, but are still societies ridden by crime and anti-social behaviour. By
2010, the prison population in Britain was around 85,000, up from 45,000
in ten years. That's an incarceration rate of about 140 per 100,000 people,
toward the highest rate in Europe. The United States is in a universe of its
own on this statistic of shame, with an incarceration rate between 500 and
750 per 100,000, depending on which statistics you consult.

The Civil Services

Any government will need effort and energy, as well as shrewdness and
charm, to be on top of its civil servants, not only because of inevitable
institutional conservatism and such factors, but more basically because
officials have as much power to resist as ministers have to command. Ministers can instruct, but officials can subvert.

In the tug of war between ministers and officials, officials have the
advantage of information. Christopher Hood takes the control of information to be a government tool, but that is to turn things upside down. Ministers have intentions, information they need others to give them. They may
have some experience and knowledge about how things work, but mostly
they rely on their officials to provide them with the information they need
to figure out how intentions might be realised. The civil service has more
and longer experience than any minister, more experience in their area of
work and more capacity to gather and put together information. They can
filter and doctor the information they pass on to their superiors. Mr. Blair

liked to be "out and about [because it was a useful way] of finding out if what I was being told in Downing Street bore any resemblance to the facts on the ground. Very often it didn't."[12] In the run-up to the war in Iraq, the CIA and Pentagon failed, possibly intentionally, to inform the secretary of state, Colin Powell, that a key source behind the claim of Saddam Hussein's bioweapons capability was known to be unreliable.

When President Obama in 2009 was working to overhaul the strategy for the war in Afghanistan, it appears that he was unable to get his defence department officials and military planners to prepare for him the alternatives he wanted to compare and choose from.[13] The result of political-administrative wrangling was a messy compromise involving an added thirty thousand troops, far removed from both what the president had wanted—an exit strategy, the planning of which was thereby delayed by two years—and what many of the planners thought might work as a surge.

Administration

Governance, says Finer, is an interplay between decision-making personnel and decision-implementing personnel. He was right to draw a line between the decision makers and those who work for them but wrong to lump all officials into a single category. While on the armed side we distinguish between the military and the police, on the civil side there is a distinction to be drawn between agencies that are central—the ministries—and those that are subordinate. Ministries do not really implement orders. They pass orders down to those who are charged with implementation and they manage oversight, follow-ups and the like. Practical implementation is done by subordinate agencies and officials on the ground. We should therefore distinguish again between administration, which is in the hands of *near* others, and implementation, which is left to *distant* others.

Ministers are intimately in touch with those who work in their central departments. There is daily contact, they see what is going on, and officials are flattered by their nearness to political bigwigs. It is comparatively easy for ministers to get these people to do the work they put to them, and since this is the work they are in touch with, they live under the delusion that their orders are followed up and acted upon. Under New Labour activism, the pace of work in Whitehall was high pressure. Blair and Brown and company no doubt sincerely believed that their policies were effective and they were confirmed in that belief by the amount of work they could see that they generated in their ministerial offices, the work Mr. Powell in *The New Machiavelli* takes as evidence of the government "making things happen." The more distant agencies are outsiders. They are not involved in decision making but are squarely on the receiving end of orders passed down to them from someone not of their kind and from up high. Ministers are not in any similar way in touch with the goings on in these agencies. They therefore do not and cannot easily see if their orders are actually being implemented where implementation needs to happen.

The management of its near others may not be a government's biggest problem, but that is not to say that it is without difficulty. Officials have interests of their own. They are not just cogs in a machinery that ministers grind, but people of flesh and blood and spirit. They have vested interests in their jobs, their pay, their titles, their status, their dignity, their turf, their say, their influence—and in their leisure and holidays and pensions. They have unions that work to pressure the government on their behalf on pay, working conditions and sometimes policies. They want their place in the sun when things go well and they want to escape blame when things go wrong. They cover their backs—the iron law of bureaucratic positioning. They identify with their unit or department or ministry, and see other units as competitors to be kept down and away. They have opinions, including about public policy, and will when given the opportunity nudge their bosses in the direction they like. They are like other people—they need stimulus and encouragement and are easily turned off if they are not treated as they think they should be. No minister ever really knows what his people think of him or what they are doing on his behalf.

"As I discovered early on," says Tony Blair, "the problem with the traditional civil service is not obstruction but inertia."[14] Mr. Blair here seems to contradict Professor Lindblom, who, as we saw in Chapter 1, rejected inertia as an explanation of government failure in favour of "the great number of other people who are vigorously trying to frustrate." But fear not: they are both right. We are just not yet deep enough into the plot to see how. It is indeed difficult for ministers to get officials to do as they bid them, but in this game the problem is mainly, although far from only, inertia. It is even more difficult for them to get citizens to obey, as we will see in the next chapter, precisely because the problem then is not so much hesitancy as enmity.

Implementation

When my colleague Jooha Lee undertook his study of social policy consequences in South Korea of the Asian economic crisis of 1997, he made two discoveries, one of substance and one of methodology. He first discovered a real upgrading in policy decisions on unemployment compensation and social assistance by the central government. However, since these central government decisions had to be implemented locally, local government and administration were crucial in turning those decisions into practical action. The government's decisions met both inability and resistance at the lower level, with the result that what was implemented locally was both different from and less than had been decided centrally.

Second, he discovered that while there is a mass of literature on the politics of decision making, there is less to be found on the politics of implementation. There is a decision-making bias in the study of public policy. When we read this literature, we read endlessly about things governments do and hospitals they run and roads they build and so on, but less about who actually does and runs and builds. In *A Worker Reads History*, Brecht asked, "Who build the seven gates of Thebes? The books are filled with the names of kings. Was it the kings who hauled the craggy blocks of stone? Caesar beat the Gauls. Was there not even a cook in his army?"

One reason for decision-making bias is central government bias. Political scientists like to study central government, where the real action is thought to be, and, with some exceptions, don't care much for local government which they think is academically unsexy. Since implementation generally is local, the neglect of local government leads to the neglect of implementation.

There are two main impediments to implementation, not counting for now resistance in the population. One is distance and the bureaucratic levels an order has to travel through before it arrives at its destination, with no end to the potential for distortion en route. The other one is competing authority. When implementation is local, local government comes into the picture, sometimes indirectly when local implementing agencies work under delegated authority of the central government but still in the vicinity of local authorities, and sometimes directly when implementation is a local government responsibility. In public policy, local and central governments *always* compete with each other, and local government, the underdog, is always jealous to protect and when possible to expand its area of authority.

Should a government work with the bureaucracy it has and try to make the most of it, or should it try to reform the system and make it more responsive? Both, no doubt, but usually in careful measure with reform. Reform can get obsessive: you persuade yourself that you must first get the system right, only to discover that you have wasted time and find yourself too late to get anything done at all. I know something about the temptation to reorganise from municipal governance in Norway, a debate I've long been intimately involved in. Municipalities there have extensive responsibilities. That makes local government demanding. The municipalities are also pretty small (about five thousand in median population size). From time to time, a discussion erupts about merging smaller municipalities into larger units, in the hope that larger municipalities would be more efficient. In fact, the job would be much the same and no less demanding: the same officials must provide the same services to the same citizens. Local politicians and officials want to do their job better and in despair fasten on what seems to be the available reform in a vain hope that just that reform will make the job easier.

Mr. Blair's deliverer-in-chief, Michael Barber, listed as one of the lessons on retiring from the post that "Flogging the system can no longer achieve these goals, reform is the key."[15] Mr. Blair himself bangs on endlessly about public sector reform in his memoirs. But their problem was that they got it wrong in the way they worked the system. Flogging, which is indeed what they did, did not work, but less because the bureaucracy was unworkable than that they worked it the wrong way. Flogging causes resentment, and resentment they got. The alternative is not only reform but working the system with the help of, in a brilliant phrase, "gentle persuasion, relentlessly applied."[16] They should have relied less on command and more on mobilisation.

HOW BUREAUCRACY AND MOBILISATION WORKS

Bureaucracy imposes discipline from above. Mobilisation creates energy from below.

Bureaucracy

There are possibly examples in history of governments trying to rule without officials, but if so that is eccentric. There are many examples, however, of governments working without bureaucracies, or at least with extremely disorganised administrations. It was the Chinese emperors who invented bureaucracy, starting with the Han empire more than two thousand years ago. As a result they were able to rule over vast and durable empires. In feudal Europe, much later, the kings had no proper understanding of administration and tried to rule through vassals and courts in systems that were hotbeds of intrigue and wastelands of inefficiency and what we now would call corruption. The bureaucracies all public workers love to hate are miracles of order.

A bureaucracy is a system of posts, levels and rules. The level says who the holder of a post reports to and who reports to him, and whom he is equal with. The rules prescribe duties, what superiors expect of him and what he can expect of subordinates, and how he is supposed to coordinate with equals.

When you join a bureaucracy, you jump onto a train in motion. Work is being done and you are immediately caught up in it. Your colleagues depend on you to do what is expected of the holder of the position you occupy.

Once inside the beast, it makes you its. When I was a student at the University of Oslo, a group of left-leaning professors and lecturers made law an unlikely hub of radicalism, in part with the idea of educating radical lawyers who would go into the Ministry of Justice and work to influence the criminal justice system in a progressive direction from the inside. This was a deadly serious plan. The right students were recruited, educated in the right way, and moved into the ministry high on idealism. There, however, from day one, in spite of themselves, they were absorbed into the prevailing culture, quickly became organisation women and men, and shifted their loyalties from big issues to practical administration. "The character of the Home Office," says Mr. Marshall-Andrews, "is one of the persistent wonders of Whitehall. Perfectly decent young men and women enter this vast part of the Civil Service, proud of their country's civil liberties and intent on a career dedicated to their nurture and propagation. What happens to them within the walls of this ancient ministry is a subject of persistent conjecture. Certain is it that they change, and certain is it that, within weeks or months, they are formulating and proposing legislation which their earlier selves would have found inconceivable."[17]

From bureaucratic organisation flows surprisingly much to shape administrative attitudes and work. First, a division of labour that not only may help toward efficiency but also ties those who work in the organisation together in mutual dependency. You are participating with your colleagues in the production of a result, you know that unless you do your part the effort will suffer, and you know that they know that you know they know. It takes extraordinary cynicism and indifference to ignore this force of collegiality.

Second, hierarchy. Any worker in a bureaucracy, unless you are at the very top, has a superior and usually superiors above superiors. The force of hierarchy, like that of collegiality, is strong. When someone in a hierarchy who is a superior expresses an expectation of a subordinate, that expectation has force. Any teacher knows this. He or she has authority in force of being the superior. I know as a university teacher: it never fails to astonish what importance a student may attach to a throwaway remark just because it comes from her appointed supervisor.

Third, systematic recruitment. Bureaucracies work by explicit rules of recruitment, the purpose of which is to replenish the organisation with people who fit in and can be expected to work well and loyally, and to keep others out. The great invention of Chinese administration was recruitment by education, merit and reasonably fair and open competition. In democratic systems, recruitment is open so that those who go into public administration do so freely, and it does not then make sense to not work loyally for the organisation one joins.

Fourth, conventions. Bureaucracies are durable organisations with cultures and work habits that have become part of what it is that defines the organisation. These conventions sit in the air and the walls and tell you how to behave. In an administrative organisation where the convention is to work long hours, new recruits take to working long hours even if not required to do so by contract. Prevailing conventions are as much a part of the structure of a workplace as are buildings and offices, and are from the individual worker's point of view inescapable facts on the ground. Bismarck said of his unhappy experience as a young man in the Prussian bureaucracy that it "confined itself to pushing the administrative machinery along the track already laid down" (and added for his own sake that he would make music he considered good, or none at all).[18]

And fifth, systems of discipline. A hierarchy brings down upon the individual worker not only rules and expectations about what to do and how to work, but also, and with the same obviousness, reactions against anyone who does not at least try to do what is expected and to reasonably perform. Disciplinary reactions are formal (punishment) or informal (bullying), fair (by the book) or unfair (slander), and range from benevolent help (if you are not able to do what you should we will humiliate you and have someone else do it for you) via being moved to another part or relieved of responsibilities, to being formally punished and ultimately fired for incompetence or insubordination.

Mobilisation

The means of mobilisation can be crude or subtle. On the crude side are "targets"—that trademark of New Labour management. The government issued targets for health officials, teachers, social workers, the police and other professionals throughout the services—in the belief, presumably, that if officials are given something to strive for they will exert themselves to reach those benchmarks. The effectiveness of governing by targets and when and how it may be productive is much in dispute.[19] The New Labour experience is that if targets sometimes work, they are as often discouraging and distorting. An extreme example is the case of Stafford Hospital where, after the health watchdog reported at least four hundred more deaths than should have been expected during the period from 2005 to 2008, various official inquiries, the final one reporting in February 2013, concluded that "appalling" care had caused "unimaginable" distress, resulting from, among other failings, managers having become obsessed by targets to the degree that patient care was neglected. Putting a target in front of a worker is not to delve deeply into human motivation, to put it carefully.

A slightly more subtle form of encouragement is with the help of incentives—that great item of faith in "new public management." The incentives available to a government are salaries, working conditions, pensions, titles, and power.

Public service has traditionally been paid less than work in the private sector, usually compensated by better job security, more relaxed working conditions and good pensions. This combination has made public service an attractive career, all the more so for steady and risk-averse workers, who are probably the workers best suited for public service. One side effect of "new public management" may have been to push up public as compared with private wage levels, something that may have eroded the old social contract and paradoxically been to the detriment of public service—not to mention of public budgets and pension obligations.

Economic incentives are also used individually in the form of performance-related pay or benefits. In my university, for example, general pay adjustments were by and large abolished in the late 1990s and replaced by performance-related awards. The utility of such award systems is anyone's guess. Some workers are possibly motivated, but the cost is new divisions within the organisation and a heavy burden of form filling and committee management.

Titles are an elegant means of encouragement because they seem to matter for workers and are cost-free for employers. When I entered government service in Norway (around 1980), officials below the level of head of section would mainly be "secretaries" or "consultants." By the time I left (ten years later) they had become "consultants" or "first consultants." In another ten years, these had become minority titles and most officials were now "advisors," "special advisors" or "senior advisors." In my university, again, when I was elected to my chair in 1990, there was a small minority of "professors" and a large majority of "lecturers." About ten years later (to facilitate the transition to performance-related pay) the title of "professor" was released and made available to all lecturers with a professorial-level record of publication, but without improvements in pay or teaching duties, so that very soon "professor" had become the majority title. It was a bit like President Mitterrand in France who, the radical he was, took on the *Légion d'honneur* not by abolishing it but by "democratising" it and handing it out more freely and to many more worthies. In Britain, the prospect of a knighthood or a peerage is of great significance. A senior civil servant of my acquaintance took early retirement when it became clear that he could not expect promotion to a knighthood post; he would have stayed on had the prospect of a gong not been removed.

But be aware of fancy titles, which are sometimes a disguise for pushing people who cannot be fired into limbo. Often, observes Finer, "the more splendid the title the less its functional importance, while at the same time, the really functional offices are bearing very humble titles: in the Persian Empire the cupbearer, for instance; in late medieval England the King's secretary."[20] Even today in Britain, the top ministers are "secretaries" (as they are in the United States as well), while the grander title of "minister" is carried by those on a lower level.

Power is a motivational aphrodisiac. One way for ministers to get officials to work with dedication, at least near officials, is to give them importance. The problem, obviously, is also giving up control. Mrs. Thatcher emasculated the civil service because she thought the mandarins were a part of "the establishment" she detested.

The use of the gift of power brings us beyond crude incentives and into the subtle means of motivation. If incentives mobilise the self-interest of officials, we are now into ways of influencing their very self-interest, into making them want and think they want to exert themselves for their master's plans. This is the most difficult form of leadership, which relies on the personality of the leader, on a keen understanding of human nature and on the deft use of signals. While targets and incentives are based on a crude view of human motivation as more or less mechanical responses to stimuli, the subtle form of encouragement works on the nature of motivation itself.

Political bosses should be motivational leaders. Crude leadership does not give much return; it goes to acceptance but does not reach the trigger of enthusiastic support. The psychologist Frederick Herzberg called it "kick in the ass management," of which he said that it produces movement but not motivation. "If I kick my dog, he will move. But when I want him to move again, what must I do? I must kick him again."

There is huge potential in motivational leadership for bosses to get the best out of their servants. People do respond to rewards and punishments, but what the one-time American presidential adviser Daniel Pink calls "drive" comes from self-direction. And self-direction again comes from what he calls "the purpose motive," that workers are able to recognise purpose in their jobs and see progress toward it in their efforts.

So leaders should be inspirational, but can they? Who can hold up a project that inspires? Who can handle the vision thing? Who has the gift of charisma? Who is a natural entrepreneur and leader? Some can and do, and we have met some of them as we have gone along: Roosevelt, Churchill, Aneurin Bevan in 1945 when he inspired his young officials to turn health care planning around, Kennedy, Reagan. We could add more: in Norway, Einar Gerhardsen, in Sweden Olof Palme, in Germany Willy Brandt, in Brazil Luiz Inácio Lula da Silva, in Greece Geórgios Papandréou who led his country in the most difficult of circumstances with remarkable strength and dignity (although it is unclear if his manoeu-vres in November 2011 that led to his resignation and the establishment of broad coalition government were ingenious scheming or a man suc-cumbing to the strain, something, if so, no one should hold against him). It is not impossible and leaders should aspire to be inspirational—but it is difficult.

Obviously, they should take care not to de-motivate. After the riots throughout England in the summer of 2011, when blame was heaped on the police, Prime Minister Cameron made a mistake he is going to long pay for of suggesting that he might shake up the London Metropolitan Police by putting the American "super-cop" Bill Bratton of New York and Los Angeles fame in charge. That was never going to happen, and he spoke where he should have stayed quiet. All he achieved was to cause of-fence to the only police service he has to work with in a counterproductive top-down command spirit worthy of his public service de-motivating New Labour predecessors.

It is not about being cuddly. Officials want clear lines, want to be made to work and want to be expected to deliver. They do not like wishy-washy bosses who try to be their friends and prefer proper bosses who come to them with proper projects and give them proper orders. But it all depends—to return to a cliché I have resorted to previously—on getting the melody right. Leaders who do not have the knack are probably better off not trying because they will only make fools of themselves. We have encountered as many bad leaders as good ones in this essay and there is no reason to name them again. But there is that always intriguing charac-ter of Mr. Blair, who since he came on to the political stage has captured our imaginations for good and bad, at least mine. He was without doubt a superb communicator and looked every bit the great leader as long as the going was good. But his leadership was not solid and, as for Lyndon Johnson, did not survive adversity.

ELUSIVE OBEDIENCE

It should be obvious: ministers order and officials do. But the message that runs through this chapter is one of *mystery,* of how difficult it is for political leaders to get things done because of how difficult it is for them to get obedience, at least with some enthusiasm, from even those who work for them. Officials do obey, at least often, at least so much that they cannot be said to disobey, at least in appearance. But when they do, the reason is not that they are ordered but that they find themselves embedded in influences which push and pull them with irresistible force, certainly bureaucratic influences, and in fortunate circumstances the influence of mobilisation.

Political leaders are themselves prisoners of the bureaucracies they need to work with. They can get nothing done without them, but also they cannot get more done than is available in the machinery they are given and have to make do with. Ministers have to work with what is there, and what is there works in its own ways with its own traditions and habits.

What leaders *can* do is to energise the women and men who occupy their bureaucracies with the help of inspirational leadership. But that too is difficult. Not all leaders are or can be inspirational, and nothing backfires like ordinary leaders trying to make themselves extraordinary. That elusive enthusiastic support is available only to exceptional leaders who have the gift of working normatively and being able to move others who are naturally sceptical of them.

HOW TO MAKE
CITIZENS OBEY

A man who is made prince by the favour of the
people must work to retain their friendship.

—The Prince, chapter 9

The government has brought to heel the officials, who then carry its orders out to the citizens. By "citizens" I mean ordinary folks: workers, taxpayers, business tycoons, political activists, teachers, philanthropists, trade union bosses, bankers, women, parents (and sometimes children). Why should those people obey what their government says?

The short answer is that they don't and they shouldn't. Citizens have rights. Ministers cannot lord over them in the way they can instruct those who on the job have given up some of their freedom by putting themselves in their employment. Look to any proper democracy and you will see people protesting, criticising, petitioning, pressuring, campaigning, ridiculing, demonstrating, striking.

But Max Weber was still right that "the dominated must obey the authority claimed by the powers that be." Laws must be abided by and taxes paid. Policies must be implemented, which finally means complied with by citizens. We need security, and rights must have protection. He was, however, careful with his wording. He did not say that the dominated "must obey," but that they "must obey the authority" that governments claim.

The difference has been explained by the economist Albert Hirschman in a famous conceptual triad: exit, voice and loyalty. In any system of authority, the dominated will be dissatisfied with much of what they are asked to accept and will try to lighten their discomfort. They can do that by voice or exit. Those who react by voice try to improve the way the system treats them. Those who react by exit have given up on the system and seek to abandon or undermine it. What determines the choice between voice and exit is loyalty. Citizens may be dissatisfied with policies but still believe in the system, in which case they are likely to consider it worth their while to voice their dissatisfaction. Or they may reject the system, in which case they will feel free to be destructive if that serves their own purpose.

So it's not about sheepish obedience, which anyway is not available. But if a government is to matter, it must have loyalty. Therein lies the shared identity between the rulers and the ruled which Carl Schmitt saw to be a condition of a functioning democracy. It's a delicate balance: citizens consenting because governments govern well; governments governing well because citizens consent. The government gives citizens what they need, and they it what it needs. That is the holy grail: the settlement of order.

DISOBEDIENCE

Citizens are a troublesome mass, the harbingers of refusal, non-cooperation, subversion and revolt. The worst that ministers usually get from officials is foot-dragging. In the citizenry, they meet enemies.

There are other ways that governors may think of citizens. They might think of them as constituencies: those who have voted for them or whose support they aim to secure. Or as people in need: those who have problems which they depend on government services to manage. All governments will have in mind those whose support they want and those they can help, but these are not the people they must manage in order to rule. They are the ones they want to do things for, but those they have to worry about are the ones they have to handle in order to do what they want for those they want to help.

The Taxpayers

Governments must first neutralise the taxpayers. Serious conflict over public policy is *always* on the tax side. We quarrel about transfers, of course, often under a cloud of ideology, but that's proxy for the fear of paying. The history of government could be written (as Finer to some degree has) as a never-ending confrontation between rulers to tax and subjects to avoid being taxed. The battle over taxes has not been suspended by modern enlightenment but is every bit as intense as it ever was. If you want to know the quality of settlement, look to taxpayer behaviour.

Governments should adopt a double strategy. They should control tax collection ruthlessly. The purpose is not only to bring in the revenue, although that too, but also to ensure that no one gets away with visible cheating that others can take as an excuse to cheat on their side—and before you know it authority evaporates. A good tax bureaucracy pursues taxpayers beyond what is cost-effective in revenue terms.

Then they should tax fairly, which is to say so that no significant group of taxpayers can reasonably claim to be taxed unfairly. A credible claim to unfairness is an excuse to justifiably refuse or evade.

Indirect taxes may be objectively unfair but have a marvellous quality of being perceived to be fair, which goes some way to explaining their popularity. Mr. Blair claims that Paul Keating, then Australian prime minister, gave him "sensible advice" on taxation: "Don't ever put up income tax, mate. Take it off them anyhow you please, but do that and they'll rip your f***ing guts out."[1]

In income taxation, there has for a while been a fad in favour of a flat-tax regime, mainly on the argument of simplicity and mainly on the political right.[2] What gives the flat-tax idea some credence is the dismal experience in some countries of a strongly progressive income tax. However, if the alternatives are a moderately progressive tax or a flat one, the good arguments are against the deceptively simple idea of taxing all citizens at a flat rate. It is not necessary. A moderately progressive tax is neither costly nor complicated. Even moderate progressivity *does* redistribute income in a useful direction and is an option that should not be given away. But the most important argument is that a flat tax would undermine the capacity of the tax regime to be seen to be fair. Most of the tax burden is carried by the middle class. A flat-rate income tax would give the majority of taxpayers an argument of some justification for persuading themselves that they are paying more than they should and the rich less than they should. The willingness of the middle-class majority to underwrite public spending depends on its perception that the rich pay at least a bit more than they do. The innocent-looking flat tax is not a technical argument about simplicity, but a Trojan horse to erode government power.

The Capitalists

The second group that no government can disregard are those who control capital and jobs. What stands between a government and governance for the public good is economic power.

The reason there was initially hope for New Labour was that it had genuinely remade itself. After its defeat in the 1979 election, the party went into the 1983 election with a manifesto that was described as "the longest suicide note in history" (by one of its own MPs, no less, Gerald Kaufman). That manifesto was loony because it was a declaration of intent to rule by disregarding the power of capital—which is like a spaceship engineer proposing to disregard the force of gravity.

By 1997, Mr. Blair had completed a process started by Neil Kinnock (from 1983) and John Smith (from 1992), and made the Labour Party electable by signalling that it would accommodate and work with capital. Unfortunately, they overdid it and, once in office, turned from flirting with the enemy to getting into bed with her. As late as in his Mansion House Speech on the 20th of June 2007, as world capitalism was about to implode, Mr. Brown heaped praise on the financial services and congratulated "the City of London on these remarkable achievements, and an era that history will record as the beginning of a new golden age [in which] a new world order was created." Capital is a dangerous friend. There is glamour in money, and most politicians, not least social democratic ones who are not used to serious money, may not notice that when you think you make them your friends, it is really they who get a hold on you.

The recent trend has been for capital to wield increasing power. Economic globalisation has made financial capital in particular, but also physical capital, more movable. That has given the capitalists extensive veto powers over policies which they see as crucial to their interests, in particular taxation and in particular the level of taxation, which they see as ultimately a cost to businesses. They have that power in the credible threat of moving their business to countries with a friendlier regime. This threat is now so obvious that it does not even have to be made explicit. My favourite story is from the 20th of June 2003 when Peter Hain, a long-standing member of the British Labour cabinet, gave a public lecture on various policy issues. On the morning of that day it became known that his manuscript included a call for a debate on taxation, including the possibility of ensuring "that hard-working middle income families and the low-paid get a better deal" and for "those at the very top of the pay scale contributing more." That resulted in what Mr. Hain called "an absolute frenzy" in government circles, and by the time this voice of the left in the government delivered his lecture in the evening the intended call for debate was dropped in favour of, "We will not raise the top rate of tax, and there is no going back to the old days of punitive tax rates to fund reckless spending."[3]

One way for governments to deal with economic power is, in theory, to eliminate it. If those who hold political power expropriate property and thereby economic power, they can get on and rule with force. The idea was once thought to be good but has proved unworkable. It creates despotism on the political side and inefficiency on the economic side, a pretty awful combination. It has been tried, failed and given up, and there is nothing more to say about it.

A second possible strategy is appeasement, to just recognise the fact of economic power, give it reassurance, and hope to be able to govern without its direct opposition. This is possibly, but not necessarily, the instinct of conservative governments, and has also been the strategy of choice of "modern progressives" such as President Clinton, Prime Minister Blair and President Obama. But any government is tone deaf if it does not recognise that there is an inescapable conflict between political and economic power. Political power wants to *do,* economic power wants *not* to be done to. While taxpayers can be persuaded (more or less), capitalists must be dominated (more or less). Economic power knows no other good than the private.

Democratic governments can with effect take on capital on the rationale of "trust-busting." That is persuasive because it is directed against arrangements that undermine the workings of competitive markets themselves, which no honest capitalist can credibly object to. Hence, President Theodore Roosevelt in the United States could seek the breakup of the big oligopolies of his time, the next President Roosevelt could break up the big banks with the Banking Act of 1933, President Eisenhower could warn against the military-industrial complex, and President Kim Dae Jung could push through *chaebŏl* reform in Korea.

Today, in the aftermath of the post-2007 economic crisis, we are in the middle of a fierce, if slow, battle between politics and capital over trust-busting in the banking and financial services industry. What we have seen so far is how difficult it is for politics to rein in even capitalist recklessness, even in the aftermath of monumental market failure, even after having salvaged the banking sector with massive subsidies. The outcome of this battle is up in the air, but the signs are that capital may come out pretty much in peace. Cautious regulations, perhaps, but trust-busting seems to be off the agenda. In Britain, a government-appointed independent commission on banking, charged with exploring structural and regulatory reforms in the banking sector, reported in September 2011 and recommended new regulations on the big banks, including to separate their investment banking and their deposit-taking functions, but not a breaking up of the big conglomerates. Whether its recommendations will be implemented and, if so, be of more consequence for savvy operators than, for example, the similar Dodd-Frank Act of 2010 has been in the United States is an open question, all the more so since it is recommended to be done on a slow timescale up to 2019 and the banks started lobbying against the proposal long before it was even put on the table by the commission.[4]

Tertiary Groups

When governments are reasonably in control of their potential enemies among taxpayers and capitalists and make them reasonably compliant, there is normal governance in a normal democracy. It is when governments lose that control, so that enemies are able to set the political agenda, instead of the other way around, that governance disintegrates into the dysfunctional. It is in these groups that interests reside that challenge loyalty. If that challenge is not held back, disobedience will spread like a contagion. Brennan and Buchanan call it "a sort of Gresham's law in social interaction such that bad behaviour drives out good and that all persons will be led themselves by the presence of even a few self-seekers to adopt self-interested behaviour."[5]

Many other groups make trouble, but usually not so that governments have much to fear. Groups like these—women, for instance, celebrities, and various lobbies such as those for gay rights, environmentalists and animal righters—may have some power by numbers, organisation or visibility but not much sway. It is sufficient to deal with them by, above all, taking care not to offend and by occasionally showing them attention and flattery.

Manifestations against democratic governments usually do not amount to much once the demonstrators have let off steam. The last successful rebellion from below in Britain was more than twenty years ago, against the poll tax, but that policy was so blatantly fraught that it was unenforceable anyway. A later attempt was against going into the war in Iraq in 2003. In February, protesters in the millions took to the streets across the country in a well-organised campaign, backed up by massive opposition to the war in public opinion, but nothing came of it.

Flattery is easily given and offence easily caused. It mattered for their bravery, we have seen, that Caesar addressed his men as "comrades" rather than "soldiers." But he could also cause massive offence by petty arrogance (until, you will remember, he was finally assassinated): "What provoked particular bitter hostility was that when one day the entire Senate, armed with an imposing list of honours they had just voted him, came to where he sat, he did not rise to greet them and grimaced angrily at Gaius Trebatius, who suggested this courtesy."[6]

On causing offence, the British election campaign in 2010 threw up a brilliant example. Gordon Brown was caught on microphone, after an exchange with a sympathetic but critical voter, referring to his interlocutor as "that woman" and as "bigoted." "Bigoted" was all over the press and derailed Labour's campaign so that Mr. Brown was forced to pay a visit to the lady and grovel for forgiveness, which he did not quite get. She on her side explained, to great effect, that what had irked her was not so much "bigoted," which she could take, as being called "that woman."

Organisation
Once there are shared interests, the next step is organisation, be it organised labour, organised capital, or organised special or single interest groups.

The resources of organised interests are numbers, money, and skills from lobbying to direct action. Of these, numbers are the least weighty. French unions are able to cause havoc throughout the country although they organise less that a tenth of the workforce. In Britain, in September 2000, a paralysing fuel crisis was brought on by an action of haulers in which "no more than a thousand protesters, using mobile phones and the Internet, nearly brought the country to a halt."[7]

For some time, a trend in many democracies has been a weakening of the position of organised labour. During the good economic years toward the end of the twentieth century and the beginning of the twenty-first, when economic growth came to be seen as given, unionisation declined and with it the clout of the labour movement. In the United States, by 2010, the percentage of organised workers had fallen toward 10, down from about 35 percent in the 1950s and still about 20 percent in the mid-1980s. The consequences of the economic crash for the position of organised labour are yet to be seen, but at least in the United States unionisation has continued to fall.

An opposite trend, more in some democracies than in others, the United States being the vanguard, is for capital to strengthen its organisation.

These two movements are of dramatic import. From a situation of division between capital relying on economic power and labour on organisational power, the trend is for capital to extend into organisation and to be without contest from opposing organised interests of comparable strength. Economic power drives a wedge between governance and the public good. The combination of globalisation and organised capital makes that a formidable wedge.

LOYALTY

Although self-interest invites citizens to resist what their governments bring down upon them and organisation gives them the means to do so, legal thinkers have settled on an optimistic view about obedience: "We must suppose that, whatever the motive, most of the orders are more often obeyed than disobeyed by most of those affected." So says H. L. A. Hart, the most respected authority in modern jurisprudence.[8]

That may well be correct as an observation, but if so, why? Hart put it down to "a general habit of obedience." His followers have tempered his optimism. If people often obey, they agree, it is still a mystery why they do so.[9] Obedience must come from something else than the order itself, something outside of the order that obliges people to react in the way that is intended in the order.

The "something else" that weighs down on citizens to mould them into loyalty is the double influence of pull and push. If government is attractive, citizens are pulled into loyalty because they do not have reasons or excuses to disobey. That pull comes from fair governance and good leadership.

It would be nice if we could count on citizens delivering their part of the settlement once the government did its part, but temptation is strong and the flesh weak. Loyalty depends, in addition, on citizens being pushed into line by institutions that are robust enough to control them. That push comes from law, constitution and political culture.

When these influences stack up, citizens are offered a deal they cannot refuse and we have a settlement. Things may then look and feel obvious and feather light as if by "habit," but that is only because the pressures on citizens, which are many and heavy, are out of sight.

Fairness

I explained in Chapter 6 that governments need to get it right if they are to get citizens to accept them and their orders as rightful. Machiavelli did not say that "laws" are a foundation of the state—he said "good laws." Aristotle did not appeal to "law" but to "law and justice," and Washington not to "order" but to "order and right." We often say that democratic governments enjoy democratic legitimacy, but that is wrong. Governments, democratic or not, that make bad policies will not be seen to be rightfully in power. In Korea, the second republic delivered improved democracy but not effective governance, and there was little sadness over the coup against it. Derek Bok is putting a marker on the legitimacy of American governments in his criticism of persistently poor and incoherent legislation.

There is no one-and-only prescription for fair governance. What is fair can be different in different countries and at different times, but some principles can be laid down. First, fair governance depends, as I've explained in Chapter 3, on both fair process and fair outcome. Governors need to persuade citizens that they are giving rightful orders in rightful ways and depend for authority on being able to claim respect for both what they do and the way they do it. Second, since it would be governance by compromise, fair public policy is almost always different from what almost everyone would see as a policy for their own private good; it is *public*. And third, since fairness includes the protection of political losers and of minorities and minority interests and rights, a fair government would maintain considerable regulations and distribute considerable transfers, and hence be in need of considerable taxes. Fair government may not necessarily be big government, but you can forget small government.

Leadership
Leadership can be steady or charismatic.

Steady leadership is not dependent on the big man or woman but is somehow inherent in a political system. Take the case of Germany, first West Germany, after the Second World War. Here was a country whose government twice in the same century had unleashed total war on its neighbours and the wider world, in the second one with hitherto unimaginable evils of genocide. It had seen its first attempt at democracy destroyed and replaced by a dictatorship of horrendous brutality which nevertheless enjoyed considerable support in the population.[10] It lost both wars and suffered economic and physical destruction as a result. Yet after the second war, it re-created itself with near incredible force. It made itself (albeit with some help from friends) the economic powerhouse of Europe. It made itself a model federal democracy. It made itself a trustworthy partner for its neighbours by tying itself down in a web of its own making of European mutual dependency and integration. It made itself a conciliator between west and east that enabled it to grasp the opportunity for reunification that arrived out of the blue. It reinvented itself morally in a cultural revolution that took the population (albeit after initial hesitation) through a soul-searching reckoning with its own past, in a way less tainted nations such as Austria and France have been unable to do. This was possible thanks to steady leadership exercised by a parade of solid politicians: Adenauer, Erhard, Kiesinger, Brandt, Schmidt, Kohl, Schröder, Merkel. Not much of flashy charisma there, with the exception of Mr. Brandt, but continuous strong leadership in a monumental national project.

Charismatic leadership is that of, say, President Roosevelt in the United States, both Presidents Roosevelt in fact, as well as Presidents

Kennedy (although his tenure did not last long enough to establish his leadership as solid) and Reagan. These were men with personal qualities that inspired others to be followers.

The American political system has not produced good leadership since Mr. Reagan left the stage (although with Mr. Obama it is too early to tell). In Britain, after Mr. Churchill, there has been neither steady nor charismatic leadership of any note. Mrs. Thatcher is sometimes seen to have been a charismatic leader, but that is false. She was never, contrary to her friend Ronald Reagan, a leader by inspiration. She won three elections, but in each case with just over 40 percent of the vote. During her first term, the country fell into an abyss of recession, unemployment and industrial unrest, her popularity collapsed, and she was heading for defeat at her first test, even against the then self-destructive Labour opposition, a destiny she avoided only thanks to the drama of the Falklands War in 1982. (James Callaghan, another one of Labour's failed leaders, was asked during the war how he thought it was going and answered as in a daze, "I wish I'd had a war, if only I'd had a war.")[11] In later mythology, it is mostly forgotten that she is one of only a few democratic leaders to have been brought down by "people power." Mr. Blair initially looked effective but his leadership proved hollow. He and his friend Mr. Clinton in the United States have in common that both presided over regressive policies while, in utter political impertinence, spinning themselves as "modern progressives" and in the process stimulating cynical disrespect for "politics."

Both Mr. Obama in the United States and Mr. Cameron in Britain set themselves the ambition of leading their countries out of combined economic and political crisis. Mr. Cameron offered to wean the British off "big government" and take them to "the big society," an ambition that stands naked after the reality of Britain's sharp social divisions made itself felt in violent riots across England in the summer of 2011. On Mr. Obama's leadership, he came to look like a smart man who may nevertheless not be an entrepreneur. His mindset is that of the intellectual.[12] Intellectuals can be good leaders, but can also fail, as in the case of President Woodrow Wilson. They may incline to theory and be without a feel for the practical. They may get into thinking too much and hesitating in action. They may be too ready to recognise the validity of counterarguments and dither. They want to be gentlemanly and may fail on necessary ruthlessness. Or they may have too much confidence in the power of argument and not appreciate the unavoidability of battle.

Law

A law is an order with an inspirational name. An order that comes with the certificate of "law" carries with it the authority that comes with that label. The authority of that label, that word, is so strong that it is to some degree independent of who the lawmaker is and whether he is democratic or not. Political thinkers all through history from the classics on have appealed to the authority of the law. Go to Aristotle's *Politics* and see how. When Machiavelli mentioned good laws (in addition to good arms) as a foundation of every state, he meant "law" and obviously not "democratic law." Even the Korean dictators (as most dictators) held themselves with national assemblies that put the stamp of "law" on the decisions they themselves made. "Law" is a certification that the order is legitimate. Although laws that are bad or incorrectly made do not enjoy full legitimacy, laws' legitimacy sits in part in the certification itself. Even very bad laws cannot usually be dismissed as invalid, and not only because obedience can be enforced with the threat of punishment.

When Mrs. Thatcher decided to rein in the power of trade union bosses to call strikes, she made it compulsory for unions to ballot members and proscribed strikes unless they had the backing of a majority of members. This was laid down in law, in the Trade Union Act of 1984. How strongly law conditions obedience was on display in April 2010 when the Unite union called a strike after balloting its members among British Airways cabin crew. The employer took the union to court on a technicality—that it had failed to notify members correctly that 11 out of 9,282 ballots had been spoiled, having given that information only on notice boards and its Web site and not by direct communication to members—and won an injunction against the strike on the ground that it had not been prepared correctly according to the letter of the law. The technicality was of no substantive consequence, but the ruling of the court was as it was and the union called off the strike. Later, it won an appeal and was able to go forward with the strike, but as long as the injunction was in effect it had to obey, however flimsy the decision of the court.

If Mrs. Thatcher had tried to lay down the same rules by force of, for example, a decree by her as prime minister, she would not have been obeyed. It is obvious that she would not have tried that, but not because there was any material difference. The Trade Union Act was a result of a decision by her government in the sense that the government was in control of Parliament and was the real decider. But it was still the fact that the decision was taken through the formalities of Parliament and thereby given the stamp of "law" that made it a fact that trade unions felt obliged to abide by.

Constitution

The constitutional system of a country is made up of formal rules and generally observed conventions about the right shape and content of political participation, decision making and governance. At the core is the constitution—the body of formal rules—but the system works equally on conventions that interpret the rules and fill in where the constitution is silent.[13]

Constitutional rules are super-laws which prescribe, among other things, the way ordinary laws should be prepared, passed and presented to the public in order to carry the authority of "law." In the United States, for example, nothing is law until it has been passed by both chambers in Congress and signed by the president, and may still be disqualified if the Supreme Court rules it to be unconstitutional.

Conventions sometimes carry the same constitutional power as rules that are written up formally. In Norway, for example, the written constitution grants the king a range of powers, including the right to appoint government ministers, but constitutional convention has long since turned that power over to the parliament, and it would be unthinkable for the king to exercise it no matter what the constitution says. If the Supreme Court were asked to rule on the matter, it would rule according to the convention and not the text.[14]

Constitutional systems differ in the degree to which they are based on written rules and how strongly they run on conventions. The United States has a written constitution, but what is accepted to be constitutional still rests in large measure on conventions. Even the powerful position of the Supreme Court, which has become constitutionally sacred, is not laid down in the text and was not the intention of those who wrote it (as far as we can know their intentions). Britain is often said to have no written constitution, but that is not correct. It is only that the written parts are found in many different acts and not gathered into a single document with "Constitution" in its heading. Constitutional systems also differ in the degree to which constitutional law is super-law. In the United States, again, the provisions of the Constitution are super-law both in trumping other law and being amendable only by special and cumbersome procedures. In Britain, constitutional laws are just laws, which can be cast aside by Parliament as with any other law.

Law and constitution work toward obedience in three ways. Government orders are given the sanction of law and the authority that comes with being constitutionally correct. Where political decision making is undertaken within the constraints of law and constitution, the government is itself bound by the law and the country governed according to "the rule of law." That gives citizens reasons to trust that government orders are reasonable and deprives them of arguments for dismissing them as something they do not have to obey. What is according to law can be taken to court. When orders are lawful, they are backed up by the threat of punishment against those who disobey.

Culture

Political culture can be thought of as the way we speak to one another about democracy, politics, politicians, governments, governance, laws, taxes and so on, and the way we think about these things. If we show respect for and trust in democracy, government and the laws, we push each other to loyalty. If we speak and behave in ways that denigrate politics and politicians, we give each other licence to exit.

The influence of political culture is strong and omnipresent. It is decisive for how leaders think about themselves and behave and use power. It is decisive for how followers are inclined to see authority and legitimacy in their leaders and for their willingness to accept leadership. It is decisive for how governors work, for example how keen or averse they are to lean on power and rely on commanding. It is decisive for the ability of governors to use signals and for the effectiveness of normative leadership. It is decisive for governments' power to tax and for taxpayers' willingness to comply with tax commands. It is decisive for the way ministers deal with officials and for how administrators and implementers respond and exert themselves. It is decisive for fair governance, for the quality of law and constitution, and through all of these influences for loyalty. It is through the political culture that citizens are, or are not, "perfected" and are made to understand "the nature of the democratic system and the subtle inter-relationship between liberty and responsibility." It contains the combined direction and coercion of social control that Morris Janowitz, the pioneer-ing theoretician of the welfare state, explained that no functioning society can do without. We could *almost* say (although it would be false) that in a good political culture even bad leaders can do no harm, and in a bad culture even good leaders no good.

The trick in a democratic culture is for it to balance on the two pil-lars of criticism and loyalty. Criticism is, of course, sound and necessary and a positive input to a democratic culture and good government. But when criticism turns to assault on loyalty, things start to look unsteady for democracy itself. The sentiment that spread through the United States in the days after the attack on congresswoman Gabrielle Giffords, judge John Roll, and bystanders in Tucson, Arizona, on the 8th of January 2011 was that political culture had failed in its protection of democratic loy-alty. The words of Clarence W. Dupnik, the local sheriff, on the "vitriolic rhetoric" and "the anger, the hatred, the bigotry that goes on in this coun-try," captured that sentiment and guided it toward a reckoning with the way Americans, or at least American political activists, had come to see each other.

A good political culture sits on a sociological foundation of cohesion and we-feeling. Upon that foundation, there is hope for the relationship between rulers and the ruled, that the rulers be committed to the public good and the ruled to consent and compliance. This is the stuff of a virtu-ous circle of vibrant two-way deliberation that breeds trust and feeds back into its own foundations.

A bad political culture is fractured from the foundation and up. Where cohesion is absent, deliberation is difficult, trust in short supply and obedience even more so. The shared identity among citizens and be-tween them and their representatives unravels and political life disinte-grates into a downward spiral. Governments falter and dysfunction feeds back into the population as a confirmation that politicians are useless and government a mess of interference, inefficiency and unfairness. In California, according to the *Financial Times,* where citizens have denied their leaders the capacity to rule them, "the more citizens tie the hands of their representatives, the more they despise them for failing to tackle their problems."[15]

How culture works is not easily said, but one channel is clearly the media. In large measure it is through the press, radio, television and the Internet that we speak to one another about politics. We of course discuss politics directly, for example among friends or in workplaces, but the big conversation depends on being broadcast.

Another influence is the capital of experience with governance and with each other. Where governance has previously been fair, honest, and effective, it is likely to be trusted again today. Where people have been used to being able to trust one another and those in power for honesty and law abidance, they are likely to trust again.

Beyond that, political culture grows out of what Finer in his long history returns to as "belief systems." In our Korean study, the country's Confucian belief system of respect comes through as a strong influence that helped leaders get the population behind their national project of modernisation.

But in the end, political culture is pretty inexplicable, and so sharp an analyst as Robert Dahl has resorted to luck to explain it: "The prospects for stable democracy in a country are improved if its citizens and leaders strongly support democratic ideas, values, and practices. The most reliable support comes when these beliefs and predispositions are embedded in the country's culture and transmitted, in large part, from one generation to the next. In other words, the country possesses a democratic political culture. Lucky the country whose history has led to these happy results!"[16]

ENMITY

Governments have enemies who are not just reluctant to obey but against settlement. They are dangerous. Disobedience is contagious.

Friends?
One might think tax-cutting and deregulating governments less likely to rub up against resistance than are tax-and-spend governments, but it's not that simple. Conservative governments are usually not as conservative as

they want to be seen as once they get down to business. "Some 1000 pages of federal regulations were added each year Mr. Bush was in office."[17] Although taxation is always resented, taxpayers can be persuaded, or forced, to accept relatively high taxes more easily than is sometimes thought. Citizens in high-tax countries are not less supportive of their governments or more inclined to disobey. In the first decades after World War II, in the democratic countries, tax and spend was the order of the day, and with it the building of modern welfare states. In Britain, Winston Churchill, whose Conservative Party was forced into opposition in 1945, made his second great contribution to social reform by not opposing the Labour government on its welfare-state plans. (His first contribution had been between 1909 and 1911, as a Liberal minister and an ally of David Lloyd George in fighting through "the people's budget," the permanent income tax, and national insurance.) In Lyndon Johnson's first term as president, he commanded enormous authority for his "great society" policies, and the public mood in America was pro-welfare-state. If Mr. Reagan and Mrs. Thatcher led tax-slashing regimes, they found that a difficult agenda to push through, being able, mythology notwithstanding, neither to curb public spending—taxes rose in seven of eight years under Mr. Reagan—nor to dismantle much of the respective welfare states.[18] In Britain after the 2010 election, the new coalition won the debate on public debt and pushed through not only spending cuts but also increased taxes, such as putting up VAT from 17.5 to 20 percent. On the 8th of February 2011, the British chancellor, George Osborne, announced a snap decision to increase a levy on banks and extract an extra £800 million from them, on the argument that their finances had turned out to be better than had previously been thought. It was not much but enough to make the bankers respond with outrage (to lay down a marker against future temptations, no doubt) and the talk the next few days was about whether financial services would now abandon the City of London for friendlier habitats. But they paid up, signed a contract of cooperation toward increased lending the next day (which never came to much), the skies did not fall in, their offices were not boarded up, and they did not get on the next plane to Switzerland. (But a month later: "After Britain's biggest bank, HSBC, was forced to deny reports that it plans to quit the UK because of the bank levy and bonus tax, the [business lobbying organisation] CBI warned

George Osborne to give a deadline for scrapping the 50p tax rate or risk losing talented business people and growing companies to cheaper locations abroad. The CBI director general, John Cridland, said wealthy business people needed to play their part in cutting the deficit but warned that top-rate tax payers would be tempted to quit the country if the 50p rate became a permanent feature."[19] And three weeks on, when Mr. Osborne unveiled his second budget in Parliament, he announced that the top income-tax rate of 50 per cent would be temporary and would be scrapped before it could do "lasting damage" to the economy. In 2012, he reduced it to 45 percent, effective from 2013.)

No government can rule by satisfying friends, which is impossible. They do not have much to give away, the money they have is tied up in entitlements, and those they might try to buy off are never satisfied. They will obviously praise the government that gives them goods or relieves them of burdens, but it is delusion for a government to think those who bring praise are faithful friends. Ruling is not about giving people goods but about governing them, devils and all. Governments do not have friends; it's enemies they need to worry about. You are better off if you are disliked, if not hated, by all than if you are liked by just some.

One man who recognised the unavoidability of battle was President Franklin Roosevelt. More than any other leader he grasped the value of charm and spin, but also understood the necessity of fighting. He relished in the enemies he made and shamed them, and paraded the hostility of the captains of finance as a way of legitimising his New Deal. There is a contrast with the next crisis president, Barack Obama. He recognised the election campaign as a battle and took it on with relish, but once in office he wanted to dispense with battle and govern with reason. His mistake was that when he did not get reason in return, he still did not do battle, and saw his authority erode, first into defeat in the midterm election, then capitulation in his first competition with the new opposition in the budget negotiations in April 2011, when the Republican majority in the House of Representatives threatened to deny him a budget and to shut down the federal government, and finally when in the summer of 2011 that same majority was able to hold a helpless president hostage by threatening to not increase the federal debt ceiling. The golden rule for forging cooperation out of competition is "tit for tat": you offer cooperation, and if you get cooperation back you cooperate again; if you don't you strike back with vengeance.[20] Tit for tat does not ensure cooperation, but if your authority is challenged nothing else can.

Enemies

Although many governments do not appreciate it, opposition is not enmity. Far from it, a vigorous opposition is essential for good government. It tempers the zeal of intemperate governments, in particular ideological ones, and contributes to sanity and common sense in governance. In Britain in recent times, pitiful oppositions have as much to answer for as bad governments.[21] During Mrs. Thatcher's years the Labour opposition was impotent and during Mr. Blair's years the Conservative opposition likewise. No wonder. Political decision making being as centralised to Downing Street as it now is, parliamentary work is of little consequence beyond mechanically ratifying what has been decided by the government. All that matters is to get into government; working in Parliament does not have much meaning.

Nor are taxpayers enemies, nor capitalists, nor organised interests, nor interested citizens, nor critics. Activism, protest and resistance are also part of the equation that makes for good government.

The enemies are those who abandon loyalty—in British parliamentary language "Her Majesty's loyal opposition." A man who showed up that kind of ruthlessness with pride was the godfather of American neoconservatism, Irving Kristol, during the advent of the neoconservative awakening: "And what if the traditionalist-conservatives are right and a tax cut, without corresponding cuts in expenditures, also leaves us with a fiscal problem? The neo-conservative is willing to leave those problems to be coped with by liberal interregnums. He wants to shape the future, and will leave it up to his opponents to tidy up afterwards."[22]

The sources of enmity are anger, greed and ideology. There are bad people out there, people who are ruthless, hateful and sometimes evil, and who direct their hatred at politicians, politics and government. There are greedy people out there—in fact we are all selfish if not "perfected" away from it. But it is ideology that makes for real enmity. Ideology combines certainty and righteousness. Those who subscribe to ideology are certain about what is right and have no space for doubt.

Exit can take two forms. You can turn your back on the system and walk away, deliberately or in apathy, or you can strike back at it with destructive intent. Anger and greed are sentiments which on their own mostly generate resentment. Ideology is what makes for hot enmity. It gels the disaffected together and turns those who are hostile into groups. It justifies destruction with a promise of perfection. It is this belief in perfection, as Isaiah Berlin argued in a lifetime of writing, and before him the great Karl Popper, that makes ideologies dangerous. This is the danger of fundamentalism, the danger that makes people believe that their truth is so strongly for the good of mankind that it should be promoted with any means possible, ultimately that they are entitled to kill those who stand in its way, as when Nazi and communist dictators killed for the good of progress, when religious fundamentalist kill for the good of faith, when fanatical anti-abortionists kill for the good of life, when unhinged libertarians bomb a federal building (as happened in Oklahoma City on the 19th of April 1995) or shoot a congresswoman and bystanders (as happened in Tucson on the 12th of January 2011) for the good of freedom. When ideological flames are fanned, there is danger afoot, ultimately the danger of mayhem and murder.

The twentieth century was, for democracy, a titanic battle with enemies from without: fascists and communists. Both of these assaults were rebuffed, and by century's end the language of democracy and human rights was the only game in town, so that even dictators (bar the North Korean ones and President Alexander Lukashenko in Belarus) were forced to pay lip service to it. Even Muammar Gaddafi, who unleashed civil war on the people of Libya, claimed to do so in defence of a genuine democracy.

Enemies from without had allies within, domestic fascists and communists who used democratic liberties to work against democracy in their respective countries. These enemies have had surprising life force. The ultra-right is on the rise in Europe, with an element of retained fascist enmity, so that, for example, an ideologically committed national terrorist in Norway in 2011 could see the killing of seventy-seven people, mostly political youths, as a necessary political act. The ultra-left, inspired by neo-Marxist ideology of various descriptions, survived until well after *real existierender Kommunismus* had lost all practical credibility.

No one who remembers the madness of neo-Marxist extremism, no less than fascism, can be in doubt about the potential for enmity against democracy from within democracy itself. A young generation in Europe had reason for radicalism, in for example entrenched authoritarianism in France—but revolution against democracy? I remember it from Norway, where there was not a shred of reason in the political system or in public policy for taking criticism into enmity but where still bright and privileged young women and men of my own generation, and some not so young, made themselves Stalinists and Maoists, called for revolution at home, and saw with their own eyes paradise in the making in East Germany, in Mao's China, in Khmer Rouge's Cambodia, and in Enver Hoxha's Albania and Kim Il Sung's North Korea.

Toward the end of the century, these enemies had been mostly defeated. But enmity did not end. While democracy was under credible attack from the left, conservatism was loyal. In the United States, for example, President Eisenhower's Republicanism is as far removed from hard Republicanism today as is any contemporary Democrat. With the demise of enmity from the left, conservatism could radicalise and split into a traditional wing—Kristol's traditionalist-conservatives—and a neoconservative wing, unbound by loyalty.

There are striking similarities between neo-Marxist and neoconservative extremism. Both are ideological movements. Both are inspired by constructs of perfection—perfect planning and perfect markets, respectively. The degree to which the belief in perfect markets is an ideological super-belief became evident with the post-2007 crash. In testifying before the House of Representatives Oversight Committee on the 23rd of October 2008, the former U.S. Federal Reserve chairman Alan Greenspan famously described himself as "shocked" at having to face up to his free-market ideology, which he had been going by for forty years or more—"the model that I perceived is a critical functioning structure that defines how the world works"—being "flawed." They both draw on their ideological conviction for aggressive self-righteousness. They both see themselves as defenders of high ideals and of ordinary people. Both would protest vigorously against being branded enemies of anything democratic, at least "genuinely" democratic. Both have been able to attract a following, or at least sympathy, beyond their own hard core. Not all neoconservatives are true believers and not all believers are extremists, but there should be no illusions about the hardness of the neoconservative movement where it is at its most determined.

There are of course differences, and not only in the brand of ideology. Neo-Marxist enmity was explicitly in favour of dictatorship. It was grounded exclusively in ideology. That proved an illusory base, and the extreme left was never successful in electoral terms, certainly not among the downtrodden it claimed to represent. It is after all not exactly a smart strategy for recruiting followers to promise them dictatorship.

The neoconservatives are more strategic. Their politics are grounded in ideology, but not only ideology. Although taxpayers and capitalists are not enemies, neoconservative enmity feeds on their self-interest and is more broadly based than was neo-Marxism, being able to appeal to both lofty ideals and down-to-earth interests. It is the voice of corporate monied interests—those who want not to be done to—wrapped in high ideals. While neo-Marxist enmity relied on organisation, the neoconservative one can draw on money as well.

Where Do They Fight?

Political combat is fought, first, in and around the legislature and government offices, and intermittently in election campaigns. Ministers depend on lawmakers for permission to govern and money to do it with, and in parliamentary systems for their jobs. Lawmakers are elected by voters who all have the same power in force of one-person-one-vote and owe allegiance to them and to no one else. Others, such as interest groups, try to influence as best they can from the side. Let's call this the *onstage arena.*

In addition, combat is fought outside of and behind the formal stage: in the media, in lobbying, by the display of economic power, by informal pressure, through think tanks, by pamphlets and tracts, and by manifestations, million-man marches and direct action. Let's call that the *backstage arena.*

These arenas differ in many ways. They differ in what is fought over. In the onstage arena, the government, the opposition and assorted supporters struggle over budgets, laws, regulations and other policies, in short over what orders are to go out to the population. In the backstage arena, the battle is mainly over ideas, over the agenda, over which issues are to be salient for policy, over the permissible domain for political orders, over what is to come on to the table onstage, over authority, over the government's position and its control of the platform from which it can rule. Ideas, said the economist John Maynard Keynes, "both when they are right and when they are wrong, are more powerful than is commonly understood. Indeed the world is ruled by little else."[23]

They differ in who the main players are. Onstage, elected representatives and government ministers have the leading roles, while others are supporting cast. Backstage, *others* hold sway, be they organisation men or women or the wielders of economic power or intellectual influence.

They differ in rules. Onstage, all who engage are constrained by formal rules and informal conventions that sit in, for example, the hallowed halls of Congress or the traditions of the Palace of Westminster. Even witnesses before committees feel this pressure and speak and behave differently and more reverently than they may feel free to elsewhere. Political activity backstage is less regimented. In the onstage arena, loyalty is a given; in the backstage arena anything goes and loyalty is at stake.

In normal democracies, the power of decision making sits in the onstage arena, and functional institutions regulate and protect that power. When things work as they should here, governance is by and large fair in process and outcome. However, that normality may be undermined by influences from backstage. Informal politicking is normal and inevitable. People are entitled to defend their interests and to work for causes they believe in. Economic power is a fact of life. But governance in fealty to the public good depends on onstage actors being able to mediate as umpires in the battle of self-interests and forge out of that battle rules and policies that are common and joint. They must make themselves the authority of the public good and claim obedience to that authority. Their ability to so do depends on the balance of power between the onstage and backstage arenas and that the former overrules the latter.

Power in the backstage arena can be engineered by those who control the relevant resources for engagement in it. Monied interests are the ones with clout. They can arrange the political architecture in three ways. The first way is to boost the *size* of the backstage arena. Those who have money can invest in it and create think tanks, committees, political action groups, Web sites, media organizations and so on. The larger the backstage arena, the smaller, relatively speaking, the onstage arena. The more forceful the influence of informal politicking, the more ideas and agendas are shaped behind the scenes and before formal politicking comes into play. I found in Chapter 4 that the smart way for enemies to make trouble for a government is to derail it from being able to give orders. The Independent Banking Commission in Britain, which I have mentioned above, backed away from recommending a breaking up of the big conglomerates. That may have been because the commission saw this to be impractical, or did not think the radical option was politically available. The bigger the backstage arena, the more exposed the government. This is where President Obama found himself in 2010 when, although he had "muscled through Congress perhaps the most ambitious domestic agenda in a generation," he still lost control of the agenda.

The second way monied interests use clout to arrange things to suit their interests is through *bias*. They can buy up the backstage arena for themselves. They can invest in organisations of their own making, such as media organisations and think tanks, and put in more money than the competition. They can pull in friendly intellectuals, give them space and resources. They can take control of the tenor of public discourse and the formation of ideas. The influence that flows from backstage politics is then their influence.

The third way is by *transgression*. In an elegant book on economics and politics titled *Equality and Efficiency: The Big Tradeoff*, published in 1975, the economist Arthur Okun argued that there are two great competing values in American culture: accumulation and equality. Fair public policy would reflect a balanced compromise between these concerns. However, warned Okun, the value of equality was losing out. The reason for that, he argued, was that economic power was transgressing into politics and creating distortions in public policy. The troubling persistence of poverty among affluence was due, he suggested, not to Americans being unwilling to see each other as equals, but to non-monied interests being denied fair political influence.

Transgression works in intricate ways. Its does not depend on money flowing to politics in an illegal way, or secretly, or for base motives. It is not through crude corruption or because money buys specific policy decisions. No doubt there is a bit of that, but even in the heavily money-dependent American system this is not the rule. It's more subtle. In a democracy, candidates for office are supposed to be beholden to the voters. Since all voters have one vote, there is political equality and no voters can make candidates more beholden to themselves than to others. Candidates will seek to win over voters in the middle who are up for grabs from either side. The "median voter" will be carefully catered for in public policy. We get compromise policies.

When, however, candidates become dependent not only on voters for their votes but also on givers for their money, they have to win over givers as well as voters. Every now and then, a careless lobbyist lets his guard down and tells it like it is: "Those who count on Hollywood for support need to understand that this industry is watching very carefully who's going to stand up for it."[24] Since givers are more likely to be rich than poor—and even Barack Obama's original strategy of relying on not only big donors but also on the many small ones did not change this—the rich get two goes at influencing candidates and public policies, one as a voter and one as a giver, while the non-rich have only the single influence of the vote. And it's actually worse than that. The poor are less likely to vote and have less voting power than they should have by their numbers. The potential givers are relatively few and the power of their money, certainly of the big money, is more than that of an additional vote. My colleague Archon Fung explained it elegantly in a memorandum. "American politics is no longer characterized by the rule of the median *voter,* if it ever was. Instead, in contemporary America the median *capitalist* rules as both the Democratic and Republic parties adjust their policies to attract monied interests."

Backstage influence is a fact of life in any democracy, and a constant dilemma, wherefore, said the political scientist Stein Rokkan, "votes count but resources decide."[25] The question, however, is how much or little votes are to count and how much resources are to decide. When backstage investment, bias and transgression reinforce each other systematically, it works like this:

1. The political use of private money becomes acceptable.
2. That makes money a political resource, lowers the value of the vote, and wipes out the political equality that is enshrined in the principle of one-person-one-vote.
3. This stimulates a demand for political investment opportunities. Monied interests want expensive politics because expensive politics is the mechanism of transgression. It is a misunderstanding to think that candidates chase money. It is money that chases candi-

dates. Most of those who invest private money in politics have more than they need or, if they are corporate investors, are spending other people's money. There is no opportunity cost to them in this use of money. The influence they are buying is real and is bought at nil or insignificant sacrifice. You can try to regulate, but private money will find its way to transgression when the political terrain allows it as unstoppably as water runs down a falling landscape.

For example: "Louisiana's biggest corporate players, many with long agendas before the state government, are restricted in making campaign contributions to Gov. Bobby Jindal. But they can give whatever they like to the foundation set up by his wife months after he took office. AT&T, which needed Mr. Jindal, a Republican, to sign off on legislation allowing the company to sell cable television services without having to negotiate with individual parishes, had pledged at least $250,000 to the Supriya Jindal Foundation for Louisiana's Children. Marathon Oil, which last year won approval from the Jindal administration to increase the amount of oil it can refine at its Louisiana plant, also committed to a $250,000 donation. And the military contractor Northrop Grumman, which got state officials to help set up an airplane maintenance facility at a former Air Force Base, promised $10,000 to the charity. The foundation collected nearly $1 million in previously unreported pledges from major oil companies, insurers and other corporations in Louisiana with high-stakes regulatory issues."[26] Or, in Chicago: "The highly acclaimed campaign-finance law that took effect seven weeks before the February 22 mayoral elections declares that no individual can give more than $5000 to a candidate, and no company can donate more than $10,000. But the Puig family wanted to see Gery Chico elected mayor, and members found a simple and apparently legal way to get around the new restrictions. The Puigs, longtime masonry contractors, pooled $30,000 for Mr Chico's ultimately unsuccessful campaign in one day in early February, writing $5000 checks in the names of six separately incorporated, family-owned businesses, state and city records show. A review of campaign-finance reports found that loopholes in the new regulations on political donations emerged almost immediately."[27]

American politicians are aware of having sunk into a murky bog of moral corruption but are trapped. President Obama said that "you cannot stand by and let the special interests drown out the voice of the American people." The Democratic Party was opposed to, for example, secret political donations, but in preparation for the 2012 elections, the Democrats copied the Republicans in using all available means to amass the biggest possible campaign chest. They did not like, they said, "the campaign finance rules, which the Supreme Court helped create, but are unwilling to cede the advantage to the Republicans."[28] And further: "Despite a pledge not to take money from lobbyists, President Obama has relied on prominent supporters who are active in the lobbying industry to raise millions of dollars for his re-election bid. At least 15 of Mr. Obama's 'bundlers'—supporters who contribute their own money to his campaign and solicit it from others—are involved in lobbying for Washington consulting shops or private companies. They have raised more than $5 million so far for the campaign. Because the bundlers are not registered as lobbyists with the Senate, the Obama campaign has managed to avoid running afoul of its self-imposed ban on taking money from lobbyists."[29]

4. Sooner or later, a point comes when politicking in the onstage arena is unable to overrule the influence that bears down from backstage. It comes to be decided behind the stage who can run for office— those who can raise the money—and what they can do in onstage politics—that which is acceptable to those who hold the sway in agenda setting backstage and who have the power and will to give or deny political money. Backstage actors win control over ideologies, ideas and agendas. There will still be lively politics onstage, so that Tocqueville's democratic formality is preserved, and even looks commanding, but the sum total of onstage and backstage politicking adds up so that not much remains of democratic reality. That is what soft despotism looks like: business as usual onstage, while the real action takes place in a backstage arena which is overpowering and systematically biased. We are no longer in a normal democracy with functional institutions that regulate and protect normal onstage decision making.

What happens when transgression from a big and biased backstage arena is institutionalised is that power shifts: from governors to others, from onstage to backstage, from political to economic resources. The ability of political power to dominate economic power evaporates, and monied interests, who cannot be pulled into a settlement by persuasion, are also not pushed into the fold by robust institutions. Fair governance breaks down and the most well-meaning attempt to rule is frustrated by the iron law of effectiveness: where there is not enough fairness there is not enough obedience, and where there is not enough obedience there is not enough ability to implementation.

This is no abstract theory. In *Winner-Take-All Politics,* Jacob Hacker and Paul Pierson describe a shift in American politics during the past thirty years or so, a reconfiguration to what they call "the politics of organised combat." Political candidacy has become forbiddingly expensive. Capital has made itself dominant backstage by strengthening its organisation and has been able and determined to boost and monopolise the pressure that is exerted from informal politicking on to formal decision making in favour of corporate monied interests. Capacity and force in the onstage arena have withered. This is *new.* American democracy has always been rough and ugly, but has not always been systematically biased by economic transgression on a monumental scale the way it now is—"hacked," says Al Gore in *The Future.* As in the Soviet economy, where *they* pretended to pay us and *we* pretended to work, in the American polity now, *they* pretend to rule and *we* pretend to obey.

If we go back to the parade of presidents from Franklin Roosevelt through Lyndon Johnson before his demise, politics was fought predominantly onstage and others were influence hawkers. Before the tectonic shift that began in the 1980s, the political question was what governments could and should do, with taxation a background constraint. The eight years of Republican rule under President Eisenhower did not challenge that regime. He was a fiscal conservative, but one for whom taxation was still a function of necessary action. Now, in American politics, combat in the backstage arena matters more than what is done onstage for the shaping of public policy. Corporate interests have grasped that influencing proceedings in the onstage arena with the help of economic power does not give them control and that to be effective they must get into the act earlier with organisational power to dominate the ideas and agendas that shape the decision game. One result is a redefinition of the political question so that taxation has become the primary parameter and government action the consequential one. That has made life difficult for governments, for whom the need to tax is the Achilles heel, and easier for enemies, who can always appeal to the pain of taxation.

What has resulted is exactly what theory predicts. From unfairness in process follows unfairness in outcome, as we will see in the next section. From a collapse of fairness follows a collapse of loyalty. From the collapse of loyalty follows exit in behaviour. If you want to know the quality of settlement, I said above, look to taxpayer behaviour. If you make that ob- servation in America today, what you see is a chronic tax revolt. President Obama was simply reflecting the fraught relationship between govern- ment and population when he observed "the number of people who don't pay their taxes." Corporate interests have the power they need in the backstage arena to get the tax code rigged to free themselves from paying fair taxes. "General Electric, the nation's largest corporation, had a very good year in 2010. The company reported worldwide profits of $14.2 bil- lion, and said that $5.1 billion of the total came from its operations in the United States. Its American tax bill? None. Its extraordinary success is based on an aggressive strategy that mixes fierce lobbying for tax breaks and innovative accounting."[30] That says something about General Elec- tric, but even more about the American tax code and the loopholes it of- fers up for exploitation. The middle class and poor have no similar power and can only react with petty cheating, which is rampant, and anger.

DYSFUNCTION

Political scientists have overestimated the force for loyalty that sits in de- mocracy itself. They have mostly thought that once a democracy is con- solidated, it has made it. Consolidated democracies are then equally good and the many differences between them only differences in form and not in quality.

But that is too optimistic a view. Democracy is not a machine which generates legitimacy once it is switched on. It is an instrument that must be played, and this can be done well or badly. Leaders need to deliver governance that citizens see as worthy of loyalty.

A few years ago I set myself to understand what it is that makes for a good democracy. I found that it depends on various conditions, primarily the degree of consolidation (rather than consolidated or not), government capacity, the delivery of fairness, and optimal trust and confidence in the political culture.

I went on to compare democratic quality thus defined by estimating an index with a range from 0 (low quality) to 8 (high quality). Taking twenty-five of the world's leading and most respected democracies, I found that they distribute from top to bottom on this scale. Countries like the Scandinavian ones, the Netherlands and New Zealand are toward the top. Australia, Canada, Germany and Switzerland, for example, are in the middle. A single European democracy, Italy, is at the very bottom on level 0. This is all reported in detail in my previous book *What Democracy Is For.*

Statistical indexing is a treacherous business, but this index is robust. It confirms what everyone knows (except some political scientists in comparative democracy), that a democracy is not a democracy and that some are better than others. It positions the observed democracies correctly in the upper, middle and lower range. Democracies, even consolidated ones, differ in how well they deliver democratic value. That the Scandinavian ones perform well is no surprise, nor that democracy in Italy does not. The index proved sensitive to relevant known features, for example the strains on governance in Germany following reunification (my timing of measurement was around the turn of the century) and imperfections in France resulting from a less than robustly free press.

The more surprising result, for me at the time, was that the two model democracies of the United States and Britain came through as performing badly, on levels 2 and 3 respectively on my scale, on a par with South Africa, Chile, Spain and Portugal.

Fairness
Nothing in my own research has influenced my thinking about public policy more strongly than my work to measure the standard of living of children, with the use of British data and hence about public policy in Britain (as reported in my book *Citizens, Families and Reform*). With colleagues, I was able to create a data set combining family income and the value and distribution of family production measured by time use, giving us a broad estimate of economic well-being. Our first observation was for the year 1976, coinciding with a turning of the overall distribution of income from a period of increasing equality, which had lasted since at least 1950, and

into a new period with an opposite trend of increasing *inequality,* which is still ongoing. Our second observation was for 1986, allowing me to analyse movements in economic well-being in the first part of the new era of combined growth and inequality. With the help of careful econometrics and endless data crunching, and using the broad estimate of well-being, I was able to follow the standard of living of children specifically (and not just of families with children). What I found was that while the economy had been growing, children had benefitted less in their economic well-being than the population on average. In an atmosphere of increasing inequality, there was an economic penalty for being a child.

The relative disadvantage of British children is also observed in more elementary measures of income poverty, as we have seen in Chapter 2. From about 1975, to repeat, the rate of relative income poverty among children increased steadily from about 15 per cent up to about the double of that twenty years later, to 30 per cent or a bit more (compared with a population average at 8 to 10 percentage points lower), a level at which it subsequently more or less stayed (until the after effects of the 2008 crash started to come through in 2010 and 2011). That measure is sometimes contested since it is based on a narrow income concept, but my work confirms the trend when using a broader measure. If children had benefitted equitably from economic growth, the rate of relative child poverty would have been stable.

A stable level of child poverty at 15 per cent through a period of economic growth in a rich country would have been scandalous. All the more scandalous is the fact of *increasing* child poverty when the nation was getting richer. In pondering how that could have happened, I concluded that it must be a result of some mistake. I do not believe Britons have wanted their children to benefit less than others from economic prosperity. I think rather, as Arthur Okun concluded for the United States, that there is something with prevailing political institutions that prevents the preferences in the population from feeding fairly into the making of public policy.

These findings have formed one basis of my view that "misrule" is an apt description of public policy in Britain. My subsequent study of the New Labour experiment has further strengthened that view. Outcomes materialise that deviate too much from what would be fair. Derek Bok, whose *The Trouble with Government* we have visited on several occasions, made the same point for the American case. The troubles he identified were, as we have seen, poorly designed legislation and oppressive regulations, but he added a third trouble, the one Okun had warned of twenty-five years earlier: that poor citizens do not have fair political influence.

One reason for increasing inequality has been that the share of the national income that goes to those at the very top has risen sharply.[31] In Britain, the top 1 per cent of families had about 7 per cent of the national income in the mid-1970s; by the turn of the century that had increased to about 13 per cent. The same movement has been observed in the United States, but even more extremely. From 1960 to 1980, the top 1 per cent steadily earned about 10 per cent of all income; then their share started to shift upward so that by 2007 it had increased to nearly 25 per cent—one per cent of the people get 25 per cent of the dollars! If income had grown at the same rate across all income groups from 1979 to 2006, all groups would have been better off in 2006 than they actually were, except the very richest. In fact, Hacker and Pierson find in *Winner-Take-All Politics,* over the last generation the rewards of economic growth in America have gone predominantly to the rich and superrich, while the rest, from the poor through the upper middle class, have fallen behind. Here, the shocking story is that in years of increasing prosperity, no one except the very rich have seen any improvement in their economic standard by way of better pay, and what improvement the non-rich have seen has come exclusively from more work, including longer hours and the shift to two-income families. In 2010, the top 1 per cent captured 93 percent of the income gains while the middle class was either treading water or seeing falling incomes. "America's dream unravels," in the verdict of the *Financial Times.*[32]

A common defence of inequality in America is that there is also a high level of social mobility. In fact, however, there is not only a widening income gap but also a widening opportunity gap.[33] Recent research has established that America is *less* socially mobile than comparable countries. A review of more than fifty studies of earnings mobility in nine countries found Canada and the Scandinavian countries to have the highest mobility and the United States the lowest (along with Britain), below Germany and France.[34]

While the British story looks like a mistake, the American one looks worse. Hacker and Pierson describe the three decades up to about 2010 as "the thirty-year war." These were years of massive and politically induced redistributions in favour of the rich to the detriment of everyone else.

"The median income of Americans today is lower than it was a decade ago, and the median income of full-time male workers is lower than it was more than four decades ago," says Joseph Stiglitz. "America used to be thought of as the land of opportunity. Today, a child's life chances are more dependent on the income of his or her parents than in Europe, or any of the advanced industrial countries for which there are data. The US worked hard to create the American dream of opportunity. But today, that dream is a myth."[35] These misfortunes are not inevitable results of market forces, but the outcome of market deregulation, ineffective and unfair taxation, and inadequate social protection.

In "the politics of organised combat" the centre of gravity has shifted from the onstage to the backstage arena and the backstage arena has been expanded and expropriated by corporate monied interests. There is not only transgression of economic power into politics but deliberate, determined and systematically biased transgression, as exemplified by the case of General Electric as we saw above.

On the 15th of April 2011, the House of Representatives by its Republican majority voted in favour of a long-term budget plan, "the Ryan plan," after its author Congressman Paul Ryan, aimed to balance the federal budget while awarding lasting tax relief to corporations and high-income taxpayers. In an editorial three days later, the New York Times observed that the vote "showed how far [the Republican] mainstream had been dragged to the right." Dragged to the right is exactly what had happened, and where that mainstream had been "dragged" is precisely in the backstage arena. The vote that day did not decide what future budgets are going to look like—the Ryan plan will never be implemented and no one expected it to be—but it established where negotiations on the matter would stand, as was to be seen in the confrontation between House Republicans and President Obama on the debt ceiling in the summer of 2011. The president was defeated not by the opposition in Congress but by a coalition of onstage and backstage oppositions. He had made the mistake of not taking ownership of the deficit problem in a situation in which it was a necessity to bring the budget back to some kind of balance, and of allowing his diverse oppositions to expropriate it and define the terms of dealing with it. Had he studied the ways of a great predecessor, Count von Bismarck in Germany, he would have learned that one thing an effective leader must never do is to fail to take on what by necessity must be dealt with.

An American renegade political activist has described American economics as "corporate crony capitalism" and Washington as "the capital of corporate welfare." "This is not the capitalism of free men and free markets, of innovation and hard work and ethics, of sacrifice and of risk. It's the collusion of big government, big business and big finance to the detriment of all the rest." You will not find a better diagnosis. This one is by Sarah Palin.[36]

On all levels, American politics has been made excessively expensive and candidates cannot but wholly exceptionally enter a race, be it for central or local office, with any hope without corporate sponsorship. Fifty years ago, President Eisenhower warned of the "economic, political and even spiritual" influence of the military-industrial complex in "every city, every statehouse and every office in the federal government." Later, Arthur Okun warned of transgression by economic power into public policy. Today, these warnings have come true, and public policy is distorted not only by the influence of a military-industrial complex but by the commanding power in the now dominant backstage arena of a politico-corporate complex.

Leadership

Times have been bad for political leaders. Prime Minister Kevin Rudd in Australia was dumped by his own party in June 2010, having come to office two and a half years earlier as the most admired politician in the country ever. His sins were an aggressive management style, control freakery, an entourage of yes men, and the pursuit of unattainable goals. In Britain, Prime Minister Gordon Brown, no stranger to control freakery and aggressive management himself, who could have retired after ten years as chancellor of the exchequer with a reputation as a master of public finance, suffered three years of agony as leader until he was relieved of the responsibility by the voters in May 2010. In France, President Nicolas Sarkozy started with a vast capital of support and promise, only to see himself reduced to a figure of ridicule for vanity and hyperactivity (control freakery again). In the United States, President Obama invited Congress and others to join him in a new era of cooperation but was rewarded with the most brutish division in Washington and throughout the country for decades.

Times have also been bad for leadership. In the early years of the new century, political leaders from one country to another persuaded themselves and their followers that economic growth would continue into the heavens and let their people down in their duty of protection. Governments, banks and households embraced debt-financed consumption in a way that destroyed financial institutions and unleashed the worst economic crisis since 1929.

What is conspicuous in this parade of poor leadership is the absence of vision. The last leaders in the United States and Britain who were able to explain in a more or less coherent way what they were in government for are Mr. Reagan and Mrs. Thatcher. Their visions were, as are all visions worthy of the name, controversial, but they did make it understandable that there was something they wanted done. For the rest, it has been a string of repetitions of President Carter's failure "to impose a clear vision that others can ascribe to."

Law

Derek Bok is right in his criticism of bad legislation and regulation in America. He should have added more explicitly the perverse tax system, which combines all possible vices, being inefficient, unfair, offensive, and discouraging and distorting to business, a system so deficient that no one, winner or loser, is able to mobilise even grudging respect for it or see any commanding reason to obey it. "The American tax code grew from 1.4 million words in 2001 to 3.8 million words by 2010," in a continuous introduction of new loopholes.[37] "If all the volumes were stacked, they would stand 5ft tall, forming a bloated set of rules often incomprehensible to all but the most expensive accountants."[38] The way national wealth has been shared in the past decades is beyond decency. "Another banana republic," in the words, correctly, of the *New York Times* columnist Nicholas Kristof.[39]

For the case of Britain, I have referred in Chapter 6 to the Hansard Society's study *Making Better Law,* which lays out the misery of "bad law" in the most persuasive way. I have given the case of the Criminal Justice Act of 2003 as an example of how bad it gets. Legislation is—and not just occasionally but as a rule—badly prepared, badly scrutinised and badly designed. There is too much of it, too much that is unnecessary, too much that is overlapping, and too much that is corrective legislation because of defects in previous legislation.

I have also referred to Tom Bingham's criticism in *The Rule of Law* of not only excessive and poorly designed legislation—he mentions the astonishing statistic that three thousand new criminal offences were created during Mr. Blair's ten years—but also of the ways laws are written and presented to the public as incomprehensible tracts of impenetrable jargon and technicality, each act written up with endless cross-references to other acts.[40] Bingham questions whether the state of law in Britain is now such that citizens can in any reasonable way know what the law is. The purpose of putting government orders in the language of "law" is to make the duty of obedience unambiguous. But that requires that the law is known and understandable. If law is not published, there is, as universally recognised, no duty to obey it. But also, if the published law is incomprehensible, there are good reasons for citizens to at least temper their own feeling about their duty of obedience.

Constitution

Constitutional systems are often thought of as stable and as being changeable only slowly and incrementally. In fact, the recent American and British experience is of radical and rapid change, sometimes by new rules but more often by changing conventions.

The U.S. Constitution is beautifully simple. At the core is Congress, envisioned as the decider but constrained by the checking powers of the president and the Supreme Court. From early on, in President Washington's second term, when the national honeymoon was over and American politics started to take on the roughness it has since had, a contest for preeminence started between these three centres of constitutional power. That contest has now been resolved, and Congress has lost. It is clear to even the cursory observer that congressional politics is ineffective and ugly. Yet, say Thomas Mann and Norman Ornstein, the sharpest of America's scholars of Congress, "it's even worse than it looks." Not only is Congress unable to make good law, it is pretty much unable to make law at all and to prevent others from doing it in its place.

From one side, the president can for all intents and purposes refuse to implement the laws that Congress passes to him, or those parts he does not like. President George W. Bush changed the American constitutional system by making extensive use of "signing statements" to accompany the signing of bills into law, statements by which he limited his own duty to implement all aspects of laws as passed by Congress. This procedure saved him the trouble of having to veto legislation he did not like and freed the presidency of some of its duty of implementation. It also deprived Congress of its constitutional right to improve on laws by having a second go and to override the president's veto. Although signing statements were not new, the extensive use of them by this president was, and served to elevate this instrument in constitutional prominence. President Obama criticised his predecessor for his use of signing statements, but he has nevertheless resorted to the same technique himself, demonstrating that once a convention has crept in it is difficult to root out. Why, one must ask, does Congress, the people's assembly, stand for its laws and itself to be so mistreated?

From the other side, the Supreme Court not only checks reactively the constitutionality of congressional decisions but actively makes law of its own. Lest there be doubt about this proposition, proof positive was provided in a ruling on the 21st of January 2010, when the Court, with a 5-to-4 majority, struck down laws that limited corporations in their ability to use their own money to support or oppose candidates for public office, on the grounds that such limitations constitute a form of censorship. The significance of that case for the present argument is less the ruling itself (although it has added dysfunction to American democracy) than that the court had a specific case before it which it, on its own volition, used to strike down a whole swath of law. The case concerned the right of a group called Citizens United to air ads for an explicitly partisan political film during the primary election campaign, something it had been prevented from doing on the argument that the film itself had the appearance of a long campaign ad and should therefore be regulated as such. The ruling of the court, however, went beyond the case and affected a wide range of existing legislation that had not been put before it and which it did not have to rule on in order to resolve the case. The majority grasped an opportunity, redefined the issue, and—in a virtual coup d'état—swept away one hundred years of legislation and made law by its own will. (Corporate political contributions were first barred in 1907, under Theodore Roosevelt's presidency.) It was criticized from within. Justice John Paul Stevens, of the minority, criticised the majority on both the ruling and procedure: "Essentially, five justices were unhappy with the limited nature of the case before us, so they changed the case to give themselves an opportunity to change the law." The court, under the control of a majority of ideologically determined justices, has been lifted out of its constitutional position of controller in the onstage arena and in some measure been turned into an actor in the backstage arena.

The bias in the present court is seen most clearly in the position that the political use of private money should not be constrained because such constraints limit the space for free expression, or constitute a censorship on freedom of expression directly. That view, however, is not only extreme but in the most elementary possible way wrong. It has nothing to do with the Constitution but is only an opinion of a court grounded in a convention of its own making. If I write an opinion article for the *Financial Times* which the editors decide not to print, I am denied the opportunity to express myself in the way I wish. But there has been no infringement in my freedom of expression. If the law prohibits me from giving five thousand dollars to a candidate I like for him to pay for political advertisements, we are both denied the kind of expression of opinion we would have liked. But there has been no infringement in our freedom of expression. After Isaiah Berlin established the distinction between negative and positive freedom, between freedom *from* and freedom *to,* it became the established conservative view that freedom should be conceptualised as freedom from, as the absence of coercion, and that the notion of freedom to is a concept particularly susceptible to perversion. Yet here is a court under conservative domination that in this matter lets itself be informed by a conception of freedom that is, in Berlin's meaning, perverse *in extremis.*

The position the Supreme Court has attained is, says Robert Dahl, an "aberrant aspect of the American constitutional system."[41] The dilemma of an overpowering court is, of course, well known. In his first inaugural address, in 1861, President Lincoln warned of the danger: "I do not forget that constitutional questions are to be decided by the Supreme Court, nor do I deny that such decisions must be binding. At the same time the candid citizen must confess that if the policy of the Government, upon vital questions, is to be irrevocably fixed by decisions of the Supreme Court, the people will have ceased to be their own rulers, having, to that extent, practically resigned their government, into the hands of that worthy tribunal." Although it remains true "that constitutional questions are to be decided by the Supreme Court," it has also become true that "the people have ceased to be their own rulers."

In the most comprehensive recent review of the British constitution, Anthony King lays out a tale of rapid upheaval. He identifies what he calls "a new constitution" which has emerged since the 1970s, in a period of "radical discontinuity."[42] The traditional constitution "no longer exists" and Britain's governing designs have been "substantially transformed" from "order" to "mess."[43]

The British used to "love their constitution," which as recently as the 1960s was "almost universally regarded as well-nigh perfect." Then occurred a convulsion of self-doubt, driven by the end of deference, new social attitudes, economic stagnation, endlessly disruptive industrial relations, and European integration. Labour lurched to the left, the postwar consensus broke down, and Margaret Thatcher came to power. Her influence in British constitutional life was strong and lasting, but unfortunately bad. It was Tony Blair who brought in the language of constitutional reform, but with one exception—devolution—his activism (as usual) mattered for little. In fact, although the constitution has been radically transformed, its transformation has been in large measure unintended and unwanted. The great shift in the making of policy has been toward a concentration of political power from the country to London (devolution notwithstanding), in London from Parliament to Whitehall, and in Whitehall from departments to Downing Street. "Local government is no longer, in any meaningful sense, a part of the British constitution." In the civil service a tradition of collaboration has been replaced by top-down managerialism and the service has been politicised with the help of a mass of political commissars called special advisors inserted between masters and officials, notably in the Blair administration. Parliament, or more precisely the House of Commons, is ignored and taken for granted. Mr. Blair hardly bothered to set foot there unless forced to. Increasingly, policy pronouncements were made through the press rather than in the House. Occasionally a backbencher would protest, but the House of Commons is now so meek that it is happy even to be humiliated.

Take the 2nd of February 2010. On that day the prime minister, Gordon Brown, announced through the press that the House would vote the next week on a bill on a referendum on electoral reform (on introducing an "alternative vote" system). And the next week the House did vote on the matter, and in support of the government's proposal. Any self-respecting legislature would have refused that overture—or, to put it differently, if the House of Commons had possessed any pride in itself as the representative body of the people, it would have been impossible for a prime minister to behave in this way towards it. First, it was bullying behaviour. When the prime minister made it known what the Commons would be dealing with the next week, most MPs had no idea that that was what they would be considering and voting on. Second, it was never a serious legislative proposal. At the time of Mr. Brown's announcement, it was known that the general election would be no later than in May and that there would not be time to take the bill through the legislative hurdles before Parliament was dissolved. The MPs knew that their vote in February was without consequence and just went along with it for a bit of pre-election-campaign shadow boxing. The matter subsequently came back on to the agenda again, but not as a result of Mr. Brown's initiative, and in February that looked unlikely. And third, the proposal was badly prepared and did not allow MPs to deliberate in an informed way on what they were voting over. The government provided no information on how an "alternative vote" system might work, for example on whether large or small parties would be likely to benefit or whether the House would become more representative. There were grumblings on the back benches, but the minister speaking for the bill, Jack Straw, brushed it aside as if to naughty children in the patronising way ministers adopt when they have become accustomed to telling the lawmakers what to do. A people's assembly that accepts to be thus trodden on should be sent packing.

Culture

Where these two democracies still do not converge is in culture. In Britain, the political culture remains firmly democratic around core values of liberty, justice and fair play. It is true, as we have seen, that these values do not properly filter through into public policy, but that is due more to faulty institutions than to a faulty culture. This is greatly significant and means that the job of repair is less of an uphill struggle in Britain than in America.

That culture, and democracy itself, enjoys the protection of a national press and of media organisations of diversity and quality, under the standard setting example of the BBC, the British Broadcasting Corporation, and of a parade of serious national newspapers of quality. British tabloid journalism has been ruthless and ugly, and a single press baron, Mr. Murdoch, was allowed to build up and abuse a position of power so as to subvert democratic process. But excess notwithstanding, the media setting ascertains that the big political conversation remains comparatively informed and civilised.

The backstage arena is made up of a mix of think tanks without any monopolistic tendency to either right or left. The mesh of money and politics is a mess of corruption. New Labour in government was caught up in a string of scandals, for example under the label of "peerages for sale" in which it appeared that big donations to the party could be an entry to a seat in the House of Lords. During its first term in government, the party was effectively bankrupt but was able to fill its coffers ahead of the 2005 elections by "loans" to the value of about £12 million from a handful of wealthy supporters, loans which the party had no ability to repay but which came with the advantage that they, being loans, would not have to be made public as donations under election laws. When the scandal broke, says Mr. Marshall-Andrews, it exposed a "sweaty relationship between New Labour and new money" which amounted to a "sale of the party."[44] Under the next government, "financiers in the City of London provided more than 50 percent of the funding for the Tories last year [2010]. This compares with 25 percent of its funding in 2005 [while the Conservative Party was still stuck in opposition]."[45] In early 2012, the co-treasurer of the Conservative Party, Peter Cruddas, was forced to resign after he was caught in a sting by reporters from the *Sunday Times* offering access to the prime minister, and an opportunity to influence policy, in return for donations to the party of up to £250,000. But for all that, transgression is not institutionalised and the political use of private money still not culturally accepted as a normal component of the constitutional system.

American democracy, on the other hand, is dysfunctional all the way to the core of political culture. American culture is rich, diverse and pluralistic, and remains defined by values such as equality, opportunity and charity. But American *political* culture is now strangely narrow and has turned its back on much of what is traditional in the American way of life. In a culture of equality, the fact of runaway economic inequality is astonishingly accepted, as is the destruction of political equality. The use of private money as a political resource has become an established feature of the political system, so much so that the strength of political campaigns is routinely reported on by the amount of money that is raised. When the effort started more than a hundred years ago to legislate against the political use of private money, the vision was of a future in which electoral politics would be free from the contaminating influence of economic power. Today, even mild regulations are successfully branded dictatorial and the very idea of economically clean politics is as good as dead.

In the place of shared identity between rulers and the ruled, there is mutual distrust. Washington is unable—or indifferent—and the heartland is in revolt. Ideological differences are sharp and deep, with no common ground in sight. Even congressional civility has broken down.[46]

The way American activists have come to speak to one another about politics is terrifying: the aggression, the divisions, the suspicions, the accusations, the distrust of all by all—it is just staggering. What remains is a political culture bereft of deliberation. There are reasons in the system for distrust, but the forms and expressions are disturbing. Here the media do not help. The big political conversation is poorly informed, and important parts of the media are partisan actors in the backstage arena and not in the business of even pretending to disseminate balanced information and feed into honest deliberation. Neither is the length and intensity of political campaigning helpful, or the degree to which it is fought through political advertisement. Political advertising is by inescapable logic negative, and once campaigns are in flow all candidates are caught up in what none of them want, of having to speak about other candidates as scoundrels, cheats and incompetents. In perpetual campaigns, innocent citizens are bombarded with disinformation, untruth, distrust and an avalanche of negativism about politics and public service. No one is unaffected by this persistent propaganda of destruction.

Decline?

Those of us who think of ourselves as defenders of democracy, and who try to observe its ways and trends through the prism of academic theory and research, tend to get excited by notions of "crisis." We should be wary of that overused scare: as long as there have been observers of democracy, there have been warnings of crisis.

What makes for crisis in any system is that it functions very badly in respect to its purpose, not just badly but *very* badly, and that it is in decline in its functionality. By these criteria, there is no crisis of democracy in the world. Democracy has been expanding and many democracies perform eminently well, some even improving from a base of good quality, as in the case of Denmark that I mentioned in Chapter 3. In reflections on democracy, it makes sense to think of most democracies as normal democracies.

However, in the American and British cases, both conditions of crisis are present. American democracy has never been a pretty sight and has from its inception been rough, brutal and corrupt. British government has been aristocratically biased, elitist and exclusive. It is not that there is a golden age in these countries to look back to in reverence, but rather that there is decline even from a base of serious imperfection. British democracy is partially dysfunctional in that a centralised system of decision making is bereft of institutions that could have prevented an epidemic of bad law and reasonably enabled shifting governments to implement their will. American democracy is fully dysfunctional with notably low quality of governance and decline in fairness, leadership, law, constitution and the political culture itself.

American Exceptionalism

America has come a long way since Alexis de Tocqueville saw it as the leading example for democrats everywhere. But already he warned against dangers of perversion, and it is his warning rather than his admiration that has best stood the test of time.

Many Americans have seen their republic as an exceptional and blessed one. Today, American democratic exceptionalism is defined by a system that is dysfunctional in *all* the conditions that are needed for settlement and loyalty.

Tocqueville warned of the possible erosion of democratic reality within a shell of democratic formality. Arthur Okun, a century and a half later, explained how that erosion could come to pass through the transgression of economic power into the domain of political decision making. He also *warned*. In a recent and disturbing literature, other observers argue that these warnings have come to pass, including in some of the works we have met on our way, such as Derek Bok's *The Trouble with Gov-*

ernment and Jacob Hacker and Paul Pierson's *Winner-Take-All Politics.* Other recent and equally disturbing works include Robert Dahl's *How Democratic Is the American Constitution?* and *On Political Equality,* Eric Lane and Michael Oreskes' *The Genius of America,* Ronald Dworkin's *Is Democracy Possible Here?* Alan Wolfe's *Does American Democracy Still Work?* Sheldon Wolin's *Democracy Incorporated,* Bruce Ackerman's *The Decline and Fall of the American Republic,* Jeffrey Sachs' *The Price of Civilization* and Timothy Noah's *The Great Divergence.*

Professor Dahl is the doyen of democracy studies in America, in his work always learned, cautious and respectful of evidence. Through a long life he has been an uncompromising defender of American democracy, including in the awful years when it was under disdain from the left by academics of a Marxist leaning. Late in life he published three beautifully composed and brief books summarising a life of learning, the two mentioned above and before that *On Democracy.* In *How Democratic Is the American Constitution?* he does not answer "not at all," but he does say "not very." In his final book, *On Political Equality,* this careful observer and persistent defender of democracy finds himself nearer to the edge: "Because of a decline of the direct influence of citizens over crucial governmental decisions, and also in the influence of their elected representatives, political inequality might reach levels at which the American political system dropped well below the threshold for democracy broadly accepted at the opening of the twenty-first century."[47] We are now well into the twenty-first century and developments since its beginning have hardly been to the shoring up of confidence in American democracy. The books I here call a disturbing literature, and I now add my own to that library, from respected political observers and constitutional experts, are, in their various ways, and more or less outspokenly, edging toward an answer in the negative to this historically tragic question: *is America still a democracy?*

9

GOOD GOVERNMENT

Nor I hope will it be considered presumptuous for
a man of low and humble status to dare to discuss and lay
down the law about how princes should rule.

—*The Prince,* Letter to Lorenzo

In a democracy, we control our governors and they rule us. Those of us who idealise democracy are much concerned with the former. We should temper our romanticism and be equally concerned with the latter. Democracy is to make rule safe, but the need for rule is not diminished by democracy. Our representatives are in our place, our betters—and they make us obey, or so they should. If they are lucky, their system is workable and they can get on with it. If they are unlucky, they inherit a dysfunctional system and should go back to base one and repair it.

PART I: NORMAL DEMOCRACIES

When you settle into a grand office surrounded by lackeys who call you "minister" and assure you of their dedication, your instincts are almost certainly wrong. You will think that you have made it, that you have won power, that you have been given the tools of government. Everything around you will confirm you in your prejudice: the imposing edifices of government, the near officials who flatter you, the machinery of administration that rolls on. You will see a frenzy of activity in every corner in the government ghetto. "We're in business," you will think.

More likely you are in trouble. If you go by your instincts, you will make bad decisions, and even your good ones you will not get implemented. One of Bismarck's qualities as a leader was his ability to distrust his own instinct and to grasp the imperative of necessity even when it went against every grain of his mind and body. He saw the emerging working class and its organisation as the enemy of the established Prussian order he as an arch-reactionary *Junker* was wedded to preserving, and his instinct was to use the powers of the state against the threat. But he soon understood that it was useless to crush what would survive, and effortlessly, and to his friends' disgust, he turned 180 degrees and gave workers voting rights and social security, recognising that, however repulsive, it was in the best interest of his state to neutralise rather than to antagonise.

You will want to get decisions made quickly, to rely on the power you have won, to impose yourself top-down through your bureaucracy. The Cameron government that came to power in Britain in 2010 started with a rush of decisions on schools, health care, constitutional matters and more. Its leaders had read Mr. Blair's memoirs, in which he regretted not having moved more quickly at the start of his tenure. It would not have helped him and his advice did not help them. Their schemes were poorly thought through. Others set themselves against them because they felt ignored, something they could do with effect since the plans were shoddy. The result for the government was a series of embarrassing climb-downs and U-turns, authority lost and time wasted. It would have been able to move faster and further by taking the time to plan prudently, putting some effort into mobilising those indispensible *others,* and concentrating on fewer priorities—the ever difficult matter of de-prioritising. It beggars belief that a new government comes in and thinks, for example, that a reorganisation of the National Health Service, one of the biggest corporations known to man, can be done by legislation without preparation. Misrule, British style!

What you should do early is to take initiatives and set processes in motion toward decision making. That will enable you to command the political high ground. But you should avoid hasty decision making, which will cause you the loss of authority that comes with having to defend impracticable policies.

So you must restrain yourself. You must put your ingenuity into working normatively. There are *others* out there. They are reluctant and sometimes hostile, yet you need them. You must get the willing collaboration of your officials if you are to make good decisions. You must get sundry more distant others on board if you are to get them implemented. Work others over instrumentally with hard power and they turn against you. Success is never guaranteed, but without the acquiescence of others it is not even possible. Control freaks fail.

You must give away power. To mobilise your officials and implementers and professionals, you must pull them on to your turf and give them real work of influence. You should aim for more than their acceptance and to get some enthusiastic support out of them. You will get none of it if you bully them with commands. Mr. Reagan was content to set the direction, left the practicalities to others and was a compromiser who did not worry about getting one hundred per cent if eighty would do. Mr. Blair and Mr. Brown flogged the system and caused public sector efficiency to implode.

You must bind yourself. You should offer your people a vision—but also put it in front of yourself to remind yourself day in and day out of your purpose. Impose on yourself rules of decision making and scrutiny to protect yourself against the destructive temptation to go it alone in a rush.

Battle

Governing is to get things done. Getting things done is to get others to do. Getting others to do is to get them to do what they do not want. Some others do not want to obey so strongly that they are your enemies. You must do battle.

Political battle is most visible around onstage decision making on matters such as taxes, regulatory laws, defence spending, agricultural subsidies, social security and the like. You are the governor and have the advantage of owning the initiative. Your initiatives meet with opposition, which can be more or less troubling depending on political constellations, such as whether or not your side has a majority in the legislature. But always there is opposition, often from within your own camp, and majority or not in the legislature matters less than is often thought.

The way to deal with opposition is to be bold and straight in your initiatives, whereby you determine what subsequent battle is going to be over, and flexible in decision making. Avoid ideology. Avoid principle. If you play your cards well initially, you will eventually get most of what you want. Bid for more than you need and give away what you do not really care about. Do not worry about what you have promised in the election campaign; that is behind you. Keep your eye on what you can get done. You will be thanked for nothing else. Initiate cooperation and make compromises. Allow the opposition their victories. If you insist on all or nothing, you are likely to get very little and to make things difficult next time because you have humiliated your opposition this time.

Only if your opposition does not respond with cooperation should you strike back with confrontation. It is then important that you know your enemy. You must know who they are and you must know their weaknesses. You must have an archive of information and intelligence to draw on. You must have prepared strategies of counterattack. You must be able to threaten. Do not worry now about being gentlemanly. You have invited cooperation and have been rebuffed. You are entitled to strike back.

However, political battle is not won or lost where it is most visible. What matters more is the prior competition over ideas and agendas, over winning or losing "the debate." President Obama did not lose the battle over the budget during the negotiations with the Republicans in Congress in the summer of 2011. He had lost that battle earlier when his opposition had taken ownership of the deficit issue. All that remained for the negotiations was how humiliating his defeat was going to be.

When the Cameron government came into office in 2010, it won the debate on the budget deficit and could push its hard austerity policies through Parliament without noticeable resistance. It did not deserve to win that debate, but it did and could then easily get its way in decision making.[1]

When President Obama got his health care bill through Congress in 2010, he won the decision but not the debate. His policy had all merit, but he failed to get that merit accepted by a single member of the opposition in Congress and broadly in the American population. The implementation of what had been decided has remained contested, and what will eventually be implemented and the degree to which it will be implemented in different parts of the country is still uncertain. In this case, much of the blame lies with the Democratic Party itself. Instead of rallying behind their leader in a landmark policy, congressional Democrats took to quibbling about details so that what was adopted, with the slimmest of majorities, was adopted grudgingly and presented itself to the American people as another mess of murky congressional horse-trading.

Power

Forget being loved—it will not happen. It is respect you want, because it is respect that will make others award you authority.

To win respect, a government must show its power. The display of power will not win you the respect you need but is necessary to define political relations, to establish you as the governor to whom others respond and to put you on the platform from which you can issue orders. If you cannot get others to accept it as a fact on the ground that you are the one to whom they respond, there is not much you can do but resign yourself to being a caretaker.

Taxation is the battleground on which to establish your power. There is no way of taxing other than through command and there is no way of ruling without the power to tax. Confrontation is a given. It is just as well to take it head on and to use the unavoidable to make yourself respected. You should tell your followers that they must pay what their government costs and you must take from them what you need and can. In a rambling conversation with General Erich Ludendorff during the peace treaty negotiations in Versailles in 1918, Max Weber (who was there as an adviser and had suggested to Ludendorff that he offer up his head for execution as a way of restoring the honour of the German officer class) explained the meaning of democracy: "In a democracy, the people choose a leader in whom they trust. Then the chosen leader says, 'Now shut up and obey me.' Later the people can sit in judgement. If the leader has made mistakes to the gallows with him."[2] That may sound outdated to sensitive ears, but is precisely where any government must start, and taxation is precisely where to tell followers to shut up and obey. Not in so many words, of course. Prudent governors, prospective governors even more, *speak* with great circumspection about taxes, but once in office they must lay down the law.

At any point in time, most of your revenues are tied up in commitments and entitlements. Although your budget is large there is not much money in it for you to work with. You can reallocate, but there is never much to go on. You must continue to tax as previously merely to balance the books. If you want to do more, you must tax more.

Therefore, never give away a penny of existing revenue. You cannot: you have nothing to give. You do not have to: you can blame the previous government. It will do nothing for you: those you give it to will come back for more the next day.

Taxing is taking and there is no way to be nice about it. You do not get enemies by claiming necessary taxes, you win grudging respect. You do not win friends by undertaxing, but reap contempt. If you are unable to stand against citizens' resistance to being taxed, you will not be able to stand against their claims on transfers, and you will preside over a growing black hole in your budget. The cost in authority of that misrule is infinitely more than you risk by standing firm on taxing.

The purpose of taxing is to raise revenue, and this is how you should think about it. You can redistribute income through taxation, but not much. You can influence behaviour through taxation, but not much. The introduction of secondary and tertiary rationales and incentives into the tax code puts loopholes into it and gives taxpayers excuses and openings to evade and avoid. That's the story of the American tax code, says the tax lawyer Pamela Olson: "We run social policy and industrial policy through the tax code and it doesn't make any sense to do that."[3] It in fact makes so little sense that the result is tax revolt and chronic undertaxing. The best you can do is to keep it simple, make it fair, and deny enemies a playground of frustration where they most want it.

Then you must be tight-fisted in spending. It is tempting to think that the more you give the more friends you make, but it is impossible to buy political friendship. Grateful recipients are never faithful friends. You win groupies but not followers who will still follow when the going gets tough.

Ministers are tempted by being able to spend other people's money. When Mr. Brown was chancellor, spending on the National Health Service became its own purpose and he heaped new money on faster than it could be absorbed. The NHS had its problems but it was a miracle of cost-effectiveness. That was lost by the way new money was poured in. Public services are efficient only when budget control is tight and wasteful when it is not. There is no end to the demands that come to you for government money and the most difficult thing for a democratic government is to withstand that pressure. You will not be able to do that unless you are tight across the board so that your tightness in individual cases is seen to be fair and unexceptional. You need to control spending in order to justify taxing. Wastefulness on your part is a reason for taxpayers to feel that they have a right to resist your demands on them.

You should be modest with yourself. "Nor was he [Augustus] given to luxurious displays, despite his overwhelming wealth," finds the historian Robert Hughes. "Few later emperors—Claudius and Hadrian being among the exceptions—would show such an understanding of the difference between *auctoritas* (authoritative influence) and *imperium* (command from above)."[4] Bismarck was forceful but, to his benefit, no show-off. His office was in size and furnishings so that "no provincial prefect in France would have been satisfied with such modest surroundings."[5] His modesty was noted, and respected.

Modern leaders have lost the touch. French national politicians typically have one or two local posts in addition to their central one, with the requisite additional salaries and perks.[6] In many capital cities, ministers shoulder their way through town in heavy limousines with a parade of motorcycle police to hold back troublesome traffic so that those who are more important than others do not have to stop at red lights (all in the name of security, of course). "To attend Prime Minister's Questions, Blair employed three armoured vehicles and two outriders to negotiate the journey of 250 yards between Downing Street and Parliament."[7] When President Obama came to Oslo on a twenty-four-hour visit to receive the 2009 Nobel Peace Price (which he should have gracefully declined), he and his party arrived in three jumbo jets to waiting limousines and helicopters at the airport for the great man to choose his transport into town, took up three city hotels, and had the entire police force of the small capital city and surrounding towns reorganised for the day and night. There are times and places for the American president to display his grandeur; this was not it. The U.S. Congress has provided that if it shuts down the federal government by denying it funds, as it did in 1995 and 1996 and was near to doing again in 2011, and suspends pay to government workers, the representatives and senators themselves will continue to be paid. It has also provided that state elected officials can, on generous terms, start collecting pensions before leaving office, hence drawing a pension and a full salary at the same time. Citizens are surprisingly tolerant of this kind of quasi graft and show-off-manship, but there is a long climb from indifference to respect.

So neither conservative nor social democratic be, but social democratic in taxing and conservative in spending. This is the recipe for respect, that what you are doing is seen to be what a government must do.

Vision

In July 1862, Bismarck, then Prussian ambassador to Paris but expecting to be appointed minister-president, met Benjamin Disraeli in London and told him what he would do when in charge: "As soon as the army shall have been brought into such a condition as to inspire respect, I shall seize the first best pretext to declare war against Austria, dissolve the German Diet, subdue the minor states and give national unity to Germany under Prussian leadership." Now, there's a vision for you. In September, he was duly made minister-president by King William and within nine years had achieved exactly what he intended in exactly the way he intended, in what his biographer Jonathan Steinberg calls "the greatest diplomatic and political achievement by any leader in the last two centuries."[8] That's what vision can do for you—at least when you can back it up with the king's authority.

Any government that is to be successful must have a vision—or project or purpose or design or narrative. If you do not have an idea of what you are in power for and what you want to do you are lost and can at best be a manager. In addition, you need to communicate your idea into one "that others can ascribe to." All leaders (except dictators, and mostly even they) are agents of some principal on whom they depend. Bismarck was the king's, later emperor's, agent and was able to rule as long as he had his goodwill (and was dismissed when he lost it). A democratic leader is the agent of, in some meaning, the people, and must have their goodwill in order to rule. Bismarck extracted authority from the king, although he despised his monarch and schemed against him behind his back, because the king was pleased with the power and position Bismarck brought him. A democratic leader must extract authority from his people. If he is to have any chance with those he must dominate, he must offer them a purpose to follow.

Without vision you can get nothing done:

- You cannot make yourself a rightful leader or government in the eyes of citizens. What right do you have to lead if you do not know where you want to go?

- You cannot lead and you cannot persuade others to be followers. Leadership, after Joseph Nye again, is "to orient and mobilize others for a purpose." No purpose, no leadership. No clarity about objectives, no good governance.
- You can win no debate, because vision is the argument you need to outdo your opponent.
- You cannot persuade citizens to part with their money for taxes unless you can persuade them that there is purpose to it.
- You cannot touch the motivational nerve of your officials and get a taste of their enthusiastic support if you cannot put a project in front of them to work for.
- You cannot formulate a credible programme of government.
- You cannot have direction and consistency in governance.
- You cannot prioritise, and even more de-prioritise, and make sense of and explain the difficult business of de-prioritising that always threatens your authority.
- You cannot give, because you have no way of knowing what to give and what to deny.
- You cannot claim a right to be obeyed, because there is no reason to obey what is without purpose.
- You cannot claim success, because there is nothing to measure success against.

All remarkable governments are governments of vision: Bismarck, Roosevelt, Johnson, Reagan, Thatcher. President Park in Korea put a modernisation project in front of his people and was able to mobilise officials, advisers, business, voluntarism and the population itself for its realisation. Governments without vision are never remarkable: Carter, Clinton, Blair, Bush, Brown.

Why is "the vision thing" so difficult? One reason for the absence of visible projects could be that some governments do not want to display their real selves. It is possible that President Bush the younger simply was an agent of the rich. If so, that was not something he could parade too ostentatiously, although he came close, most carelessly at a fundraising dinner for wealthy supporters on the 15th of June 2006, when he in his speech took delight in the company of not only "the haves but the have-mores" and in reassuring his audience that "some people call you the élite. I call you my base."

But many governments are simply in confusion about what they are for. Whatever one might say about President Carter, manipulative he was not. It is quite possible that Mr. Brown was genuinely bewildered about his purpose when he found himself prime minister after ten years as number two. It is intellectually difficult to articulate idea and purpose clearly and persuasively, even to oneself. That is true for any enterprise. Any author knows it. To be asked what the book you are working on is about and what you want with it is enough to bring out a cold sweat and is likely to produce at best muddled evasiveness. Mr. Blair failed to genuinely *see* the vision that was sitting in front of him waiting to be taken up, and that he would even speak about on festive occasions—to turn the tide on Thatcherite injustice—and got himself into a muddle as "moderniser." A clear vision is capable of being explained in a simple way and preferably captured in a slogan such as "new deal" or "great society"—and possibly "the big society." If you cannot give your vision a concise expression, it is not yet a clear idea in your head.

Prospective governments better have given the vision thing thought before they get into office. Once there, events will take over and there will be no time, and those who have not done their homework find themselves without purpose however much they think they have it.

The other reason, specifically in our time, is a loss of confidence in the very idea of government. Mr. Reagan in the United States and Mrs. Thatcher in Britain were not successful in their intentions to cut back public spending and taxation, but they were influential in shaping *ideas* about government and capitalism. Anthony King, in his review of upheavals in the British constitution from around 1970, ascribes a good deal to new social and political attitudes, including "Thatcherism." Mr. Reagan, the communicator he was, defined the new era with striking simplicity in his first inaugural address in 1981: "Government is not the solution to our problem, it *is* the problem." This Reagan-Thatcher paradigm grew out of many influences much beyond that of two leaders, but these two took on the job of being its ideological midwives and did that with brilliance. Their influence in public policy was modest, but in culture great. They helped to overturn what had been a broadly shared pragmatic confidence in government as an instrument of order and good. With that confidence gone, it is difficult for a leader to stand up and say with pride: here is what I'm going to put government to work for.

Nigel Hamilton, in *American Caesars,* dithers about including Ronald Reagan in the pantheon of great presidents and in the end does not. He was right. Mr. Reagan was an inspired leader and an influential statesman, but at the core of his world view he was wrong. He prepared the ground for the unravelling of American political culture. Bad government is obviously a problem but there is no order without good government.

It has sometimes been thought that the age of great visions is in the past and that government is now mere management. We now know that nothing could be further from the truth. Capitalism has collapsed into crisis in an orgy of deregulation. Money is transgressing into politics and undermining democracy itself. Economically destructive distributional injustice is rampant and increasing. Public poverty persists among private affluence. Global financial services exercise monopolistic power over national policies, unchecked by any semblance of global political power. Trust is haemorrhaging. The European Union, the greatest ever experiment in super-national democracy, is imploding.

Signals

Ministers have only two tools in their tiny box: commands and signals. Once you have shown your power, you must restrain your urge to command. Remember President Bush the younger, who was fond of calling himself "the decider." He reaped only failure. Your game is now about encouraging and outwitting. Remember President Reagan who was the most easygoing of leaders and did not push people around. He got what he wanted. You must engage your people in deliberation with you and each other. You must educate them about the subtlety of democratic government and their responsibilities within it. You must touch their ideas and preferences and make them better citizens than they are inclined to be. You must let officials and citizens know what you are for and that there is purpose to your regime. You must let people see what you are doing and impose yourself on the world around you. You must define the terms of political combat and control the agenda.

Spin is inescapable. There are two simple rules to square the circle: (1) you must always spin, loudly, dominantly, aggressively, incessantly and outspin everyone else, and (2) you must never overdo it.

But there is more to it than spin. You are a democratic government. You are an agent of your people. You must "discern." You must engage in deliberation with them. You must involve the citizens in your plans and make them participants. You depend for your doings on a settlement in which they accept being dominated. You must do your part to preserve a democratic culture and if possible to improve on it. You must create that shared identity between government and people that is a condition of democratic rule. It falls on you. People are reluctant. You must pull them into your embrace and give them reasons to be loyal. You must govern fairly, first of all, but you must also explain and educate. You must be their leader and make them want to be followers.

Leadership

Leadership comes from the top. If you do not have it in you to be a leader whom others will follow, you are better off not trying. Mr. Brown did— and destroyed his reputation.

A party or movement that aims for government should find itself an effective leader to carry the banner. They should choose leaders who are capable of leading. Their policies matter less, the stuff of leadership more. The Labour Party in Britain has a tradition of choosing leaders according to whether they are three inches to the right or the left and hence of choosing ineffective leaders who have been most remarkable for losing elections. Before the 1997 election, the choice was between Mr. Blair and Mr. Brown and the party for once made the right choice. It may be difficult today to remember the promise that came with Mr. Blair, and he went on to win three commanding elections, something no previous Labour leader had been near to achieving. But he lost the grip and made himself a follower, of the captains of finance at home and the American presidents abroad.

A leader must impose himself. He has enemies who want to frustrate. The way to make yourself imposing and get others to sit up and listen is by displaying courage. Great leaders, said de Gaulle, are those who are able to grasp opportunities that present themselves and to take risks.[9] "The great thing about Steve Jobs," said his biographer Alan Deutschman when Jobs was forced by ill health to step down as head of the Apple corporation, "is not his genius or charisma, but his extraordinary risk-taking. Apple has been so innovative because Jobs takes major risks, which is rare in corporate America."[10] True, if you if you stand up against those who want to hold you down and take the risk of doing battle you may lose, but if you don't you can't win.

On the 25th of December 1776, George Washington famously crossed the Delaware River in ferocious weather with a ragtag army, and defied all odds to inflict defeat on superior Hessian forces at Trenton. The American forces had suffered a string of beatings and were on the run and mutinous. Washington feared that his already small army would fall apart and the revolutionary war disintegrate. Something spectacular was needed, an opportunity presented itself and Washington grasped it with full awareness that it was win or lose for the American cause and that losing was the more likely outcome. The battle at Trenton stiffened American political and military morale, kept the American effort alive, and established Washington as a leader beyond reproach.

When Abraham Lincoln faced reelection in 1864, the smart strategic advice was appeasement of the anti-emancipation lobby. By that time, however, after much agonising, Lincoln had come down in favour of full emancipation and decided, against his advisers and in awareness of the risk of defeat, to stand his ground and face down the opposition—and beat the odds to be firmly reelected and to establish himself as the undisputed master (until he was shot dead just a month after his second inaugural).

When Eisenhower took up the presidency in 1953, he inherited war in Korea. His advisers wanted a decisive escalation and promised victory—the argument that would later carry the day in Vietnam. But Eisenhower recognised that the war was unwinnable by any conventional means and that an armistice was the best available outcome. He passed a message through to the Chinese and Russians that he would accept a settlement where the armies stood, without concession, but no continued stalemate, and that if his offer was rejected he was prepared to use nuclear weapons. The threat was believed and the war ended.

After his party's losses in the 2010 midterm elections, Barack Obama faced the question of final approval of a new arms control treaty with Russia in the Senate, for which he needed Republican votes. Again, the smart strategic advice was to give it up and not risk loss in a hostile Congress, which would paralyse an already weak president. Instead, Mr. Obama decided to take one of the biggest gambles in his presidency, insisted that the Senate approve the treaty by year's end, and launched a campaign to rally the necessary vote. He prevailed, in perhaps his finest hour of leadership, and a president who had looked weak was by a stroke of courage strong again.

But a short year later, in the standoff in the summer of 2011 with an opposition majority in Congress over increasing the federal debt ceiling, he chose not to confront and lost both the battle and much of his authority. Had he risked confrontation, he might still have lost, but by avoiding risk he made failure inevitable.

Ahead of local elections in Germany in March 2011, fallout from a nuclear reactor in Japan, following a huge earthquake and tsunami, propelled the vexed question of nuclear energy to the forefront of German political and campaign awareness. The chancellor, Angela Merkel, who had been a proponent of continued nuclear energy, decided to shut down seven of the country's seventeen nuclear plants. This was shortly after their operating lives had been extended with the chancellor's assurance that they were safe. The move was seen as cowardly and opportunistic and the Christian Democratic Union suffered a humiliating defeat in the solidly conservative state of Baden-Württemberg, losing the ruling majority it had held for fifty-eight years. The party might have lost anyway, but to lose an election is not to lose respect.

Half a year later, however, the chancellor brilliantly displayed risk taking and leadership, in the early hours of the 27th of October, as European leaders were negotiating a complicated deal to reassure the markets and save the euro, just before the Asian markets were to open. "For hours, negotiators had been trying to persuade the banks [through their representatives at the meeting] to accept a 'voluntary' 50 percent loss in the face value of their Greek bond holdings. The banks, which had already agreed to a 21 percent write-down, had dug in their heals. But Mrs. Merkel called the banks' bluff. Accept the 50 percent write-down, she told the bankers, or bear the consequences of a default. In effect, she was willing to risk a credit event, and to place the blame for the fallout on them."[11]

The demands on political leadership that I have lined up in this treatise are horrendous. The leader must manage, represent, negotiate, sort out personnel issues, be strategically intelligent, deflect crisis, be respected, stand the storm, be courageous, be visionary, know everything, handle the press, be charming, display confidence, and give the appearance of being relaxed and liking it. Well, if you want to be a political leader you must accept. It is your choice and if you make it you surrender your person to the job. You will be hounded by a press with no mercy and you have no right to complain. You are no longer a private person, you no longer have a private life, your family is no longer your private family. Mrs. Thatcher's husband, Denis Thatcher, played the role of consort to perfection and gave even the iron lady a patina of human touch. Mr. Brown built a wall between his public and family life and was seen as cold and distant. When on the day he left office he walked past the cameras with his two little sons in hand, there was not a dry eye in the country and no one who did not ask themselves why he had not previously shown some of his human side.

PART II: DYSFUNCTIONAL DEMOCRACIES

Britain is not going to get a government better set to rule than New Labour in its good years. But it was unable. America is not going to get a more worthy and able president than Barack Obama. But his promise was ground down by a system that took revenge. No doubt, there are other dysfunctional democracies to pick on, but these are the ones worth confronting. It is right to say that they *are* dysfunctional. Policy is not made, or if made not in the service of the public good, or if in the service of the public good not implemented. It is right to say that they *have gone* dysfunctional. Until recently, these were normal democracies. In Britain, the constitutional system declined from "order" to "mess" after the 1970s. In the United States, normal onstage political battle has been displaced after the 1980s.

The British Predicament

The two questions for reform are: what is to be done and who should do it? In the American case, as we will see, these are both difficult questions, the second one in particular. The British case is by comparison simple. What needs to be done is far from revolutionary. The agent of reform is Parliament, which has the power to reform as it wishes.

True, Parliament needs to assert itself. The House of Commons is not in control of its own agenda. The Speaker does not direct parliamentary affairs, except for chairing debates in the chamber. The post known as "Leader of the House" is held by a cabinet minister who, as the government's commissar, manages the House's business. There is some movement for the House to take more control of its own affairs. In 2010, an ad hoc committee on parliamentary business, the Wright committee, recommended the establishment of a permanent House of Commons Business Committee. That may happen. The 2010 government indicated that it might favour the establishment of such a committee within three years. The strange thing, of course, is that the establishment of a committee of the House of Commons, on the recommendation of a committee of the House of Commons to conduct House of Commons business, would depend on the *government's* say-so. If this is what the House of Commons, the highest authority in the land, wants, it should just do it. So although Parliament is supreme, the House of Commons has some way to go to make itself wish to use the power it has.

There are many problems in the British constitutional system and each observer has his or her favourite one to remedy. Underlying all of it, however, is a single basic defect: the concentration of political power to the prime minister in Downing Street and the inevitable misrule that flows from such centralisation of decision making and administration.

In three public lectures in London under the auspices of the Royal Society for the Arts and the Hansard Society I have outlined an agenda of constitutional reform.[12]

1. The House of Commons should establish itself as an equitable partner to the government in political decision making and should exercise effective scrutiny in legislative and budgetary decisions. Many parliamentary reformers in Britain set their sight on the House of Lords—an easy target since it is unelected—but reform is more urgent in the House of Commons.
2. Political funding should be redesigned to prevent the consolidation in Britain of an overpowering politico-corporate complex.
3. Local government with serious autonomy and responsibility should be reconstituted as a counterweight to the concentration of political power to London.

In the House of Commons, no more is needed for a major improvement than a minor change in its working order. As the House works, it can barely be said to legislate at all in any real meaning of the term. It mainly ratifies what has been decided in Whitehall, which, since Mrs. Thatcher, increasingly means Downing Street. It does not do enough work on the legislation that passes through it to say meaningfully that it makes law. It would be good if we could say that it prevents bad law, but it does not even do that other than exceptionally. Compared with normal legislative and budgetary work in other democratic national assemblies, the House of Commons is conspicuously passive. It receives proposals from the government, has a cursory look at them in haste, and votes them through, with many MPs often not even knowing what they are voting for or against.

British MPs are held in low esteem in the public, in particular after the "claims scandal" in 2009, which revealed widespread moral and some legal corruption, and there is a view that the House of Commons cannot be trusted with authority because its members are not of the necessary calibre. But that is mistaken. The House performs admirably when given real work to do. This is in evidence in the select committees—in the work they are allowed to do—and also in the Chamber when there is a free vote so that members can and must make up their own minds. We then get debates of outstanding integrity and quality. But not surprisingly, when, as in most debates, the respective whips instruct MPs on what to mean and how to vote, we get the tepid debate which is inevitable when only sheepish behaviour is expected and available.

For better decision making the House needs arrangements whereby, first, it can turn away proposals from the government which are wrong, unnecessary or badly prepared, and second, double-check, improve and correct proposals it wishes to deal with. Those not familiar with the way "the mother of parliaments" works may be surprised to learn that it has none of these powers.

The House has roughly a select committee for each government department. These committees do excellent work, but for the most part after the fact. They explore the experience of how laws have worked once they have been in operation for a while—and publish the critical reports about how badly most things work that those of us who live in Britain are used to hearing about on the morning news. They *can* also engage in before-the-fact scrutiny, meaning to look into the details of how a government proposal might work before it is put through the legislative hurdles, but that is at the government's discretion (except that the excellent House of Lords sometimes steps in and does it unasked). Ordinary bills are debated but not subject to before-the-fact scrutiny. Only "draft bills" get this treatment, and recent governments have almost never published draft bills.

The solution is a simple modification in the passage of bills through the House of Commons so that they first go to the relevant select committee for scrutiny before they continue through the rest of the legislative procedure, not just occasionally but always (with obvious exceptions for emergency legislation). The committee would be able to return to the government proposals that are deemed unnecessary or ill prepared. It is essential that the power be to return a bad proposal to the government, and not to shelve it, a matter to which we return in the American case. This power is crucial, but is one that in a parliamentary system would almost never be used because governments that know their proposals will be worked over would not make the kinds of proposals that would be dismissed. The Criminal Justice Act of 2003, for example, which I discussed in Chapter 6, would never have seen the light of day. The committee should be obliged to double-check those proposals it accepts for consideration and go through them in detail. That provision would make for both greater legislative discipline and better legislative quality. This is considered a radical proposal in British politics but is in reality no more than for Parliament to take control of its own business and make itself a normal legislature.

An orderly system for the funding of politics is also eminently possible. Democracy needs money to operate, and a good deal of it. British democracy is unfunded, except for fees from a diminishing number of party members. Into this void flows private money from unions, businesses, and individuals in a semi-secret bog of political, moral and, presumably, legal corruption. Downing Street is the magnet for money, for its power of patronage, as evidenced by the boost in the Conservative Party's ability to attract generosity once in power with the premiership after the 2010 elections.

My proposal is in two steps: First, the necessary funding of parties and campaigns should come from the public purse and all other forms of political money should be considered corruption in law, be it from businesses or unions, from individuals, or from candidates' own means. This would both provide the funds that are needed and break the link of transgression between the seekers of office and the givers of money. Taxes are what we use to fund public goods. Democracy is a joint matter that we should pay for jointly and equally. If you think about it, you will easily see it to be perverse to leave the running of democracy to be dependent on private largess.

However, public funding creates its own problems and is in itself not exactly an enterprising proposal. If the parties that are represented in the national assembly would have access to funds from the state budget, which they control, they would be likely to help themselves lavishly at the expense of smaller parties and parties not yet represented. This can be seen in for example Germany and Scandinavia. Also, straight public funding of parties fails to exploit a lucky potential for improvements in the quality of democracy. No democracy can escape the dilemma of economic power, but public funding of politics can be designed so as to democratise some economic power.

The second part of my proposal is that public funds for politics be turned into a political resource in the hands of voters so that those seeking elected office be dependent on the voters for financial means as they already depend on them for votes. The extra influence of political money should not only be removed from a rich minority but redistributed equally to all voters. There would be *two* beneficent results: voters would count more and minority resources decide less. Citizens would hold the control from below that is prescribed in democratic theory in two ways, in votes and in money. The principle of one-person-one-vote, now one-person-one-influence, would be practical reality. There would be political equality, not just in theory but in fact.

I have previously suggested that this should be done with the help of vouchers to voters for them to pass on the parties or candidates of their choice or to throw away, just as they now do with their votes.[13] I still think this a theoretically elegant idea, but I have come to the view that it is practically too complicated. It would require a huge administrative apparatus. The vouchers would be worth, say, a dollar per voter per year, and it might be difficult to get voters to find it worth their while to participate (although most voters have no difficulty in recognising the importance of voting in spite of their individual votes being of no discernible influence).

My suggestion now is to institute an annual survey of voters to record the distribution of preferences for the allocation of the public allotment to pay for politics and then to distribute it accordingly. The U.S. Constitution made the census a constitutional tool. I now suggest the survey as a constitutional tool. This is a practical, effective and inexpensive way of putting economic power into the hands of voters. Modern survey techniques are perfectly up to the task in precision and robustness. There is a bonus of anonymity: no direct contact between givers and getters and no scope for corruption. Parties and candidates would face an annual competition in front of the voters on whom they would be dependent for the funds they need to do political campaigning.[14]

The difficult matter in my British agenda is that of local democracy. As it is, Britain does not have proper local units to devolve power to—which is one reason why "local government is no longer a part of the British constitution." Across Europe, municipalities have on average about 10,000 inhabitants or fewer. In rural Britain, districts have an average size of about 110,000 inhabitants and metropolitan boroughs more than 300,000. These units are unwieldy and not really local, and have now also been deprived of any vestige of autonomy, the last to go being the remaining local authority over local schools. The result is disengagement, as seen in very low levels of voter turnout in local elections, often down to below 20 per cent (less than a third on average throughout the country in the 2012 local elections). These exercises look like elections, but really are not, as I know from my own district. A few voters go to the polls, but there is no process, no discussions in neighbourhoods and no involvement. British democracy needs a system of municipalities and many more elected politicians to represent citizens' interests.

My recommendation is a whole-scale restructuring of local government, something that would be equally beneficent democratically as administratively. The British should be given the benefit of some of that "municipilization" that Quinton Mayne found had served the Danish people so well. Local units—municipalities—should be small, there should be more of them, and they should have more power and responsibility. British democracy has too few elected representatives, fewer proportionally than any other democracy in Europe. There are too many Members of Parliament in London but too few elected representatives throughout the country. There is no counterbalance to the concentration of political power in London and Downing Street.

But, regrettably, I am unable to entertain much hope that this might happen. Strangely enough, in the most centralised system of government in Europe, there is no appetite in the population or among elites for local democracy, and no provocation, at least that I have found, seems able to ignite any interest in it. Mr. Cameron may be an advocate of "localism" but that does not mean localism of political power. It seems that what he and his colleagues have in mind does not have anything to do with local government at all, but is rather a matter of localising responsibility—to whom?—without localising power, which is a recipe for further misrule and erosion of local government.

The American Predicament

Constitutional redesign is often thought to be prohibitively difficult in America because of the rigidities of the Constitution itself. Even so reform-minded an observer as Robert Dahl has, for that reason, in his recent critical works, felt able to suggest very little of practical reform.[15] Jacob Hacker and Paul Pierson, in *Winner-Take-All Politics,* are radical in diagnosis but have next to nothing to offer in prescription. American political writing is in paralysis, critical but despondent. In a review of two central books, the Reuters columnist Felix Salmon writes: "This is now a country run by the rich for the rich. And nothing in either of these books gives me any reason to believe that there is any hope of changing that."[16] That sounds glib, but is correct both on the American predicament and the intellectual response to it.

This reticence is misplaced. The American constitutional system has been in constant evolution and is not set in stone. The Republic was born in revolution and has continued to live revolution. At critical junctures, America, rather than falling into paralysis, has been conspicuous for its ability to reinvent itself. After the passing of the Constitution, there have been four political revolutions. The Revolution of 1800, following Thomas Jefferson's election as president, was not only regime change with the dismissal of the Federalists, but also represented a shift in values and mindsets so that it has come to be seen as a democratic consolidation. Later in that century, under President Lincoln's guidance, a counterrevolution was prevented and a progressive one assured when the country went to the extreme of civil war to preserve and improve the Constitution, with the ending of slavery and the emancipation of the African American people as the eventual outcome. In the twentieth century, President Roosevelt's New Deal, and President Reagan's revolution in the opposite direction, were of consequence not only for practicalities of public policy but equally for the way Americans came to think about politics and government. The New Deal revolution endured until its consolidation failed in the tragedy of President Johnson's tenure. President Reagan inspired a counterrevolution—unregulated monopoly capitalism underpinned by a cult of inequality and anti-government ideology—in which we are still living.

There is a progressive continuity in American political history, from the Declaration of Independence through the Constitution and on to the first three of the post-Constitution revolutions. President Reagan's counterrevolution interrupted that continuity but has failed to produce a new settlement and instead brought on disorder and crisis. The American way of life is disintegrating in an orgy of inequality and stalled mobility, and democracy is being eaten up from inside by the virus of transgression.

"Counterrevolution" might be thought alarmist and exaggerated language, but it is not. What is in motion in America is of monumental proportions. At the core of the progressive continuity has been the building of more inclusive institutions, politically and socially.[17] A culture built on inclusiveness is what makes for national progress. It is this direction of progress in the social and political fabric of American life that is the source of the success that has been the envy of the world.

This is the tradition that is being overturned today. What Mr. Reagan unleashed was not finally a critique of "big government" but an assault on inclusiveness. With democracy withering, political inclusiveness is going: resources decide everything and votes count for nothing. With inequality rising and mobility declining, social inclusiveness is going, and with it the nation's cohesion. It is not only that a minority is confiscating the nation's wealth and destroying political equality, it is doing that at great cost to the nation's engine of strength.

So the Republic is at a crossroads. Is the counterrevolution to be consolidated with ever less of democratic reality and more of soft despotism? Or is it to be rebuffed so that America reconnects with the progressive tradition and finds its way to a new settlement of government for the public good? The stakes could hardly be higher, for America and for the democratic world.

Some of America's constitutional upheavals have come about through changes in the Constitution itself. No sooner was it adopted than it was redesigned by ten amendments that came to be known as the Bill of Rights. The abolishment of slavery was finalised in a constitutional amendment. Later amendments introduced, for example, direct election of the Senate, voting rights for women, and the lowering of the voting age to eighteen. There are now twenty-seven amendments added to the original text. The thrust of these amendments, although not all of them, has been toward more democratic arrangements, confirming the progressive continuity. The Constitution today is radically different in both philosophy and practice from the one adopted in 1787.

But as much has been done without changes in the Constitution, either by way of ordinary legislation (even in issues of basic principle: universal suffrage was secured as late as 1965, by the Voting Rights Act) or through changing conventions in the political culture. The four post-Constitution revolutions have in common that they went not only to new political arrangements but also, and primarily, deep into the political culture.

So change and ability to change is a constant in the American system. Today, that system is ripe for redesign again. The two necessary conditions of reform are present: there is crisis and there is awareness of crisis. The crisis is that democracy is eroding and the American dream of opportunity and mobility has been extinguished by oppressive inequality. The awareness of crisis is seen in the contempt in which "Washington" and "politics" are held throughout the nation. "The latest NYT/CBS poll [finds] Americans' distrust of government at its highest level ever."[18] The Tea Party and Occupy Wall Street movements are cuts of the same cloth: a deep loss of confidence in the nation's political and economic institutions. The tax system—the heart of public policy—is distrusted in the citizenry and the business community alike.[19] To take a leaf out of Mr. Reagan's book: Washington is not the solution to our problem, it *is* the problem.

Political insiders wish to think of distrust in government as something that happens in the citizenry, but that is usually wrong. Citizens are as they are; when they lose trust in their institutions, that is usually because those institutions are becoming unworthy of trust. This is certainly the case in the now fraught relationship between Washington and the rest of the country. The insiders interpret social movements as pressure groups for specific directions in public policy and scramble to accommodate them, but that is a misunderstanding. The Tea Party in particular, but also the Occupy (Wall Street) groups, if they can keep up their momentum, are great movements of rebellion in the American revolutionary tradition. They are one to the right and one to the left, obviously, but more basically their discontent is a shared one with the political system. It is dysfunction that gives these movements credence and life force. They are also movements that give voice to a dissatisfaction that sits deep in the citizenry and hence movements of loyalty. The enemies of American democracy are elsewhere. They are the agents of the politico-corporate complex who have abandoned loyalty and work backstage. The loyal rebellions stand against that enmity. They speak from within and for American culture against the decline in American political culture. To regain a shared identity between the rulers and the ruled, their energy should be mobilised and not rejected.

An enumeration of dysfunctions in the American system (as in the British one) would make up a long list, but the core defects are easy to pinpoint. No doubt, there are faults in the Constitution itself, but none of what is needed to pull American democracy out of its decline depends on changes in the Constitution. The problems stick deep, but sit mainly in conventions. The Constitution does not stand in the way of repairing what it does not regulate and can be left in peace. The defects are in four layers.

First, of the main constitutional powers, only the presidency is in working order. Congress is bereft of capacity. The Supreme Court has taken on powers it should not have.

The disability of Congress was on stark display in November 2011 when its "super-committee" on deficit reduction failed in its task and gave up. Congress had recognised its own disability to deal with the most pressing problem in public policy in front of it, had established an extraordinary arrangement to deal with what it was unable to handle through its ordinary procedures, and had put that ad hoc committee under the threat that if it failed to produce a plan, deficit reduction would be taken out of the legislators' hands and go forward, if at all, on autopilot. But nothing came of it. At the end of 2012, Congress's impotence was on display again in its dealing with the imperative of the "fiscal cliff."

Francis Fukuyama has named it "vetocracy." "Checks have metastasised . . . the result is paralysis."[20] Congress has allowed ever more byzantine and irrational procedural rules to take hold so that everyone and anyone—speakers, majority leaders, minority leaders, committee chairmen, sub-committee chairmen, intransigent individual lawmakers, filibusterers (in the Senate), minorities (in the Senate again)—can prevent action. The House of Representatives freed itself of filibuster in 1842. Why is it still there in the Senate?

The problem is the opposite one of that in Britain's Parliament. There, the House of Commons has too little power in the legislative process. In Congress, there is too much power to prevent and too little capacity to do. Congress should be obliged to decide on proposals from the government without undue delay, or to return them for more work, but should not have the ability to bury proposals in non-action.

The Supreme Court is excessively activist and inadequately checked. It is too eager to rule too easily. Judicial review is established in the U.S. Constitution, but it is a provision that requires, for sound practice, restraint on the part of the courts. The Supreme Court should guard against the unlikely eventuality that Congress might act unconstitutionally, but should not set itself up to exercise general veto over legislation. Decisions made correctly in the legislature should by default be considered constitutional and should normally not be reexamined by courts. It should take strong judicial grounds both to accept correct decisions for revision and, if reviewed, to overrule them. Strong judicial grounds should be expected to be broadly recognised as such by qualified judicial expertise. The Supreme Court, engaged in the review of the constitutionality of decisions by the legislature, should require of itself broad agreement of opinion and should not accept ruling by simple majority. If the best judicial expertise in the land divides more or less equally on an issue of apparent constitutionality, it can be taken that the issue is political and not judicial and that it should be left to be decided politically.

There are too few justices—nine—with too much power. So much power should not sit in the hands of so few appointed officials who feel that nothing can remove them from office. It should be diluted in a larger court to enforce more demanding judicial deliberation. The size of the Court has varied between at first six justices and at the most ten. President Roosevelt wanted to increase its size but did not prevail. It is time to raise the issue again.

To restrain the Court from excessive activism, there should be a requirement of qualified majority ruling. There should be no more embarrassing 5-to-4 majority decisions in important constitutional matters. Increasing the number of justices to ten and requiring six for a ruling would be a considerable step forward, although I would recommend a larger Court and a more demanding qualified majority rule.

However, an activist court is not likely to restrain itself. For serious constitutional reform, therefore, a showdown with the Supreme Court is inevitable. The difficulty under current conventions is that the Court is likely to claim the power to overrule attempts from outside to restrain it. What reform is up against, then, is a prevailing understanding in the political culture of the role and position of the Court in the constitutional system.

As it happens, the Supreme Court is much less powerful than it is often or sometimes thought to be. The other powers have a considerable arsenal to bring to a confrontation with it. The Court can be put under the moral pressure of well-argued criticism. There are now strong grounds for such criticism. While upholding various esoteric principles of its own definition, principally the unrestricted right for private money to transgress into politics, the Court is failing in its higher duty to protect democracy as such. It is fortifying selected trees while setting the forest on fire. The historical experience is that the Court responds to well-argued criticism. President Roosevelt attacked the Court for its resistance to his New Deal measures. That has been thought a political failure, but it was not. He may have wanted to pack the Court with additional justices, as he threatened. In that he failed, if ever it was a serious intention, but by 1937, and before he was able to change its composition, he had a compliant Court.[21]

It is sometimes thought a weakness in the Constitution that it gives the Court the power to check Congress and the executive but that the Court is itself unchecked. But that is not what the Constitution says. The court "shall have appellate Jurisdiction, both as to Law and Fact, with such Exceptions, and under such regulations as Congress shall make" (Article III, Section 2). If it is assumed that the framers were concerned to create a system of checks and balances, it should be assumed that they wanted to include the Supreme Court in the scheme, and that the power of Congress to impose exceptions and regulations on the Court was the mechanism for Congress to check the Court that checks it. Congress could, for example, impose on the Court a qualified majority rule.

It is even a misunderstanding that justices once appointed are protected from being removed. They hold the post "during good Behavior" (Article III, Section 1). That clause is interpretable. Take, for example, the case of Justice Clarence Thomas. His rulings are often, by broad judicial agreement, eccentric, unpredictable and original in the sense of displaying apparently novel and surprising legal theory. Yet he has remained unwilling to engage in serious deliberation on or explanation of his line of ruling. In 2012, it was the seventh year that he had not spoken during court argument.[22] He has shied away from qualified judicial debate outside of the Court. When on turn he has announced opinions, he has tended to rely on legalistic and technical jargon ill suited for comprehension or enlightenment outside the courtroom, or even within it. It could be argued, in the spirit of modern and open democracy, that a man who accepts the power held by a justice of the Supreme Court and who delights in its use has a duty to engage with and educate the public on his exercise of that privilege, and that the refusal to so engage, which is unusual among the justices, represents a contempt of both the Court and of the democratic system that falls short of good behaviour on the part of a person in a position of authority.

Both Congress and the president have powers to overrule, to some degree, decisions by the Court. Congress can do this in subsequent law to "correct" Court decisions. When the Court invalidated the Agricultural Adjustment Act in 1936, three years after it was passed, the government rewrote and preserved its main provisions in the Soil Conservation and Domestic Allotment Act of 1936 and the Agricultural Adjustment Act of 1938. The Civil Rights Act of 1991 overturned nine Supreme Court decisions that had narrowed interpretation in previous law. The executive on its part implements Court rulings in public policy and can, as with law, influence the impact of rulings through interpretation. On the 2nd of December 2011, for example, President Obama annulled a Bush-era interpretation of recent Court rulings on affirmative action in college admissions that warned against considering race at all. Using other aspects of the rulings, he issued new guidelines more in support of affirmative action. Of course, the Court can strike back, but until it does the executive interpretation stands, and if it seems inclined to it can be restrained by well-argued criticism.

Finally, in a hardened confrontation, the Court is not in control of its purse. The justices have a right to compensation, but Congress is not obliged to increase the compensation beyond where it stands, or to pay justices a salary for life on retirement, or any other pension for that matter, or to fund the lavish Court administration.

A confrontation with the Supreme Court in which the other powers mobilised all the potentials in their arsenal, down to the threat of withholding means, is perhaps unlikely. But it is worth making the point that the elevated position the Supreme Court now holds in its own and other people's minds is not laid down in the Constitution but is a matter of convention that the other powers have ample means to challenge, if they should wish to.

The second level of defect is in the quality of decisions that come out of the broken system of decision making. Not only is there paralysis: what breaks through the paralysis is of bad quality. That can be seen in a federal budget that is out of political control and unable to stand up to a spell of low growth, and in the blight of command-and-control regulations and incoherent legislation. Nowhere is this defect more apparent than in taxation, which, to repeat, combines *all* the vices that are possible in a bad tax system.

The third level of defect, which explains the lack of capacity of decision making and the persistent low quality of public policy, is in the availability of transgression by private money into the domain of politics, with the resulting breakdown of political equality and the distortion of power between the onstage and backstage arenas of political combat. Congress now is not autonomous. The women and men who serve there are not straightforwardly delegates of their constituencies but also dependents of financial sponsors. Policies that might seriously threaten the flow of political money are at a disadvantage, or unavailable, while policies that might attract such money have a selective advantage. Near to a century ago, when America was in a crisis not unlike the present one, Justice Louis Brandeis of the Supreme Court warned: "We may have democracy, or we may have wealth concentrated in the hands of a few, but we can't have both." There is an obvious contradiction between political equality and economic inequality, and the more extreme the inequality the starker the contradiction. But democracy *can* be protected from the potentially erosive force of economic inequality. It is not easily done, but it is possible. It would take a Chinese wall between the market, where economic inequality is inevitable and has a role to play, and the domain of politics, where political equality is an imperative. If so, democracy can live with even quite extreme economic inequality. What we cannot have, however, is democracy with both extreme economic inequality and the institutionalisation of private money as a political resource. Under those conditions, democracy dies. That is no theoretical construct. It is empirical fact. It is not what might happen, it is what *is* happening.

Finally, at the fourth level is a political culture which is distorted and inadequate in its defence of democratic values and principles. The other defects have come to be broadly accepted as normal. There is anger at Washington in the population, but in an anger that is without direction. Congress may be despised but is not under pressure to reform itself. A politicised Supreme Court is let off scot-free before the tribunal of the people. The Constitution is mistakenly thought of as a bequest of wise founding fathers and a holy text in the hands of a high priesthood of jurists. The wilful destruction of political equality, which is a condition of a functioning democracy, is accepted to be a right.

The elections of 2012 were uplifting. Fundamentalists were rejected in the Senate race, ethically tainted incumbents dismissed in the House race, ballot issues decided pragmatically throughout the states, and Mr. Obama was reelected. No wonder liberals have started to feel good about politics—but they deceive themselves. What that election shows is that there is good sense out there in the population. But in Washington, the systemic dysfunction persists unabated.

The two questions for reform are, to repeat, what is to be done and who should do it? The first question is roughly answered in the above. The difficulty is in the second question. The reason there is reticence about constitutional reform in America is that it is difficult to see how it could come about. There is no shortage of awareness of disrepair, but how to get from awareness to action? Those who wish to promote reform need to ask the right question. We can discuss endlessly what *should* be done, but nothing can come of it unless we first find a way through which it *could* be done.

To illustrate: In a recent book, *Republic, Lost,* Lawrence Lessig has suggested a mechanism of political funding by way of vouchers held by voters, not unlike my previous proposal discussed above. That idea has merit.[23] But any notion, in prevailing conditions, that the president might bring legislation to that effect to Congress, and Congress pass it, is not of this world. Before there is any chance that Congress could be moved to any such reform, there would have to be a change in the prevailing conditions within which it works.

In the end, only Congress can decide. But the right question to start from in the American case is not what Congress should do but how Congress could be brought about to doing anything at all. The paralysis that Francis Fukuyama identified is not limited to Congress but is entrenched in a multi-layered dysfunctionality in the political system around Congress, down to the political culture. That level of dysfunction is, to repeat, *new.* It is the legacy of Mr. Reagan's counterrevolution. What is at stake is not pie-in-the-sky but the restoration of democracy in America enough for the country to rejoin the family of normal democracies and before it is no longer a democracy at all.

The who-should-do-it-question comes up against a very specific paralysis. Let's call it *the Washington bind:*

1. The constitutional institutions, notable Congress and the Supreme Court, are in need of radical reform.
2. That reform can come only from and through those selfsame institutions.
3. Those institutions are unable (Congress) or disinclined (Supreme Court).

This is the Gordian Knot that needs to be untied *first,* before we can get on to the question of what more practically to do. "Reform," then, is too weak a concept. The question for America, now as at previous junctures, is: revolution or not? The Republic needs to be salvaged from succumbing to counterrevolution. There needs to be better constitutional arrangements, but before that and in order to bring better arrangements about, the Americans need, yet again, to shake themselves up in the way they *think* about government, politics and their Constitution.

The term "cultural revolution" is tainted by having been attached to Mao's dictatorship in China, but that was an aberration. America taught the world about cultural revolution long before the Chinese abused the concept. Political revolution in America has always come by way of cultural revolution. In this treatise, we have seen the power of cultural revolution in other countries as well. In Korea, the leaders built a new nation in part by mobilising the country in a cultural revolution of participation and self-betterment. It was by cultural revolution that Germany reinvented itself to moral authority in Europe. We have also seen the absence of cultural revolution where it should have been called for. In Britain, Mr. Brown wanted

to abolish child poverty by technocratic decree without first investing politically to change Britain's culture of accepting poverty and mobilising the
population for a great cause. In America, reform will not be generated in
Washington by the constitutional powers but must be mobilised from the
country as a force to be brought down upon those powers. This is the way
it has happened previously and how it can be done again. It will depend
on the vitality of American culture being mobilised to breath new life into
a sclerotic political culture.

If that is the task for the American people, the burden I have brought
upon myself is to propose a way that cultural revolution could come about.
You may feel that I, as a non-American, have said more than I should already. But the ways of American governments affect not only Americans
but all of us, and I feel I have a right to be concerned with matters that are
of consequence also for friends beyond your shores. What I have started
I must finish. There is not much experience to draw on and I can do no
better than to imagine one way—and there are possibly others—in which
cultural revolution could be made.

The first step is to identify the catalyst that could release the energy
that is latent in the American people for, in the words of the Constitution,
"a more perfect Union." This is where the paralysis sits in contemporary
political writing. Authors like Hacker and Pierson, Paul Krugman (in *End
This Depression Now!*) and Joseph Stiglitz (in *The Price of Inequality*) are
good at explaining problems and pointing out the necessity of reform, but
silent on how to ignite reform up against entrenched vetocracy. Hedrick
Smith (in *Who Stole the American Dream?*) wants a "popular rebellion"
but does not suggest how that could come about. Sanford Levinson (in
Framed) wants a new constitutional convention, but how could that be
brought to happen? Al Gore (in *The Future*) correctly diagnoses American democracy as "hacked" and Congress as "incapable," but suggests no
way out of the Washington bind. Cultural revolution is a matter of popular mobilisation for a cause. That depends, as always, on leadership. That
leadership should come from the remaining institution of integrity, from
the presidency. Political revolution in America has always been inspired
by presidents of great authority.

American democracy is in need of a president who sees himself or
herself as a political entrepreneur of the way policy is made and who is
able and willing to engage with the risks that come with confronting the

system he or she is part of. A president who is to be transformative would recognise that in America now, before there can be better policy, there must be a better system, and would invest the great authority of the Office of the President of the United States of America into the enterprise of bringing that about. He or she would break through the Washington bind, bypass the other constitutional powers in the capital, and mobilise the country into a deep reflection on the state of its constitutional system, in an exercise in deliberative democracy writ large and of proportions never before seen in the world. The entrepreneurial president would be the initiator to unleash cultural revolution. This leader would inspire and guide that revolution, and control it to some degree, but could not and should not define its outcomes. He would inspire, as leadership always does, through vision. That vision would go both to the restoration of democracy and, beyond that and deeper, to salvaging the American dream.

President Obama is now in his second term and has the freedom of action of not having to worry about another election. He can already look forward to retiring from what will be seen as a great presidency: America lifted out of depression, universal health insurance established, the country extracted from the wars in Iraq and Afghanistan. But it is not yet, as he aimed it to be, a transformative presidency. America still lives in the darkness of the Reagan counterrevolution and has not been brought back into the light of its progressive tradition. The economic crisis should have enabled that transformation, but this has so far not been made to happen.

The second step would be for the president to assemble a coalition to ignite cultural revolution and drive it forward. That coalition will not be found in Washington. The other constitutional powers are to be rescued from themselves. Allies will have to be found deeper inside the broader culture.

Those allies should be mobilised from America's formidable community of national foundations and charitable organisations. These are institutions of moral authority: the nation's conscience of the public good. The president should mobilise their assistance and present his initiative to the American people as one grounded both in the presidential office and in the best of civil society. The foundations' contribution should include the funding of the apparatus of revolution, so that the president would not have to go to Congress and thereby allow it the financial lever to deflect the initiative.

The third step would be for the president, with the support of his coalition, to build that apparatus of revolution. How can a democracy be made to revolutionise itself, down to its political culture? It will not be done, obviously, by fighting in the streets, but only through careful deliberation.

The president should appoint a series of presidential commissions to explore core aspects of the constitutional system. There should be commissions for these areas:

- *On Congress.* This commission, as the subsequent ones, should start from first principles and elucidate the role and responsibility of Congress in the constitutional system and then work its way through to practical details of working procedures in the two chambers. The reference should be to find arrangements that preserve Congress's power to check the executive without the paralysis of vetocracy.
- *On the Supreme Court.* This commission should engineer the broadest possible exploration of a rational role for the Supreme Court under the provisions of the Constitution and again work its way through from first principles to practical details of procedure. The reference should be to seek out the balance President Lincoln was alluding to in his elegant recognition that "constitutional questions are to be decided by the Supreme Court" but not so that "the people will have ceased to be their own rulers."
- *On taxation.* This commission would invite deliberation on the meaning of taxation as the bond between the ruled and their rulers and between citizens themselves. It should explore all aspects of taxation, personal and corporate, direct and indirect, federal and local. There would be much attention to indirect taxes, since effectiveness in the raising of revenue in a modern economy depends crucially on indirect taxation. The American tax system has been allowed to falter, with endemic tax revolt the result. That needs to be broken. The reference should be not just the tax code but a totally new system that is simple, effective and fair.
- *On how to pay for politics.* This commission would explore the relationship between the imperative of political equality and the way democratic politics is funded, and how political equality can be protected from the force of economic inequality. The reference should

be President Obama's call to not "stand by and let the special interests drown out the voice of the American people." Of course,
the problem of soft despotism is the drowning out not only of the
people's voice, but more basically of their *say*.

- *On constitutional conventions.* This would be a super-commission to
guide the work of the other commissions and to which they would
report. It would be able to put matters to the other commissions to
be explored and would in due course pull together and interpret the
work and outcomes from the other commissions.

Each commission should have a wide, open and ambitious remit.
The president's control would lie in his decision on the compositions of
the commissions and in the framing of their terms of reference. Beyond
that, he should release them to their task, inspire the process from the
side, and get on with his ordinary business of governing. The commissions should be made up of respected citizens from academia, civil society and the business community. There should be no members from
federal or state legislative, executive or judicial institutions. Each commission should be asked to prepare a string of studies for a duration of,
say, five years, starting from first principles and working gradually toward
practical proposals. They should be asked to look beyond America and
to infuse deliberation at home with the ways and experiences of other
democracies. They should bring their work to the American people and
into American cultural life. Their studies should be distributed to federal,
state and local authorities throughout the land, and to non-governmental
organisations and associations, who should all be asked to produce comments and suggestions. There should be town meetings, hearings and con-
sultations throughout the land. Schools, colleges and universities should
be engaged to contribute. Sundry groups—in neighbourhoods, churches,
workplaces and formal associations—should be pulled into the exercise
and encouraged to initiative. Social media should be mobilised to maximum effect. A constitutional overhaul should be unleashed for all Americans to engage in.

President Eisenhower identified the embryo of America's dysfunction in his prophetic warning about the military-industrial complex and its
"economic, political, even spiritual" influence that was "felt in every city,
every statehouse, every office of the federal government." This is the crisis

that has now befallen American democracy. It is as deep as Eisenhower saw it might be—economic, political, spiritual—and its effects are as wide as he thought they might be, including every city, every statehouse, every federal office. It is in this understanding of the depth of the crisis that it should be confronted and it is in this understanding of the breath of its effects that it should be resolved.

A personal confession: It has been difficult, to put it carefully, to devise a prescription for untying the Washington bind. No less than anyone else do I recognise that "commissions" is not exactly a triumph of bold imagination. But: (1) The knot has to be untied. (2) I challenge anyone to suggest a better way and would be delighted to see it. (3) It happened that my reflection on these matters coincided with the four hundredth anniversary of the King James Bible, one of the greatest intellectual achievements in human history. That achievement was realised by a cumbersome apparatus of royal committees and super-committees. By this procedure the king not only got the Bible he wanted, what he got was also a work of supreme integrity and beauty. The commemoration of that achievement today has forever refuted the prejudice that the combination of "committee" and "genius" is a contradiction in terms.[24]

NOTES

1. THE POWERLESSNESS OF POWERFUL GOVERNMENT

1. First published in German in July 1919 and later in English as *Politics as a Vocation,* ref. Gerth and Mills, *From Max Weber.*

2. *The Politics,* 1253a25 (the Benjamin Jowett translation).

3. Cohen, *Nothing to Fear.*

4. *International Herald Tribune,* 19 February 2009.

5. *International Herald Tribune,* 27 February 2009.

6. In summing up a weeklong "austerity debate" in the comments pages of the *Financial Times* with contributions from some of the world's leading academic and government economists, I concluded that these "are some of the things they find no consensus on: Has recovery taken hold or are we heading for a double dip? If we are in recovery, have economic policies contributed? If economic policies have contributed, is that due to fiscal or monetary policies? Should governments now consolidate or add more stimulus? If more stimulus, what form should that take?" (*Financial Times,* 27 July 2010).

7. *Financial Times,* 12 July 2012.

8. Truman, *Harry S. Truman,* pp. 551–52.

9. Powell, *The New Machiavelli,* p. 29.

10. Lindblom, "The Market as Prison," p. 329.

11. Kissinger, *On China,* p. 13.

12. *International Herald Tribune,* 8 April 2011.

13. Schmitt, *The Crisis of Parliamentary Democracy,* p. 27.

14. Crozier et al., *The Crisis of Democracy,* Introduction note.

15. On democracy prospering, see *The Human Development Report* 2002. It was long a widely prescribed theory that democracy outcompetes autocracy on fairness, but that autocracy prevails on efficiency, certainly in respect to serious problems such as underdevelopment or overpopulation. The experience, however, is that democracy (generally, if not always) outcompetes autocracy on both fairness and efficiency. The evidence is summarized in Dahl, *On Democracy.*

16. The term "dysfunctional" has now become standard in mainstream discussion on democratic government. In a comment on the need for reform in the U.S. Senate, for example, former vice president Walter Mondale describes the Senate as "arguably more dysfunctional that at any time in recent history" (*New York Times,* 4 January 2011). When the governor of New York, Andrew Cuomo, celebrated his own achievements in his first "state of the state" address, on the 7th of January 2012, he congratulated himself for having ended "the dysfunction of state government." In a critical article on California's government, the *Financial Times* awarded the state "the gold medal for dysfunctional democracy" (11 June 2012).

17. Like many generalisations about America, this one is not entirely fair. The press all considered is in a sad state, but also some of the best papers and other outlets anywhere are to be found there.

18. There is also a sociological influence from the great Norwegian sociologist Eilert Sundt and the French sociologist Emile Durkheim. On these links and on "togetherness" and "social anchorage," see my *What Democracy Is For,* chapter 6 and appendix G.

19. Gerth and Mills, *From Max Weber,* p. 55. The technical term is "methodological individualism."

CHAPTER 2. HOW TO DO IT WELL AND BADLY

1. I use the concept of "institutions" in the broad and fuzzy way that is now established in social theory, such as in "institutional economics," to mean, for example: "organised patterns of socially constructed norms and roles, and socially prescribed behaviours expected of occupants of those roles, which are created and re-created over time—any arrangement that co-ordinates the behaviour of

individuals in society" (Goodin, *The Theory of Institutional Design*, p. 55). Institutions are physical, say courts, or moral, say norms.

2. This chapter draws on work that is reported and sourced in more detail in Ringen, *The Economic Consequences of Mr. Brown: How a Strong Government Was Defeated by a Weak System of Governance*, and Ringen et al., *The Korean State and Social Policy: How South Korea Lifted Itself from Poverty and Dictatorship to Affluence and Democracy.*

3. Blair, *A Journey*, p. xvi.

4. Marshall-Andrews, *Off Message*, pp. 9, 56.

5. As can be seen in a collection of his major speeches, in Brown, *Moving Britain Forward.*

6. See also e.g. Jenkins, *Thatcher & Sons.* Mr. Blair himself, on several occasions in his memoirs, positions his own project as a continuation of what Mrs. Thatcher had started but not carried through, for example: "Thatcher had done the right thing in liberating enterprise and industry, but in becoming so obsessed with Euroscepticism, I felt she had indulged the country in a view of itself that was simply no longer compatible with where we needed to be now." (*A Journey*, p. 288).

7. Powell, *The New Machiavelli*, p. 71.

8. See Hills, *Towards a More Equal Society.*

9. For rates of child poverty, see IFS, *Poverty and Inequality in the UK.*

10. As documented in reports by the Parliamentary Ombudsman, the Audit Commission and the National Audit Office, cf. Ringen, *The Economic Consequences*, p. 40. For a case study in the convolution of targeting, see Ringen, *What Democracy Is For*, pp. 88–91.

11. The distribution of income in Britain had changed from moving toward equality to moving toward inequality around 1975. From then on, children as a group benefitted less from economic growth that the population average and rates of child poverty escalated quickly. Cf. Ringen, *Citizens, Families and Reform.*

12. On reign of terror, see Rawnsley, *The End of the Party*, and Darling, *Back from the Brink*, and prior to 2007, Powell, *The New Machiavelli.*

13. The term "control freak" is said to have come into use during Jimmy Carter's presidency. Hamilton, *American Caesars*, pp. 337–38.

14. The seminal work is Amsden, *Asia's Next Giant.*

15. Nye, *The Future of Power*, pp. 212, 218.

16. Park, *The Country, Revolution and I*, p. 177.

17. Blair, *A Journey*, pp. xvi–xvii.

18. Hamilton, *American Caesars,* p. 337. Hamilton here draws on Bourne, *Jimmy Carter.*

19. This is according to Herodotus, *The Histories.*

20. Suetonius, Divus Augustus, 48.

21. Davies, *Europe,* p. 841.

22. Suetonius, Tiberius, 31.

CHAPTER 3. HOW TO USE POWER

1. Hacker and Pierson, *Winner-Take-All Politics,* p. 99.

2. In an interview with Thomas L. Friedman, *International Herald Tribune,* 22 April 2010.

3. Mayne, *The Satisfied Citizen,* pp. 454–55.

4. I am grateful to Joseph Nye for allowing me to use this quote.

5. Actually, the OED's definition is "governing a state," but I reword it slightly.

6. Levi, "Why We Need a New Theory of Government," p. 13.

7. See e.g. Peters and van Nispen, *Public Policy Instruments,* Bemelmans-Videc et al., *Carrots, Sticks and Sermons,* and Salamon, *The Tools of Government.*

8. According to Barber, *Instruction to Deliver,* p. 71.

9. The term "behemoth" I have borrowed from Horowitz, *Behemoth.*

10. Rose, "On the Priorities of Government."

11. Powell, *The New Machiavelli,* p. 17.

12. Weber, *The Theory of Social and Economic Organization,* p. 152.

13. Coleman, *Foundations,* p. 133.

14. Aron, *Peace and War,* p. 47.

15. Nye, *Soft Power.*

16. Hodge, *Collaborators,* pp. 61–62.

17. As argued in Berlin, *Many Thousands Gone.*

18. As confirmed by Boyce in conversation with the author.

19. Fenby, *The General,* p. 241.

20. Chernow, *Washington,* p. 331.

21. Havel's essay was written in 1978 and published in English in a volume under the same title in 1985.

22. According to Barber, *Instruction to Deliver,* p. 72.

23. Montefiore, *Jerusalem,* pp. 244–45.

24. Chernow, *Washington,* pp. 121, 530.

25. See Steinberg, *Bismarck.*

26. Hamilton, *American Caesars,* p. 123.

27. *The Prince,* ch. 4.

28. Suetonius, Divus Julius, 55.

29. Blair, *A Journey,* p. 217.

30. Chernow, *Washington,* ch. 15.

31. *World Development Report 2006,* Foreword.

32. Suetonius, Divus Julius, 74.

33. Hamilton, *American Caesars,* p. 213; Goldman, *The Tragedy of Lyndon Johnson.*

34. Nye, *The Powers to Lead,* p. 19.

CHAPTER 4. HOW TO BE A GOVERNMENT

1. Blair, *A Journey,* p. 304. He was referring to the great English controversy over fox hunting with hounds.

2. Barber, *Instruction to Deliver,* p. 114.

3. Blair, *A Journey,* p. 10.

4. Powell, *The New Machiavelli,* p. 23.

5. Pressman and Wildavsky, *Implementation.*

6. Webster, *The NHS.*

7. Powell, *The New Machiavelli,* p. 184.

8. Fenby, *The General,* p. 564.

9. Terum, *Grenser for sosialpolitisk modernisering.*

10. Perry Link in the *New York Review of Books,* 24 March 2011, p. 22.

CHAPTER 5. HOW TO GIVE ORDERS

1. When I was researching *The Economic Consequences of Mr. Brown* I consulted a range of such Web sites and gradually came to see how infested they were with the culture of spin. Factual information was difficult to get at, hidden away beneath layers of propaganda with very poor signposting, as if added in afterthought by programmers who had more important promotional matters on their minds. Also, it was usually difficult (as generally with that government) to separate actual action from plans, schemes, initiatives, aspirations and other matters of hot air. The exception was the then Department for Children, Schools and Families, which somehow had slipped up and produce an informative Web site.

2. Saich, *Providing Public Goods,* pp. 50, 55, 70.

3. Ziegler, *Edward Heath,* pp. 233–34.

4. Peter Baker, "What Does He Do Now?" *New York Times Magazine* 17 October 2010, p. 42.

5. I am grateful to my then student Dayoon Lee for this example.

6. Norman Rockwell Museum, Stockbridge, Massachusetts.

7. Baker, "What Does He Do Now?" p. 46.

8. Finer, *The History of Government,* p. 383.

9. *Economist,* 30 July 2011.

10. House of Lords Science and Technology Committee, Second Report on Behavioural Change (19 July 2011, www.parliament.uk/hlscience).

11. Suetonius, Divus Julius, 44.

CHAPTER 6. HOW TO GET IT RIGHT

1. Taleb, *The Bed of Procrustes.*

2. Schulz, *Being Wrong,* p. 63.

3. *International Herald Tribune,* 5 July 2010.

4. Rawnsley, *The End of the Party,* p. 144.

5. As conceded by Mr. Blair: "That the plan for the aftermath was inadequate is well documented. . . . The US effort . . . was a mess." (*A Journey,* pp. 441, 448.)

6. Blair, *A Journey,* pp. 441–42.

7. On "moralistic mindsets," see Lionel Barber's review of Bush, *Decision Points,* in the *Financial Times,* 13 November 2010.

8. Gawande, *The Checklist Manifesto.*

9. This example is from a domestic between my wife and myself. We now have another new sofa.

10. Hamilton, *American Caesars,* p. 98.

11. Hamilton, *American Caesars,* pp. 122–23.

12. See Bertelsmann Stiftung: *Sustainable Governance Indicators, 2009 and 2011,* www.sgi-network.org.

13. Chernow, *Washington,* p. 604.

14. Hamilton, *American Caesars,* p. 113.

15. Tuchman, *The March of Folly,* p. 383.

16. Fox and Korris, *Making Better Law.*

17. House of Commons, Committee of Public Accounts, *Managing the Defence Budget and Estate* (14 December 2010, quotes from summary).

18. Powell, *The New Machiavelli,* pp. 58, 62.

19. Marshall-Andrews, *Off Message,* p. 34.

CHAPTER 7. HOW TO MAKE OFFICIALS OBEY

1. Hamilton, *American Caesars,* p. 377.

2. According to Roberts, *Masters and Commanders,* p. xxxvii.

3. www.22julikommisjonen.no.

4. Finer, *The History of Government,* pp. 295–96.

5. Blair, *A Journey,* p. 220.

6. *New York Times,* 5 August 2011.

7. *The Prince,* ch. 12.

8. Hamilton, *American Caesars,* p. 111.

9. Hamilton, *American Caesars,* p. 144.

10. Fenby, *The General,* pp. 378, 380.

11. Suetonius, Divus Julius, 67–69.

12. Blair, *A Journey,* p. 291.

13. Woodward, *Obama's Wars.*

14. Blair, *A Journey,* p. 19.

15. Barber, *Instruction to Deliver,* p. 193.

16. A term as good as this one must have an origin but I have been unable to find it.

17. Marshall-Andrews, *Off Message,* p. 115.

18. Steinberg, *Bismarck,* p. 51.

19. See Hood, "Gaming in Targetworld."

20. Finer, *The History of Government,* p. 491.

CHAPTER 8. HOW TO MAKE CITIZENS OBEY

1. Blair, *A Journey,* p. 97.

2. See e.g. Hall and Rabushka, *The Flat Tax.*

3. As reported in the *Guardian,* 21 June 2003.

4. The Dodd-Frank Act is a monster of 848 incomprehensible pages. The Banking Act of 1933 was 37 pages and created order in American banking until deregulation at the end of the century. The act of 2010 has imposed a massive, costly and near-unmanageable burden of rigid regulations on American banks, for probably little effect in terms of its purpose, and so far stands as an exercise in the futility of regulating big conglomerates as an alternative to breaking them up. See the *Economist,* 18 February 2012.

5. Brennan and Buchanan, *The Reason of Rules,* p. 60.

6. Suetonius, Divus Julius, 78.

7. Powell, *The New Machiavelli,* p. 44.

8. Hart, *The Concept of Law,* pp. 23–24.

9. I here lean on Raz, *Between Authority and Interpretation* and *The Authority of Law,* and Galligan, *Law in Modern Society.*

10. But never majority support. The last free elections in Germany were in November 1932. The NSDAP then got 33.1 per cent of the vote, down from 37.3 per cent in the previous election in July. After the November elections, an attempt to form a government without Hitler failed, and Hitler was appointed chancellor by President Hindenburg in January 1933, in a coalition government with the Conservatives. "New elections were called again. Just before the election the Reichstag building was set afire. The National Socialists declared the Communists responsible and proceeded to arrest leaders of that party as well as some Social Democrats. With the National Socialists in control of the police throughout the Reich and now using the SA as police auxiliaries, the March 1933 election was not exactly a free contest. Even then, however, they fell short of the majority they had long sought (they got 43.9 per cent). In the months that followed, the dictatorship was consolidated, the remaining parties dissolved, and the institutions of the republic dismantled." (Hamilton, *Who Voted for Hitler?* p. 484.)

11. In conversation with Simon Jenkins, as confirmed by Jenkins to the author.

12. According to Kloppenberg, *Reading Obama.*

13. In the "Constitution" and "constitutional system" terminology, I follow Dahl, *How Democratic Is the American Constitution?*

14. The court would in this case refer to *forfatningen,* which would be seen to stand above *grunnloven.* This linguistic distinction, for example in German between *die Verfassung* (constitutional system) and *das Grundgesetz* (basic law), does not exist in English or Latin languages.

15. *Financial Times,* 11 June 2012.

16. Dahl, *On Democracy,* pp. 157–58.

17. *The Economist,* Special Report on the Future of the State, 19 March 2011.

18. See Pierson, *Dismantling the Welfare State?*

19. *Guardian,* 7 March 2011.

20. See Axelrod, *The Evolution of Cooperation.*

21. Another case is that of Italy under Silvio Berlusconi. When he resigned on Saturday the 12th of November 2011, the opposition that had never exercised its duty to oppose disgraced itself further by jeering the outgoing prime minister, however much the jeering was deserved.

22. Irving Kristol in the *Wall Street Journal*, 16 May 1980, quoted in Hacker and Pierson, *Winner-Take-All Politics*, p. 233.

23. Keynes, *General Theory*, last page.

24. Christopher J. Dodd, president of the Motion Picture Association of America, in the *New York Times*, 15 February 2012.

25. Rokkan, "Numerical Democracy and Corporate Pluralism," p. 105.

26. *New York Times*, 3 March 2011.

27. *New York Times*, 13 March 2011.

28. *New York Times*, editorial, 8 May 2011.

29. *New York Times*, 28 October 2011.

30. *New York Times*, 25 March 2011. There is some dispute about whether General Electric's 2010 federal tax liability was "none" or only "small," depending on how its accounts are read (*Economist*, 30 April 2011).

31. These statistics are from Hacker and Pierson, *Winner-Take-All Politics*, pp. 18–27. The best source for similar statistics for Britain is the Institute for Fiscal Studies (IFS).

32. *FT Magazine*, 31 March 2012.

33. This use of "opportunity gap" is from the *New York Times* columnist David Brooks (9 July 2012), summarising ongoing research by the Harvard sociologist Robert Putnam and colleagues which shows that the children of affluent and less affluent parents are raised in ways that are increasingly different, including the time and resources that parents invest in their children and in the activity level of the children themselves.

34. Corak, "Do Poor Children Become Poor Adults?" Even the British school system, with its unusually high degree of social segregation, now produces more upward social mobility than does the American system (OECD: "Education at a Glance 2012," www.oecd.org/edu/eag2012).

35. Joseph Stiglitz, *Financial Times*, 2 June 2012.

36. At a Tea Party meeting in Indianola, Iowa, on the 3rd of September 2011.

37. *Economist*, Special Report on the Future of the State, 19 March 2011.

38. *Financial Times*, 5 October 11.

39. *International Herald Tribune*, 10 November 2010.

40. Marshall-Andrews disputes the three thousand number as containing a good amount of double counting, but also finds that "in thirteen years, the New Labour government passed more criminal justice legislation than became law in the whole of the nineteenth century." (*Off Message*, p. 102.)

41. Dahl, *How Democratic Is the American Constitution?* p. 55.

42. All quotes from King, *The British Constitution.*

43. For a similar and parallel non-constitutional analysis, see Moran, *The British Regulatory State.*

44. Marshall-Andrews, *Off Message,* pp. 75, 78.

45. *Guardian,* 9 February 2011, based on a study by the Bureau of Investigative Journalism.

46. So at least says Congressman Barney Frank who, after thirty years of service, gave this as one of his reasons when he announced his decision to resign from the House earlier than he had intended (on the 28th of November 2011). And Senator Olympia J. Snowe, who announced (on the 28th of February 2012) her decision, after thirty-three years in Congress, to not seek a reelection she would easily have won, citing a lack of comity in the current Congress and an atmosphere of polarization which she saw no prospect of changing over the short term.

47. Dahl, *On Political Equality,* p. 94.

CHAPTER 9. GOOD GOVERNMENT

1. The British government did not have a debt problem, and still does not. In the aftermath of the 2008 crash, it had a growth problem and consequently a revenue problem. The gap between revenues and spending would have to be dealt with, but did not require a rushed and brutal slashing of expenditures. It could have been done more softly while retaining more public spending stimulus into the economy. There was no worry about British government debt in the markets, credit is cheap, and an alternative plan would have created no worry. But the outgoing Labour administration had forfeited authority in the matter, lost the debate they should have won, and were unable to oppose.

2. Gerth and Mills, *From Max Weber,* p. 42.

3. *Financial Times,* 5 October 2011.

4. Hughes, *Rome,* p. 75.

5. Steinberg, *Bismarck,* p. 188.

6. "Une Assemblée de cumulards," according to *Le Monde* (9 June 2012): 83 per cent of the deputies in the French National Assembly have also at least one local post.

7. Marshall-Andrews, *Off Message,* p. 183.

8. Steinberg, *Bismarck,* pp. 174, 184.

9. Fenby, *The General,* p. 5.

10. *New York Times,* 25 August 2011.

11. *New York Times,* 28 October 2011.

12. "How to Repair Democracy in Britain" (31 January 2008), "The Economic Consequences of Mr. Brown" (14 September 2009), and "Whatever Has Become of the Mother of Parliaments" (26 January 2011), all in the Royal Society for the Arts. See also my "Constitutional Authority in British Democracy" and *The Economic Consequences of Mr. Brown.*

13. In *What Democracy Is For,* pp. 227–28.

14. The devil-in-the-detail issue is to determine who would be eligible for a share of the public allotment, including how individual and party-independent candidates would have access to political funds.

15. The critical works in question are *How Democratic Is the American Constitution?* and *On Political Equality.* "For that reason": in conversation with the author.

16. *New York Times,* 13 June 2012. The two books in question are Timothy Noah's *The Great Divergence* and Paul Krugman's *End This Depression Now!*

17. The terminology and logic of "inclusive institutions" is from Acemoglu and Robinson, *Why Nations Fail.*

18. *New York Times,* 26 October 2011.

19. *Financial Times,* Analysis, 5 October 2011.

20. *Financial Times,* 22 November 2011.

21. See Shesol, *Supreme Power.*

22. On the 14th of January 2013, Justice Thomas broke his silence by, apparently, cracking a joke during court proceedings, enough for some words to be recorded in the court transcript. Even his silence, which had lasted since the 22nd of February 2006, had not been absolute. He is known to have exchanged banter with colleagues next to him. His joke on this day was little more and did not amount to any question or contribution of substance to ongoing deliberations.

23. Lessig's more detailed proposal, however, does not have much merit. He suggests a fifty-dollar voucher for each voter, in order for public to outcompete private funding, whereby there would be no need to limit or regulate private funding. But that is a colossal amount of money. (By comparison, the running of Congress costs between five and ten dollars per capita.) Congress needs to have its authority boosted, not undermined further. As long as there is expensive politics, transgression will find its way. A fifty-dollar voucher would represent a noticeable tax rise and put a visible price of discontent on democracy.

24. From the vast celebratory literature on the King James Bible, I recommend Nicolson, *When God Spoke English.*

BIBLIOGRAPHY

Acemoglu, Daron, and James A. Robinson, *Why Nations Fail: The Origins of Power, Prosperity, and Poverty* (New York: Crown 2012).

Ackerman, Bruce, *The Decline and Fall of the American Republic* (Cambridge: Harvard University Press 2010)

Amsden, Alice H., *Asia's Next Giant: South Korea and Late Industrialization* (New York: Oxford University Press 1989).

Aristotle, *The Politics.*

Aron, Raymond, *Peace and War* (New York: Praeger 1967).

Axelrod, Robert, *The Evolution of Cooperation* (New York: Basic 1984).

Barber, Michael, *Instruction to Deliver: Tony Blair, Public Services and the Challenge of Achieving Targets* (London: Politico's 2007).

Barr, Nicholas, *The Economics of the Welfare State* (Oxford: Oxford University Press 1998).

Barzelay, Michael, *The New Public Management: Improving Research and Policy Dialogue* (Berkeley: University of California Press 2001).

Bemelmans-Videc, Marie-Louise, Ray C. Rist, and Evert Vedung, eds., *Carrots, Sticks and Sermons: Policy Instruments and Their Evaluation* (New Brunswick; Transaction 1998).

Berlin, Ira, *Many Thousands Gone: The First Two Centuries of Slavery in North America* (Cambridge: Harvard University Press 1998).

Berlin, Isaiah, *The Crooked Timber of Humanity,* ed. Henry Hardy (London: John Murray 1990).

Berlin, Isaiah, *Liberty* (Oxford: Oxford University Press 2002).

Bessette, Joseph M., *The Mild Voice of Reason: Deliberative Democracy and American National Government* (Chicago: University of Chicago Press 1994).

Bingham, Tom, *The Rule of Law* (London: Allen Lane 2010).

Bird, Graham, ed., *A Companion to Kant* (London: Wiley-Blackwell 2006)

Blair, Tony, *A Journey* (London: Hutchinson 2010).

Blondel, Jean, *Political Leadership: Towards a General Analysis* (London: Sage 1987).

Bojer, Johan, *Den siste viking* (Copenhagen: Gyldendal 1921).

Bok, Derek, *The Trouble with Government* (Cambridge: Harvard University Press 2001).

Bourne, Peter G., *Jimmy Carter: A Comprehensive Biography from Plains to Post-presidency* (New York: Scribner 1997).

Brennan, Geoffrey, and James M. Buchanan, *The Power to Tax* (Cambridge: Cambridge University Press 1980).

Brennan, Geoffrey, and James M. Buchanan, *The Reason of Rules: Constitutional Political Economy* (Cambridge: Cambridge University Press 1985).

Brinkley, Alan, *Franklin Delano Roosevelt* (New York: Oxford University Press 2010).

Brown, Gordon, *Moving Britain Forward: Selected Speeches, 1997–2006,* ed. Wilf Stevenson (London: Bloomsbury 2006).

Bush, George W., *Decision Points* (New York: Virgin 2010).

Butler, David, Andrew Adonis, and Tony Travers, *Failure in British Government: Politics of the Poll Tax* (Oxford: Oxford University Press 1994).

Campbell, John, *Margaret Thatcher: Iron Lady,* vol. 2 (London: Jonathan Cape 2003).

Caro, Robert A., *The Passage of Power: The Years of Lyndon Johnson* (New York: Knopf 2012).

Chernow, Ron, *Washington: A Life* (New York: Penguin 2010)

Cohen, Adam, *Nothing to Fear: FDR's Inner Circle and the Hundred Days that Created Modern America* (New York: Penguin 2009).

Coleman, James S., *Foundations of Social Theory* (Cambridge: Harvard University Press 1990).

Collier, Paul, *The Bottom Billion: Why the Poorest Countries Are Failing and What Can Be Done About It* (Oxford: Oxford University Press 2007).

Corak, Miles, "Do Poor Children Become Poor Adults? Lessons from a Cross Country Comparison of Earnings Mobility,"*Research on Income Inequality* 13, no. 1 (2006), pp. 143–88.

Croissant, Aurel, and Wolfgang Merkel, eds., "Consolidated or Defective Democracy?" in *Democratization* 11, no. 1 (2004), special issue.

Crozier, Michel, Samuel P. Huntington, and Joji Watanuki, *The Crisis of Democracy* (New York: New York University Press 1975).

Cumings, Bruce, *Korea's Place in the Sun: A Modern History* (New York: Norton 1997).

Dahl, Robert H., *On Political Equality* (New Haven: Yale University Press 2006).

Dahl, Robert H., *How Democratic Is the American Constitution?* (New Haven: Yale University Press 2001).

Dahl, Robert H., *On Democracy* (New Haven: Yale University Press 1998).

Darling, Alistair, *Back from the Brink: 1000 Days at Number 11* (London: Atlantic 2011).

Davies, Norman, *Europe: A History* (London: Pimlico 1997)

Diggins, John P., *Ronald Reagan: Fate, Freedom, and the Making of History* (New York: Norton 2007).

Dunn, John, *The Cunning of Unreason* (London: HarperCollins 2000).

Dworkin, Ronald, *Is Democracy Possible Here? Principles for a New Political Debate* (Princeton: Princeton University Press 2006)

Eliasson, Sven, ed., *Building Civil Society and Democracy in the New Europe* (Newcastle: Cambridge Scholars Publishing 2008).

Elster, Jon, *Explaining Social Behaviour: More Nuts and Bolts for the Social Sciences* (Cambridge: Cambridge University Press 2007).

Fenby, Jonathan, *The General: Charles de Gaulle and the France He Saved* (London: Simon & Schuster 2010).

Finer, S. E., *The History of Government,* vols. 1–3 (Oxford: Oxford University Press 1997).

Foner, Eric, *The Fiery Trail: Abraham Lincoln and American Slavery* (New York: Norton 2010).

Fox, Ruth, and Matt Korris, *Making Better Law* (London: Hansard Society 2010).

Fukuyama, Francis, *The Origins of Political Order: From Prehuman Times to the French Revolution* (New York: Farrar, Straus and Giroux 2011).

Galligan, Dennis J., *Law in Modern Society* (Oxford: Oxford University Press 2007).

Gawande, Atul, *The Checklist Manifesto: How to Get Things Right* (New York: Metropolitan 2009).

Gerth, H. H., and C. Wright Mills, *From Max Weber: Essays in Sociology* (New York: Oxford University Press 1946).

Goldman, Eric F., *The Tragedy of Lyndon Johnson* (New York: Knopf 1969).

Goldstein, Gordon M., *Lessons in Disaster: McGeorge Bundy and the Path to the War in Vietnam* (New York: Holt 2008).

Goodin, Robert, *The Theory of Institutional Design* (Cambridge: Cambridge University Press 1996).

Gore, Al, *The Future: Six Drivers of Global Change* (New York: Random House 2013).

Gutman, Amy, and Dennis Thompson, *Why Deliberative Democracy?* (Princeton: Princeton University Press 2004).

Hacker, Jacob, and Paul Pierson, *Winner-Take-All Politics: How Washington Made the Rich Richer and Turned Its Back on the Middle Class* (New York: Simon & Schuster 2010).

Hall, Robert E., and Alvin Rabushka, *The Flat Tax,* 2nd ed. (Stanford: Hoover Institution Press 1995).

Hamilton, Nigel, *American Caesars: Lives of the U.S. Presidents from Franklin D. Roosevelt to George W. Bush* (London: Bodley Head 2010).

Hamilton, Richard, *Who Voted for Hitler?* (Princeton: Princeton University Press 1982).

Hart, H. L. A., *The Concept of Law* (Oxford: Oxford University Press 1961).

Hastings, Max, *Winston's War: Churchill, 1940–1945* (New York: Knopf 2009).

Havel, Václav, et al., *The Power of the Powerless: Citizens Against the State in Central-Eastern Europe,* ed. John Keane (London: Hutchinson 1985).

Held, David, *Models of Democracy* (Palo Alto: Stanford University Press 2006).

Henken, Louis, *How Nations Behave: Law and Foreign Policy* (New York: Columbia University Press 1979).

Herodotus, *The Histories.*

Herzberg, Frederick, "One More Time: How Do You Motivate Employees?" *Harvard Business Review* 46, no. 1 (1968), pp. 53–62.

Hirschman, Albert O., *Exit, Voice, and Loyalty* (Cambridge: Harvard University Press 1970).

Hobbes, *Leviathan.*

Hodge, John, *Collaborators* (London: Faber and Faber 2011).

Hölldobler, Bert, and Edward Q. Wilson, *The Superorganism: The Beauty, Elegance, and Strangeness of Insect Societies* (New York: Norton 2008).

Holms, Stephen, *Passions and Constraint* (Chicago: University of Chicago Press 1995).

Hood, Christopher C., *The Art of the State: Culture, Rhetoric, and Public Management* (Oxford: Oxford University Press 1998).

Hood, Christopher C., "Gaming in Targetworld: The Targets Approach to Managing British Public Services," *Public Administration Review* 66, issue 4 (2006), pp. 515–21.

Hood, Christopher C., *The Tools of Government* (London: Macmillan 1983).

Hood, Christopher C., and Helen Z. Margetts, *The Tools of Government in the Digital Age* (London: Palgrave Macmillan 2007).

Horowitz, Irving L., *Behemoth: Main Currents in the History and Theory of Political Sociology* (New Brunswick: Transaction 1999).

Hughes, Robert, *Rome* (London: Weidenfeld & Nicolson 2011).

Huntington, Samuel P., *Political Order in Changing Societies* (New Haven: Yale University Press 1968).

IFS, *Poverty and Inequality in the UK, 2010* (London: Institute for Fiscal Studies 2010).

Janowitz, Morris, *Social Control of the Welfare State* (New York: Elsevier 1976).

Jenkins, Roy, *Churchill* (London: Macmillan 2001).

Jenkins, Simon, *Thatcher & Sons: A Revolution in Three Acts* (London: Penguin 2006).

Kahneman, Daniel, *Thinking, Fast and Slow* (New York: Farrar, Straus and Giroux 2011).

Keane, John, *The Life and Death of Democracy* (New York: Simon & Schuster 2009).

Keynes, John Maynard, *The General Theory of Employment, Interest and Money* (London: Macmillan 1936).

Kim, Taekyoon, *Controlling the Welfare Mix: A Historical Review of the Changing Contours of State-Voluntary Relations in Korea* (University of Oxford, DPhil dissertation 2007).

King, Anthony, *The British Constitution* (Oxford: Oxford University Press 2007).

Kissinger, Henry, *On China* (New York: Penguin 2011).

Kloppenberg, James T., *Reading Obama: Dreams, Hopes, and the American Political Tradition* (Princeton: Princeton University Press 2010).

Kristol, Irving, *The Neoconservative Perspective,* ed. Gertrude Himmelfarb (New York: Basic 2011).

Krugman, Paul, *End This Depression Now!* (New York: Norton 2012).

Kwon, Huck-ju, *The Welfare State in Korea: The Politics of Legitimation* (London: Macmillan 1999).

Lane, Eric, and Michael Oreskes, *The Genius of America: How the Constitution Saved Our Country and Why It Can Again* (New York: Bloomsbury 2007).

Lee, Jooha, *Welfare Reform in Korea After the Economic Crisis* (University of Oxford, DPhil dissertation 2008).

Lessig, Lawrence, *Republic, Lost: How Money Corrupts Congress—and a Plan to Stop It* (New York: Twelve 2011).

Levi, Margaret, *Consent, Dissent, and Patriotism* (Cambridge: Cambridge University Press 1997).

Levi, Margaret, "Why We Need a New Theory of Government," *Perspectives on Politics* 4 (2006), pp. 5–19.

Levinson, Sanford, *Framed: America's 51 Constitutions and the Crisis of Governance* (New York: Oxford University Press 2012).

Lindblom, Charles E., "The Market as Prison," *The Journal of Politics* 44, issue 2 (1982), pp. 324–36.

Lindblom, Charles E., *Politics and Markets: The World's Political Economic Systems* (New York: Basic 1977).

Lipset, Seymour M., *Political Man* (NewYork: Doubleday 1960).

Lipset, Seymour M., and William Schneider, *The Confidence Gap: Business, Labor, and Government in the Public Mind* (New York: Free Press 1983).

Lipsky, Michael, *Street-Level Bureaucracy: Dilemmas of the Individual in Public Services* (New York: Russell Sage 1980).

Lukes, Steven, *Power: A Radical View* (London: Palgrave Macmillan 2005).

Machiavelli, *The Prince* (Penguin Classics 1961).

Mann, Thomas E., and Norman J. Ornstein, *It's Even Worse Than It Looks: How the American Constitutional System Collided with the New Politics of Extremism* (New York: Basic 2012).

Marshall-Andrews, Bob, *Off Message* (London: Profile 2011).

Mayne, Quinton, *The Satisfied Citizen: Participation, Influence, and Public Perceptions of Democratic Performance* (Princeton University, Department of Politics, PhD dissertation 2010).

Mommsen, Wolfgang J., ed., *The Emergence of the Welfare State in Britain and Germany* (London: Croom Helm 1981).

Montefiore, Simon Sebag, *Jerusalem: The Biography* (London: Weidenfeld & Nicolson 2011).

Moran, Michael, *The British Regulatory State: High Modernism and Hyper-Innovation* (Oxford: Oxford University Press 2003).

Newton, Jim, *Eisenhower: The White House Years* (New York: Doubleday 2011).

Nicolson, Adam, *When God Spoke English: The Making of the King James Bible* (London: Harper Press 2011).

Noah, Timothy, *The Great Divergence: America's Growing Inequality Crisis and What We Can Do About It* (New York: Bloomsbury 2012).

Nye, Joseph S., Jr., *The Future of Power* (New York: Public Affairs 2011).

Nye, Joseph S., Jr., *The Powers to Lead* (New York: Oxford University Press 2008).

Nye, Joseph S., Jr., *Soft Power: The Means to Success in the Modern World* (New York: Public Affairs 2004).

O'Connor, James, *The Fiscal Crisis of the State* (New York: St. Martin's Press 1973).

Offe, Claus, *Contradictions of the Welfare State* (London: Hutchinson 1984).

Okun, Arthur M., *Equality and Efficiency: The Big Tradeoff* (Washington D.C.: Brookings 1975).

O'Neill, Onora, *A Question of Trust* (Cambridge: Cambridge University Press 2002).

Park Chung Hee, *The Country, Revolution and I* (Seoul: Hollym Corporation 1963).

Peters, B. Guy, and Frans K. M. van Nispen, eds., *Public Policy Instruments: Evaluating the Tools of Public Administration* (Cheltenham: Edward Elgar 1998).

Pierson, Paul, *Dismantling the Welfare State? Reagan, Thatcher and the Politics of Retrenchment* (Cambridge: Cambridge University Press 1994).

Pink, David H., *Drive: The Surprising Truth About What Motivates Us* (New York: Riverhead 2009).

Popper, Karl, *The Open Society and Its Enemies,* vols. 1–2 (London: Routledge & Kegan Paul 1945).

Porter, Michael, *Competitive Strategy* (New York: Free Press 1980).

Powell, Jonathan, *The New Machiavelli: How to Wield Power in the Modern World* (London: Bodley Head 2010).

Pressman, Jeffrey L., and Aaron Wildavsky, *Implementation: How Great Expectations in Washington Are Dashed in Oakland; or, Why It's Amazing that Federal Programs Work at All* (Berkeley: University of California Press 1973).

Rawnsley, Andrew, *The End of the Party: The Rise and Fall of New Labour* (London: Viking 2010).

Raz, Joseph, *The Authority of Law* (Oxford: Oxford University Press 1979).

Raz, Joseph, *Between Authority and Interpretation* (Oxford: Oxford University Press 2009).

Reeves, Richard, *President Reagan* (New York: Simon & Schuster 2005).

Rimlinger, Gaston V., *Welfare Policy and Industrialization in Europe, America and Russia* (New York: Wiley 1971).

Ringen, Stein, *Citizens, Families and Reform,* 2nd ed. (New Brunswick: Transaction 2005).

Ringen, Stein, "Constitutional Authority in British Democracy," in *Towards a New Constitutional Settlement,* ed. Chris Bryant (London: The Smith Institute 2007).

Ringen, Stein, *The Economic Consequences of Mr. Brown: How a Strong Government Was Defeated by a Weak System of Governance* (Oxford: The Bardwell Press 2009).

Ringen, Stein, *The Liberal Vision and Other Essays on Democracy and Progress* (Oxford: The Bardwell Press 2007).

Ringen, Stein, *The Possibility of Politics,* 3rd ed. (New Brunswick: Transaction 2006).

Ringen, Stein, "Robert A. Dahl: Defender of Democracy," *Society,* 45, no. 3 (2008).

Ringen, Stein, *What Democracy Is For: On Freedom and Moral Government* (Princeton: Princeton University Press 2007).

Ringen, Stein, Huck-ju Kwon, Ilcheong Yi, Taekyoon Kim, and Jooha Lee, *The Korean State and Social Policy: How South Korea Lifted Itself from Poverty and Dictatorship to Affluence and Democracy* (New York: Oxford University Press 2011).

Rose, Richard, "On the Priorities of Government: A Developmental Analysis of Public Policy," *European Journal of Political Research* 4, no. 3 (1976), pp. 247–89.

Sachs, Jeffrey, *The Price of Civilization: Economics and Ethics After the Fall* (New York: Random House 2011).

Saich, Tony, *Providing Public Goods in Transitional China* (New York: Palgrave Macmillan 2008).

Salamon, Lester M., *The Tools of Government: A Guide to the New Governance* (New York: Oxford University Press 2002).

Schmitt, Carl, *The Crisis of Parliamentary Democracy* (orig. pub. 1923; Cambridge: MIT Press 1988).

Schulz, Kathryn, *Being Wrong: Adventures in the Margin of Error* (London: Portobello 2010).

Schumpeter, Joseph A., *The Theory of Economic Development* (Cambridge: Harvard University Press 1934).

Shesol, Jeff, *Supreme Power: Franklin Roosevelt vs. the Supreme Court* (New York: Norton 2010).

Skocpol, Theda, and Vanessa Williamson, *The Tea Party and the Remaking of Republican Conservatism* (New York: Oxford University Press 2011).

Smith, Hedrick, *Who Stole the American Dream?* (New York: Random House 2012).

Steinberg, Jonathan, *Bismarck: A Life* (New York: Oxford University Press 2011).

Stiglitz, Joseph, *The Price of Inequality: How Today's Divided Society Endangers Our Future* (New York: Norton 2012).

Stone, Deborah, *Policy Paradox: The Art of Political Decision Making* (New York: Norton 2002).

Suetonius, *The Twelve Caesars.*

Taleb, Nassim Nicholas, *The Bed of Procrustes: Philosophical and Practical Aphorisms* (New York: Random House 2010).

Terum, Lars Inge, *Grenser for sosialpolitisk modernisering* (Oslo: Universitetsforlaget 1996).

Thaler, Richard H., and Cass R. Sunstein, *Nudge: Improving Decisions About Health, Wealth, and Happiness* (New Haven: Yale University Press 2008).

Thatcher, Margaret, *The Downing Street Years* (London: HarperCollins 1993).

Tilly, Charles, *Democracy* (Cambridge: Cambridge University Press 2007).

Tocqueville, Alexis de, *Democracy in America* (orig. pub. 1835, 1840).

Truman, Margaret, *Harry S. Truman* (New York: Morrow 1972).

Tuchman, Barbara, *The March of Folly: From Troy to Vietnam* (New York: Ballantine Books 1985).

Tyler, Tom R., *Why People Obey the Law* (New Haven: Yale University Press 1990).

Weber, Max, *Economy and Society: An Outline of Interpretive Sociology,* ed. Guenther Roth and Claus Wittich (Berkeley: University of California Press 1978).

Webster, Charles, *The NHS: A Political History* (Oxford: Oxford University Press 1998).

Wildavsky, Aaron, *Speaking Truth to Power: The Art and Craft of Policy Analysis* (New York: Little, Brown 1979).

Wolin, Sheldon S., *Democracy Incorporated: Managed Democracy and the Specter of Inverted Totalitarianism* (Princeton: Princeton University Press 2008).

Woodward, Bob, *Obama's Wars* (New York: Simon & Schuster 2010).

Wolfe, Alan, *Does American Democracy Still Work?* (New Haven: Yale University Press, 2006)

Yi, Ilcheong, *The Politics of Occupational Welfare in Korea* (Fukuoka: Han-Syoin Press 2007).

Ziegler, Peter, *Edward Heath* (London: Harper Press 2010).

ACKNOWLEDGEMENTS

This book was brought towards completion during a year of research leave from the University of Oxford. I'm grateful to many colleagues there for helpful exchange, in particular Christopher Hood, Dennis Galligan, Laurence Whitehead, and Tim Garton Ash (for a liberating discussion on "dysfunctional" democracy).

During a marvelously productive and hospitable stay at the Ash Center of the Kennedy School at Harvard, I had the benefit of collaborating with Tony Saich, Archon Fung, Quinton Mayne, Jorrit de Jong and the other members of the democracy group. For helpful discussions then and previously, I am most grateful to Joe Nye.

During an equally productive stay at the Wissenschaftszentrum in Berlin, I was welcomed into the friendship and stimulus of another adventurous democracy research group. I am in debt to all its members and affiliates, in particular Wolfgang Merkel, Bernhard Wessels, Sonia Alonso, Andrea Volkens, Andreas Schedler, Thamy Pogrebinschi, Tamar Hermann and Gudrun Mouna. Outside of this group at the WZB, Jutta Allmendinger, Jens Alber, Chiara Saraceno and Gunnar Folke Schuppert were helpful interlocutors, as were Christine Landfried, with whom I share an affiliation with the WZB, Ellen Kennedy, then a fellow of the

American Academy in Berlin, and Kai Wegrich and Stein Kuhnle of the Hertie School of Governance. I have been in exchange on matters that have worked their way into this book for years with Claus Offe, and again during this period in Berlin. Pieter Vanhuysse solved a terminological difficulty for me of which he will be aware.

My colleagues Huck-ju Kwon, Ilcheong Yi, Taekyoon Kim and Jooha Lee in the study of the Korean state that is summarised in Chapter 2 have generously allowed me to make use of our joint work and been greatly supportive in many other ways.

In a home away from home at Lillehammer University College, many colleagues have given generously of time and ideas, in particular Bente Ohnstad, Ole Gunnar Austvik, Noralv Veggeland, Jon Helge Lesjø and Dag Leonardsen.

The Royal Society for the Arts and the Hansard Society, both in London, have enabled me to present ideas in progress in public lectures, for which I am grateful to Matthew Taylor and Fiona Booth, and to discussants on those occasions: Andrew Tyrie MP, Paul Skidmore, Polly Toynbee, Zac Goldsmith MP, Margaret Hodge MP, and George Parker. My publishers, Maura Roessner at Oxford University Press and Peter Hamilton at the Bardwell Press, have generously allowed me to refer at some length to previously published work.

Alan Wolfe read a draft manuscript and offered perceptive comments and suggestions which were greatly helpful, as did an anonymous reader.

At Yale University Press, I am grateful to my editor, Bill Frucht, to Jaya Chatterjee and Phil King, who took the manuscript in hand, and to their other colleagues during the process for their support and excellent collaboration.

Many friends have tolerated long discussions, or pontifications, and given generously of criticism and guidance. Bill Schwarz, during a lively dinner, saved me from a mistake of which he will not be aware. My wife and writing companion, Mary Chamberlain, has, as always, been a constant and marvelous moral and intellectual support.

INDEX

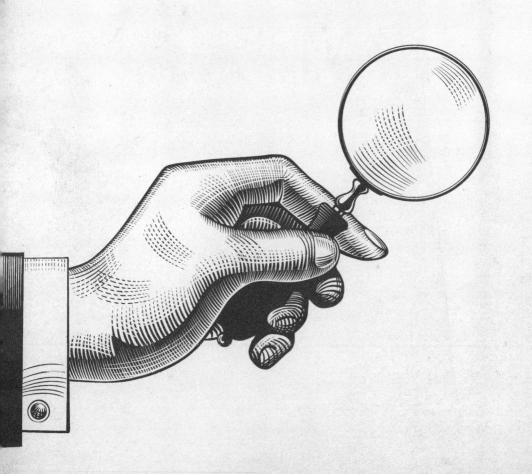

SHERLOCK HOLMES'
BOOK OF
CONUNDRUMS

SHERLOCK HOLMES'
~ BOOK OF ~
CONUNDRUMS

Inspiring | Educating | Creating | Entertaining

Brimming with creative inspiration, how-to projects, and useful information to enrich your everyday life, Quarto Knows is a favorite destination for those pursuing their interests and passions. Visit our site and dig deeper with our books into your area of interest: Quarto Creates, Quarto Cooks, Quarto Homes, Quarto Lives, Quarto Drives, Quarto Explores, Quarto Gifts, or Quarto Kids.

© 2018 Quarto Publishing plc

This edition published in 2018 by Chartwell Books
an imprint of The Quarto Group,
142 West 36th Street, 4th Floor,
New York, NY 10018, USA
T (212) 779-4972 F (212) 779-6058
www.QuartoKnows.com

QUAR.LATP

Conceived, edited, and designed by
Quarto Publishing plc
an imprint of The Quarto Group
The Old Brewery
6 Blundell Street
London N7 9BH

Editor: Kate Burkett
Designer: Hugh Schermuly
Art director: Caroline Guest
Creative director: Moira Clinch
Publisher: Samantha Warrington

Chartwell Books titles are also available at discount for retail, wholesale, promotional, and bulk purchase. For details, contact the Special Sales Manager by email at:
specialsales@quarto.com or by mail at: The Quarto Group, Attn: Special Sales Manager, 401 Second Avenue North, Suite 310, Minneapolis, MN 55401, USA.

10 9 8 7 6 5 4 3 2 1

ISBN: 978-0-7858-3584-4

Printed in China

MIX
Paper from
responsible sources
FSC® C104723

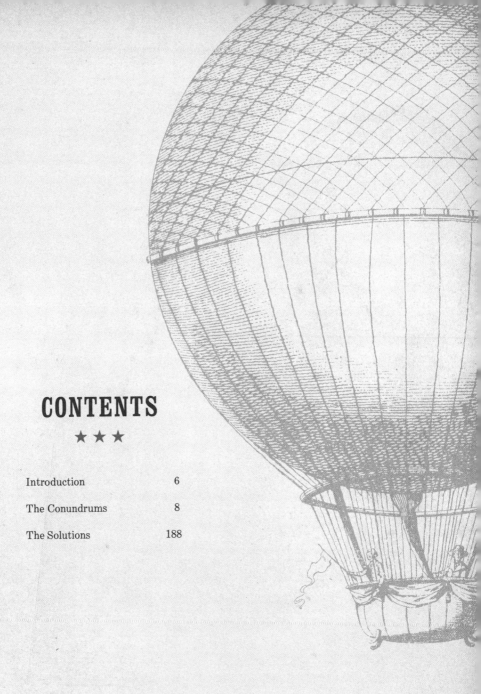

CONTENTS

★ ★ ★

INTRODUCTION

★ ★ ★

Upon being commissioned to write a book of Sherlock Holmes- and Victorian-era-inspired puzzles, my mother presented me with her well-worn copy of the *Complete Sherlock Holmes*. Spending much of the day reading these enjoyable stories, while feeling suitably virtuous as it also counted as work, has been a rare pleasure. As there are 56 short stories and only four novels, the majority of the canon can be read in a single sitting and invariably demonstrate Sherlock's most singular crime-solving prowess, with only the occasional failure.

While the pipe-smoking detective, his sidekick Dr. Watson, and his arch-enemy Moriarty have proved enduringly popular, recent movie and TV adaptations have resulted in even greater interest in Arthur Conan Doyle's creation. It is a fair bet you will be familiar with the Sherlock stories, having purchased this book. However, apart from in one or two rare instances, no actual knowledge of the world of Sherlock Holmes is required to solve the puzzles herein.

There are various categories of puzzle in this book, including memory, problem solving, math, creativity, and lateral thinking. Solutions to all puzzles are given at the back of the book, with the exception of the creativity puzzles, which are all about letting your creative juices flow and being as imaginative as you possibly can. A solution is given for each of the lateral-thinking puzzles, but in each case this is only a suggested answer, and you may well come up with alternative explanations for a given scenario that are also entirely plausible.

The puzzles range from the fairly short and simple teaser that will take just a minute or two to solve, through to more complicated, time-consuming conundrums. Therefore, whether you just have a few minutes to spare or half an hour, there will be a suitable puzzle to tackle. Difficulty gradings are not given with the puzzles; this is so that you can decide how easy or hard you find each teaser yourself without having set expectations.

There is an exception to this rule: there are two particularly tough puzzles that are marked as such. To find the answers to these should you get stuck, or once you have cracked them and wish to check your answers, you must tear open the sealed pages at the back of the book. These two questions test different solving skills: one will require methodically working through a large number of options to find the answer, while the other will require you to unleash your inner code-cracking abilities, as you try to decipher a seemingly random pattern.

There is no right or wrong way to work through the puzzles in this book: you should feel free to solve them in any way you wish, whether that is working systematically from start to finish, picking your favorite puzzle type and solving each of those first, or indeed just opening the book randomly and solving the puzzles you find on that page.

I hope you enjoy the puzzles and that you are inspired to read the Sherlock Holmes stories, if you haven't already done so. Happy solving, and to paraphrase Sherlock's words in *The Sign of Four*, when you have eliminated the impossible, whatever remains, however improbable, must be the answer.

★ ★ ★

OFF THE RAILS

Lateral Thinking

It was a stormy night in November 1888, and Clarence was traveling by train with his son Algernon. Suddenly the train lurched from side to side, being buffeted visibly by the ferocious wind. Moments later, the locomotive derailed, and the impact of the train hitting the ground killed Clarence instantly. Algernon survived, but was rushed to the infirmary in a critically ill state. The surgeon gasped on seeing Algernon and said, *"I cannot operate on this child for he is my son!"* How is this possible?

THE GUNSLINGER

Lateral Thinking

The Unicorn, an old sailing inn just yards from the East India Docks, was particularly busy one misty night, as the locals sought refuge from the elements. Suddenly the doors of the inn flew open. Voices hushed as a man walked up to the counter and demanded a glass of water. Moments later, the innkeeper pulled out a gun and pointed it directly at him. *"Thanks very much,"* said the man, and he promptly turned around and left. Can you explain this unusual sequence of events?

TEA CLIPPERS

Problem Solving

★ ★ ★

The Master at the workhouse decided to give the wretched beggars a break from their physically punishing work with a little mental workout instead. The aim of the game was to deduce the position of 10 Tea Clippers of varying length in the grid, based on the clues provided. Anyone who solved the puzzle in under 10 minutes was allowed an extra pint of beer with their supper. Would you be one of the lucky few who successfully completed the challenge and had the extra beer to sup with their supper?

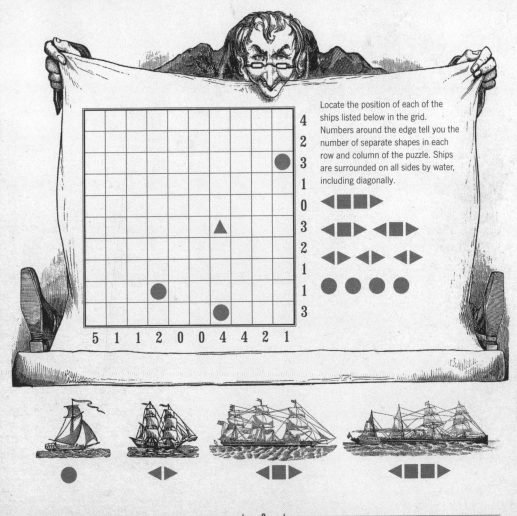

Locate the position of each of the ships listed below in the grid. Numbers around the edge tell you the number of separate shapes in each row and column of the puzzle. Ships are surrounded on all sides by water, including diagonally.

FAMILY ALBUM

Perception Puzzle

★ ★ ★

Study the panel of images below for 15 seconds. Then look at the opposite page. Without looking back at the left-hand page, can you ascertain which two images have been swapped over?

1.

2.

3.

4.

5.

6.

7.

8.

9.

1. 2. 3.

4. 5. 6.

7. 8. 9.

MRS BEETON'S RABBIT PIE

Perception Puzzle

★ ★ ★

Read the recipe below for Mrs Beeton's Rabbit Pie. Study the list for just 30 seconds, and then answer the questions underneath without referring back to the list. You may find it easier to cover the recipe with a piece of paper after reading through it to resist the temptation to cheat!

RECIPE

1 rabbit

a few slices of ham or bacon

salt and white pepper, to taste

2 blades pounded mace

½ tsp grated nutmeg

a few balls of forcemeat

2 hard-boiled eggs

½ pint gravy

puff pastry crust

QUESTIONS

1. How much mace is required?

2. Complete the line "a few slices of..."?

3. What type of crust does the rabbit pie have?

4. How many hard-boiled eggs are needed?

5. Complete the line "a few balls of..."?

IN A PUDDLE

Logic Puzzle

★ ★ ★

Sherlock Holmes had been called to a stately home, where a burglary had been committed the night before. While inspecting the grounds, he came across a puddle very close to the window where the burglar was suspected to have gained entry to the property. As meticulous as ever in his study of all the little details that others thought superfluous to a case, he resolved to measure the area of the puddle.

Sherlock had in his pocket a tape measure and noticed a pile of garden stakes leaning against a nearby outbuilding. How did he calculate the area of the puddle using just these items?

THE BAKER STREET IRREGULARS

Math

★ ★ ★

The Baker Street Irregulars have been helping Sherlock with his investigations, tracking a couple of somewhat shady suspects. Sherlock has given the Irregulars a generous allowance of £1 a day, and today they have decided to spend their sleuthing revenue on a choice selection of sweets.

At the local confectionery store, gobstoppers are 2.5d each, barley sugars are 1.75d each, and a giant bag of sherbet dips is 1.5s.

> *Use the following information to help you:*
>
> 12d = 1s, and 20s = £1, where 1d is 1 old penny and 1s is 1 old shilling.

The Irregulars buy five gobstoppers, 12 barley sugars, and one giant bag of sherbet dips.

QUESTION

How much change is left from the £1 Sherlock gave them once they have purchased the candy?

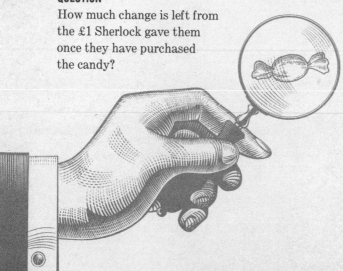

A THREE PIPE PROBLEM
Problem Solving

★ ★ ★

While working on a particularly tricky conundrum, Sherlock reached for one of his Meerschaum pipes to smoke. He had built up quite a collection, many of which were given to him as gifts, and now had a pipe tray containing no less than 17 different pipes. There were five beige, eight brown, and four light brown-colored pipes on the tray. If Holmes takes pipes randomly from the tray, without looking at them, how many pipes must he take to be guaranteed to have selected at least one pipe of each of the three colors?

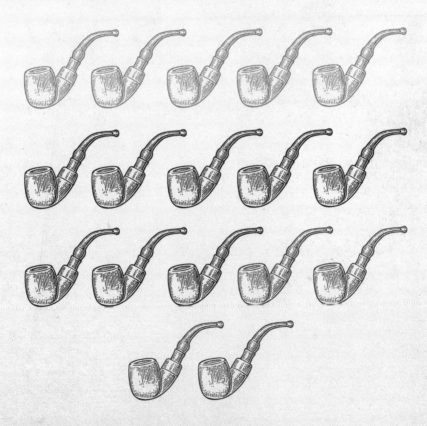

THINK TANK

Problem Solving

★ ★ ★

❝*I overheard this conversation at the tavern yesterday, Holmes, and couldn't for the life of me get to the bottom of it,***"** said Watson.

"A gentleman mentioned to the landlord that he had a rather large tank full of water that weighed 55 pounds. He put something in the tank that is jolly unusual—it actually made it weigh less! But he wouldn't say what it was. For the life of me I can't work it out."

Sherlock immediately smiled to himself and said, *"My dear Watson, the whole truth will be revealed to you if you would only persevere."*

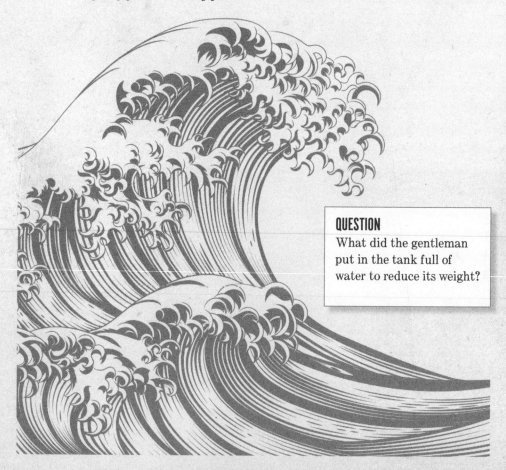

> ## QUESTION
> What did the gentleman put in the tank full of water to reduce its weight?

A PIECE OF THE PUZZLE

Problem Solving

★ ★ ★

"*Often when solving a crime, Watson, you are provided with, or are able to ascertain, the various pieces of the jigsaw and must fit them together. However, at other times you must work out the constituent parts from the whole,*" explained Holmes.

Can you split the blocks below into four shapes that are exactly the same as each other? You may need to rotate the shapes in order to do this.

A LEMON ENTRY

Problem Solving

★ ★ ★

Sherlock and Dr. Watson approached a row of five houses, with brightly colored doors. In no particular order, the five front doors were brown, orange, yellow, blue, and purple in color. From the clues below can you deduce the colors of each door number from 1–5 correctly? Try to solve the puzzle without writing anything down.

If the colors of the doors on houses 3 and 5 are mixed together, you get green.

One of the even-numbered houses has a brown door, and does not neighbor either the yellow-doored or purple-doored house.

THE PSYCHIC DREAMER

Problem Solving

★ ★ ★

Psychic Phyllis was an ever-present draw during the age of Victorian spiritualism. People came from far and wide to hear her predictions, which, it was alleged, were unerringly accurate. She used to compare the personalities of people who came for a reading to different animals. One psychic debunker tenaciously visited the psychic under four different guises throughout the year.

On March 1, the debunker was compared to a fish, while on May 1 the comparison was with a bull. On July 1, she was compared to a crab. What was she compared to on November 1?

KING'S JOURNEY

Problem Solving

★ ★ ★

The members of a London Chess Club loved to play and discuss chess in the local coffee houses. They enjoyed a variety of chess-related puzzles in addition to playing matches, and did so just as competitively as in the modern era, timing how long it took them to solve various teasers. See if you can solve these two chess-related puzzles within 10 minutes each:

A chess king has visited every square on the grid just once, from 1 to 100 (marked in gray). However, only certain squares along the path have been marked in the grid. Your task is to complete the grid, writing the correct number in each blank square, in order to completely log the king's journey from square 1 to 100. The king can move one square at a time in any direction, including diagonally.

	4					28	98	99	
	5		14				100		
1	9		18			94			
10				32		91	92	86	
		20	24		89			83	
						81			72
		35			77	76			
		43		64		69	70		
	40	44	48		63		61	57	56
	39					52			

KNIGHT'S TOUR

Problem Solving

★ ★ ★

Now try tackling this tricky teaser. The idea is the same as the king's journey puzzle, but here the 100 moves from square 1 to square 100 record the movement of a knight, who again visits each square on the grid exactly once. Can you recreate the rest of the knight's tour across the board? On each move, the knight can move two squares horizontally followed by one square vertically, or two squares vertically followed by one square horizontally.

17			52		40	57	36		38
	51	18		56	61				
			70	63		67			22
50			91				81		
	44	73	76						32
72			65	96		88			1
45	14			87		79			24
		48	93			28			83
13			6			99			30
10				100					3

LOOK CLOSELY

Problem Solving

★ ★ ★

Can you solve this tricky puzzle and reveal an item associated with Sherlock Holmes?

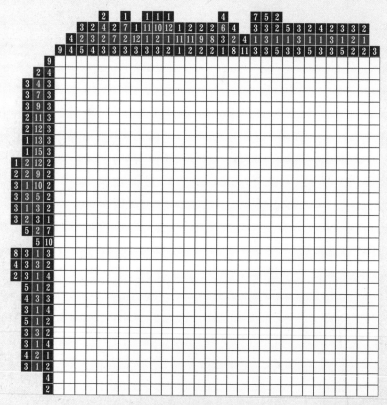

Numbers around the edge of the grid tell you how many squares should be colored-in in each row and column of the grid. There are two colors—blue and brown. A clue at the start of a row or column that reads 2 (blue), 2 (brown) tells you that the region contains zero-or-more blank squares, followed by two blue squares, followed by zero-or-more blank squares, then two brown squares, then any remaining squares up to the end of the region are empty. Note that where the same color appears next to itself in a row/column, there must be a gap of at least one blank square between them. Thus if the clue were 2 (blue), 2 (blue), then there must be at least one blank square between the shaded regions. The puzzle can be solved with logic alone, you do not need to guess.

SAFE HOUSE

Problem Solving

★ ★ ★

"*C*an you open the safe, Watson, and hand me the document inside it please?"
"*Certainly Holmes, but I do rather need the entry code!*"
"*Here's everything you need to know, my dear chap. Now—the document please...*"

Use the clues below to work out the four-digit code that will open the safe, bearing in mind that the four numbers are all different.

1. The first and last digits add up to 10.
2. The second and third digits when multiplied together give an odd number between 30 and 40.
3. The second digit is five greater than the first digit.

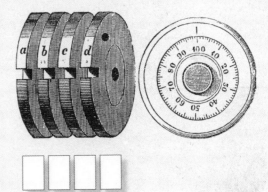

MR. WATSON, COME HERE!

Problem Solving

★ ★ ★

A lexander Graham Bell made the world's first telephone call in 1876 to his assistant, saying, "*Mr. Watson, come here! I want to see you!*" The Watson in question was, of course, different to Sherlock Holmes' Watson. If the telephone call took place 123 days before July 11, on which date did it take place? Try to calculate the answer mentally.

PLAYING THE VIOLIN

Problem Solving

★ ★ ★

Sherlock was playing his violin absent-mindedly while thinking deeply about a case. Watson noted that he was continually playing the notes A, B, C, D, E, F, G, then going back down to A, then back up to G, and so forth. Thus the sequence of notes was A, B, C, D, E, F, G, F, E, D, C, B, A, B, C, D, E, F, G... and so forth up and down.

If Holmes plays 750 notes in total, following this sequence exactly and starting on A, on which note does he finish playing?

FOREVER FAITHFUL

Problem Solving

★ ★ ★

Jones was a friendly, jovial man, and had a large number of female friends. He had also married several women, yet had never once been divorced! However, Jones had never been accused of bigamy, nor was he a bigamist. How is this possible?

BOOBY TRAPS

Problem Solving

One of Sherlock's many adversaries had booby-trapped various rooms in a warehouse Holmes had been using to observe a criminal operation. Can you find all the booby-trapped rooms, shown as individual squares in the grid below? Put a filled circle in each room that contains a booby trap. A room that contains a number cannot also contain a booby trap. A number in a room tells you how many adjacent rooms (include diagonally-touching rooms) contain a booby trap. The puzzle can be solved logically.

1		1		0			1
					3		
		0	2		3		
	0		2		3		1
		0				2	3
		3			1		
	2			2	3		2
	1		3				2
0	2				3	5	
		2			3		

QUICK GETAWAY

Problem Solving

★ ★ ★

Sherlock and Dr. Watson were staking out a crime scene from what appeared to be a large disused building that was something of a labyrinth. However, looking out of the window, Sherlock could see the prime suspect in the case in the distance, and he was walking in the direction of the very same building. They needed to make a quick getaway before they were trapped inside.

Can you find your way out of the building? You are currently located on the second floor of the building (the left-hand of the two floors shown adjacent to each other below), where the letter "X" is in the top row. Can you exit the building at the bottom right of the first floor, labeled "exit?" When you encounter the > symbol you may choose to use a ladder and go down to the first floor in the corresponding position, or simply ignore it and carry straight on, and likewise when you see the < symbol you may choose to go up to the second floor or simply carry on.

MARK THE DATE

Problem Solving

★ ★ ★

Sherlock Holmes was called away on some mysterious business overseas. He left on May 1 and returned to England a full 111 days later. What was the date of his return? Try to work out the answer in your head.

FRUIT STALL

Math

★ ★ ★

At the market the fresh fruit and vegetables were proving particularly popular. The stallholder had a large selection out on display. He had 91 apples and pears on his stall in total. There were 2.5 times as many apples as there were pears. Given this, how many apples and how many pears were on his stall?

IN the BALANCE

Math

At the local candy store, some of the tasty Victorian treats came in pre-prepared bags, all of different weights.

On the weighing scales, one bag of toffees balanced with two bags of bonbons. In turn, one bag of bonbons weighed the same as three bags of pear drops. Two bags of pear drops weighed the same as one bag of humbugs.

QUESTIONS

Given this, can you work out the following:

1. How many bags of pear drops weigh the same as three bags of toffees?
2. How many bags of humbugs weigh the same as four bags of bonbons?
3. If there are two bags of toffees and two bags of bonbons on the left-hand side of the scales, and three bags of humbugs on the right-hand side, how many bags of pear drops must be added to the right-hand side to balance the scales?

CONCEALED ITALIAN

Problem Solving

★ ★ ★

"*S*ometimes there is more to cracking a puzzle than there appears to be on initial inspection, Watson, and the puzzle can have hidden depths that are not immediately apparent," observed Holmes.

"Here's an example. Can you solve this number search puzzle and subsequently tell me the famous Italian hidden within?"

```
6 4 5 5 5 8 6 0 6 , 6 1
8 , 0 1 6 7 6 8 7 5 5 ,
7 5 2 3 , 3 9 1 8 7 , 5
6 6 , 7 4 4 0 9 5 2 8 6
8 0 , 6 6 9 9 7 7 9 8 7
1 6 1 8 6 9 8 6 3 4 0 9
3 8 0 7 9 6 6 7 3 3 9 5
3 9 2 6 6 , 4 3 3 2 6 4
2 1 , 8 7 3 9 9 6 1 7 3
4 , 5 6 8 4 1 3 3 5 6 2
2 6 7 8 6 7 8 , 8 9 8 ,
1 4 7 8 6 3 0 6 1 4 7 4
```

To solve a number search, find each of the numbers in the grid. They may appear horizontally, vertically, or diagonally and in either a forward or backward direction.

68555
96786
109672
123492
147863
363337
403498
687575
689468
768762
986065
999856
2345976
6067486
6768755
6876813
7687686
9767393
80967687
98649180

SHERLOCK SUDOKU

Problem Solving

★ ★ ★

In this puzzle, can you place the eight letters that make up "SHERLOCK" exactly once in each row, column, and 4 x 2 bold-lined box in the grid to solve the puzzle?

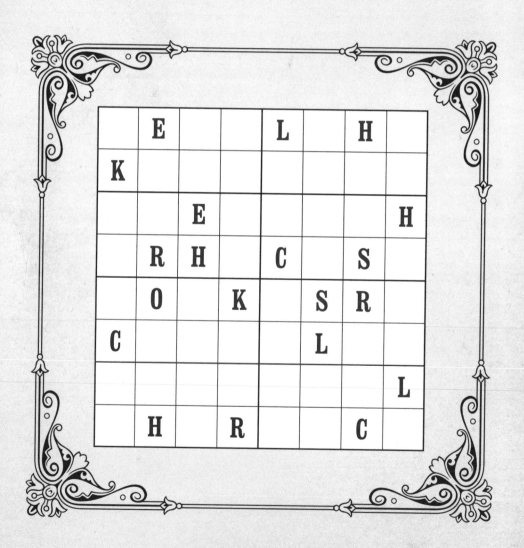

MONEY BOX

Problem Solving

★ ★ ★

Lined up on the table there were four small wooden boxes. *"One of these boxes contains a gold coin, Watson, while the other three are empty. I know which box contains the coin but you don't. Pick a box!"* said Sherlock. Watson duly picked a box, and selected number one. Sherlock proceeded to open box two to show it to be empty, and likewise with box three.

"The question, my dear doctor, is simple: now you know these two boxes are empty, would you like to open box one as you initially chose, or change your mind and open box four instead?"

"Well I should very much like the gold coin, of course," replied Watson, *"but it makes not a jot of difference which box I open as there is a 50/50 chance now that it is in either box, so I shall stick with box one."*

Is Dr. Watson right and it makes no difference whether he changes his mind or not, or is he more likely to get the gold coin by either sticking with box one or changing his mind and opening box four?

"S" FOR SHERLOCK

Math

★ ★ ★

Can you solve this S-shaped number crossword? Numbers in light brown squares indicate the sum total of the white squares in the relevant row/column. You can use the numbers 1–9 only and cannot repeat a number within a run. Therefore if the total 4 is to be made from two white squares, those squares must contain 1 and 3 in some order, not 2 and 2.

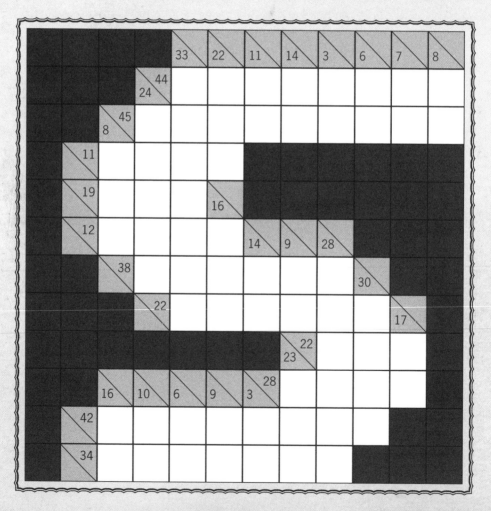

MARBLE-OUS

Problem Solving

★ ★ ★

*"*ometimes, my dear Watson, one must think several steps ahead in one's mind in order to follow a chain of reasoning through to its logical conclusion."

Can you solve this puzzle in your head, mentally logging the steps in order from start to finish? You must guide the marble from the starting square at the top left of the grid through to the finishing square at the bottom right, marked with a dimple. You must imagine tilting the board left, right, up, and down. Each time the marble rolls and hits the edge of the grid or one of the walls (marked with thicker white lines), the marble stops, and the grid must be tilted to make it move again.

Can you reach the dimpled square in a total of 15 rolls?

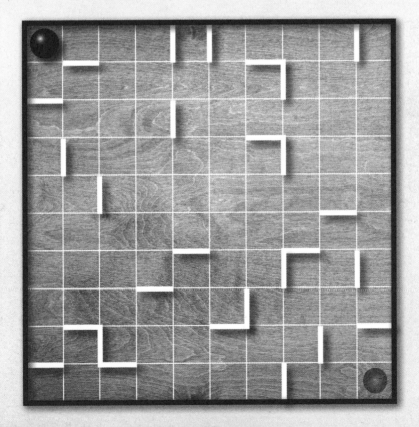

SHERLOCK SEARCH

Problem Solving

★ ★ ★

Can you find all the numbers listed hidden in the grid? They all appear in the shape of the letter "S" for Sherlock, as per the example given. The numbers may run forward or backward within each "S" shape.

2	7	0	7	7	2	7	1	0	2	6	8	0	5	4	0
3	4	8	5	2	3	5	8	0	5	2	6	0	2	5	0
0	6	7	0	3	6	5	4	7	1	9	6	3	1	1	8
2	0	7	6	4	8	0	5	8	1	3	7	2	6	2	3
1	2	2	7	4	8	1	8	3	7	9	1	3	3	9	9
7	1	4	6	8	4	7	1	3	8	0	4	4	9	0	1
4	1	6	1	8	6	2	8	2	5	8	2	1	5	0	7
0	3	7	0	9	4	4	1	1	2	4	1	8	9	2	3
9	6	5	0	5	3	0	9	6	2	8	7	0	5	6	0
5	3	8	5	6	5	5	7	7	0	9	1	4	9	3	2
2	1	3	8	9	9	1	9	1	1	5	4	6	5	9	0
0	8	1	6	3	6	2	9	8	2	3	2	3	1	8	8
9	4	7	1	2	2	7	0	9	7	5	5	2	9	5	6
8	6	8	0	1	5	3	3	6	0	6	2	9	2	9	8
0	0	9	5	1	8	0	2	7	6	1	7	9	5	5	1
2	9	2	9	2	1	7	1	8	6	6	4	0	0	6	

08629632319	31724116775	75524510287	84676846490
22174167569	48105632727	81163991705	86616069823
24124087137	49362981490	81329295000	90359199072
26321530712	68016181385	82587385471	95680959560

HOT-AIR BALLOONS

Problem Solving

Interest in hot-air balloons had really started to take off, and Arthur was at the park to watch a hot-air balloon race, among a crowd containing hundreds of well-dressed Victorian gentlemen and ladies. There were five balloons in the race, each sporting a different symbol. They were a dragon, a shield, a rose, a saltire, and a lion. From the information given below, can you deduce the finishing position from first to fifth place of each of the balloons?

1. The dragon balloon didn't win and the lion balloon didn't finish last.

2. The balloon sporting a rose beat the balloon featuring the saltire.

3. The balloon with the shield wasn't last, but did finish behind the lion balloon.

4. The balloon with the saltire beat the balloon sporting the lion.

GAME, SET, AND MATCH

Lateral Thinking

★ ★ ★

Henry was feeling not a little aggrieved. He had worked up quite a sweat in his lawn tennis match against his French opponent, Cedric. He had played very well too, and had won more points than his opponent. Despite this, Cedric was declared the winner of the match. How is this possible, given Henry was not disqualified?

BOXING HARES

Math

★ ★ ★

A brace of Victorian gentlemen were walking through the fields while indulging in a spot of shooting. Their eyes were drawn toward some hares energetically boxing in the long grass. If there were nine hares, and hares only box in pairs, how many possible boxing matches between different hares were there?

A WEIGHTY PROBLEM

Problem Solving

★ ★ ★

"*T*here are often many ways to solve a problem, Watson, but one should always aim to solve it as efficiently as possible," explained Holmes.

"For instance, a company that makes weights recently encountered a small problem—some of their 1-pound weights actually weighed 1.1 pounds by mistake."

"That's far from ideal," observed Watson.

"Indeed. Imagine this set-up: there are seven piles, each containing nine weights. The weights in six piles all weigh 1 pound, while those in the other pile all weigh 1.1 pounds. Given accurate weighing scales, how many weighings do you need to perform to discover for certain which pile contains the heavier weights?"

"A weighty problem indeed," said Watson wryly, "I'm quite sure I don't know the answer."

Can you help Watson out and provide the answer?

WATCH THE BALL

Problem Solving

★ ★ ★

Aconman operating on a popular London thoroughfare was hiding a ball under one of three cups, then moving them around quickly. The challenge to the passer-by was simple: pay a penny and state correctly where the ball ended up, in order to win tuppence. To illustrate how the game worked, he gave the following run-through before taking a bet, with the ball starting off under the middle cup in the starting position below. Keeping track of the location of the ball in your head alone, where did it end up?

1. Swap the cups in positions A and B.

2. Swap the cups in positions B and A, then those in positions C and A.

3. Swap cups in positions B and C, then those in positions A and C.

4. Before any of the above swaps were performed, cups in starting positions B and C were swapped.

5. The ball actually started under the right-hand cup (position C), not the middle cup (position B).

QUESTION

Where did the ball finish, given this information?

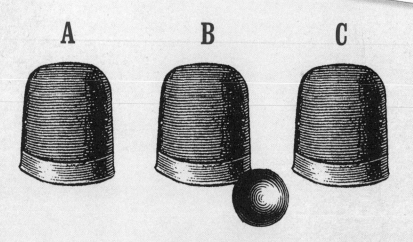

A **B** **C**

RING, RING

Perception

★ ★ ★

Can you mentally rearrange the 11 rings in order from smallest to largest? Once done, you will reveal the name of a character in the Sherlock Holmes stories.

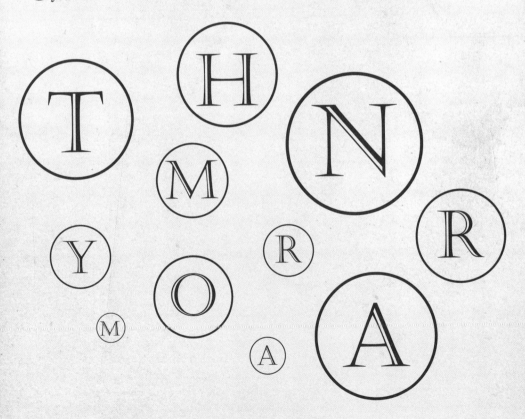

AS EASY AS RIDING A BIKE

Math

★ ★ ★

Albert is learning to ride a penny-farthing, and is a little daunted. For every full revolution of the big wheel, the small wheel rotates fully three times.

The first time Albert attempts to ride the bike, the big wheel goes round 13 times before he falls off. On the second attempt, the little wheel revolves 27 times before he falls off. Progress was being made. On his third attempt, the big wheel revolves 112 times—Albert was jolly pleased he was starting to get used to riding his penny-farthing.

Across the three attempts, how many times did the wheels revolve in total?

THE **MYSTERIOUS NOTE**

Memory

★ ★ ★

In the story *A Scandal in Bohemia*, Holmes receives a note. Read the passage of text below, discussing this note, carefully. Then answer the questions underneath without looking back at the text.

"The man who wrote it was presumably well to do," I [Watson] remarked, endeavoring to imitate my companion's processes. *"Such paper could not be bought under half a crown a packet. It is peculiarly strong and stiff."*

"Peculiar—that is the very word," said Holmes. *"It is not an English paper at all. Hold it up to the light."*

I did so, and saw a large "E" with a small "g," a "P," and a large "G" with a small "t" woven into the texture of the paper.

"What do you make of that?" asked Holmes.

"The name of the maker, no doubt; or his monogram, rather."

"Not at all. The 'G' with the small 't' stands for 'Gesellschaft,' which is the German for 'Company.' It is a customary contraction like our 'Co.' 'P,' of course, stands for 'Papier.' Now for the 'Eg.' Let us glance at our Continental Gazetteer." He took down a heavy brown volume from his shelves. *"Eglow, Eglonitz—here we are, Egria. It is in a German-speaking country—in Bohemia, not far from Carlsbad. 'Remarkable as being the scene of the death of Wallenstein, and for its numerous glass-factories and paper-mills.' Ha, ha, my boy, what do you make of that?"* His eyes sparkled, and he sent up a great blue triumphant cloud from his cigarette.

QUESTIONS

1. Watson said about the paper: "It is peculiarly ___ and ___." Which two words fill the blanks?

2. Which German word did Holmes say the "G" with the small "t" stands for?

3. We are told Egria is in Bohemia, not far from where?

4. What color was the cloud of triumphant smoke from Holmes' cigarette?

SPEEDY EXIT

Problem Solving

Help Holmes exit the maze in as few moves as possible, starting at the top left square and exiting at the bottom right square. You may move to another square in the same row or column that is either of the same color or contains the same object as the square you are currently on.

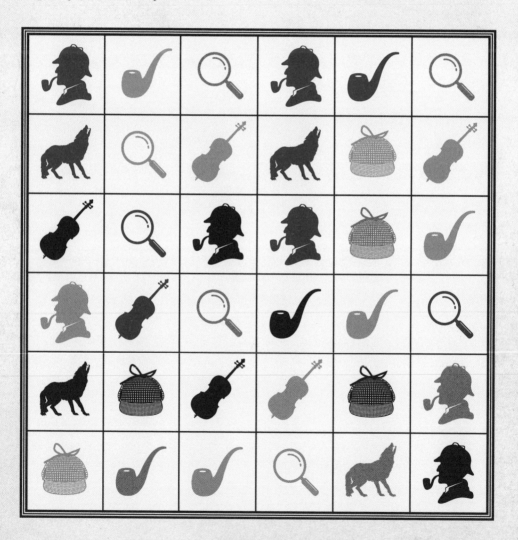

THE **RED-HEADED GANG**

Problem Solving

★ ★ ★

Sherlock Holmes had been investigating a gang of men who all had red hair, but he was uncertain how many members there were in the gang, and was therefore trying to ascertain the correct figure. An informant told him that there were an odd number of members, and that they could all fit around a rectangular table which was 6.5 feet wide and 8.2 feet long. If the men sat around the table in such a way that each man occupied between 3 feet and 2.5 feet, how many men were in the red-headed gang?

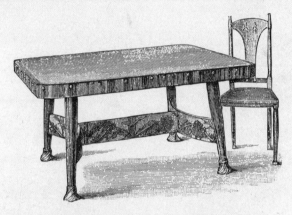

AT THE WORKHOUSE

Math

★ ★ ★

At a Victorian workhouse, a scheme was trialed whereby the destitute of the parish were split into three groups, depending on how much they were in favor with the Masters. Those in the most-favored group were allowed one day off their hard work every eight days, the second group were allowed a day off every 10 days, and the third group were allowed a day off only every 15 days.

How frequently did all three groups have a day off at the same time?

CAUGHT on CAMERA

Perception

★ ★ ★

Alice was one of the first Victorian photographers, and took a picture of her friends. She took another one a few moments later. Can you spot the six differences between the two pictures?

NINE SQUARED

Problem Solving

★ ★ ★

*"*S*ometimes the obvious answer to a case is the correct answer, Watson, while at other times there is more to it than first meets the eye. For instance, how many squares do you see in the grid below?"*

"Why, there are 81 squares, quite as truly as 9 x 9 = 81," Watson replied.

"Ah—but look again—there are many squares of all different sizes, including the one large square that contains all the others. So I ask again—how many squares are there below?"

QUESTION

Can you count up all the squares in the grid and find the answer to Sherlock's teaser?

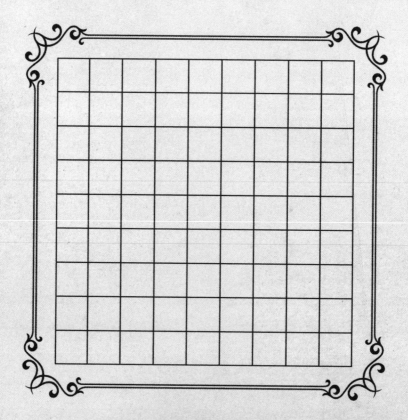

DAYLIGHT ROBBERY

Lateral Thinking

★ ★ ★

Two men were fleeing from a robbery, where they had stolen an extremely expensive gold ring from one of London's finest Victorian jewelry stores. The police were hot on their tails, and saw them run into a small outbuilding. The officers watched the building carefully, but the men did not emerge. A short while later, they decided to enter the outbuilding and catch the men red-handed, rather than apprehending them when they left the building.

However, on entering the building, the two men were there, but the gold ring was nowhere to be seen. They searched thoroughly and were confident no one had entered or exited the building, but it seemed the gold had disappeared into thin air. The room was full of all sorts of paraphernalia, including what appeared to be many books, tables, food and drink, chairs, games, several items of clothing such as gloves and hoods, and several maps on the wall. But no matter how hard they looked, the gold ring was nowhere to be seen. What had happened?

TRIPLETS

Lateral Thinking

★ ★ ★

Clara, Bessie, and Margaret were the best of friends, and had been since their birth in the workhouse. All three girls were born within a few minutes of each other to the same mother, and they even looked identical. What's more remarkable is that, despite all appearances to the contrary, they were not actually triplets. How can that be possible?

THE SCENE OF THE CRIME

Creativity

★ ★ ★

The police detectives arrived at the scene of a reported crime to be confronted with the following: a man lying dead on the floor, with a pool of strangely colored liquid next to him. What could have caused him to meet his maker in this fashion? Let your creativity flow and come up with five possible scenarios for what had happened before the police detectives arrived at the scene.

HOLMES SUDOKU

Problem Solving

★ ★ ★

In this puzzle, can you place the six letters that make up "HOLMES" exactly once in each row, column, and 3 x 2 bold-lined box in the grid to solve the puzzle?

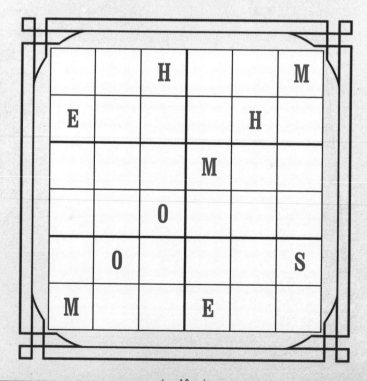

COUNT TO 25

Math

★ ★ ★

The children at a Victorian school had been using their abacuses to help them with their sums. Can you use your mathematical skills to complete the number diamond below?

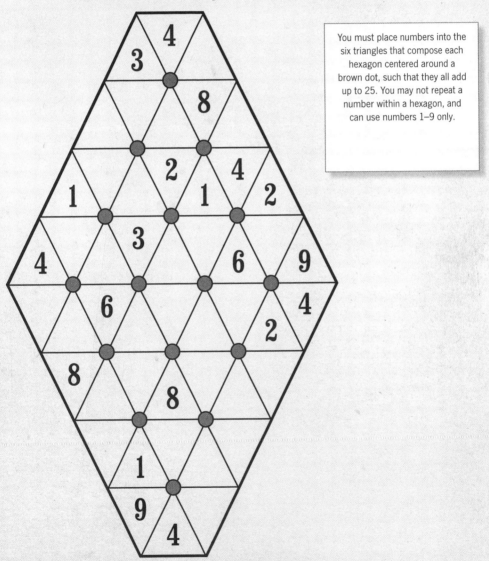

You must place numbers into the six triangles that compose each hexagon centered around a brown dot, such that they all add up to 25. You may not repeat a number within a hexagon, and can use numbers 1–9 only.

ILLUMINATION IN THE DARKNESS

Lateral Thinking

★ ★ ★

Lord Smith was avidly reading a gripping and illuminating novel after dark, from the comfort of his study. Reading once the sun had set was no problem now that many houses had been fitted with gas lights. Suddenly, however, the gas light in Lord Smith's room failed, plunging it into darkness. Lord Smith was perfectly aware of this, but strangely was able to continue reading without issue, despite the light level being negligible. How was this possible given he did not light a candle or rely on any other form of illumination?

THREE PIPE-BOX PROBLEM

Problem Solving

★ ★ ★

Dr. Watson wanted a new pipe, so headed to the tobacconist's store with Sherlock Holmes. Inside there was something of a kerfuffle, as the tobacconist threw his arms in the air in exasperation and exclaimed, *"I've no idea how it's happened, but all my pipe boxes are labeled incorrectly!"* He sold two types of pipe: clay pipes and briar pipes.

There were three boxes on the shelf he pointed to, labeled "Clay Pipes," "Briar Pipes," and "Clay and Briar Pipes."

"Not to worry," said Watson, *"we'll take out all the pipes from all the boxes and place them in the correct boxes for you, one by one."*

"That will be quite unnecessary, Watson," said Holmes. *"I can simply take one pipe from one box and we can then relabel the three boxes quite correctly."* Can you work out how?

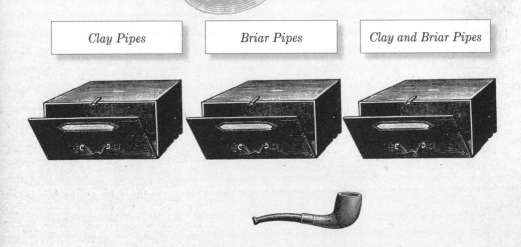

THE HAPPY ROBBER

Lateral Thinking

★ ★ ★

Abank robber, acting alone, was intent on getting as rich as he possibly could. He entered a bank fully intending to commit robbery. However, he left a short while later with no money on his person whatsoever. Despite this, he was quite happy. Why?

A FRUITFUL PLANT

Lateral Thinking

★ ★ ★

Allotments were introduced by the Victorians, and John, a factory worker, seemed to have particularly productive strawberry plants. The rest of the allotment holders were envious, as these plants bore great fruit. If he had nine plants, and each yielded 11 fruits per day, how many raspberries did the plants bear over the course of 27 days?

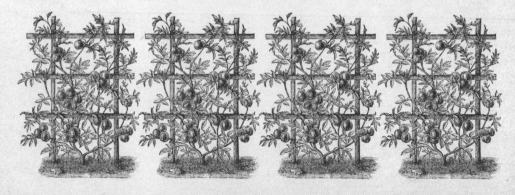

SUBTRACTION

Lateral Thinking

★ ★ ★

Children wrote on slates with chalk in the Victorian classroom, but for this teaser from a Victorian math teacher, they had to solve the puzzle in their head without writing anything down. Can you do the same? The question is: how many times can you subtract seven from 197?

GOING FOR GOLD

Lateral Thinking

★ ★ ★

Archibald was a particularly good athlete, and was competing in an athletics contest along with several other sporting young gentlemen. He won the high jump and also the long jump. He won the events fair-and-square and was not disqualified. Despite this, he didn't win any gold medals. Why was this?

ELEMENTARY, MY DEAR WATSON

Problem Solving

Sherlock left Dr. Watson the following note. Can you crack the code to find out the name of the person Sherlock is following?

My Dear Watson,

I'm hot on the heels of a suspect—should you not hear from me for a few hours, please let the police know his name, which I've written in the most elementary fashion below:

74, 1, 53, 52, 67, 92, 34

Yours,

Sherlock

OPERATING TABLE

Lateral Thinking

A brave man is on the Victorian operating table, and there is no anesthetic to numb the pain. He had been in a fistfight that had quickly escalated and led to him subsequently being shot several times. The surgeon removed a bullet from the man's leg, yet he did not cry or show any signs of pain, despite being conscious. How is this possible?

INVENTION TEST

Problem Solving

★ ★ ★

The grid below contains four Victorian inventions: the sewing machine, the penny-farthing, the light bulb, and the gramophone.

Can you divide the grid into groups of four, with each group containing one of each of the different inventions?

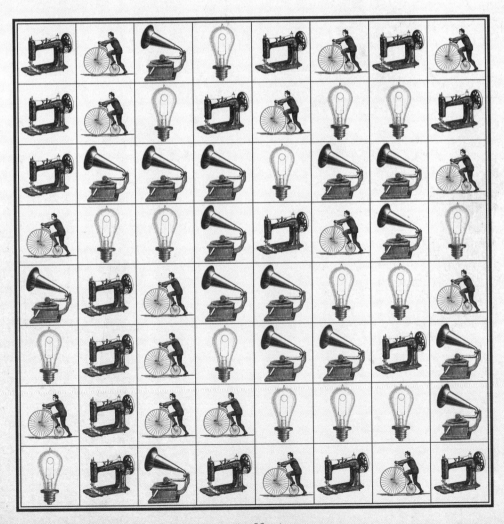

"WEIGHT" AND SEE

Problem Solving

★ ★ ★

Lestrade had rounded up three possible suspects for a crime, and hauled them into the police station. The first suspect weighed 154 pounds while the second weighed 162 pounds. The average weight of the three suspects was 155 pounds.

Sherlock arrived at the police station and pronounced, *"Based on the depth of the footprints in the mud at the scene of the crime, the person who committed this crime weighed no more than 150 pounds."*

Could the criminal be one of the three men Lestrade suspected?

QUEEN OF HEARTS

Math

★ ★ ★

A few Victorian gentlemen were smoking their pipes and idly playing some card games, while waiting for the fourth member of their bridge team to arrive. Evidently his hansom was delayed en route.

One of the gentlemen posed this teaser—can you answer it?

"I take a card at random from a standard deck of 52 cards, and place it face down on the table. I then do the same again. Now, on turning them over, I see that the first card I picked is the Ace of Hearts and the second is the Queen of Hearts. What is the chance of me taking these two cards from the pack in this order?"

PILE OF PIPES

Problem Solving

★ ★ ★

Apile of Sherlock's pipes are lying in a stack. Can you work out which of the pipes is at the bottom of the pile?

THE DAY OF TRUTH

Problem Solving

Victorian morality may be well known, but Algernon is a born liar, and every word that comes out of his mouth is a fib. Apart from on Fridays, when he reconciles himself to telling the truth for just one day. His wife Beatrice is much better, and tells the truth for a full five days of the week, only lapsing into nothing but lies on Thursdays and Fridays.

If you were to ask Beatrice, *"What day is it today?"* and she were to reply, *"Friday,"* then what day is it?

If you were to ask Beatrice, *"What day is it today?"* and she were to reply, *"Saturday,"* and then you put the same question to Algernon and he said, *"It is indeed Saturday,"* then what day is it?

A GROWING PROBLEM

Math

There was unprecedented population growth in Britain during the Victorian era. The population was 13.9 million in 1831, while by 1901 it had risen dramatically to 32.5 million. What was the percentage increase in the population during this period, to the nearest one percent?

NAME TRACKING

Problem Solving

★ ★ ★

Sherlock requested the services of an expert tracker to help solve a crime. By looking at the differences in the two grids below carefully, can you deduce the name of that expert tracker?

83	20	27	50	45	48	9	46	60	97	28	40	30
76	21	58	67	39	61	89	1	24	10	70	6	49
22	56	22	37	72	50	48	58	99	58	62	93	46
68	17	42	69	49	4	69	9	17	78	93	89	78
97	27	92	97	48	43	94	22	54	6	76	9	41
1	20	29	99	7	23	30	36	90	91	22	57	54
40	67	85	33	85	69	26	31	70	83	10	10	94
92	41	76	9	11	74	98	62	63	56	83	70	2
2	30	94	62	19	2	2	97	32	95	48	68	44
50	93	44	96	68	55	57	21	86	4	4	17	4
49	6	23	22	91	66	55	69	88	21	88	45	53
8	5	61	64	26	65	73	33	76	46	15	25	37
84	10	74	98	55	38	64	86	13	14	34	15	64

4	26	63	63	84	48	66	40	22	16	86	40	30
76	21	95	67	39	61	77	1	24	10	54	6	49
22	56	79	37	72	50	8	58	99	58	95	93	46
68	17	81	69	49	4	27	9	17	78	10	89	78
97	27	41	97	48	43	18	63	19	34	38	9	41
1	20	29	99	7	23	30	36	90	91	22	57	54
96	73	4	21	40	69	65	31	70	83	25	10	94
50	41	76	9	98	74	55	62	63	56	30	70	2
76	30	94	62	70	2	77	61	32	8	96	68	44
73	93	85	6	68	55	57	9	1	87	4	17	4
79	6	23	22	32	66	55	69	95	21	88	45	53
9	5	61	64	87	65	73	33	74	46	15	25	37
25	29	45	44	74	38	64	86	19	14	34	15	64

ROMAN LESSON

Math

★ ★ ★

The pupils at a Victorian school were learning about Ancient Rome and Roman numerals. The teacher set a math puzzle to familiarize the children with Roman numerals. Can you complete the puzzle? Enter the Roman numerals for the numbers 1–9 once into the grid (I through to IX) in order to complete the sums (shown in the brown squares around the edge of the grid). Perform the math sums from left-to-right across the rows and top-to-bottom down the columns rather than in strict mathematical order. One number (III, the Roman numeral for 3) has been placed to start you off.

	×		−	**XLIV**
+		×		÷
	+		−	**XI**
×		+		÷
	+	**III**	÷	**VI**
XCIX		**LIX**		**II**

THE KEY CLUE

Problem Solving

★ ★ ★

The Baker Street Irregulars had handed Sherlock an unusually jagged key that a burglary suspect they were following had inadvertently dropped from his coat pocket. Does the key match any of those of the houses that the ne'er-do-well was suspected of burgling, and so provide incriminating evidence?

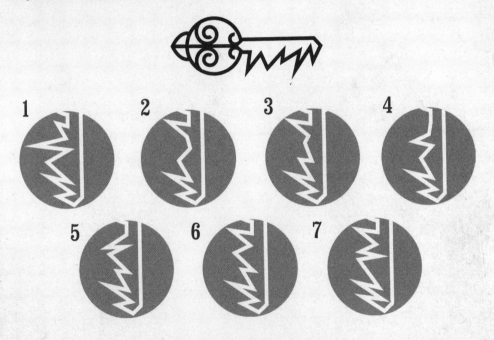

WHAT'S THE SCORE?

Lateral Thinking

★ ★ ★

If Mycroft is 28, Sherlock is 32, and Watson is 24, what is Moriarty?

DEERSTALKER

Math

★ ★ ★

A very singular deerstalker, wearing of course a deerstalker hat, had a sporting sense of fairness—if he missed a deer with his first shot, he took no further shot at it and allowed it to escape. If the deerstalker had a 25 percent success rate, with one in four of his shots hitting its intended target, what is the chance that he fired five shots and four hit their cervine targets?

SHORT-CHANGED

Problem Solving

Three shorter-than-average criminals (5 ft. 1 in., 5 ft. 2 in., 5 ft. 3 in. respectively) had been conning people out of money in a cunning Victorian street game, with one acting as a shill for a game run by the other two where the odds were bent heavily in their favor. Can you work out the height and age of each of the three criminals from the clues below? The ages are 30, 37, and 44. Try to write the solution directly into the grid below without making any notes before doing so.

The youngest of the three criminals was not the shortest nor the tallest. Lester was not the tallest nor the oldest. Harvey was not the oldest nor the youngest nor the tallest.

Name	Height	Age
Harvey		
Russell		
Lester		

NAPOLEON'S STORMY PETREL

Problem Solving

In the Sherlock Holmes stories, Napoleon is to Moriarty as a stormy petrel is to who?

A KEY PROBLEM

Problem Solving

★ ★ ★

Twelve keys are lying stacked in a pile. The key at the bottom of the pile opens a strongbox containing some important documents relating to a police case—which key should the police use to open the strongbox?

THE FIVE ORANGE PIPS

Math

★ ★ ★

Five orange pips were arranged in the shape of an "X" in nine miniature boxes, as shown below:

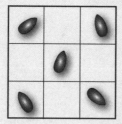

How many ways are there of placing five pips into the nine boxes, if all five pips must always be placed in a box and each pip must occupy its own box?

THE DETECTIVE'S DESK

Problem Solving

★ ★ ★

Look at the two pictures of Sherlock's desk below. Can you find the nine differences between the two images?

THUMBPRINT

Problem Solving

★ ★ ★

Sherlock has been examining some thumbprints (shown in light brown below and labeled A–E) to see if they match that of a known criminal (shown in dark brown below). Can you reveal the identity of the criminal?

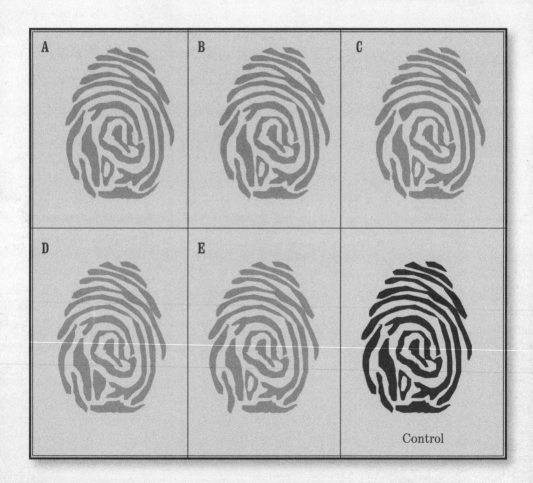

Control

SIGNIFICANT DATES

Problem Solving

★ ★ ★

Find the 16 numbers listed to the right of the puzzle in the grid of numbers. The answers may be found by moving continuously from square to adjacent square horizontally or vertically one square at a time; no square is visited more than once per answer. Once you have found all 16 answers, you will find 12 particularly busy squares. Reading from left-to-right and top-to-bottom, three important dates will be revealed to you in these squares. What are they, and what is their significance?

1	3	5	0	2	4	9	2	8	8
6	2	4	4	5	6	8	0	4	2
2	8	0	2	1	9	1	3	8	4
5	9	6	3	3	4	7	7	1	5
0	7	2	7	7	2	4	2	8	3
2	1	7	4	8	1	1	5	2	5
2	8	9	0	2	3	9	3	4	8
2	7	3	2	0	3	8	2	5	0
8	6	1	8	0	9	1	1	7	2
0	5	7	0	9	7	6	7	8	9

022890
11935
135428
16259
17738
2451835
24680
276175
3342427
48209
79328
81678920
88481
91125
913772
98191

MEMORY GRID

Memory

★ ★ ★

Study the grid below carefully for 30 seconds. Then, without looking back at the grid, answer the three questions underneath.

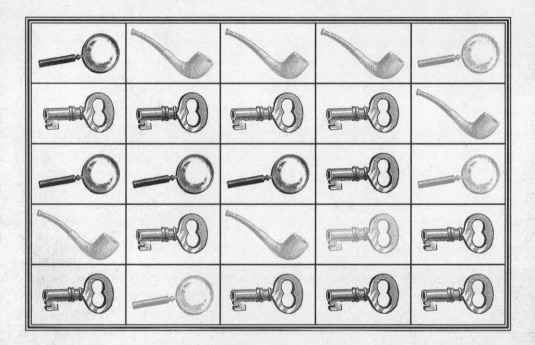

QUESTIONS

1. Which object features the most: key, pipe, or magnifying glass?
2. Which color features the most: brown, dark blue, or light blue?
3. Which object features exactly seven times?

EXHIBITION ART

Math

★ ★ ★

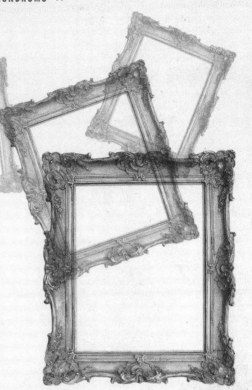

A pair of artists were commissioned to create a series of pictures all themed around the Great Exhibition of 1851, and created art continuously for the duration of the exhibition. One artist specialized in creating watercolors, the other in oil paintings.

In total they created 92 paintings, and there were 24 more watercolors made than oil paintings. How many paintings of each of the two types did the artists create?

MYSTERIOUS GENTLEMAN

Laterel Thinking

★ ★ ★

A mysterious Victorian gentleman was standing on a street corner, offering a curious proposition: he was offering people a £1 note for a shilling, which on the face of it seemed too good to be true. It didn't seem possible for the man to be able to do anything but lose money through this most singular venture. Yet the man was a millionaire. How is this possible?

SAFE SPACE 1

Problem Solving

★ ★ ★

"*Being able to visualize problems, and hence work through a series of steps quickly in your head, is an important problem-solving skill, Watson,*" said Holmes.

Can you study the grid below and find the single safe square as quickly as you can?

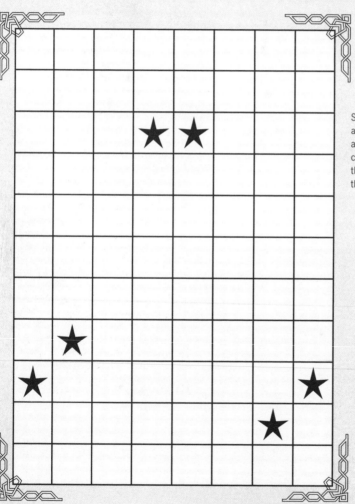

Squares that contain stars are attack squares, and threaten any square in the same row, column, or diagonals as themselves. Try to solve the puzzle mentally.

SAFE SPACE 2

Problem Solving

★ ★ ★

The rules are the same as in Safe Space 1, with one exception: squares that contain circles are also attack squares, but only threaten squares in the same row and column as themselves. Solve the puzzle mentally in order to find the single safe square.

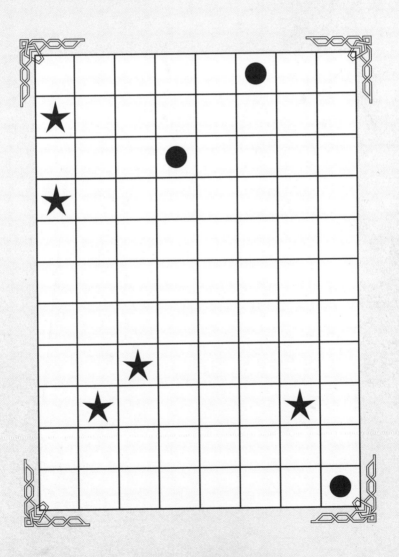

VALUABLE NAMES

Lateral Thinking

★ ★ ★

If SHERLOCK scores 150 points; HOLMES scores 1,050 points; and LESTRADE scores 550 points, then how many points is MORIARTY worth?

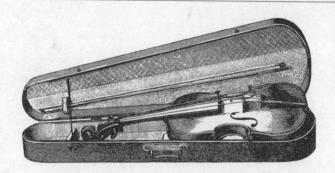

MUSICAL MURDERS

Lateral Thinking

★ ★ ★

Sherlock was investigating a most gruesome case, in which it was suspected that a former violin maestro had gone crazy and was going around killing members of the orchestra he used to belong to, seemingly at random. Sherlock wanted to find a pattern in the killings to anticipate who would be targeted next and ensure a trap could be laid for the madman.

So far, three murders had been committed, all at the homes of the victims, and in each case a maid had reported hearing a violin playing which aroused their suspicion; however, the murderer had always fled by the time they entered the room where the murder had taken place. The three murdered orchestra members were called Ada, Gabe, and Fae. Which one of the following three orchestra members is in danger of being next on the hit list: Eula, Gale, or Bea?

MOURNING

Math

★ ★ ★

Queen Victoria wore only black for the whole of her reign after the death of her husband, Prince Albert, who died on December 14, 1861. Queen Victoria died on January 22, 1901. How many days apart are these two dates? The first leap year in the period was 1864; the year 1900 was not a leap year.

THE GREAT ELM

Math

★ ★ ★

Born into a rich family, the math tutor of a Victorian boy had taken to walking the child around the family estate and asking him to calculate the height of all the trees.

Today the boy was tasked with measuring the height of a great elm tree, the most famous tree on the whole estate. The boy flew his kite at an angle of exactly 60 degrees with the ground. The kite had a string length of exactly 120 feet, and the end of the string reached precisely to the top of the tree whilst the kite was at the 60-degree angle to the ground. Given this, how tall was the great elm?

A HANSOM CHAP

Problem Solving

★ ★ ★

Ahansom cab driver is known to have acted as getaway driver for an acquaintance of Moriarty. Which of these seven men, labeled A–G, is the driver? They are standing in height order, with A the shortest and G the tallest. Solve the puzzle mentally.

The driver is not positioned two men away from the man in the middle. The men two away from the man in the middle are not standing two away from the driver. The driver has men standing either side of him, with more people to his right than his left.

TOUR OF EUROPE

Lateral Thinking

★ ★ ★

Awealthy Victorian gentleman was traveling around Europe in order to broaden his cultural horizons. When he went to Scotland, he wore a blue shirt and white trouser pants. In Denmark, he kept the pants, but decided to wear a red shirt. In Greece he reverted to the outfit he wore in Scotland. Which two colors did he wear during the final part of his trip to Sweden?

MISSING LINKS...

Problem Solving

★ ★ ★

In this simple puzzle, shade squares in the grid to reveal an object invented during the Victorian era. Squares containing 1 may be shaded in straight away. All other numbered squares come in pairs and mark the end points of a group of shaded squares of the stated number. You must link them together by shading in the appropriate number of squares (e.g. if linking a pair of 5s, shade the two squares and three others in between the pair to make a set of five continuous shaded squares in total). Paths move horizontally and vertically only, and each square in the grid may only be part of one path.

...MISSING NEIGHBORS

Problem Solving

★ ★ ★

In this harder puzzle, shade squares in the grid to reveal another object invented during the Victorian era. Numbers in squares tell you how many neighboring squares (those that are adjacent and diagonally touching, and additionally the square containing the number itself) are to be shaded in. So a "0" in a square means that the square containing the "0" and all neighboring squares, including diagonally-touching squares, are to be left blank, whilst a "9" would mean the opposite: that the square itself and all eight numbers should be shaded in. Solve the puzzle logically.

1					3	3			
	5		3			3	5	3	
		6	4	3	3	3		5	
6	5				3	3	5	6	
		4	3		3		6		
3	5	4	0	0		0	2	5	
		4	2				2	4	1
	3		3			4	3		
0	3	3			6	6			
0		3			3		5	3	3
			5		6	3			
			2		3		2	3	
0		3		6	7			3	
			3			3			
0	3		3		4	6		3	
						3	3		0
	3		3		6				
			3		2	5			
		3	3		7	5	3	3	0
0				4		4	2		
0	3			3		5		3	0
	3		0		5				
	4	4		3	5	8	0	4	4
3	6	6			5		8	3	5
			3						3

PERCEPTION DETECTION

Problem Solving

★ ★ ★

Put your detective skills to the test with this pattern recognition test—how quickly can you track down the single occurrence of this pattern in the colorful mosaic?

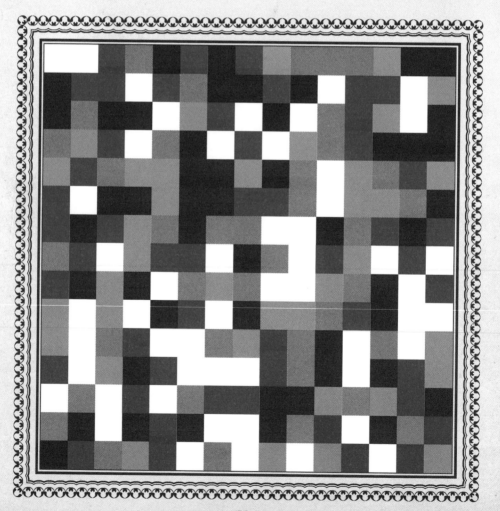

TRAINSPOTTING

Problem Solving

★ ★ ★

Trainspotting was a popular activity in the Victorian era. One young enthusiast was at a station waiting to espy three most characterful trains, called the Steam Dream, Piston Pusher, and Coal Chugger respectively. One of the trains had a top speed of 55mph, another 60mph, and the third 65mph. One was predominantly red in color, another blue, and the third train was green. Can you work out the color and top speed of each train from the clues below and complete the table? Try to solve the puzzle in your head, then write the solution down directly.

The Coal Chugger was not the fastest train, nor the Steam Dream the slowest. The blue train was the slowest. The green train was the fastest, and wasn't called Piston Pusher. The Coal Chugger was red.

Train name	Top speed	Color
Steam Dream		
Piston Pusher		
Coal Chugger		

KILLER SUDOKU

Problem Solving

★ ★ ★

Solve this killer sudoku and then find the name of a killer in a Sherlock Holmes story. One of the numbers holds the key. To solve a killer sudoku, place the numbers 1–9 once in each row, column, and 3 x 3 box. Dotted lines around groups of squares have a number in the top-left square which is the sum total of the squares bounded by that dotted line. A number may not repeat within a dotted group of squares.

L	C	J	A	V	E	Z	F	M
O	X	N	L	O	E	E	K	K
T	J	L	D	F	M	E	K	C
E	J	E	L	C	F	M	M	K
D	S	E	U	I	S	Z	K	E
R	K	N	L	W	K	I	K	R
O	H	O	S	A	P	A	O	S
A	O	V	N	K	T	D	M	A
F	S	A	N	S	P	B	N	K

Killer sudoku grid:

Row 1 clues: 15, 17, 8, 9, 22, 6
Row 2 clues: 11, 20, 15
Row 3 clues: 5, 9, 13, 10
Row 4 clues: 23, 17, 13
Row 5 clues: 12, 5, 10, 6
Row 6 clues: 17, 11
Row 7 clues: 11, 10, 11, 14
Row 8 clues: 19, 16, 12, 5, 13
Row 9 clues: 10, 10

WHAT A CHARACTER

Problem Solving

★ ★ ★

Look at the list of names (right). They have one thing in common—they are all characters that appear in the Sherlock Holmes stories, including the great private detective himself. There is another person concealed within—who is it?

MACDONALD

COOK

WINDIBANK

BRADSTREET

RANCE

ANDERSON

STONER

ROYLOTT

HOLMES

GREGORY

MURDER MOST FOWL

Lateral Thinking

★ ★ ★

From the Industrial Revolution onward and throughout the Victorian era, farming grew more and more sophisticated. But some things remained the same, such as the threat that foxes pose to chickens.

One particularly pesky fox seemed to be able to gain access to the chicken coop at a farm at will, no matter what defenses were put in its way. The fox killed five chickens on January 4, then 12 on the March 9, and 17 on May 12.

How many chickens did it kill on April 17?

A SUSPECT QUESTION

Problem Solving

★ ★ ★

Holmes had tasked the Baker Street Irregulars with following three people: Griggs, Wakefield, and Chattoway. Can you work out the hair color and age of each person from the clues below? One has brown hair, another blonde hair, and the third man has red hair. The ages of the men are 24, 34, and 44. Try to solve the puzzle in your head and then write the solution directly into the table below.

The person with the shortest name is not 34 years old. The 44-year-old has blonde hair. The 24-year old has not got brown hair. Chattoway is not in his thirties. Griggs is a redhead.

Name	Hair color	Age
Griggs		
Wakefield		
Chattoway		

THE POISONED CHALICE

Creativity

★ ★ ★

With a quivering hand, an old man drank a glass of wine that he knew contained poison. Given he didn't want to die, and that there was no danger to his life, and no threat had been made against him or anyone he held dear to him, why did he put the glass to his lips? Be as creative as you can, and try to come up with at least three reasons why he took this course of action.

CIRCLE THE ANSWER

Problem Solving

★ ★ ★

Can you mentally rearrange the 11 circles in order from smallest to largest? Once done, you will reveal the name of a person associated with the Sherlock Holmes stories.

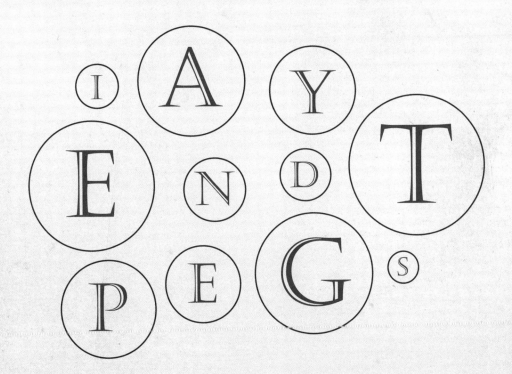

BUILDING BRIDGES

Problem Solving

★ ★ ★

Duimg the Industrial Revolution, modern bridge-building started in earnest. And it continued apace throughout the Victorian era. Can you do some bridge-building of your own by solving this bridges puzzle?

Connect every island (represented by circles) into a single interconnected group. To do this, draw bridges between the islands. The number in each circle states how many bridges must be connected to that island. Bridges cannot cross each other, can only be drawn horizontally or vertically, and there can only be a maximum of two bridges between any pair of islands.

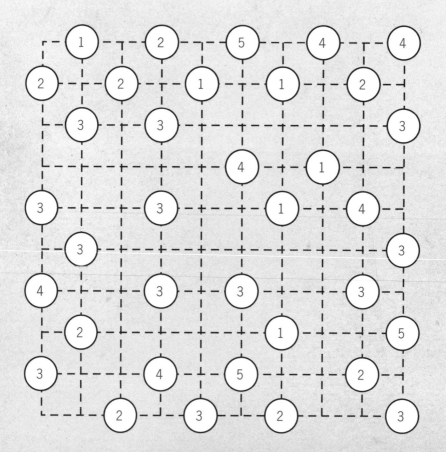

VALUABLE INVENTIONS

Problem Solving

★ ★ ★

Four Victorian inventions are displayed in the grid below: the gas lamp, a photograph, a steamship, and a postage stamp. Each has been assigned a number from 1–10. Can you work out the value of each of the four inventions? Numbers around the edge of the grid tell you the sum total of the objects in the respective row/column.

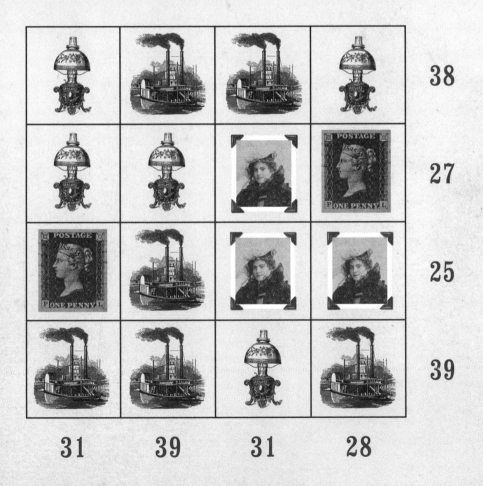

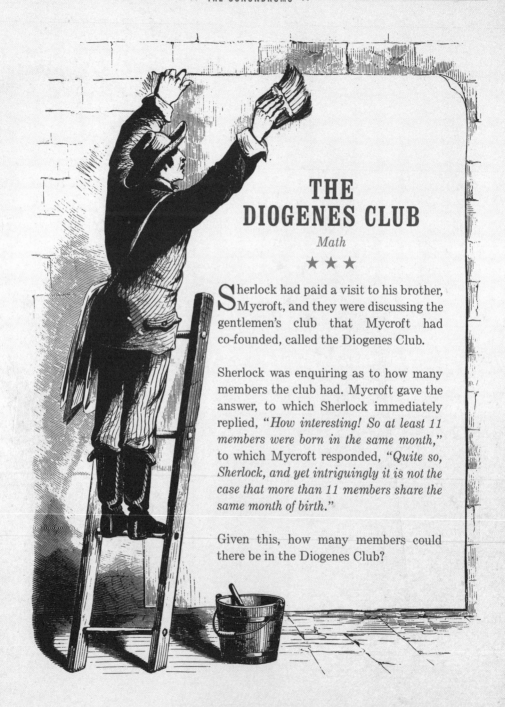

THE DIOGENES CLUB

Math

★ ★ ★

Sherlock had paid a visit to his brother, Mycroft, and they were discussing the gentlemen's club that Mycroft had co-founded, called the Diogenes Club.

Sherlock was enquiring as to how many members the club had. Mycroft gave the answer, to which Sherlock immediately replied, *"How interesting! So at least 11 members were born in the same month,"* to which Mycroft responded, *"Quite so, Sherlock, and yet intriguingly it is not the case that more than 11 members share the same month of birth."*

Given this, how many members could there be in the Diogenes Club?

SPLITTING UP

Problem Solving

★ ★ ★

Can you mentally rearrange the silhouette below of an object associated with Sherlock Holmes that has been split into four pieces, and thus reveal what that object is?

FOUR CANDLES

Problem Solving

★ ★ ★

The Victorian era saw the greatest amount of church building since the Middle Ages. One devout parishioner was helping the vicar work out the most economical way to buy white candles for a recently built church. There were four options:

a. A box of 24 candles that lasted 1.5 hours each that cost a penny each.

b. A box of 36 candles that lasted 2 hours and cost tuppence each.

c. A box of 18 candles that lasted 2.5 hours each and cost 1.5 pence each.

d. A box of 42 candles that lasted 3 hours each and cost 2.5 pence each.

The vicar is purely interested in getting the longest burn time out of a box of candles at the lowest price. Given this, which box should the parishioner recommend?

PIECING IT TOGETHER

Problem Solving

★ ★ ★

Dr. Watson was unable to sleep, and decided to divert himself with the following puzzle. Can you solve it? The aim is to move the blue block from the entrance at the top-middle of the grid to the exit at the bottom-middle. The six colored pieces can move horizontally or vertically but cannot pass over each other. You will need to determine the sequence in which to move the various colored blocks in order to enable the blue block to reach the exit. You may wish to cut out the page and the individual blocks so you can slide them around, or alternatively copy out the page onto a piece of paper, then cut out the shapes in order to play this sliding blocks game.

Entrance

Exit

FALLING LIKE DOMINOES

Problem Solving

★ ★ ★

"*When considering the evidence in a case, my dear Watson, one must train oneself to sift through all that is irrelevant and fix upon only those points which are relevant and pertinent to the case in question. Then an explanation of events may fall into place like a series of falling dominoes,*" instructed Sherlock.

Can you solve this one-player dominoes puzzle? A set of dominoes from 0–0 to 6–6 have been placed in the grid. You must work out logically where each of the dominoes has been placed in the grid. Use the answer key to the right of the puzzle grid to cross off each of the 28 dominoes as you place them.

1	4	0	0	1	6	3	3
1	6	2	1	1	2	4	5
3	3	2	3	4	6	0	6
0	5	0	3	3	0	6	4
1	1	2	3	6	2	5	5
5	2	2	0	6	5	0	2
4	4	5	6	5	4	1	4

	0	1	2	3	4	5	6
6							
5							
4							
3							
2							
1							
0							

COIN CRIME

Problem Solving

The police had called in Sherlock to assist them in investigating a gang suspected of illegally minting coins. The gang members all had a very curious tattoo that the police officer was explaining to Sherlock. Can you recreate the tattoo?

To recreate the tattoo, move four coins from their starting squares in the left-hand grid below into blank squares in order that every coin touches (either horizontally, vertically, or diagonally) exactly two others. Leave the other four coins in their starting positions.

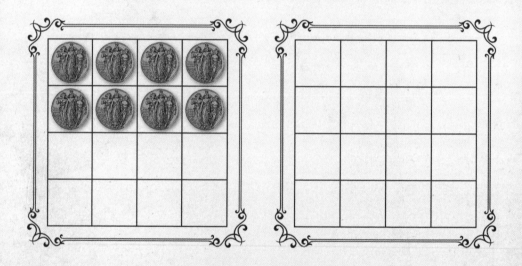

ALL THE THREES

Lateral Thinking

The pupils had their slates and chalk out in math class, and the teacher was testing them on a range of different sums. At the end of the class, he asked them to write down the following number: thirty-three thousand, thirty-three hundred, and thirty-three. What is the answer?

SEE THE LIGHT

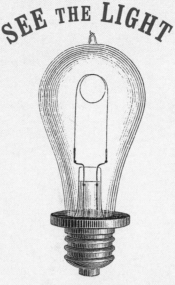

Lateral Thinking

" *I'm reading about a most intriguing situation in the morning paper, Holmes,"* said Watson. *"Listen to this interesting event that occurred just last night: Walter Jones was sitting quietly in his room, when suddenly he was plunged into darkness as the light went out. It was an extremely dark night and the moon was hidden behind clouds. Walter had no plans to go out, and was not expecting any visitors. However, he knew that the light going out was an extremely dangerous event."*

"I hardly think this is quite so intriguing as you intimated, my dear doctor," Holmes retorted.

"Here's the intriguing element of the story, Sherlock—the article is asking for readers to write in with their guess as to Walter's occupation!"

"The answer is so simple as to be mere child's play," said Sherlock, whilst puffing at his long pipe.

Can you deduce what Walter's job is?

ARISE, SIR SHERLOCK

Lateral Thinking

★ ★ ★

Sherlock had tasked the Baker Street Irregulars with following two men, and reporting back to him what they were up to. A couple of the Irregulars followed the two men and saw them entering a small house with a large garden. The house had one door downstairs, no downstairs windows, and an inaccessible roof. One of the Irregulars stayed behind as a sentry to continue observations, taking up position immediately adjacent to the front door to try to listen for any conversations taking place, which proved difficult as there were a couple of cats fighting noisily nearby, while the other reported back to Holmes in case he wanted to come and observe the men for himself.

An hour later, Holmes and Watson turned up at the house, and the sentry reported what little had happened, but there was still no sign of activity inside, and it became clear that the men had somehow left the building without being observed. Sherlock examined the building and could see there was no obvious escape route, with solid flooring throughout, no access to the roof from the upstairs window, and a jump from the window would have led at best to broken limbs. Sherlock could see there were no footprints in the mud on the ground below the window, ruling out that method of escape.

"Why," said Watson, *"this is a most strange affair—they seem to have escaped from an inescapable house. If you can solve this one, Sherlock, you deserve a knighthood!"*

"On the contrary, the solution is quite clear, my dear Doctor," replied Holmes. How had the men escaped?

WAITING for HOLMES

Problem Solving

★ ★ ★

Dr. Watson was waiting for Sherlock to return from one of his meetings with the Baker Street Irregulars. While sitting in front of the fire, his eyes caught sight of a little brainteaser in the evening newspaper. Can you solve it?

You must find your way through the maze as quickly as possible. You must start at the top left square and finish at the bottom right square. Numbers in squares indicate how many squares you may move in any direction (horizontally, vertically, or diagonally) when you land on that square. Can you solve this little teaser in 10 steps?

3	1	2	3	2
4	2	4	4	2
3	2	3	4	3
2	3	4	3	3
4	2	3	3	4

THE COLORFUL SHERLOCK HOLMES

Problem Solving

★ ★ ★

Can you find the odd one out in the image below within 20 seconds?

HOLMES	HOLMES	HOLMES	HOLMES
SHERLOCK	HOLMES	SHERLOCK	HOLMES
SHERLOCK	SHERLOCK	HOLMES	SHERLOCK
HOLMES	SHERLOCK	HOLMES	HOLMES
SHERLOCK	HOLMES	SHERLOCK	SHERLOCK
HOLMES	SHERLOCK	HOLMES	HOLMES
SHERLOCK	HOLMES	SHERLOCK	HOLMES
HOLMES	SHERLOCK	HOLMES	HOLMES
HOLMES	SHERLOCK	HOLMES	HOLMES
HOLMES	SHERLOCK	SHERLOCK	SHERLOCK
SHERLOCK	HOLMES	SHERLOCK	HOLMES
SHERLOCK	SHERLOCK	HOLMES	SHERLOCK
HOLMES	HOLMES	HOLMES	HOLMES

THE GREAT EXHIBITION

Math

★ ★ ★

The Great Exhibition of 1851 was organized by Henry Cole and Queen Victoria's husband, Prince Albert. The event was greatly anticipated and grand in scale, taking place at The Crystal Palace.

If one exhibit was of five exquisitely beautiful colored diamonds, arranged in order from cheapest to most expensive, with the cheapest being worth £2,000 and the value of each successive diamond being 1.5 times that of the previous one, how expensive was the fifth and final diamond? Try to complete the calculation in your head.

HAPPY FAMILY

Lateral Thinking

★ ★ ★

The average Victorian family was notably larger than today, often with five or six children. Sidney's family was particularly large, as he had seven sisters, and each of his sisters had a brother. How many children were there in Sidney's family in total?

COLORFUL CHEMICALS

Problem Solving

★ ★ ★

As usual, Dr. Watson had returned to Baker Street to find Sherlock totally absorbed in his scientific experiments, with various pungent chemicals on the go in several different jars. Can you use the clues below to work out the color of each chemical—labeled solution X, solution Y, and solution Z respectively—and what it appeared to smell like to Watson? One chemical was orange, another pink, and the third yellow; one smelt of fish, another of onions, and the third of chicken. Try to solve the puzzle in your head and then write the solution directly into the table below.

The pink solution smelt of onions. Solution Y did not smell of chicken, nor was it yellow in color. Solution Z smelt of fish, and was not orange.

Chemical Name	Color	Smell
Solution X		
Solution Y		
Solution Z		

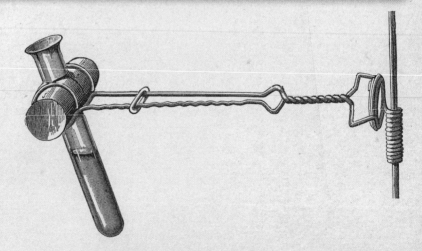

CARD CHEAT

Problem Solving

★ ★ ★

Sherlock was investigating a scandal in which a card cheat was suspected of murdering one of his playing partners for threatening to reveal the scam he was operating. During his surreptitious investigation, Sherlock stumbled across the following puzzle at one of the gentlemen's clubs he visited, where the suspect regularly played. Can you solve it?

Place one club, one diamond, one heart, and one spade in each row and column of the grid; the remaining two squares in each row and column are to be left blank. Cards at the start/end of rows/columns around the outside of the grid tell you which card is encountered first/last in that row/column. For instance, the diamond at the start of row one tells you the first card you encounter in that row is a diamond, therefore the first square must either contain a diamond or be one of the two blank squares in the row.

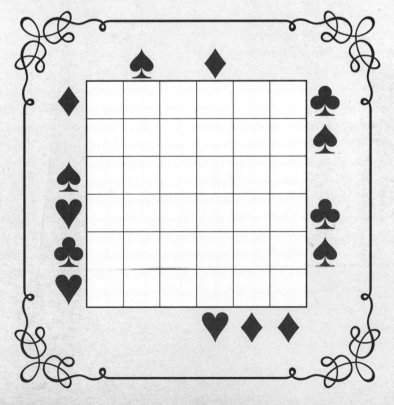

GOLD RUSH

Lateral Thinking

★ ★ ★

Three adventurous Victorian prospectors had found six small nuggets of what they believed to be gold-bearing rock in an exotic country. However, they were in a rush as, in their search, they had disturbed some savage-looking animal that was now chasing them. They ran back to the river where they had left their very simple boat, and hastily made their getaway. The boat could only take a total weight of 601 pounds before starting to sink. However, each man weighed 199 pounds and the gold nuggets weighed a pound each. How did they manage to escape in the boat with all six nuggets on board without the boat starting to sink and thus no man or any gold getting wet, given the weight limit?

TIME IS OF THE ESSENCE

Problem Solving

★ ★ ★

Sherlock Holmes arose early, in order to travel across the country to visit a mansion where a most unique happening had occurred. He left Baker Street at 5:03am, walked for 29 minutes to the train station, whereupon he spent 8 minutes waiting for his train to leave. The train journey took 2 hours and 47 minutes, whereupon Sherlock spent 21 minutes in a hansom cab to get to the mansion. He spent 1 hour 35 minutes walking around the grounds, then a further 2 hours 6 minutes inside the mansion speaking to the police and witnesses. At what time did he finish his work? Try to solve the puzzle in your head without writing down any intermediate timings.

TREE LINE

Problem Solving

★ ★ ★

Dr. Watson was reporting back to Holmes, having returned from a country house where he had been tasked with observing who entered and exited the property as part of one of Sherlock's enquiries. Watson reported back that there was a most singular arrangement of trees at the back of the property which had been a hotbed of activity, with various surreptitious meetings having taken place. There were nine trees arranged in a 7 x 7 plot, such that there were eight rows of three trees (that is, three trees in a straight line horizontally, vertically, or diagonally). All possible diagonal lines are shown in the diagram at the bottom.

"Here's a little puzzle for you, Holmes," said Watson *"I have placed nine trees in the left-hand grid below. Can you move the position of three of the trees, leaving the other six where they are, in order to recreate the arrangement of trees I have mentioned above?"*

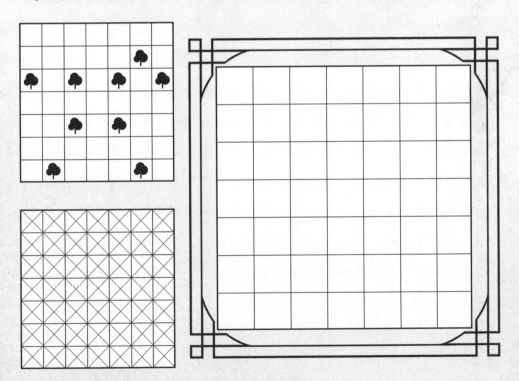

THE ARROW OF CRIME

Problem Solving

★ ★ ★

Sherlock had just helped the police bring a particularly nasty murderer to justice in an extremely singular case; the criminal used arrows rather than a pistol to shoot his victims.

Can you complete this puzzle which features many arrows? Place each number from 1–9 exactly once in each row, column, and 3 x 3 bold-lined box that compose the grid. There are several brown arrows in the grid. The cells placed along the body of an arrow add up to the number given in the circled cell at the start of that arrow. A number may repeat along the path of an arrow, as long as repeating it does not break the rule that no number can repeat in any row, column, or 3 x 3 box.

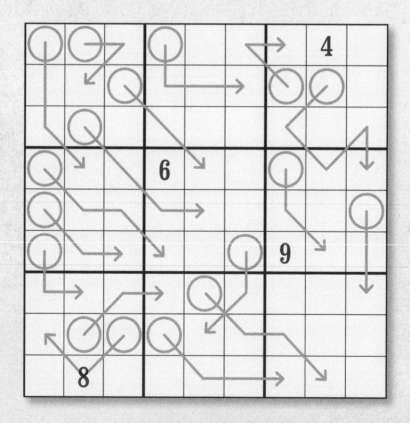

HEXACODE

Problem Solving

★ ★ ★

Can you solve the puzzle to reveal who Sherlock Holmes has been thinking about of late? Complete the hexagonal grid so that each of the 16 letters underneath the grid appears in one of the 16 blank hexagons. You must fill the grid in such a way that it is possible to move from hexagon to adjacent hexagon to spell out each of the series of letters alongside the grid. Thus it must be possible to move from the hexagon containing "N" to the hexagon containing "M" and then from the "M" to the hexagon containing "X" to spell out "NMX" and so forth. The shaded squares will reveal the answer.

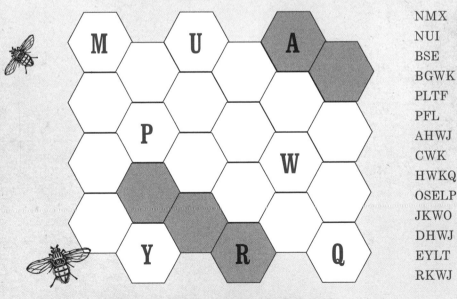

NMX
NUI
BSE
BGWK
PLTF
PFL
AHWJ
CWK
HWKQ
OSELP
JKWO
DHWJ
EYLT
RKWJ

BCDEFGHIJKLNOSTX

CHARACTER PUZZLE

Problem Solving

★ ★ ★

Can you fit all these Sherlock Holmes characters into the grid exactly once? There is only one way of doing this.

4 letters
Pike

5 letters
Adler
Lomax
Moran
Rance

6 letters
Holmes
Hudson
Martha
Watson
Wilson

7 letters
Gregson
McMurdo
Pollock
Porlock
Simpson
Wiggins

8 letters
Anderson
Lestrade
Leverton
Sherlock

HERE BE TREASURE!

Math

★ ★ ★

Inspector Hopkins, a student of Sherlock Holmes' methods, had become suspicious about a significant rise in activity at a Victorian candy store, which had recently come under new ownership. After a few weeks of observation, he began to suspect it was being used as a front for a criminal organization as most customers were not schoolchildren. Late one night he gained access to the property, and in the storeroom at the back of the property he systematically searched the 100 or so jars of brightly colored candy. Sure enough, he found disguised among them a jar containing what appeared to be a hoard of coins made out of precious metals. There were three types of coins: one was brilliant white in color, another silver, and the third type was gold.

Using the scales in the store, he was able to ascertain the coins were extremely dense and heavy, and that two white coins weighed the same as five silver coins, which in turn weighed the same as nine gold coins. If all three coins weighed an integer number of ounces, what is the least total weight that one white, one silver, and one gold coin can add up to?

INTO PIECES

Problem Solving

★ ★ ★

Can you mentally rearrange the silhouette (right) of a Victorian invention that has been split into four pieces to work out what that invention is?

HELP!

Problem Solving

★ ★ ★

It was now an hour since Holmes had left Baker Street to pursue a lead, leaving Watson with a note and the clear instruction: *"If I am not back within the hour, please contact the person below for help."* Who should Watson contact?

a. Nine sets of Ancient Wonders of the World

b. First prime number greater than 80

c. Number of faces on four icosahedrons, then add five

d. Tantalum

e. Six and a half years in months

f. 18 sets of Wise Men, less one

g. Seven zodiacs, less three

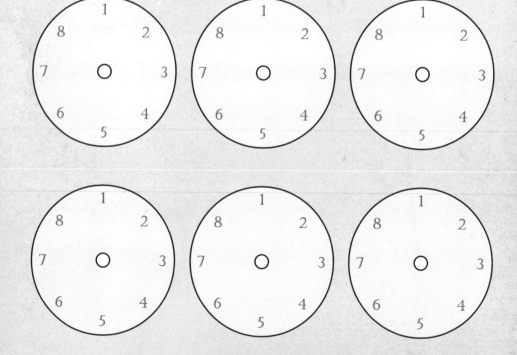

FIND YOUR WAY HOLMES

Problem Solving

★ ★ ★

How many times can you find "HOLMES" spelled out in the grid below? You may move from each letter horizontally or vertically to an adjacent letter only (not diagonally).

RECURRING NUMBERS

Problem Solving

★ ★ ★

L ook at the list of years below:

1607	**1682**
1758	**1835**
1910	

Only one of these, 1835, falls in the lifetime of Queen Victoria. What is the next number in this sequence after 1910, and what does the sequence represent?

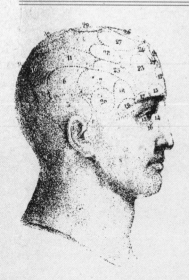

IT'S ALL IN THE MIND

Creativity

★ ★ ★

P hrenology was a respectable scientific theory in early Victorian society, and very much in vogue. By studying the skull of an individual, a phrenologist could ascertain their psychological attributes.

Can you think of five other ways that it might be possible to find out about a person, and how each method would work? Try to be as creative as you possibly can, avoiding well-known existing methods such as staring into a crystal ball.

MEMORY TEST

Memory

Read the following passage taken from *The Sign of Four* for no more than two minutes, then answer the questions below without referring back to the text:

> *"My practice has extended recently to the Continent,"* said Holmes after a while, filling up his old briar-root pipe. *"I was consulted last week by François le Villard, who, as you probably know, has come rather to the front lately in the French detective service. He has all the Celtic power of quick intuition but he is deficient in the wide range of exact knowledge which is essential to the higher developments of his art. The case was concerned with a will and possessed some features of interest. I was able to refer him to two parallel cases, the one at Riga in 1857, and the other at St. Louis in 1871, which have suggested to him the true solution. Here is the letter which I had this morning acknowledging my assistance."*
>
> He tossed over, as he spoke, a crumpled sheet of foreign notepaper. I glanced my eyes down it, catching a profusion of notes of admiration, with stray *magnifiques*, *coup-de-maîtres* and *tours-de-force*, all testifying to the ardent admiration of the Frenchman.

QUESTIONS

1. What type of pipe did Sherlock fill up?

2. Who consulted Sherlock last week?

3. Name the location and year of one of the two parallel cases Sherlock referred to.

4. What did Sherlock toss over as he spoke?

SHER...

Problem Solving

★ ★ ★

Can you place each of the four letters S, H, E, R twice in each row and column, and once in each of the rectangles containing four squares into which the grid is divided? The same letter cannot be placed in adjacent squares.

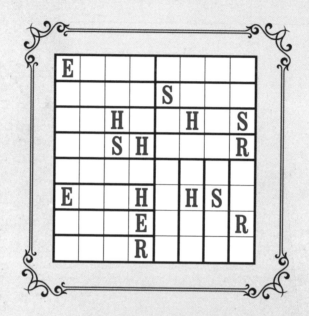

OPEN CONFESSION

Creativity

★ ★ ★

With several peelers in attendance, Arnold admitted to a crime most treacherous. Despite this, the police officers did not arrest him. Why? Try and come up with five reasons why this might have been the case. For instance, perhaps Arnold confessed in a foreign language and therefore the police officers did not understand the confession.

...LOCK

Problem Solving

★ ★ ★

Can you place each of the four letters L, O, C, K, twice in each row and column, and once in each of the rectangles containing four squares into which the grid is divided? The same letter cannot be placed in adjacent squares.

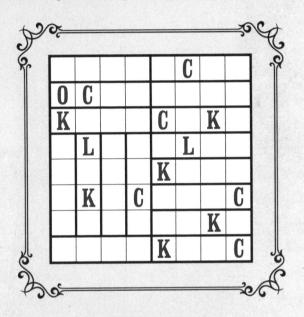

IT MUST BE FÊTE

Math

★ ★ ★

At a Victorian fête, two of the attractions were games of luck. In the first of the games, the player paid a farthing and could win a guinea if they correctly guessed the numbers on five balls drawn from a set of 30 balls numbered from 1–30. In the second game, the set-up was the same, but this time the player had to match eight balls successfully from a set of 20 balls numbered 1–20. If an attendee at the fête wants the best chance of winning, which of the two games should they play?

ODD ONE OUT

Lateral Thinking

★ ★ ★

Which of these four Victorian inventions is the odd one out? The answer is nothing to do with the words themselves.

Telephone

Postage stamp

Safety match

Typewriter

PRINCE ALBERT

Problem Solving

★ ★ ★

Prince Albert was the husband and consort of Queen Victoria, and she depended on him greatly for guidance and support during his lifetime.

Can you place each of the six letters of "Albert" once into each row, column, and jigsaw-shaped region bounded by thick lines in the grid below?

SAFE INSIDE

Problem Solving

★ ★ ★

Dr. Watson was looking at a safe in a room, while waiting for Sherlock to return from inspecting some cigar ash elsewhere in the property. Next to the safe was the following chart:

1	0	3	7	●	●	
2	7	9	8	●	●	
4	7	0	6	●	●	●
2	7	6	0	●	●	●

The safe required a four-digit code, and each individual digit could be 0–9. However, no digit was allowed to repeat: for instance, a code of 2766 would not be valid. If each blue dot indicates that a digit in the corresponding row is both of the correct value and in the correct position as the safe's code, and a brown dot indicates that a digit is correct, but not in the correct position, what is the four-digit code for the safe?

THE SILVER BLAZE

Problem Solving

A t a Victorian fireworks show, there were three types of firework that were all silver in color. They were called the Gunmetal Rocket, the Gray Sparkle, and the Silver Blaze. The fireworks could reach heights of 10 feet, 20 feet, and 40 feet, and lasted for 15 seconds, 20 seconds, and 25 seconds respectively. Can you complete the table below, filling in the duration of each firework and the height it reached when set off? Use the clues below to help you, but try to solve the puzzle in your head and then write the solution down directly.

The gunmetal rocket did not last for the shortest time, while the silver blaze did not reach the highest height. The gray sparkle reached higher than the silver blaze, but did not last as long as the gunmetal rocket. The firework that lasted the longest reached the highest height, lasting five seconds longer than the firework that reached half its height.

Firework Name	Burn time	Height Reached
Gunmetal Rocket		
Gray Sparkle		
Silver Blaze		

A DATE WITH DESTINY

Problem Solving

★ ★ ★

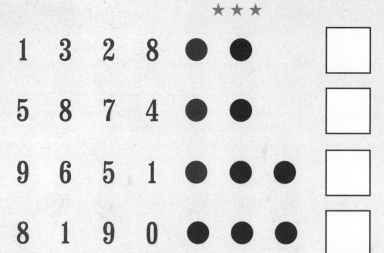

Can you use the information given above to work out a four-digit number of great significance to this book? No digit is allowed to repeat in the code: for instance, a code of 3455 would not be valid. If each blue dot indicates that a digit in the corresponding row is both of the correct value and in the correct position, and a brown dot indicates that a digit is correct, but not in the correct position, what is the four-digit number, and can you ascertain its significance?

CHARACTER COUNT

Lateral Thinking

★ ★ ★

If Sherlock = 6.2, Watson = 4.2, and Lestrade = 5.3, what is the value of Moriarty?

MIRROR IMAGE

Perception

★ ★ ★

Sherlock caught a glimpse of a suspect he was pursuing (shown below on the left) in a mirror, before he got away. Which of the options A–D is a mirror image of the man?

A   B

C   D

SCHOOL MONEY

Math

★ ★ ★

A good deal of mathematics in Victorian classrooms dealt with learning to use pounds, shillings, and pence, and the ability to perform calculations that involved adding and subtracting different sums of money.

If pence are designated by "d," shillings by "s," and pounds by "£," and there are 12 pennies in a shilling and 20 shillings in a pound, can you calculate this answer to a typical schoolroom sum?

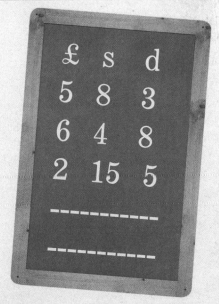

£	s	d
5	8	3
6	4	8
2	15	5
—	—	—
—	—	—

VICTORIAN NAMES

Problem Solving

Can you find these famous names from the Victorian era in the grid? They may run horizontally, vertically, or diagonally and in either a forward or backward direction.

T	E	S	Q	S	E	S	X	N	H	J	D	A	E
H	D	O	O	N	P	U	A	W	I	E	S	F	N
B	T	X	I	E	I	V	E	A	S	W	W	P	O
A	Y	Q	E	X	X	T	A	L	Z	F	R	L	T
B	E	L	A	G	N	I	T	H	G	I	N	A	S
B	N	T	E	D	I	C	K	E	N	S	X	D	D
A	Q	U	E	E	N	V	I	C	T	O	R	I	A
G	I	R	T	N	A	K	E	T	T	X	S	A	L
E	L	Y	O	D	N	A	N	O	C	R	Y	L	G
Z	N	A	J	H	L	Y	A	D	A	R	A	F	R
C	Z	W	S	B	S	Z	S	E	J	X	T	Z	T
F	J	A	E	W	A	L	L	O	R	R	A	C	U
L	L	R	R	Y	T	I	Z	V	N	C	R	A	F
S	T	E	V	E	N	S	O	N	T	D	G	A	F

BABBAGE	DISRAELI	PRINCE ALBERT
CARROLL	FARADAY	QUEEN VICTORIA
CONAN DOYLE	GLADSTONE	STEVENSON
DARWIN	NIGHTINGALE	TENNYSON
DICKENS	PEEL	

VICTORIAN NAMES 2

Problem Solving

★ ★ ★

Can you find these names that were popular in the Victorian era in the grid? They are all placed in the shape of a letter "V" for "Victoria." However, the "V" may be rotated. One name, Miles, has been placed in the grid to get you started

R	C	I	S	C	N	R	S	R	E	U	A	E	T	Q
S	C	C	L	A	Z	I	E	E	C	M	L	R	I	I
E	V	I	Y	A	L	P	D	L	D	Y	A	R	A	B
S	A	T	G	S	Q	A	D	F	E	G	I	L	Y	P
V	Y	T	F	F	I	A	A	I	L	L	C	A	J	C
H	I	X	E	E	Y	W	S	A	G	Y	A	R	O	Q
X	P	H	F	E	A	J	O	I	H	E	D	E	L	X
C	R	L	T	B	L	L	N	I	B	I	L	E	E	K
P	A	A	A	I	I	S	L	R	A	T	W	E	G	X
R	U	S	D	B	I	V	P	D	U	A	M	R	R	M
P	Y	E	I	E	G	N	E	I	A	I	R	I	W	A
J	T	P	P	L	O	V	E	L	I	O	G	T	L	R
N	T	A	D	E	A	Q	S	C	Y	R	X	E	S	I
P	I	L	D	O	Z	I	S	O	A	R	S	W	J	V
T	A	W	S	I	R	R	B	B	I	N	F	S	A	D

ALICE	DAISY	EDWIN	HILDA	OLIVE
BASIL	DORIS	ELSIE	LYDIA	PERCY
CLARA	EDGAR	EWART	~~MILES~~	RALPH
CYRIL	EDITH	GRACE	NIGEL	SILAS

TOO MANY COOKS

Problem Solving

★ ★ ★

Three chefs are preparing a tasty meal for an exquisite Victorian banquet. Can you work out the type of meat each chef is cooking, and how many years' cooking experience each chef has? Try to solve the puzzle in your head.

Of the three meats (pork, beef, and mutton), Theodore chose to cook the pork. The chef with 15 years' cooking experience is not Silas. One chef has only five years' experience, but it isn't Phineas, who has more experience than Theodore. The chef with 10 years' cooking experience did not cook beef: that meat was cooked by the most inexperienced of the chefs.

Chef's name	Meat	Experience
Theodore		
Silas		
Phineas		

VICTORIAN ISSUE

Math

★ ★ ★

Queen Victoria had nine children. If her first child were to have had one child, her second child to have had two children, and so on, how many children and grandchildren would Queen Victoria have had in total? Calculate the answer in your head.

READ ALL ABOUT IT

Memory

★ ★ ★

Read through this passage of text from *The Adventure of the Red Circle*. Then, without looking back at the text, answer the four questions underneath the passage:

> How is any news or any message to reach him from without? Obviously by advertisement through a newspaper. There seems no other way, and fortunately we need concern ourselves with the one paper only. Here are the *Daily Gazette* extracts of the last fortnight. "Lady with a black boa at Prince's Skating Club"—that we may pass. "Surely Jimmy will not break his mother's heart"—that appears to be irrelevant. "If the lady who fainted on Brixton bus"—she does not interest me. "Every day my heart longs—" Bleat, Watson—unmitigated bleat! Ah, this is a little more possible. Listen to this: "Be patient. Will find some sure means of communications. Meanwhile, this column. G." That is two days after Mrs. Warren's lodger arrived. It sounds plausible, does it not? The mysterious one could understand English, even if he could not print it. Let us see if we can pick up the trace again. Yes, here we are—three days later. "Am making successful arrangements. Patience and prudence. The clouds will pass. G." Nothing for a week after that.

1. Which newspaper is mentioned in the passage?

2. Who will surely not break his mother's heart?

3. A lady fainted on which bus?

4. Fill-in the blank: "That is two days after Mrs. ___ lodger arrived"

A SWEET TOOTH

Math

★ ★ ★

Inspector Lestrade was bending Sherlock's ear about a rather grizzly murder that was proving quite intractable to solve. While doing so he was quickly getting through the contents of a bag of candy he had purchased en route to Baker Street.

During the conversation Lestrade ate a third of the sweets and then another half of what was left. After doing so, the bag contained 12 pieces of candy in total. How many sweets were in the bag originally?

DISH WASHER

Math

★ ★ ★

Mrs. Hudson strongly approved of the new-fangled machine for washing dishes—anything to make her life easier! The generous gift from Holmes meant that she had more time to herself. She spent some time trying to find out how to get the most benefit from the machine and the most economical way to pack it.

She found that she could fit 24 flat plates into the machine before it was fully loaded. Assuming that two soup dishes take up the same amount of space as three flat plates, how many soup dishes would be able to fit in the machine?

FOOD MIXER

Perception

★ ★ ★

The image below contains nine foods that were popular in the Victorian era. Study the image on the left for 30 seconds, then cover it up and look at the second image on the right. Four pairs of items have been swapped over: can you pick out the pairs?

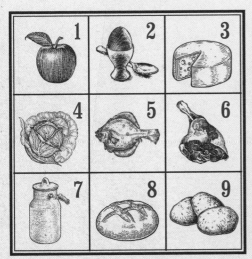

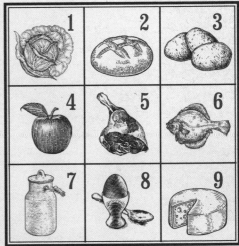

AT THE FARM

Lateral Thinking

★ ★ ★

A cockney family was excited to be visiting one of the most famous farms in Victorian London, full of anticipation as to what they would see there. The owner was known to have a more diverse range of animals than one would typically expect at a farm.

They first saw an enclosure full of large, intimidating snakes that the owner collected as a curiosity. Next, they moved to a more traditional area of the farm and saw some horses, and then walking a little farther saw some noisy goats. Wandering to a separate section of the farm, they were surprised and delighted by an enclosure containing some monkeys—not a typical farmyard animal! Then, going back to the main area of the farm, they saw some roosters and then a couple of farmyard dogs lazing around in the sun. What animal did they encounter next?

THE INVENTIVE TYPE

Perception

★ ★ ★

C an you mentally rearrange the silhouette on the left of an invention of the Victorian era that has been split into four pieces, and thus reveal what that object is?

A LIGHT IN THE DARKNESS

Problem Solving

★ ★ ★

An eccentric Victorian nobleman was having the latest gas lighting installed in one wing of his mansion. The wing consisted of 100 small square rooms in a 10 x 10 arrangement. As a true eccentric, instead of simply instructing the engineers where he wanted the gas lights installed, he drew the following grid. Can you deduce the desired location of each gas light by putting a circle in the relevant squares?

A blue square containing a number shows how many adjacent squares (horizontally and vertically) must contain a gas light. Some white squares that are not adjacent to numbered blue squares may also contain gas lights. All squares that the nobleman has left white must end up being illuminated: a square containing a gas light illuminates itself and all other squares in its row and column until a blue square is reached. No two gas lights can "see" each other: thus the light from one gas light cannot hit another gas light directly.

GRID REFERENCE

Memory

★ ★ ★

Study the grid below carefully for 30 seconds. Note that it is divided into 12 segments, from A1 through to C4. Try to remember the object located in each segment together with its color. Then, cover the grid and try to remember where the listed objects A–D are located in the grid.

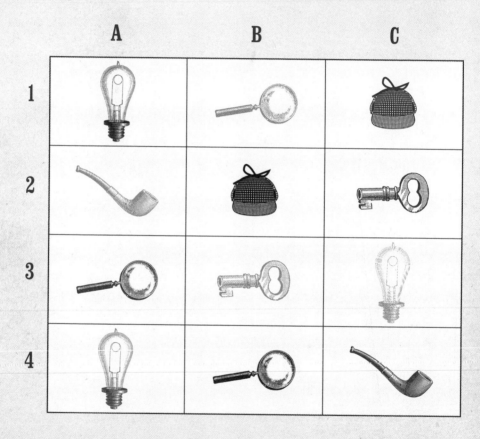

A   B   C   D

THE HOUND OF THE BASKERVILLES

Perception

★ ★ ★

Look at the five light brown outlines below (labeled A–E) carefully, and see how quickly you can find which one exactly matches the dark brown silhouette of *The Hound of the Baskervilles*.

MURDEROUS MANOR

Problem Solving

★ ★ ★

Six gentlemen went to a country manor for a dinner party. Only five returned alive. Sherlock has been asked by the police to investigate, and first he needs to know some basic details about the five living dinner party guests. Using the clues below, can you determine the surname, height and occupation of each of the diners?

1. Gilbert, the shortest of the quintet, does not have the surname Lynch. Baxter, the optician, is best friends with the 5 ft. 7 in. tall doctor.

2. Mr E. Morris is neither a lawyer, nor is he 5 ft. 6 in.

3. The bailiff, Mr. Lynch, sat next to the tallest person at the dinner party, Mr. Brewer.

4. The lawyer is not called Mr. Wright. Henry is a doctor by trade.

	Brewer	Godwin	Lynch	Morris	Wright	Actuary	Bailiff	Doctor	Lawyer	Optician	5 ft. 4 in.	5 ft. 5 in.	5 ft. 6 in.	5 ft. 7 in.	5 ft. 8 in.
Baxter															
Clarence															
Edmund															
Gilbert															
Henry															
5 ft. 4 in.															
5 ft. 5 in.															
5 ft. 6 in.															
5 ft. 7 in.															
5 ft. 8 in.															
Actuary															
Bailiff															
Doctor															
Lawyer															
Optician															

First Name	Surname	Job	Height

MURDEROUS MANNER

Lateral Thinking

★ ★ ★

You should solve "Murderous Manor" before tackling this puzzle.

Sherlock was trying to ascertain how the murder was committed. He found a severed bell pull in the study, and on inspection saw that the rope had been cut quite high up. This meant that the murderer was agile enough to clamber up a tallboy nearby in order to reach the top of the bell pull. Surmising that the furniture would not be regularly cleaned, Sherlock clambered up himself to see, sure enough, a light footprint in the dust on top of the tallboy.

Having measured the foot size of the five suspects, Sherlock found that the two shortest men had feet that were too small to match the length of the footprint. Therefore the murderer was among the three tallest men. However, all three denied being the murderer or having any knowledge of who the murderer was under police questioning.

Sherlock had the good fortune to overhear the following conversation between the three men as they sat at a standard rectangular table in the police station. Two of the men sat on one side of the table, the third sat on the facing side of the table. Who should Sherlock tell the police to charge with murder, assuming they were all telling the truth in what they say?

Clarence said, *"I didn't do it, and just one of us is sitting directly opposite the person who committed the murder."*

Baxter said, *"We're all friends, so I think we should stick together and protect the identity of the murderer who clearly got carried away in the heat of the moment."*

"Agreed," said Henry, *"none of us deserves to end up on the gallows for this. Let's shake on this to show we all agree to protect each other."*

Clarence shook hands with Baxter across the table, then stood up and shook hands with Henry across the table. The conversation continued for a short while, then Baxter and Henry also stood and the three walked off together.

SMART ALEC

Problem Solving

★ ★ ★

In the final Sherlock Holmes novel, *The Valley of Fear*, Inspector Alec MacDonald of Scotland Yard is involved in trying to solve the case.

Can you prove yourself to be a smart alec by tracing the name "ALEC" from the light brown cell at the top left of the grid below to the light brown cell at the bottom left of the grid? You must move from A→L→E→C in turn, then back to "A" again and so forth, tracing the name out nine times consecutively in the grid. You may move one square at a time, horizontally, vertically, or diagonally, visiting each square exactly once.

A	L	L	C	E	A
C	E	A	E	C	L
A	L	C	C	A	E
C	E	C	A	E	L
E	A	A	E	L	L
C	L	L	E	C	A

A USEFUL INVENTION

Perception

★ ★ ★

Can you mentally rearrange this silhouette of an invention of the Victorian era that has been split into four pieces, and thus reveal what that object is?

A PIECE OF CAKE

Lateral Thinking

★ ★ ★

Inspector Bradstreet and Inspector Gregson had bought a cake to celebrate the solving of a particularly grizzly and complicated murder. They were going to share the cake with the other six police officers who worked on the case, so they needed eight pieces in total. How could they cut the cake into eight pieces with just three cuts?

SAFE NUMBER

Math

★ ★ ★

One of the most famous gentlemen of the Victorian era, no less than an eminent former cabinet minister, had been the victim of a break-in at his country residence. Fortunately, his safe had remained secure as the burglars had not been able to deduce the four-digit code required to access it.

Look at the numerical sequence below. Can you work out the next two numbers in the sequence that replace the question marks? Once you have done so, multiply those two numbers together in order to ascertain the four-digit safe code.

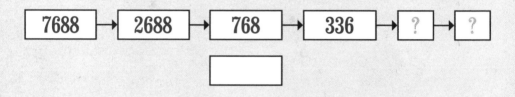

$$7688 \rightarrow 2688 \rightarrow 768 \rightarrow 336 \rightarrow ? \rightarrow ?$$

LIAR, LIAR!

Problem Solving

★ ★ ★

Inspector Lestrade had pulled in three ne'er-do-wells who had all been implicated in a series of petty thefts across London. However, all three protested their innocence under his questioning. He asked them each the following question: *"Who is telling lies?"* From their answers below, can you work out who is telling the truth and who is lying?

Adelia

Agatha

Alice

"Agatha is lying."

"Alice is lying."

"They're both lying."

GUESSING GAME

Lateral Thinking

★ ★ ★

"*T*ell me, Watson," said Holmes, "*whether you think your ability to spot patterns has improved since you started assisting me in my work?*"

"I should like to think so," said Watson.

"*Indeed. Then please tell me what I might be thinking of on Friday, if on Tuesday I think about gloves, on Wednesday I ponder the Wise Men, and on Thursday I am very much taken with the seasons of the year?*"

LIFE EXPECTANCY

Lateral Thinking

★ ★ ★

In 1851 life expectancy at birth for a Victorian man was about 40 years. Although he didn't know this statistic, Percy was feeling a little depressed at the thought he was getting old—and so quickly, too! The day before yesterday he was 39 and yet next year he would turn 42. What day of the year is it?

PROFESSOR JAMES MORIARTY

Creativity

★ ★ ★

Professor James Moriarty is introduced in *The Final Problem* as Holmes' greatest opponent, and a true criminal mastermind.

What do you think Moriarty would have looked like? Sketch what you see in your mind's eye when thinking of Moriarty in the empty box below:

A MEMORABLE PUZZLE

Memory

★ ★ ★

Focus on the objects in the grid below for 30 seconds, then cover the grid and, without looking, answer the following questions:

1. Which object features the least: hat, sewing machine, or dog?
2. Which color features the most: brown, dark blue, or light blue?
3. Which object features exactly eight times?

SUSPECT VISITS

Problem Solving

★ ★ ★

Sherlock and Dr. Watson are in a race against time to solve a particularly unpleasant crime, and need to interview six suspects as quickly as possible. They all live in different locations, labeled B–G in the diagram opposite. Sherlock and Dr. Watson start their trip as always from Baker Street, labeled A. They have their hansom cab ready to go, and need to visit each other location B–G once and then return to Baker Street.

Can you find the length of the quickest route in order to help them complete the journey as efficiently as possible? The numbers in small circles in the diagram between each pair of locations tell you the number of miles between them.

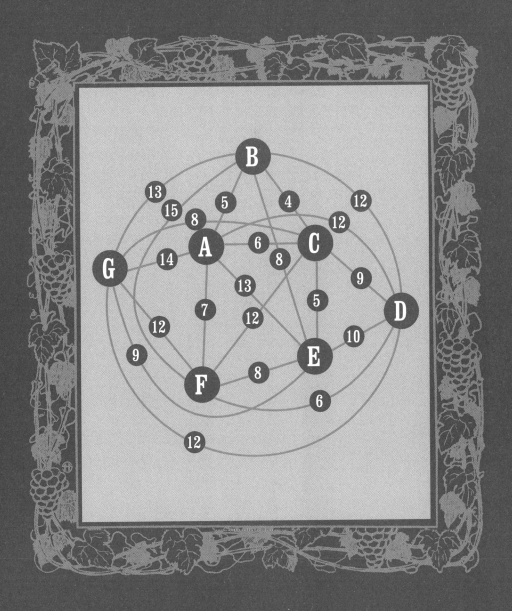

FIENDISHLY DIFFICULT

SYMBOLIC ACCESS

Problem Solving

★ ★ ★

Dr. Watson has tracked down a suspect and found a locked case with a four-character code required to open it. Can you solve the puzzle opposite to reveal the correct combination and unlock the case? Each set of characters must appear in the filled grid once. The code will appear in the tinted squares reading from left-to-right, top-to-bottom once the grid is filled.

6 characters	7 characters	8 characters
##*@££	#??£@@#	#*****£@
#*?@£$	$#**#$£	#*?*@*£$
$#@£@#	$#@$#@£	#*?@££$$
$£?*@#	$#@£*@£	?*@*£*##
£$*?@£	$$£*@*#	?*@£@#$$
	?@£*#	?@*@##*£
	?#**#@£	
	?#*@£@#	
	@*?*?#£	
	@£*£#*#	

BAKER STREET TO VICTORIA...

Math

★ ★ ★

Sherlock wanted to catch the hansom cab that would get him to Victoria from 221B Baker Street in the shortest time, in order to pursue a lead in a case. This meant that he had to reach Folkestone as quickly as possible. Outside Baker Street there was a cab with an old, slow horse which could move at 10mph. Around the corner, at a distance of a ¼ mile (and ¼ mile closer to Victoria station), was a cab with a younger, faster horse that could move 20 percent faster than the old horse. It would take Holmes four minutes to reach the younger horse on foot.

If the total distance from Baker Street to Victoria is 2.5 miles, which of the two options—a cab ride with the older horse outside Baker Street or a four-minute walk followed by a shorter cab ride with the younger horse—would get Holmes there faster?

...VICTORIA TO FOLKESTONE

Memory

★ ★ ★

Once at Victoria, Holmes saw that he had the option of three trains: St. Peter, number 5378, St. James, number 2839, and St. Paul, number 4713.

Study the above numbers for 30 seconds and commit them to memory, before reading on and solving the rest of the question without looking back at them.

The number for the fastest train observed the following three conditions:

a. The sum of the first and last digits was a prime number.

b. The multiple of the second and third digits was a multiple of seven.

c. The sum of the first and third digits was half the sum of the second and fourth digits.

Given this, which train was fastest and therefore the one that Holmes should catch?

CAUGHT IN A LOOP

Problem Solving

★ ★ ★

Can you complete this "S-" (for "Sherlock") shaped loop puzzle? You must make a single, continuous loop that visits every square of the "S-"shaped grid and does not cross itself at any point.

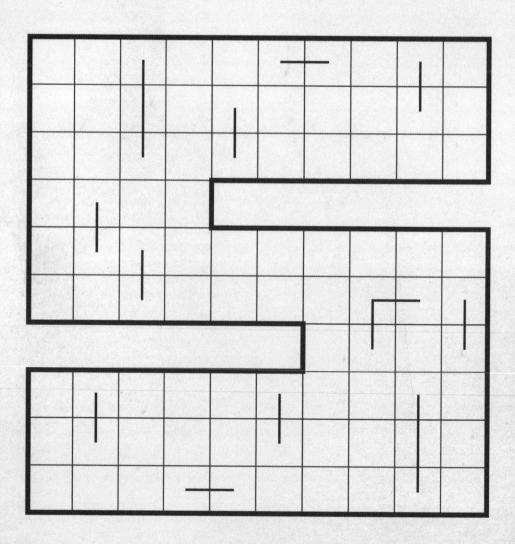

MAGIC SQUARE

Problem Solving

Complete the magic square (right) so that the total of the numbers in each row, column, and the two main diagonals is 102. Each number from 18–33 appears once in the grid.

What is the significance to Sherlock Holmes of the date formed by the numbers in the squares shaded light brown?

			22
18		26	
31		21	20
		23	

A FARE PUZZLE

Lateral Thinking

Sherlock and Dr. Watson were traveling quickly to Victoria station in a landau cab. Sherlock wanted to ask the cab driver if he had noticed anything suspicious around the streets of London during his work that day, and shouted out several questions to him loudly. However, although Sherlock was convinced the driver was able to hear his questions, the driver completely ignored him. Indeed, the driver did not turn around once during the whole journey, even when Holmes and Watson first got into the cab.

When they arrived at Victoria, the driver stated the payment he required and, on receipt of payment, drove off without saying a word. *"Gosh, what a rude driver,"* said Sherlock, frustrated at the experience. *"You never know, Sherlock, perhaps he is deaf and simply did not hear your questions,"* suggested Watson. Sherlock replied, *"That is not the reason, my dear Watson, I know for sure the driver could hear me."* How did Sherlock know the driver of the landau was not deaf?

EXPLORE ALL ANGLES

Perception

★ ★ ★

"*When looking at the scene of a crime, it is always worth exploring it from a range of viewpoints and angles. Sometimes that which is completely obvious from one position is hidden from another. If you look from every angle, you will view the scene of the crime from the eyes of both the victim and the criminal,*" Sherlock explained to Watson.

Can you rotate the collection of shapes inside the large square 90 degrees to the left in your mind's eye, and correctly select whether you would see A, B, C, or D as a result?

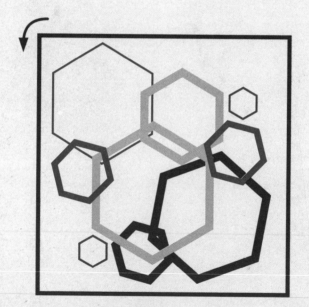

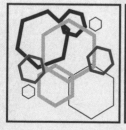

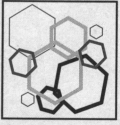

A   B   C   D

A STUDY IN SCARLET

Creativity

A well-to-do Victorian gentleman came downstairs to breakfast one day and announced to his family, *"Today I shall paint my office and everything inside it scarlet!"* This was quite unexpected, particularly since the gentleman didn't even particularly like the color scarlet. Can you come up with five reasons why he might have come to this colorful decision?

A LIGHT BULB MOMENT

Problem Solving

One of the most important inventions of the Victorian era was the incandescent light bulb.

Look carefully at the light bulb shown right. Can you shine a light on which of the options 1–7 matches the bulb exactly?

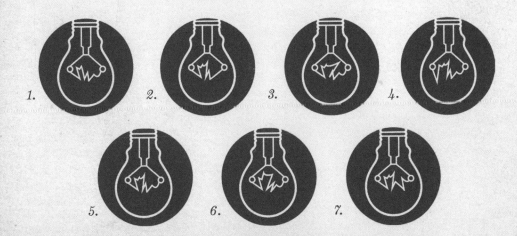

1. 2. 3. 4.

5. 6. 7.

UP, UP, AND AWAY

Problem Solving

★ ★ ★

Can you spot the six differences between these two images?

GET YOUR SKATES ON

Math

★ ★ ★

Monsieur Dubugue of the Paris police was a keen ice-skater and often frequented his local Parisian ice rink. He was getting annoyed at how frequently he was knocked into by other skaters. He decided to see how many collisions occurred between skaters on the ice, so started counting.

When there were 50 skaters on the ice, 10 collisions occurred. With 75 skaters, there were 15 collisions, while with 90 skaters on the ice, there were 18 collisions. Calculate mentally how many collisions there would be if, one extremely busy Saturday evening, there were 160 skaters on the ice.

GOING ROUND IN CIRCLES

Problem Solving

★ ★ ★

Sherlock is literally going around in circles while working on a case that he just can't crack. Can you complete the puzzle grid below, placing each of the eight letters of SHERLOCK into the circular grid such that each letter appears exactly once in each of the eight concentric circles and each of the eight spokes?

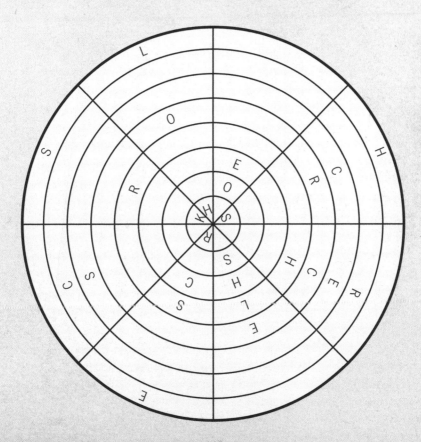

ROOM WITH A VIEW

Problem Solving

★ ★ ★

Inspector Gregory of Scotland Yard had been tracking a gang of forgers for several months. The leaders of the gang seemed to be based in a very large house with stunning views across London. The police had been able to deduce some information about the building, as shown in the diagram below.

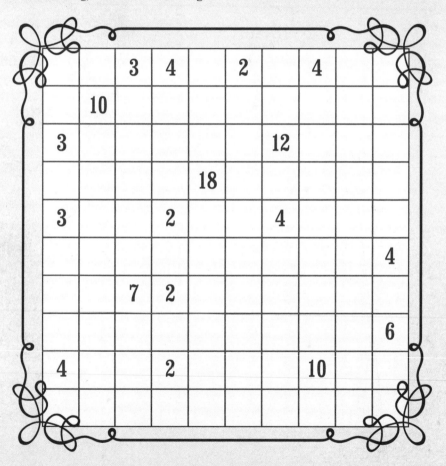

Can you complete the diagram with bold lines to show clearly all the room boundaries? All rooms are rectangular or square in shape. Squares containing a number in the diagram are part of a room containing the stated number of squares; each number belongs to just one room.

QUICK GETAWAY

Problem Solving

★ ★ ★

Moriarty and four of his partners in crime were trying to escape as quickly as possible from the scene of a crime under cover of darkness, knowing it was quite likely that Sherlock was hot on their heels. However, some of his gang were not as sprightly as they once were, and moved very slowly. They came to an extremely narrow and muddy walkway between two fields of bulls that they dared not enter for risk of getting gored. Only two of them could cross at any one time and, furthermore, they needed the light of a portable torch to find their way. They only had one portable torch—a recent invention—between them.

The five men could cross the muddy walkway in 2, 4, 7, 10, and 12 minutes respectively. What is the quickest time in which all five men could cross the muddy walkway given that a maximum of two could cross at any one time, and the single torch was required for every crossing and thus each time two people crossed the muddy walkway someone had to return the torch back to the other side?

DOTTY INVENTION

Problem Solving

★ ★ ★

Join the dots in the image below to reveal a Victorian invention. Use a blue pencil for the blue dots and a brown pencil for the brown dots. Start from dot 1 and draw a line to dot 2, then dot 3, and so on. When you hit a hollow dot, the line stops and starts again elsewhere in the image with another hollow dot. There are 280 dots in total.

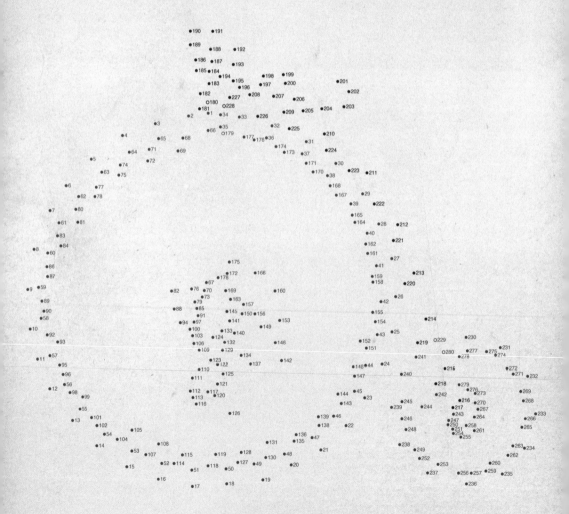

CHASING YOUR TAIL

Problem Solving

★ ★ ★

Holmes had engaged a police dog, Elsie, to try to pick up the scent of a slippery suspect who Scotland Yard had failed to track down after he escaped from the scene of a crime. However, while Elsie initially picked up the scent, after a while she started going around in circles, much to the frustration of Holmes, and appeared to be literally chasing her tail.

How many times can you find "Elsie" in the grid below, moving from letter to adjacent letter (horizontally or vertically) to spell out the name? Remember Elsie is chasing her tail, so only instances of "Elsie" that start and end on the same letter E count as valid: thus the first five letters across the first row of the puzzle do not count as a valid instance of "Elsie" as they contain two different Es.

E	L	S	I	E	L
I	S	I	E	E	L
S	S	I	E	L	E
S	L	E	I	S	S
I	E	S	L	S	I
S	L	I	E	L	E
E	L	S	I	S	S
I	S	L	E	L	S

AUTOMATIC SCULPTING MACHINE

Math

★ ★ ★

This amazing machine was used to replicate a model in whatever size you wished. Watson decided, as a fun present and talking point, that it would be amusing to sculpt a copy of Holmes' deerstalker hat. He took the hat to the sculpting machine operator and asked him to increase all the dimensions of the hat by a factor of 2.5.

If the hat had measurements of 8 in. (height) x 10 in. (width) x 12 in. (depth), then what is the volume, in cubic feet, of the sculpted copy that was produced? 12 in. = 1 foot.

THE ALIBI

Problem Solving

★ ★ ★

Inspector Gregson was visiting a petty criminal who had been accused of committing theft a few nights ago. However, the criminal had a detailed alibi that was corroborated by his friend. The petty criminal said:

"It couldn't have been me Inspector, as I was here at home, with God as my witness. I was playing this devilish little game that my friend presented me with as a birthday present— would you like a go? You must place 31 dominoes on this board in order to cover all 62 of the squares.

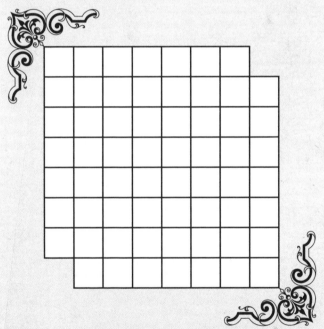

"Anyhow, I remember clearly how I found it a little trickier than it at first appeared, so I spent the evening in question absorbed in completing the task. I must admit to having a little celebratory tipple upon its successful completion!"

"Yes, it was just as he described," added his friend, *"Why, I remember the very moment he punched the air with delight when he finally solved it!"*

Is the petty criminal's alibi watertight, or should Inspector Gregson smell a rat?

WHERE ARE YOU, MRS. HUDSON?

Problem Solving

★ ★ ★

Sherlock urgently needed to speak to Mrs. Hudson as he had been away from Baker Street for a short while in order to attend to some pressing business, and he wanted to know if anyone had called round to see him while he was out. However, he couldn't find her anywhere.

How quickly can you track down the word "HUDSON" in the grid below, displayed in a 3 x 2 set of squares as illustrated on the right?

H	U	D
S	O	N

D	D	U	U	U	N	U	O	U	D	D	S	O	H
N	O	D	H	H	H	H	U	D	D	O	O	U	U	D
S	H	N	N	S	U	O	U	U	S	N	D	H	N	D
S	H	U	O	S	U	N	U	U	N	U	H	U	D	O
U	D	O	O	S	D	S	O	S	H	N	S	U	N	O
O	H	O	S	H	U	S	D	H	N	N	O	H	S	N
U	O	O	U	N	H	U	U	O	D	H	D	O	N	H
N	O	U	O	D	O	S	U	D	H	O	H	D	O	O
H	N	U	N	O	S	H	S	D	N	H	D	O	D	H
S	H	S	U	O	O	D	O	O	S	U	O	D	H	S
D	U	H	U	O	O	U	H	U	D	N	U	N	N	N
N	U	D	D	D	N	O	S	O	N	S	U	N	N	H
N	U	O	U	U	U	D	D	H	S	D	S	O	S	U
D	N	H	S	H	S	O	H	D	N	D	S	U	H	S
N	H	S	O	S	U	D	N	U	O	S	S	U	D	N

THE REICHENBACH FALLS

Math

★ ★ ★

Sherlock Holmes and Moriarty were fighting with each other at The Reichenbach Falls. They swayed back and forth near the edge, but suddenly Holmes found his foot slipping on a stone and moments later he fell backward toward the Falls. Seven seconds after Holmes fell over the edge, Moriarty heard a loud splash and thought, *"Hurray, that is the end of the accursed Mr. Holmes."* Given acceleration due to gravity of 32 feet per second, what distance (in feet) did Sherlock fall before plunging into the water at the bottom of the Falls?

THE TELEPHONE EXCHANGE

Problem Solving

★ ★ ★

Sherlock Holmes needed to telephone his brother Mycroft urgently at his government office. He couldn't remember the number, but he did know that it contained four non-zero digits, and that all the digits were different. The telephone operator told him that all government department telephones started with 75, so that just left two more to find. Holmes racked his brains and then remembered Mycroft had mentioned the digits in his telephone number added up to his day of birth, which was the last day of February 1836. Given this, what are the possible telephone numbers for Mycroft?

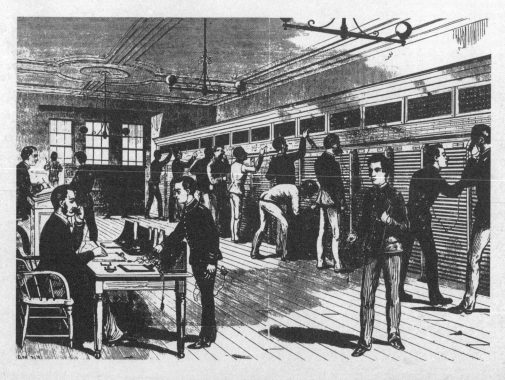

PHOTOGRAPHIC MEMORY

Memory

★ ★ ★

Look at the image, right, carefully for 30 seconds. Then, cover the image, and try to answer the questions below correctly.

QUESTIONS

1. How many maids are working in the kitchen?

2. How many rooms in the house are empty?

3. Did you notice anything odd about this house?

4. Can you name four items from the cellar?

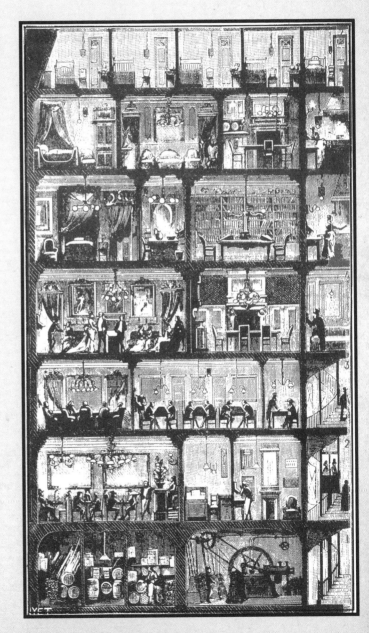

A LOT OF HOT AIR

Perception

★ ★ ★

Sherlock, Dr. Watson, and Inspector Lestrade were at a hot-air balloon festival, watching a race between three different balloons. Each of them favored a different balloon—Holmes the light blue, Watson the brown, and Lestrade the dark blue.

By following the strings, can you see which number is connected to each balloon?

MEMORABLE TEXT

Memory

R ead through this passage of text from *The Adventure of Wisteria Lodge.* Then, without looking back at the text, answer the five questions underneath the passage.

> *"The note is written upon ordinary cream-laid paper without watermark. It is a quarter-sheet. The paper is cut off in two snips with short-bladed scissors. It has been folded over three times and sealed with purple wax, put on hurriedly, and pressed down with some flat oval object. It is addressed to Mr. Garcia, Wisteria Lodge. It says: 'Our own colors, green and white. Green open, white shut. Main stair, first corridor, seventh right, green baize. Godspeed. D.' It is a woman's writing, done with a sharp-pointed pen, but the address is either done with another pen or by someone else. It is thicker and bolder, as you see."*
>
> *"A very remarkable note,"* said Holmes, glancing it over. *"I must compliment you, Mr. Baynes, upon your attention to detail in your examination of it. A few trifling points might perhaps be added. The oval seal is undoubtedly a plain sleeve-link—what else is of such a shape?"*

QUESTIONS

1. What type of scissors had been used?
2. Wax of which color had been used to seal the note?
3. To whom was the note addressed?
4. Fill in the blank: "Main stair, first corridor, ___ right, green baize."
5. Who did Sherlock compliment for his attention to detail?

AGE PROBLEM

Math

★ ★ ★

An Inspector from Scotland Yard was updating his fellow officers on a reported crime. An eccentric Victorian lady had reported the theft of some valuable jewelry from her household, but had proved rather troublesome to glean information from, as she did not answer questions in a straightforward manner. When asked her age, for instance, she answered as follows:

If to my age there added be,
One half, one third, and three times three,
Six score and 10, the sum you'll see.

How old is the eccentric Victorian lady?

THE MESSENGER

Math

★ ★ ★

Eager to get a message to Sherlock Holmes as quickly as possible, but with no money in his pocket for a cab, an associate of Holmes decided to jog to Baker Street. He jogged at a speed of 6mph, delivered the message to Holmes, and then walked back over the same route at a speed of 4mph. What was his average speed while on the move?

SNOOKERED

Problem Solving

★ ★ ★

Dr. Watson was at the snooker club, excited to try out his new cue. Cues were getting thinner during the Victorian era and he was eager to try out his new cue with just a ½ in. tip.

A fan of trick shots, he set up the table below. Can you work out how you can strike the white ball to travel around the table and knock the blue ball into the pocket? Draw your solution directly onto the table below.

IN SEQUENCE

Math

★ ★ ★

Mrs. Hudson was dutifully undertaking the cleaning at 221B Baker Street. She always had to be careful what to throw out, as some of the most inconsequential looking papers she came across turned out to be of the most value to Sherlock Holmes. She came across the following scrap of paper on the floor. Curious, she tried to work out what came next in the sequence. However, after a few minutes of head-scratching, she had to admit defeat. What is the answer?

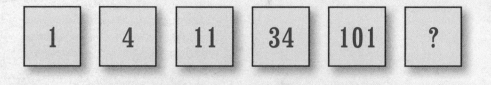

| 1 | 4 | 11 | 34 | 101 | ? |

THINKING SEQUENTIALLY

Lateral Thinking

★ ★ ★

Dr. Watson was trying to improve his lateral thinking, in an attempt to hone his detective skills. He was struggling with the following puzzle—can you work out what could come next in the sequence?

TRIANGLE TEASER

Problem Solving

★ ★ ★

Inspector Baynes of the Surrey constabulary was trying to improve his visual awareness and creative thinking, knowing that these would help him solve the increasingly perplexing cases he was being presented with in his police work. However, he was stuck on the following triangle teaser: can you work out what comes next?

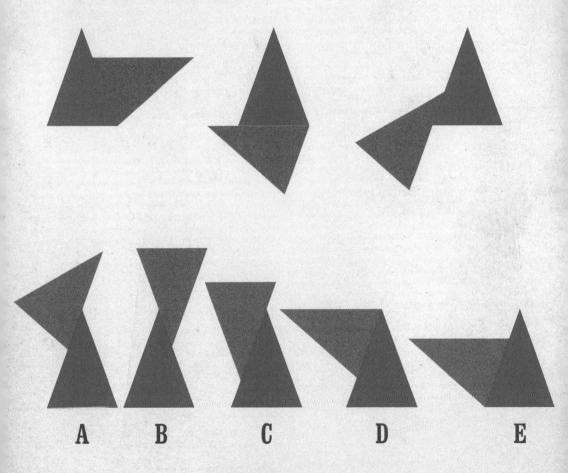

A   B   C   D   E

ON THE RIGHT TRACK

Perception

★ ★ ★

Look at the train silhouettes below. How quickly can you find the odd one out?

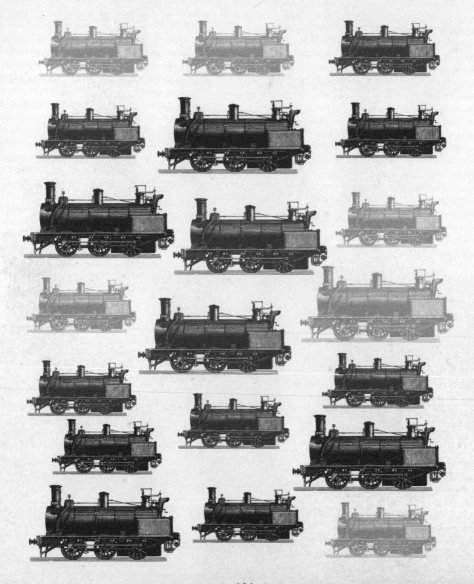

AT THE MARKET

Problem Solving

Three stallholders at a Victorian market were having a slow day selling their wares. Can you work out what each stallholder sold (clothes, jewelry, and vegetables) and the number of sales they made during the day (2, 5, 14) from the clues below? Try to solve the puzzle in your head and then write the solution directly in the table below. Wilfred had the most sales, and was not the jewelry seller. Owen did not have vegetables on his stall, and Herbert, the clothes seller, did not make the least sales.

Name	Item sold	Number of sales
Herbert		
Owen		
Wilfred		

ATTACHMENT PUZZLE

Lateral Thinking

Inspector Lestrade and his colleagues were discussing the following conundrum, but were having difficulty answering it. Can you suggest the most efficient solution?

You have a candle, a box of thumbtacks, and a book of matches. With just these items, your task is to attach the candle to a wooden door so that it throws out enough light to be able to read by.

CHARACTER SQUARES

Problem Solving

The names of various characters in the Sherlock Holmes stories have been hidden in the grid below, going clockwise or counterclockwise around the sides of a square. Can you find all the characters? One has been placed to start you off.

```
A  M  A  C  R  E  R  H  L  I  W  F  O  U  T
P  M  T  U  P  M  E  L  E  D  O  P  V  O  Y
R  A  A  T  T  T  F  E  R  A  V  D  K  E  B
U  R  D  W  G  A  Q  S  T  R  G  B  R  S  O
F  E  M  E  S  R  W  I  F  E  V  M  E  T  N
L  R  I  L  D  A  V  E  R  D  W  A  T  E  P
W  I  V  A  L  P  E  Z  T  Z  P  R  Y  P  M
I  L  E  J  E  K  L  N  O  V  U  P  R  R  O
J  R  T  L  W  S  F  J  Y  P  B  A  S  P  M
C  Q  L  C  A  U  D  O  T  X  Y  C  O  T  A
H  T  D  T  A  L  N  D  C  U  R  U  V  P  A
M  A  Q  I  B  T  N  Q  G  K  T  N  E  R  W
A  O  U  W  A  K  S  H  Y  T  R  O  S  R  T
T  S  Z  A  T  C  S  E  M  P  A  N  R  E  M
U  F  T  M  K  O  L  R  O  R  I  A  N  D  Y
```

ANDERSON	LEVERTON	PETERSON
COVENTRY	MERIVALE	SHERLOCK
~~LESTRADE~~	MORIARTY	

CROSSING THAT BRIDGE

Problem Solving

★ ★ ★

There was a very significant burst of bridge-building during the Victorian era. Can you navigate your way around this bridge maze, entering at the top-right and exiting at the bottom-left? The normal rules of a maze apply, but there are also plenty of bridges that you can walk under or over as you navigate your way through the maze. Bridges are in light brown.

TATTOO

Problem Solving

★ ★ ★

Sherlock had tasked the Baker Street Irregulars with following a suspect in a crime. He informed them that the man had a tattoo of a particular object. Solve the maze to reveal what that object is.

MISSING MONEY

Math

★ ★ ★

Inspector Bradstreet was investigating a break-in at a manor house, where a safe had been forced open and the cash inside it had been taken. He needed to ascertain how much money had been stolen. It transpired that four members of the household had stored some money inside the safe.

Charles had £50 in the safe. Benjamin had 20 percent more than Charles. George had 50 percent of the amount that Charles and Benjamin have. Frank has 20 percent of the amount that Benjamin and George have.

So how much money was in the safe?

CLIFF-HANGER

Creativity

★ ★ ★

After Sherlock Holmes had deduced the identity of a murderer in a particularly unusual case, the police wasted no time in tracking the perpetrator down. This led to a perilous chase on foot, and running along the edge of a cliff to avoid capture, the murderer fell over a 100 feet. Despite this, he lived to tell the tale. Can you come up with five ways in which this is possible? Be as creative as you can.

CIRCULAR LOGIC

Problem Solving

★ ★ ★

Can you help Sherlock find his way through this circular maze?

VICTORIAN RAILWAY

Perception

★ ★ ★

Transport was revolutionized during the Victorian era, particularly by rail, which rapidly became a key means of transport for goods and people.

In the image below, many trains are stacked up in a pile. Can you work out which of the trains is at the bottom of the pile?

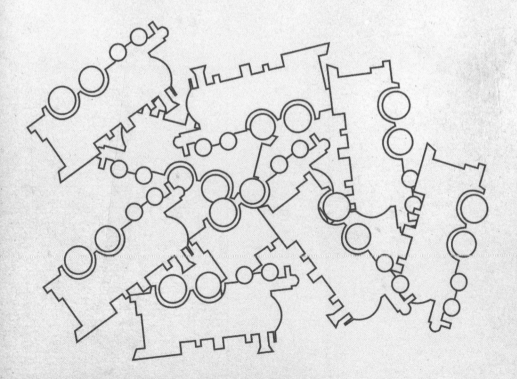

THE JEWEL THIEF

Problem Solving

★ ★ ★

The accomplice of a notorious jewel thief had been arrested by the police. However, try as they might, they failed to elicit the location of the thief during questioning. Upon searching the accomplice, they found a crumpled piece of paper in his pocket. On one side were the words:

Latitude AB . CD
Longitude EF . GH

On the other side, there was a grid of numbers, shown right. In which European city should the police expect to find the jewel thief? You will need to complete the grid by placing 1–9 once in each row, column, and 3 x 3 bold-lined box.

1	7				8	A		
6	2	B					7	
		9			7		5	C
				D	5			
7		4				2	E	8
			2	7			F	
	4		6	G		9		
	9	H					3	6
			5				2	4

MEMORY TEXT

Memory

★ ★ ★

Carefully read through this passage of text from *The Man with the Twisted Lip*, then answer the questions underneath it without looking back at the text:

The Man With The Twisted Lip

I groaned, for I was newly come back from a weary day.

We heard the door open, a few hurried words, and then quick steps upon the linoleum. Our own door flew open, and a lady, clad in some dark-colored stuff, with a black veil, entered the room.

"You will excuse my calling so late," she began, and then, suddenly losing her self-control, she ran forward, threw her arms about my wife's neck, and sobbed upon her shoulder. *"Oh, I'm in such trouble!"* she cried; *"I do so want a little help."*

"Why," said my wife, pulling up her veil, *"it is Kate Whitney. How you startled me, Kate! I had not an idea who you were when you came in."*

"I didn't know what to do, so I came straight to you." That was always the way. Folk who were in grief came to my wife like birds to a light-house.

"It was very sweet of you to come. Now, you must have some wine and water, and sit here comfortably and tell us all about it. Or should you rather that I sent James off to bed?"

35

QUESTIONS

1. What color veil was the lady clad in some dark-colored stuff wearing?

2. What was the name of the veiled lady?

3. Complete the sentence: *"Folk who were in grief came to my wife like birds to a ..."*

4. What liquid refreshment was offered to the lady?

GOOD SHOT!

Problem Solving

★ ★ ★

Three entrants into the Wimbledon gentlemen's singles tennis tournament were discussing their performance over a drink at the bar. From the clues below, can you deduce each player's best shot (forehand, backhand, serve) and the round of the tournament they reached (second, third, quarter final)? Try to solve the puzzle in your head and then write the solution directly into the table below.

Vernon did not lose in the second round, and his best shot is not his forehand. The player who went out of the tournament the earliest is known for his brilliant serve. The quarter finalist's best shot is his forehand. Randolph has a poor serve.

Player's name	Best shot	Round reached
Julian		
Randolph		
Vernon		

INSPECTOR BAYNES

Problem Solving

★ ★ ★

Inspector Baynes, a character in *The Adventure of Wisteria Lodge,* was rare among police inspectors in being complimented on his abilities by Sherlock Holmes, who said of him: *"You will rise high in your profession. You have instinct and intuition."*

How quickly can you track down the word "BAYNES" in the grid below, displayed in a 3 x 2 square as illustrated to the right?

B A Y
N E S

```
E Y B A S B E A B Y B Y A Y B
B N A B N Y S S A B B B B B B
E A A A E E Y E B Y N S A Y N
N A A B E E Y S E B Y A B S A
B E S A A E A S E E A B Y B B
Y E N A B A A A Y E E B S E Y
A B N A Y S S E E B Y N S N B
A Y N N Y A E B Y Y B S N B Y
A S S E B Y B A S Y B N E A B
A B E Y Y B S S S N S S E S E
S E B B A Y B A Y Y E B A S Y
S Y E S E A N E S N B S E A Y
B N A Y A A N E B N Y B Y S S
B E B S S A E Y E S B E A S S
A B N A S E Y Y E B N A N S S
```

THE FINANCE MINISTRY

Math

★ ★ ★

Charles, the British Finance Minister, was in a parlous state, having been involved in an accident that knocked him unconscious. Unfortunately, urgent access to his safe was needed in order to retrieve a document relating to a treaty that was due to be signed imminently, and that had received the Queen's personal seal of approval.

The Deputy Finance Minister was summoned, and remembered that Charles once told him the code was stored at the back of his diary. On opening the diary at the back page, the following partially filled tower of numbers appeared. The shaded square will reveal the three-digit code. What is it?

PATTERN RECOGNITION

Perception

★ ★ ★

Using your powers of perception, how quickly can you track down the single occurrence of this pattern in the colorful mosaic below?

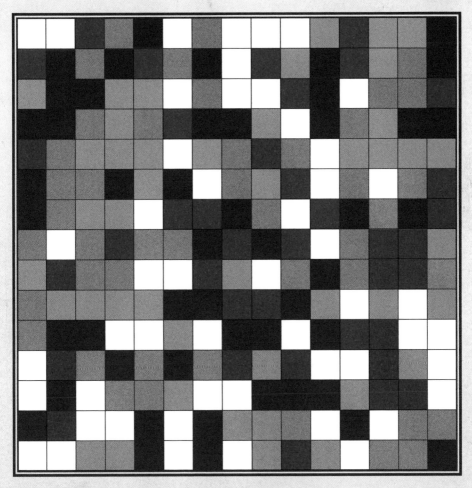

MESSAGE FOR WATSON

Problem Solving

★ ★ ★

On arrival at 221B Baker Street, Dr. Watson saw a scrawled note from Holmes. Knowing that Holmes was working on a case, Watson assumed that the note would convey a piece of information relevant to the case. What is that piece of information?

???	????	??????	????	?	??	?????	?????
	???	???	?????		?????	?????	?????
????	???	?????			???	?????	?????
??	?????	??			????	?????	?????
????		?			????		?????
		?					

FAMILY NAMES

Lateral Thinking

★ ★ ★

In one Victorian family, Mary had three brothers called Arthur, Bernard, and Clarence. Arthur was born first, then Bernard, and Clarence was the youngest of the three brothers. Can you work out which letter of the alphabet the parents decided to use as the first letter of their fourth child's name?

| Arthur | Bernard | Clarence | ? |

CRACK THE CODE

Problem Solving

★ ★ ★

Can you crack the code below? Each letter of the alphabet from A–Z has been randomly swapped with another letter (or possibly with itself). However, the same letter in the coded message always represents the same letter in the decoded message: for instance, every "S" in the code below might stand for the letter "P," and so forth.

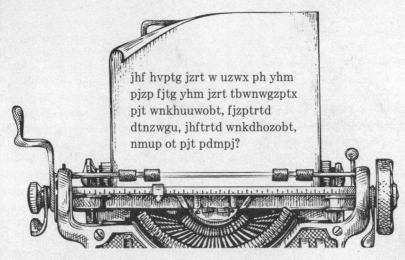

jhf hvptg jzrt w uzwx ph yhm
pjzp fjtg yhm jzrt tbwnwgzptx
pjt wnkhuuwobt, fjzptrtd
dtnzwgu, jhftrtd wnkdhozobt,
nmup ot pjt pdmpj?

WHAT'S THE SCORE?

Problem Solving

★ ★ ★

While waiting for more information on a case, Sherlock, Watson, and the detectives Lestrade and Gregson played a game. If Watson scored 92, Lestrade scored 84, and Gregson scored 85, what did Sherlock score?

I SAY, A BOOK!

Problem Solving

★ ★ ★

Which Sherlock Holmes story is being referred to cryptically below?

0.06975647

THE PROBLEM OF THE SCRAMBLED STORIES

Problem Solving

★ ★ ★

The letters in the titles of three Sherlock Holmes stories have been scrambled. Can you unshuffle the anagrams and reveal the titles of the stories?

1. Overheat flyleaf (4 words)

2. Casual dentistry (4 words)

3. Marooned ketch (3 words)

THE REIGATE PUZZLE

Problem Solving

★ ★ ★

How many times can you find the word "REIGATE" hidden in the grid below? The word may appear horizontally, vertically, or diagonally and in either a forward or backward direction.

E	E	R	G	A	E	A	E	E	E	E
A	E	T	R	E	I	G	A	T	E	E
G	R	R	A	E	I	T	I	E	A	E
E	E	T	E	G	I	E	T	A	T	T
E	R	I	R	E	I	R	R	A	A	I
T	E	E	A	E	R	E	G	T	E	I
A	I	R	I	A	I	I	R	A	A	R
G	G	A	E	G	E	G	T	A	R	E
I	A	E	E	R	A	A	A	R	E	T
E	T	R	G	T	T	T	E	T	R	E
R	E	T	R	R	E	E	E	G	E	I

NUMBER LINK

Math

★ ★ ★

Mrs. Hudson was tidying 221B Baker Street when Sherlock and Dr. Watson were out on a case. She came across a piece of paper on the table. It contained nothing but the following:

B, C, E, G, K, M, Q, ?

QUESTION

Can you work out what the sequence represents, and which letter should come next, and fill the place of the question mark?

WHAT'S THE CONNECTION?

Problem Solving

★ ★ ★

Imagination and the ability to spot connections are undoubtedly important parts of detective work such as that undertaken by Sherlock Holmes. Put your own powers to the test with this teaser.

Which of the following five words is the odd one out, and why:

SCHADENFREUDE

VAGABOND

ZEITGEIST

INCUBATION

ANTIPERSPIRANT

THE MISSING THUMB

Problem Solving

In *The Adventure of the Engineer's Thumb*, the hydraulic engineer Victor Hatherley has his thumb cut off. Can you find the word "thumb" hidden in the grid below?

It appears just once, and may be hidden either horizontally, vertically, or diagonally, in either a forward or backward direction.

```
T  B  H  B  T  B  U  H  M  B  T
H  H  H  H  T  U  H  H  H  B  H
M  M  U  U  H  T  M  U  U  M  B
T  H  H  B  H  H  U  B  T  U  H
H  T  U  T  T  U  H  U  H  H  M
H  B  T  M  T  U  T  H  M  T  T
M  M  T  H  U  U  H  M  B  M  U
H  B  U  T  B  T  M  T  T  T  U
H  B  T  T  B  M  H  M  T  M  U
T  T  T  H  M  B  U  H  T  M  M
M  M  T  U  M  H  M  M  H  B  B
```

A GAME OF DARTS

Problem Solving

★ ★ ★

Dr. Watson was practicing darts at a public house. Who was on his mind?

GET A SHIFT ON

Creativity

★ ★ ★

If WATSON = CGZYUT, MORAN = RTWFS, and MYCROFT = TFJYVMA, what does Sherlock equal?

WHAT NEXT?

Problem Solving

★ ★ ★

Can you work out what comes next in this letter sequence, in place of the question marks?

W	A	T
V	X	Y
U	U	D
T	R	I
?	?	?

FOLDED PAPER

Problem Solving

★ ★ ★

On this folded piece of paper is the name of a Victorian invention.

Can you guess what it is?

TYPEWRITER

A MOST SINGULAR CASE

Problem Solving

★ ★ ★

Holmes and Watson were staring at what really was quite the most unusual-looking case you could expect to come across. A suspect in an investigation had dropped it while running away from an area near to a crime scene.

The case required a four-digit code to open it, and each digit could be from 0–9. Faced with the laborious task of trying all 10,000 options, the police officer who had summoned Sherlock asked if he could shed any light on the matter and help them open the case.

"Gosh," said Watson, *"the owner of this case is quite the extrovert who must love to court attention!"*

"On the contrary," replied Sherlock, *"the owner is a French amnesiac, and I can certainly assist you in opening the case, officer."*

How was Sherlock able to help?

THE SOLUTIONS

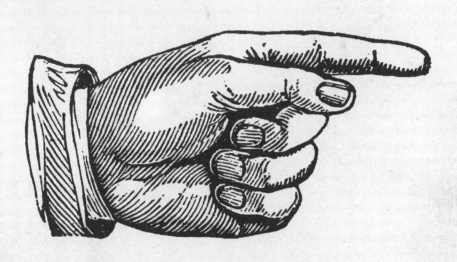

THE SOLUTIONS

Page 8

Off the Rails – The surgeon is Algernon's mother. [This is the classic lateral-thinking puzzle based on gender stereotyping and people assuming surgeons are always male. In the original puzzle the father is involved in a car crash; here it is rephrased in terms of a train derailing to suit a time period before the motorcar.]

The Gunslinger – The man had hiccups and hence had requested a glass of water to drink from upside down. The innkeeper knew that giving someone a fright is an effective cure for hiccups, and so pulled the gun on the man in order to scare him, successfully curing him of his hiccups in the process.

Page 9
Tea Clippers

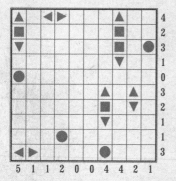

Page 10–11
Family Album – 2 and 4 have been swapped.

Page 12
Mrs Beeton's Rabbit Pie

1. 2 blades
2. Ham or bacon
3. Puff pastry
4. 2
5. Forcemeat

Page 13

In a puddle – Lay the stakes across the puddle, making sure they are an equal distance apart. Measure the length of each from top to bottom of the puddle, and add the measurements together. Divide the figure by the number of stakes lying across the puddle, and then multiply that figure by the width of the puddle to calculate the area.

Page 14
The Baker Street Irregulars – 15s and 8.5d.
5 x 2.5d = 12.5d, which is 1s and 0.5d. 12 x 1.75d = 21d = 1s and 9d. 1.5s = 1s and 6d. Add together to get 4s and 3.5d. Since £1 is 20s, then what is left is 20s—4s and 3.5d which gives us the answer of 15s and 8.5d.

Page 15

A Three Pipe Problem – 14 pipes. The figure seems surprisingly high as there are only 17 pipes in total. However, Sherlock could by chance select first all eight black pipes and the five brown pipes: therefore he needs to select 14 to guarantee having picked one of each color.

Page 16

Think Tank – The gentleman put a hole in the tank, draining out the water, and therefore making it considerably lighter.

Page 17

A Piece of the Puzzle

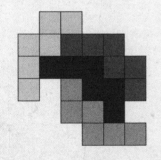

Page 18

A Lemon Entry
Door number 1 is orange.
Door number 2 is brown.
Door number 3 is blue.
Door number 4 is purple.
Door number 5 is yellow.

Page 19

The Psychic Dreamer – A scorpion. The comparisons are to the signs of the zodiac in the respective months: Pisces (fish), Taurus (bull), Cancer (crab), and finally Scorpio (scorpion).

Page 20

King's Journey

3	4	6	7	15	16	28	29	98	99
2	5	8	14	17	27	30	95	100	97
1	9	13	18	26	31	93	94	96	85
10	12	19	25	32	90	91	92	86	84
11	20	24	33	79	89	88	87	83	73
21	23	34	66	78	80	81	82	74	72
22	35	42	65	67	77	76	75	71	59
36	41	43	49	64	68	69	70	60	58
37	40	44	48	50	63	62	61	57	56
38	39	45	46	47	51	52	53	54	55

Page 21

Knight's Tour

17	42	55	52	19	40	57	36	21	38
54	51	18	41	56	61	20	39	58	35
43	16	53	70	63	90	67	60	37	22
50	71	64	91	66	69	62	81	34	59
15	44	73	76	89	80	95	68	23	32
72	49	92	65	96	75	88	33	82	1
45	14	77	74	87	94	79	98	31	24
8	11	48	93	78	97	28	85	2	83
13	46	9	6	27	86	99	4	25	30
10	7	12	47	100	5	26	29	84	3

Page 23

Safe House – 2758

Mr. Watson, Come Here!
The telephone call took place on March 10.

Page 22

Look Closely

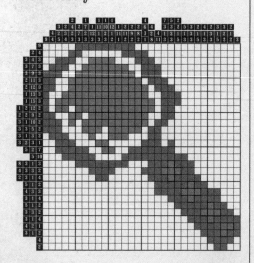

Page 24

Playing the Violin
The 750th note is an F. If you write out the notes in order, you will get the following:

A	B	C	D	E	F	G	F	E	D	C	B
1	2	3	4	5	6	7	8	9	10	11	12
13	14	15	16	17	18	19	20	21	22	23	24

So the same note repeats every 12 steps. 750 / 12 = 62.5. We know therefore that 62 x 12 = 744 notes on from the first note is another A (note 745). Therefore we simply move on five to find the 750th note, which is F.

Page 24

Forever Faithful – Jones was a priest who had married several women to their husbands in marriage ceremonies. The large number of female friends were members of his congregation at Church.

Page 25

Booby Traps

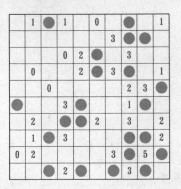

Page 26

Quick Getaway

exit

Page 27

Mark the Date – Sherlock returned to England on August 20.

Fruit Stall – There are 65 apples and 26 pears.

Page 28

In the Balance
1. Eighteen bags of pear drops
2. Six bags of humbugs
3. Twelve bags of pear drops

Page 29

Concealed Italian – The hidden Italian is the mathematician Fibonacci. Once the number search is complete, the remaining unused entries in the grid read out the first 13 terms in the famous Fibonacci sequence when read from left-to-right, top-to-bottom.

0, 1, 1, 2, 3, 5, 8, 13, 21, 34, 55, 89, 144

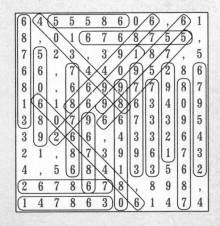

Page 30
Sherlock Sudoku

R	E	S	O	L	C	H	K
K	L	C	H	S	O	E	R
S	K	E	C	O	R	L	H
O	R	H	L	C	K	S	E
H	O	L	K	E	S	R	C
C	S	R	E	H	L	K	O
E	C	K	S	R	H	O	L
L	H	O	R	K	E	C	S

Page 31

Money Box – Dr. Watson is incorrect. He should change his mind and open box four. There is not a 50/50 chance as he surmised. There is a ¾ chance the coin is in box four and only a ¼ chance the coin is in box one, so he should definitely opt to open box four if he wants the best chance of getting the gold coin.

Page 33

Marble-ous – 15 steps: R4, D64, R67, U37, L32, D72, R76, U6, R9, D49, L43, D83, R88, D98, R100.

Page 32
"S" for Sherlock

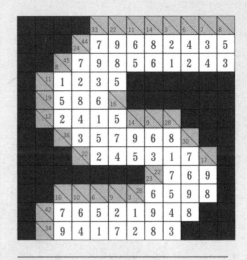

Page 34
Sherlock Search

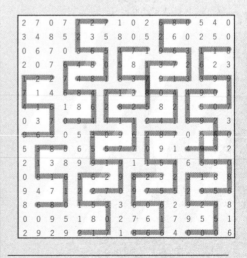

Page 35

Hot-air Balloons – From first-to-last: rose, saltire, lion, shield, dragon.

Page 36

Game, Set, and Match – Due to

the way the scoring system works in tennis (with games and sets as opposed to just a points tally), it is possible to win more points than your opponent and yet lose the match. Henry suffered this exact fate in his match against Cedric, winning more points but still losing.

Boxing Hares – There were 36

possible matches.

Page 38

Watch the Ball – The ball

finishes under the cup in the left-hand position, A, on the table.

Page 37

A Weighty Problem – Only one weighing is

needed. The key is to take a different number of weights from each of the seven piles. There are various ways to do this as there are nine weights in each pile but only seven piles in total. The simplest option is to take one weight from the first pile, two weights from the second pile, and so on, through to seven weights from the seventh pile. If all weights were 1 pound, then the weight would be $1 + 2 + 3 + 4 + 5 + 6 + 7$ pounds, which is 28 pounds. Now, we subtract this from the actual weight we measured to find which pile contains the heavier weights. For instance, if the total weight is 28.1 pounds, then the weight difference is 0.1 pounds and we know the first pile contains the heavy weights (since we placed one weight from that pile on the scale) while if the total weight is 28.7 pounds, then we know the seventh pile contains the heavy weights, as we placed seven weights from that pile on the scales.

Page 39

Ring, Ring – Once ordered from

smallest to largest, the rings spell out the name "MARY MORSTAN," who was introduced in *The Sign of Four* and became the wife of Dr. Watson.

Page 40

As Easy As Riding a Bike – 536 times.

Attempt one: big wheel 13 times, little wheel 39 times.
Attempt two: big wheel nine times, little wheel 27 times.
Attempt three: big wheel 112 times, little wheel 336 times.

Page 41

The Mysterious Note

1. Strong and stiff
2. Gesellschaft
3. Carlsbad
4. Blue

Page 42

Speedy Exit – There are many paths

through the maze. The quickest has nine steps (eight moves from the starting square): 1, 4, 16, 14, 20, 24, 6, 30, 36.

Page 43

The Red-headed Gang – Only two people can fit on the shorter sides of the table, while depending on the spacing, either two or three could sit on the longer sides. Therefore the total number around the table is either 4 + 4, 4 + 5, or 4 + 6. Only one of these numbers is odd, therefore there must be nine members in the gang.

At the Workhouse – Every 120 days. This is the lowest common multiple of 8, 10, and 15.

Page 44

Caught on Camera

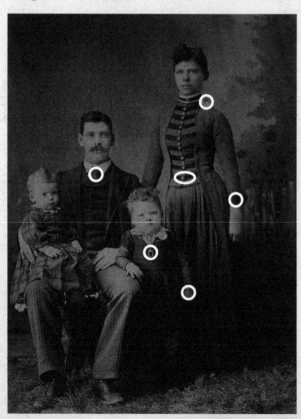

Page 46

Nine Squared – There are 285 squares in total, as follows:

one square that is 9 x 9, four squares that are 8 x 8, nine that are 7 x 7, 16 that are 6 x 6, 25 that are 5 x 5, 36 that are 4 x 4, 49 that are 3 x 3, 64 that are 2 x 2, 81 that are 1 x 1.

Page 47

Daylight Robbery – What the police thought was a drink holds the key to this mystery. A dark liquid that they mistook for tea was actually aqua regia, a powerful combination of acids that can dissolve gold, and the gold ring had indeed been dissolved in it. The gloves and hoods were safety equipment to enable them to mix the aqua regia and stop them breathing in the toxic gases released. The thieves had planned on reforming the gold ring at a later date when it was safe to do so.

Triplets – They had another sister, Emma, who was born a few minutes later, and were therefore actually quadruplets rather than triplets.

Page 48

The Scene of the Crime –
This is a Creativity Conundrum. There is no correct answer.

Holmes Sudoku

O	L	H	S	E	M
E	S	M	O	H	L
S	E	L	M	O	H
H	M	O	L	S	E
L	O	E	H	M	S
M	H	S	E	L	O

Page 49

Count to 25

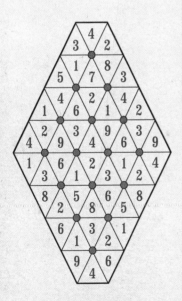

Page 50

Illumination in the Darkness –
Lord Smith was blind, and was reading from a Braille book; therefore the light failing was no obstacle to his continued reading. He was aware the gas light failed as he could no longer hear the sound of the gas burning.

Page 51

Three Pipe-box Problem –
The one pipe must be taken out of the box labeled "Clay and Briar Pipes." Since we know all three boxes are currently labeled incorrectly, then if we remove a clay pipe, this box can be relabeled "Clay Pipes." The box labeled "Briar Pipes" can then be renamed "Clay and Briar Pipes" while the box originally labeled "Clay Pipes" must therefore contain the briar pipes. Similarly, if the one pipe was a briar pipe, the "Clay and Briar Pipes" box would be relabeled "Briar Pipes," the "Clay Pipes" box is relabeled "Clay and Briar," and the "Briar Pipes" box is relabeled "Clay Pipes."

Page 52

The Happy Robber –
He did not leave with any money, but he did leave with several gold bars in his pockets that he had procured from stealthily gaining access to the bank's vaults.

A Fruitful Plant –
None—they were strawberry plants, not raspberry plants.

Page 53

Subtraction – Only once—to get 190. After that you are subtracting 7 from 190, and so on.

Going for Gold – Archibald was taking part in the decathlon, and while he won these two events, his scores in the other eight events were not sufficient for him to come first overall, hence he did not receive a gold medal.

Page 54

Elementary, My Dear Watson

WHITEHOUSE is the name of the person Sherlock is tracking. In this elementary puzzle, the code is the atomic numbers of several elements. To solve the code, look up the element in the periodic table and write down its symbol to get W + H + I + Te + Ho + U + Se for tungsten, hydrogen, iodine, tellurium, holmium, uranium, and selenium respectively.

Operating Table – The man had a wooden leg that the bullet was removed from, along with a couple of others. He was on the operating table to treat a wound from the fistfight on his body that required some stitches.

Page 55

Invention Test

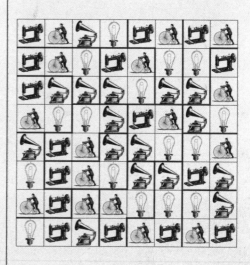

Page 56

"Weight" and See – Yes. Given an average weight of 155 pounds, the three together weigh 465 lbs. Subtracting the weights of the first two criminals leaves 149 pounds, which is therefore the weight of the third suspect. As we know, the person who committed the crime weighed no more than 150 pounds, so the third suspect could be the criminal.

Queen of Hearts – There is a 1/52 chance the first card taken from a standard deck is the Ace of Hearts, and then a 1/51 chance the second card is the Queen of Hearts. Therefore the chance is 1/2652.

Page 57
Pile of Pipes

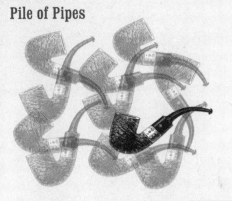

Page 58
The Day of Truth – Thursday, on both occasions.

A Growing Problem – The percentage increase is 134% to the nearest percent.

Page 59
Name Tracking

4	26	63	63	84	48	66	40	22	16	86	40	30
76	21	95	67	39	61	77	1	24	10	54	6	49
22	56	79	37	72	50	8	58	99	58	95	93	46
68	17	81	69	49	4	27	9	17	78	10	89	78
97	27	41	97	48	43	18	63	19	34	38	9	41
1	20	29	99	7	23	30	36	90	91	22	57	54
96	73	4	21	40	69	65	31	70	83	25	10	94
50	41	76	9	98	74	55	62	63	56	30	70	2
76	30	94	62	70	2	77	61	32	8	96	68	44
73	93	85	6	68	55	57	9	1	87	4	17	4
79	6	23	22	32	66	55	69	95	21	88	45	53
9	5	61	64	87	65	73	33	74	46	15	25	37
25	29	45	44	74	38	64	86	19	14	34	15	64

Page 60
Roman Lesson

VI	×	VIII	–	IV	XLIV
+		×		÷	
V	+	VII	–	I	XI
×		+		÷	
IX	+	III	÷	II	VI
XCIX		LIX		II	

Page 61

The Key Clue – Yes—the key matches number 6.

What's the Score?   32. Each letter in the name is worth four points. "Moriarty" contains eight letters, therefore the value is 8 x 4 = 32.

Page 62

Deerstalker – 15/1024 (or 0.0146, calculated as ¼ x ¼ x ¼ x ¼ x ¾ x 5).

Page 63

Short-Changed

Name	Height	Age
Harvey	5 ft. 1 in.	37
Russell	5 ft. 3 in.	44
Lester	5 ft. 2 in.	30

Napoleon's Stormy Petrel

Dr. Watson. Sherlock Holmes describes Moriarty as the "Napoleon of Crime" in *The Final Problem*, and Dr. Watson as the "Stormy Petrel of Crime" in *The Naval Treaty*.

Page 65

The Detective's Desk –

Page 64

A Key Problem

The Five Orange Pips – There are 126 possible combinations. You can solve the puzzle by carefully counting the options one by one, or use the following formula: n! / r!(n-r)! where "!" is the factorial symbol (3! = 3 x 2 x 1), n is the number of boxes (9), and r is the number of pips (5). So this gives 9! / 5! X 4! which is 362880 / 2880 = 126.

Page 66

Thumbprint – The answer is B.

Page 67

Significant Dates – White circled cells appear in one answer, gray circled cells appear in two (or more) answers and are the squares described as particularly busy in the instructions. These give the three dates 1819, 1837, 1901. These are respectively the year in which Queen Victoria was born, the year in which she became Queen, and the year of her death.

Page 68

Memory Grid
1. Key
2. Light blue
3. Magnifying glass

Page 69

Exhibition Art – 58 watercolors and 34 oil paintings.

Mysterious Gentleman – The gentleman did lose money quite significantly through this venture, but he was a (richer) millionaire before he started acting in this way. Aware that some people were too proud to accept outright charity, he disguised his philanthropy in this unusual manner.

Page 70

Safe Space 1
Square 46 is the only safe square in the grid.

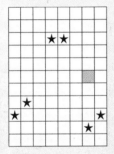

Page 72

Valuable Names – 1,001 points. Simply count up the value of the Roman numerals in each name, and ignore the other letters, thus Sherlock = L + C = 50 + 100 = 150; Holmes = L + M = 50 + 1000 = 1,050; Lestrade = L + D = 50 + 500 = 550 and Moriarty = M + I = 1,001.

Musical Murders – Bea is in danger. Sherlock realizes that the mad maestro is playing the name of each victim on his violin after killing them; therefore only orchestra members whose names can be played on the violin (containing the letters A–G) are in danger. Hence Eula and Gale are safe, but Bea is in danger.

Page 71

Safe Space 2
Square 37 is the only safe square in the grid.

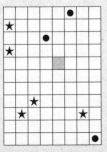

Page 73

Mourning – We need to calculate all the days in the years 1862–1900. This is a span of 39 years. There are nine leap years in the period + 30 standard years; so 30 x 365 + 9 x 366 = 10,950 + 3,294 = 14,244. Now we add the 22 days of 1901 and the 17 final days of 1861 to get the answer, 14,283 days.

Page 74

The Great Elm
The tree is 104 feet high (to the nearest foot). The puzzle can be solved using trigonometry: sin 60 = tree height / 120. So 0.866 x 120 = tree height = 103.9 feet.

Page 75

A Hansom Chap – The cab driver is E. The first clue rules out B and F; the second clue rules out D; the third clue rules out A and G firstly, then the second half of the clue rules out C, as we are told there are more people to his right than left.

Tour of Europe – Blue and yellow (or gold). The shirt and pants colors correspond to the flag of the country: Scotland and Greece have blue and white flags, Denmark's flag is red and white, while Sweden's flag is blue and yellow (or gold).

Page 76

Missing Links...
Light bulb.

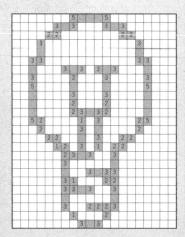

Page 77

...Missing Neighbors
Mailbox.

Page 78

Perception Detection

Page 79

Trainspotting

Train name	Top speed	Color
Steam Dream	65mph	Green
Piston Pusher	55mph	Blue
Coal Chugger	60mph	Red

Page 80

Killer Sudoku – Once the killer sudoku has been solved, the number 2 in the solved grid holds the key to finding the identity of the killer (circling the letters in the letter grid corresponding with any other number will lead to nonsense answers). Circle all the squares in the letter grid in the corresponding positions to the 2s to find the identity of the killer: JEFFERSON. Jefferson Hope is a character in *A Study in Scarlet* who kills to avenge the kidnapping and death of his fiancée.

8	3	2	4	5	7	9	6	1
7	9	6	3	8	1	2	4	5
1	5	4	6	2	9	7	8	3
4	1	5	8	9	2	6	3	7
9	6	7	5	4	3	8	1	2
2	8	3	7	1	6	5	9	4
6	4	1	8	7	8	3	5	9
5	2	8	9	3	4	1	7	6
3	7	9	1	6	5	4	2	8

Page 81

What a Character – Conan Doyle, the author of the Sherlock Holmes stories. Look at the third letter of each character name:

MACDONALD
COOK
WINDIBANK
BRADSTREET
RANCE
ANDERSON
STONER
ROYLOTT
HOLMES
GREGORY

Murder Most Fowl – 21. Simply add the day it attacked to the month of the year (January = 1 and so forth) to get the answer. So 17 + 4 (April) = 21.

Page 82

A Suspect Question

Name	Hair color	Age
Griggs	Red	24
Wakefield	Brown	34
Chattoway	Blonde	44

The Poisoned Chalice – This is a Creativity Conundrum. There is no correct answer.

Page 83

Circle the Answer – Once ordered from smallest to largest, the circles spell out the name "SIDNEY PAGET," who was a famous British illustrator best known for his illustrations of Sherlock Holmes stories.

Page 84
Building Bridges

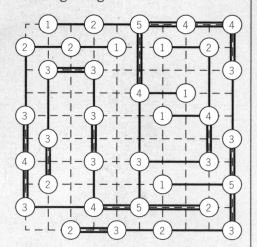

Page 86
The Diogenes Club

The Diogenes Club – The possible range of members of the Diogenes Club is 121–132. If there were 120 members, then it would be possible for there to be exactly 10 members whose birthday was in each of the 12 months. However, if there are 121 members, then at least one month must have 11 or more people born in that month, matching Sherlock's statement. Likewise if there are never more than 11 people who share a month of birth, as Mycroft says, then the upper limit is 11 x 12 = 132.

Page 85
Valuable Inventions

Gas lamp: 9
Photograph: 6
Steamship: 10
Postage stamp: 3

Page 87
Splitting Up

Four Candles – Box C, as that offers the longest burn time per penny.

Page 88
Piecing it Together

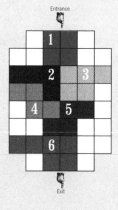

1 left	5 down	5 right
3 up	5 left	1 down
5 right	5 left	4 left
4 down	5 down	4 up
2 down	5 left	1 up
1 down	2 up	5 up
1 left	2 up	6 right
3 left	4 up	6 up
3 up	4 up	6 right
5 up	5 down	1 down
5 up	1 down	1 down
5 up	3 left	5 left
2 right	2 up	5 left
2 right	4 left	6 up
2 right	4 up	1 right
4 right	5 right	1 right
4 right	1 down	1 down,
4 right	4 left	and out
4 down	2 down	
2 down	3 right	

Page 89

Falling Like Dominoes

1	4	0	0	1	6	3	3
1	6	2	1	1	2	4	5
3	3	2	3	4	6	0	6
0	5	0	3	3	0	6	4
1	1	2	3	6	2	5	5
5	2	2	0	6	5	0	2
4	4	5	6	5	4	1	4

Page 90

Coin Crime

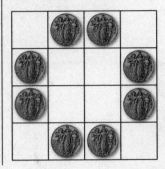

All the Threes – The answer is 36,333, not 33,333.

Page 91

See the Light – Walter is a lighthouse keeper. He knows there is great danger as the light going out could lead to ships crashing on the rocks.

Page 92

Arise, Sir Sherlock – An accomplice had been sitting in the large garden behind the property in a hot-air balloon ready to take flight. The two men ran to the upstairs window, whereupon the accomplice lifted the balloon into the air, threw the men a rope for them to hold onto, ascending as slowly as he could while the two men climbed aboard, then made their escape. The sentry did not hear the noise from the hot-air balloon's burners due to the cat fight and, being positioned right by the front door, only saw the house when he looked up, having no vision of the balloon rising into the sky and making its getaway.

Page 93

Waiting for Holmes

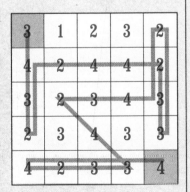

Page 94

The Colorful Sherlock Holmes – Every instance of "Sherlock" is a shade of blue and every instance of "Holmes" is white, apart from the instance circled right that is therefore the odd one out

HOLMES HOLMES HOLMES HOLMES
SHERLOCK HOLMES SHERLOCK HOLMES
SHERLOCK SHERLOCK HOLMES SHERLOCK
HOLMES SHERLOCK HOLMES HOLMES
SHERLOCK HOLMES SHERLOCK SHERLOCK
HOLMES SHERLOCK HOLMES HOLMES
SHERLOCK HOLMES SHERLOCK HOLMES
HOLMES SHERLOCK HOLMES HOLMES
HOLMES SHERLOCK HOLMES HOLMES
HOLMES SHERLOCK SHERLOCK SHERLOCK
SHERLOCK HOLMES SHERLOCK HOLMES
SHERLOCK SHERLOCK HOLMES SHERLOCK
HOLMES HOLMES HOLMES HOLMES

Page 95

The Great Exhibition
The fifth diamond was worth £10,125.

Happy Family
– There were eight children: Sidney and his seven sisters (each sister had Sidney as their brother).

Page 96

Colorful Chemicals

Chemical Name	Color	Smell
Solution X	Orange	Chicken
Solution Y	Pink	Onions
Solution Z	Yellow	Fish

Page 97

Card Cheat

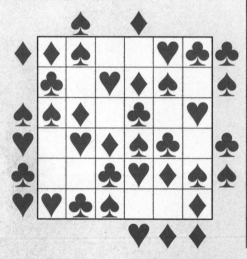

Page 98

Gold Rush
– The six nuggets of gold took the men 2 pounds over the weight limit. Therefore two of the men juggled three of the nuggets each, ensuring two were always in the air at any given time (one nugget per man), while the third man rowed their simple craft to escape the savage animal.

Time is of the Essence
– Sherlock finished his work at 12:29.

Page 99

Tree Line

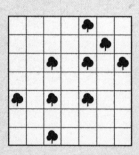

Page 100

The Arrow of Crime

Page 101

Hexacode

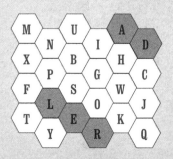

Page 102

Character Puzzle

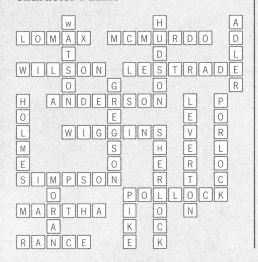

Page 103

Here Be Treasure! – 73 ounces. 2 white coins = 5 silver coins = 9 gold coins. The lowest common multiple of these three numbers is 90. So the lowest possible weight for 2 white coins = 90 ounces, 5 silver coins = 90 ounces, 9 gold coins = 90 ounces. Therefore a single coin of each color weighs 45 ounces, 18 ounces, and 10 ounces respectively, so 73 ounces in total.

Into Pieces

Page 104

Help! – The answers to the sums/questions (63, 83, 85, 73, 78, 53, 81) should be used to draw hands pointing to the appropriate positions on each of the dials in turn—for instance, if the answer is 63 (9 x 7 wonders of the Ancient World), one hand should be drawn pointing to the 6 from the dot in the middle of the corresponding dial, and another to the 3. Once complete, the seven dials read out a semaphore message, one letter per dial, spelling out M-Y-C-R-O-F-T.

Page 105

Find Your Way Holmes – There are 62 ways to spell out "HOLMES" in the grid.

Page 107

Memory Test

1. A brier-root pipe
2. Francois le Villard
3. Riga (1857) or St. Louis (1871)
4. A crumpled sheet of foreign notepaper

Page 106

Recurring Numbers – 1986. It is a list of years in which Halley's Comet was visible to the naked eye from Earth, starting in 1607.

It's All in the Mind – This is a Creativity Conundrum. There is no correct answer.

Page 108
Sher...

E	H	R	S	H	R	S	E
H	S	E	R	S	E	R	H
S	R	H	E	R	H	E	S
R	E	S	H	E	S	H	R
H	R	E	S	H	R	E	S
E	S	R	H	R	H	S	E
R	H	S	E	S	E	H	R
S	E	H	R	E	S	R	H

Open Confession – This is a Creativity Conundrum. There is no correct answer.

Page 109
...Lock

L	K	O	C	O	C	L	K
O	C	L	K	L	K	C	O
K	O	C	L	C	O	K	L
C	L	O	K	O	L	C	K
L	C	K	O	K	C	L	O
O	K	L	C	L	K	O	C
K	O	C	L	C	O	K	L
C	L	K	O	K	L	O	C

It Must Be Fête

The more attractive odds come from the second game, choosing eight balls from a set of 20, so that is the game that offers the best chance of winning. The chance of winning the games are 1/142,506 (five balls from 30) and 1/125,970 (eight balls from 20).

Page 110

Odd One Out – The safety match—the other items are all numbered (e.g. a penny black says "ONE PENNY," a telephone had the numbers 0–9 on a rotary dial to enable calls to be made, and a typewriter likewise has numbers on some keys).

Page 111
Prince Albert

B	E	A	R	T	L
L	A	T	B	R	E
T	B	R	E	L	A
A	R	E	L	B	T
E	L	B	T	A	R
R	T	L	A	E	B

Page 112

Safe Inside – The safe code is 2047.

Page 113
The Silver Blaze

Firework Name	Burn time	Height Reached
Gunmetal Rocket	25 seconds	40 feet
Gray Sparkle	20 seconds	20 feet
Silver Blaze	15 seconds	10 feet

Page 114

A Date with Destiny – The number is 1859—the year that Arthur Conan Doyle was born.

Page 114

Character Count
– 5.3. The value is a count of the number of consonants in the name, followed by a dot, then the number of vowels in the name. Moriarty contains five consonants and three vowels, hence the answer 5.3.

Page 115

Mirror Image
– D is the mirror image.

School Money
– £14.8s.4d.

Page 116

Victorian Names

Page 117

Victorian Names 2

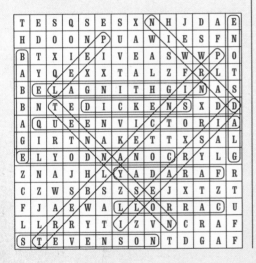

Page 118

Too Many Cooks

Chef's name	Meat	Experience
Theodore	Pork	10 years
Silas	Beef	5 years
Phineas	Mutton	15 years

Victorian Issue
– 9 + 1 + 2 + 3 + 4 + 5 + 6 + 7 + 8 + 9 = 54.

Page 119
Read All About It
1. *The Daily Gazette*
2. Jimmy
3. Brixton bus
4. Warren's

Page 120
A Sweet Tooth – There were 36 sweets in the bag originally.

Dish Washer – 16.

Page 121
Food Mixer
1. Pictures 1 and 4
2. Pictures 2 and 8
3. Pictures 3 and 9
4. Pictures 5 and 6

Page 122
At The Farm – Pigs.
The animals they see follow the order of the Chinese zodiac, from the snake onward (there were no dragons in Victorian England).

The Inventive Type

Page 123
A Light in the Darkness

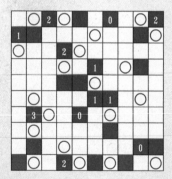

Page 124
Grid Reference
a. A3
b. A2
c. A1
d. C1

Page 125
The Hound of the Baskervilles – C.

Page 126
Murderous Manor

First Name	Surname	Job	Height
Baxter	Brewer	Optician	5 ft. 8 in.
Clarence	Lynch	Bailiff	5 ft. 6 in.
Edmund	Morris	Actuary	5 ft. 5 in.
Gilbert	Godwin	Lawyer	5 ft. 4 in.
Henry	Wright	Doctor	5 ft. 7 in.

Page 127

Murderous Manner – Baxter is the murderer. Given that what they each say is true, then Clarence is not the murderer, and the person sitting opposite him is. We know from the final paragraph that Clarence is sitting on his own with the other two men sitting facing him, as he shook both their hands across the table. The three men, sitting on two sides of the rectangular table, form a right-angled triangle. The person sitting directly opposite Clarence is closer to him than the person sitting alongside the person opposite (who is on the hypotenuse of the triangle). We know that Clarence shook the hand of Baxter directly across the table, but had to stand up in order to shake Henry's hand, presumably leaning across the table to do so. This means Henry is farther away than Baxter, and therefore Baxter must be the person directly opposite him, and thus the murderer.

Page 128
Smart Alec

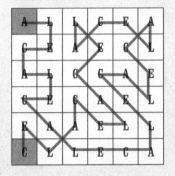

Page 129
A Useful Invention

A Piece of Cake – First cut the cake vertically into two equal pieces; secondly, cut the cake vertically at a 90-degree angle to the first cut so you now have four equal pieces. Finally, cut the cake horizontally rather than vertically, thus splitting the cake into four upper slices and four lower slices, resulting in the required eight slices with just three cuts.

Page 130

Safe Number – The numbers are 54 and 20, so the safe code is 1080. To crack the numerical sequence, simply multiply the digits in each number together to calculate the next number: for instance, 7688 is followed by 2688 because 7 x 6 x 8 x 8 = 2688.

Liar, Liar! – Agatha is telling the truth, Adelia and Alice are lying. The question can be answered by considering the options as to who is telling the truth and who is lying, and looking for a non-contradictory set of statements: if Adelia is telling the truth, Agatha is lying, which means that Alice is telling the truth (since it is then a lie that Alice is lying). That leads to a contradiction whereby Adelia is both telling the truth and lying at the same time! However, if Adelia is lying then Agatha is telling the truth and Alice is lying: this is now a consistent state of affairs and hence the answer.

Page 131

Guessing Game – The senses, or anything else associated with the number five: gloves come in pairs, there were Three Wise Men, and there are four seasons. Therefore on Friday Sherlock might think about the five senses.

Life Expectancy – It is New Years' Day. His birthday is December 31. So the day before yesterday (December 30), he was 39, then he turned 40 on December 31. This year he will therefore turn 41, and next year 42.

Page 132

Professor James Moriarty
Adam Worth (1844–1902), was called the "Napoleon of Crime," because of his international criminal career. He is said to be the model for that Arthur Conan Doyle character, Professor Moriarty. Ca. 1890.

Page 133

A Memorable Puzzle
1. Dog
2. Brown
3. Hat

Pages 134–137 **Suspect Visits** and **Symbolic Access** – These are fiendishly difficult and the answers can be found in the sealed pages at the end of the book.

Page 138

Baker Street to Victoria… – The older horse travels 2.5 miles at 10mph = 15 minutes. The younger horse travels 2.25 miles at 12mph = 11.25 minutes, + 4 minutes for Holmes to reach the cab = 15.25 minutes total. Therefore Holmes should take the older horse.

Page 140

Caught in a Loop –

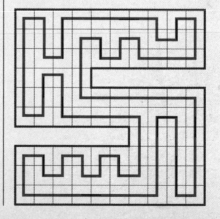

Page 139

…Victoria to Folkestone – St. Paul: number 4713.

Page 141

Magic Square – The numbers are 19 and 30. 1930 is the year in which Sherlock's creator, Arthur Conan Doyle, died.

A Fare Puzzle – The landau cab driver had taken Sherlock and Dr. Watson to their desired destination correctly, so he must have been able to hear their request to take them to Victoria when they first got on board the landau cab. It is stated that the cab driver did not turn around at any point until they had arrived, so lip-reading their request to go to Victoria can be ruled out.

Page 142

Explore All Angles – B.

Page 143

A Study in Scarlet– This is a Creativity Conundrum. There is no correct answer.

A Light Bulb Moment – Number 5 matches the light bulb.

Page 144

Up, Up, and Away

Page 146

Get Your Skates On – 32.

Page 147

Going Round in Circles

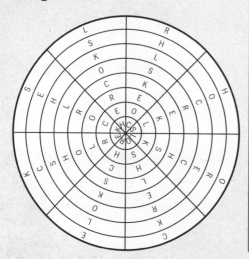

Page 148

Room with a View

		3	4		2		4		
	10								
3						12			
			18						
3			2			4			
									4
		7	2						
									6
4			2				10		

Page 149

Quick Getaway – If the quickest person participates in every muddy crossing, taking each person across in turn, then returning with the torch, the total time would be 4 + 2 + 7 + 2 + 10 + 2 + 12 = 39 minutes, comprising seven crossings of the muddy walkway.

However, it is possible for Moriarty and his partners to get across in only 35 minutes. The trick is to reduce the number of crossings the quickest person makes, and crucially to have the two slowest people cross the muddy walkway together. If we label the five people from quickest (A), who takes 2 minutes, to slowest (E), who takes 12 minutes, then the crossings are:

A and B (4 minutes)
A returns with the torch (2 minutes)
A and C (7 minutes)
A returns with the torch (2 minutes)
D and E (12 minutes)
B returns with the torch (4 minutes)
A and B (4 minutes)
The order of some of these crossings can, of course, be swapped around.

Page 150

Dotty Invention

Penny-farthing.

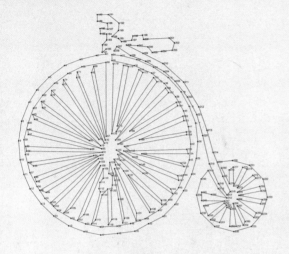

Page 151

Chasing Your Tail – There are 11 instances of "Elsie" starting and ending with the same letter in the grid.

E	L	S	I	E	L
I	S	I	E	E	L
S	S	I	E	L	E
S	L	E	I	S	S
I	E	S	L	S	I
S	L	I	E	L	E
E	L	S	I	S	S
I	S	L	E	L	S

Page 152

Automatic Sculpting Machine

Multiply each dimension by 2.5, divide by 12 to convert to feet, and then multiply the three answers together. $20/12 \times 25/12 \times 30/12 = 15000/1728$ (or 8.68) cubic feet.

Page 153

The Alibi – The criminal was lying: it is impossible to solve the puzzle, as the 31 dominoes cannot be placed on the board in such a way as to cover all 62 squares. The petty criminal would have known this if he had really been trying to solve it that night.

Page 154

Where Are You, Mrs. Hudson?

D	D	U	U	U	N	U	O	U	D	D	S	O	H
N	O	D	H	H	H	U	D	D	O	O	U	U	D
S	H	N	N	S	U	O	U	U	S	N	D	H	N	D
S	H	U	O	S	U	N	U	U	N	U	H	U	D	O
U	D	O	O	S	D	S	O	S	H	N	S	U	N	O
O	H	O	S	H	U	S	D	H	N	N	O	H	S	N
U	O	O	U	N	H	U	U	O	D	H	D	O	N	H
N	O	U	O	D	O	S	U	D	H	O	H	D	O	O
H	N	U	N	O	S	H	S	D	N	H	D	O	D	H
S	H	S	U	O	O	D	O	O	S	U	O	D	H	S
D	U	H	U	O	O	U	H	U	D	N	U	N	N	N
N	U	D	D	D	N	O	S	O	N	S	U	N	N	H
N	U	O	U	U	U	D	D	H	S	D	S	O	S	U
D	N	H	S	H	S	O	H	D	N	D	S	U	H	S
N	H	S	O	S	U	D	N	U	O	S	S	U	D	N

Page 155

The Reichenbach Falls He fell 784 feet. The distance is given by the formula 0.5 x g x t^2; therefore the distance is 0.5 x 32 x (7 x 7) = 784 feet.

Page 156

The Telephone Exchange – There are only two possibilities: 7589 and 7598. 1836 was a leap year (it is divisible by four); therefore Mycroft's day of birth was February 29, so the final two digit sum is 29 - 12 = 17.

Page 157

Photographic Memory

1. Two; 2. Twelve; 3. It's fitted with an electric lift; 4. Any of the following: generator, barrels, wood, servants, storage boxes, wine, electricity.

Page 158

A Lot of Hot Air

1 = Watson.

2 = Holmes.

3 = Lestrade.

Page 159

Memorable Text

1. Short-bladed scissors
2. Purple
3. Mr. Garcia
4. Seventh
5. Mr. Baynes

Page 160

Age Problem – 66 years old. 66 + 33 (1/2 of 66) + 22 (1/3 of 66) + 9 (3 x 3) = 130 = 6 score (a score is 20) + 10

The Messenger – 4.8mph. Imagine the man ran a total of 6 miles. That would mean his jog to reach Baker Street took 1 hour. Then walking back at 4mph, it would take him 1.5 hours to get home. Therefore the total journey of 12 miles takes 2.5 hours. 12 / 2.5 gives the average speed of 4.8mph.

Page 161

Snookered

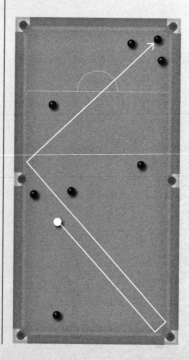

Page 162

In Sequence – 304. The sequence runs
x 3 + 1, x 3 – 1; therefore the next
number is 101 x 3 + 1 = 304.

Thinking Sequentially – Sailboat, or
anything else that resembles the number
4. The sequence is a list of objects whose
outline resembles the numbers 0, 1, 2, 3,
and so on.

Page 163

Triangle Teaser – C. The blue triangle
does not move. The brown triangle
moves clockwise around it, pivoting on
its leading edge.

Page 164

On the Right Track –

Page 165

At the Market

Name	Item sold	Number of sales
Herbert	Clothes	5
Owen	Jewelry	2
Wilfred	Vegetables	14

Attachment Puzzle – Although there
are various ways to attach the candle to
the door, the most efficient method is to
empty all the thumbtacks out of their
box, and then pin the box to the door
with the thumbtacks. Next put the
candle in the box and light it. Thus the
problem of wax dripping on the floor is
avoided, the risk of the candle falling
out of the box is minimized, and it can
be adjusted to emit light in the desired
direction.

Page 166

Character Squares

A	M	A	C	R	E	R	H	L	I	W	F	O	U	T
P	M	T	U	P	M	E	L	E	D	O	P	V	O	Y
R	A	A	T	T	T	F	E	R	A	V	D	K	E	B
U	R	D	W	G	A	Q	S	T	R	G	B	R	S	O
F	E	M	E	S	R	W	I	F	E	V	M	E	T	N
L	R	I	L	D	A	V	E	R	D	W	A	T	E	P
W	I	V	A	L	P	E	Z	T	Z	P	R	Y	P	M
I	L	E	J	E	K	L	N	O	U	P	R	R	O	M
J	R	T	L	W	S	F	J	Y	P	B	A	S	P	M
C	Q	L	C	A	U	D	O	T	X	Y	C	O	T	A
H	T	D	T	A	L	N	D	C	U	R	U	V	P	A
M	A	Q	I	B	T	N	Q	G	K	T	N	E	R	W
A	O	U	W	A	K	S	H	Y	T	R	O	S	R	T
T	S	Z	A	T	C	S	E	M	P	A	N	R	E	M
U	F	T	M	K	O	L	R	O	R	I	A	N	D	Y

Page 167

Crossing that Bridge

Page 168

Tattoo

Page 169

Missing Money – £188 in total.
Charles: £50
Benjamin: £50 + 20% = £60
George: 50% x (£50 + £60) = £55
Frank: 20% x (£60 + £55) = £23
Adding £50 + £60 + £55 + £23 gives £188.

Cliff-Hanger – Please note that this is a creativity puzzle, so there is no correct answer.

Page 170
Circular Logic

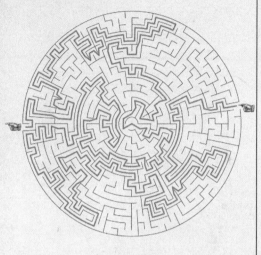

Page 171
Victorian Railway

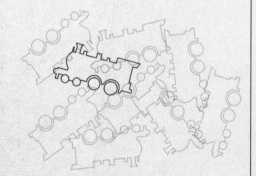

Page 172
The Jewel Thief

Vienna. Upon completing the sudoku, the numbers in the eight shaded squares are 4 8 2 1 1 6 3 7. Looking up latitude 48.21, longitude 16.37 will reveal that the jewel thief is in Vienna.

1	7	5	9	2	8	6	4	3
6	2	8	4	5	3	1	7	9
4	3	9	1	6	7	8	5	2
2	6	3	8	1	5	4	9	7
7	5	4	3	9	6	2	1	8
9	8	1	2	7	4	3	6	5
5	4	7	6	3	2	9	8	1
8	9	2	7	4	1	5	3	6
3	1	6	5	8	9	7	2	4

Page 173
Memory Text

1. Black
2. Kate Whitney
3. Light-house
4. Wine and water

Page 174
Good Shot!

Player's name	Best shot	Round reached
Julian	Serve	Second round
Randolph	Forehand	Quarter final
Vernon	Backhand	Third round

Page 175
Inspector Baynes

```
E Y B A S B E A B Y B Y A Y B
B N A B N Y S S A B B B B B
E A A A E E Y E B Y N S A Y N
N A A B E E Y S E B Y A B S A
B E S A A E A S E E A B Y B B
Y E N A B A A A Y E E B S E Y
A B N A Y S S E E B Y N S N B
A Y N N Y A E B Y Y B S N B Y
A S S E B Y B A S Y B N E A B
A B E Y Y B S S S N S E S E
S E B B A Y B A Y Y E B A S Y
S Y E S E A N E S N B S E A Y
B N A Y A A N E B N Y B Y S S
B E B S S A E Y E S B E A S S
A B N A S E Y Y E B N A N S S
```

Page 176
The Finance Ministry – 764

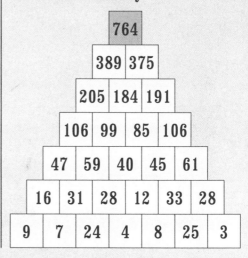

Page 177
Pattern Recognition

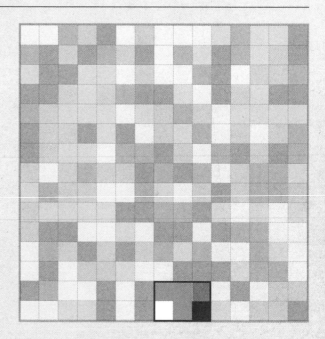

Page 178

Message for Watson – The message is MORIARTY, the name of the person Holmes was investigating. The code is straightforward: simply count the number of occurrences of the question mark in each column. The number references the position of each letter of the alphabet (A = 1, B = 2, C = 3, and so forth). Therefore the code is 13, 15, 18, 9, 1, 18, 20, 25, corresponding to MORIARTY.

Family Names – Not "D" as you may think—the fourth child's name is already given as Mary, so the answer is "M."

Page 179

Crack the Code – How often have I said to you that when you have eliminated the impossible, whatever remains, however improbable, must be the truth? (Said by Sherlock Holmes, in *The Sign of Four*.)

What's the score – The game was to turn their name into a number, with each letter from A–Z in their name scoring from 1 to 26 points respectively. Thus Sherlock scored 91.

Page 180

I Say, a Book! – *The Sign of Four*. The number given is the sine of 4 degrees, which when said sounds like "the sign of four."

The Problem of the Scrambled Stories
1. The Valley of Fear
2. A Study in Scarlet
3. The Crooked Man

Page 181

The Reigate Puzzle
The word "REIGATE" appears eight times.

Page 182

Number Link – S, the 19th letter of the alphabet. The sequence is the prime numbers represented by letters of the alphabet: 2 (B), 3 (C), 5 (E), 7 (G), 11 (K), 13 (M), 17 (Q).

What's the Connection? – Zeitgeist is the odd one out: the others all contain the names of countries within them (sCHADenfreude, vaGABONd, inCUBAtion, and antiperspIRANt).

Page 183

The Missing Thumb

T	B	H	B	T	B	U	H	M	B	T
H	H	H	H	T	U	H	H	H	B	H
M	M	U	U	H	T	M	U	U	M	B
T	H	H	B	H	H	U	B	T	U	H
H	T	U	T	T	U	H	U	H	H	M
H	B	T	M	T	U	T	H	M	T	T
M	M	T	H	U	U	H	M	B	M	U
H	B	U	T	B	T	M	T	T	T	U
H	B	T	T	B	M	H	M	T	M	U
T	T	T	H	M	B	U	H	T	M	M
M	M	T	U	M	H	M	M	H	B	B

Page 184

A Game of Darts – Hudson, referring to Mrs. Hudson, the landlady of 221B Baker Street. The scores on the six dart boards are 8, 21, 4, 19, 15, and 14 respectively. These correspond to the letters H, U, D, S, O, N in the alphabet where A = 1 and Z = 26.

Page 185

Get a Shift On – APMZTWKS. Simply shift each letter in the name forward through the alphabet by the number of letters in the word. Since "WATSON" contains six letters, each letter is shifted forward six characters (wrapping back around to A once Z is reached), so "W" becomes "C," "A" becomes "G," and so forth. Therefore each letter in Sherlock is shifted forward by eight characters.

What Next? – SON, and thus the puzzle starts with "WAT" and ends with "SON." There are three separate letter sequences: the first letter moves down the alphabet one at a time (W,V,U,T), the second letter moves down the alphabet three letters at a time (A,X,U,R), and the third letter moves up the alphabet five letters at a time (T, Y, D, I), leading to the answer "SON."

Folded Paper – TYPEWRITER.

Page 186

A Most Singular Case

– The unusual pattern on the case is not meaningless. It is actually a code. Each letter from A–Z is represented by the numbers 1–26. These decimal digits are then represented in ternary (base three, which uses 0, 1, 2 only). Holmes realized this, converted the ternary code to decimal, and then turned 1 to A and so on, to reveal the message "anniversaire."

The case is a 12-column by 3-row grid, with each column representing one of the letters of "anniversaire." Dark blue represents a value of 2, light blue a value of 1, and white a value of zero. Therefore the first column (light blue, white, white) represents 1,0,0 which corresponds to $(1 + (3^1 \times 0) + (3^2 \times 0)) = 1$ in decimal, which is therefore the letter A. The next column is dark blue, light blue, light blue which represents 2,1,1 which corresponds to $2 + 3^1 \times 1 + 3^2 \times 1$ which is $2 + 3 + 9 = 14$ in decimal representing N in the alphabet, and so on for each letter.

"Anniversaire" is the French word for birthday. From this, Holmes surmised the owner was a French speaker with a poor memory, who used this message as a secure hint to remind him of the nature of his access code—his own birthday. Further, knowing this would be in the format DD/MM, Sherlock knew that the first two digits must be in the range 01–31 and the second pair of digits in the range 01–12, therefore meaning only 366 valid dates had to be tried as possible entry codes in the worst case, rather than the full 10,000 combinations, and vastly speeding up the process of unlocking the case and revealing what was inside.

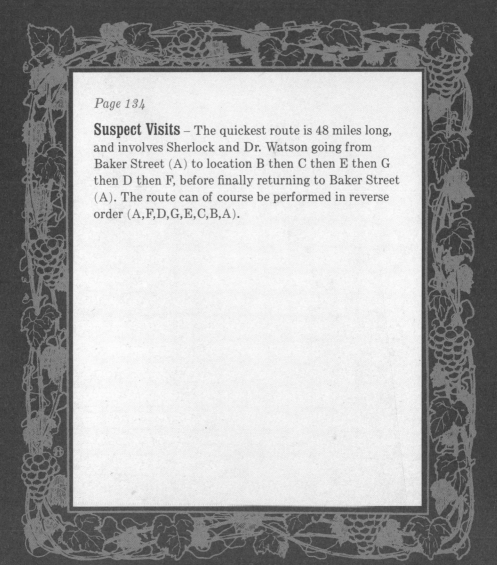

Page 134

Suspect Visits – The quickest route is 48 miles long, and involves Sherlock and Dr. Watson going from Baker Street (A) to location B then C then E then G then D then F, before finally returning to Baker Street (A). The route can of course be performed in reverse order (A,F,D,G,E,C,B,A).

FIENDISHLY DIFFICULT SOLUTIONS

Page 136

Symbolic Access – The code is £*£@

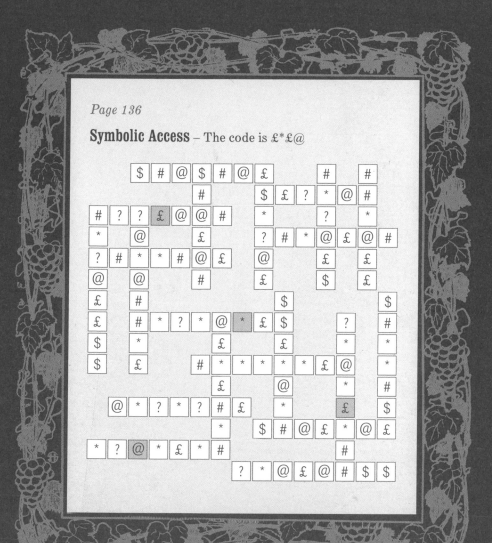